THE POST-WAR WORLD

THE
POST-WAR WORLD

DAVID HARKNESS

M.A., Ph.D.

SENIOR LECTURER IN HISTORY
UNIVERSITY OF KENT AT CANTERBURY

VISITING FELLOW IN HISTORY
UNIVERSITY OF IBADAN, NIGERIA
1971–2

MACMILLAN

First published 1974

Published by
MACMILLAN EDUCATION LTD
*Basingstoke and London
Associated companies and representatives
throughout the world*

*Set in Monophoto Baskerville
by Asco Trade Typesetting Ltd., Hong Kong*

For Hilary

Printed in Hong Kong
by Chap Yau Offset Printing Factory

Contents

List of Plates

List of Diagrams

List of cartoons and other illustrative material

Acknowledgements

I acknowledge with gratitude the prompt response to my pleas for information given by the Embassies of Brazil, China, Cuba, Japan, South Africa, The Soviet Union, The United States of America and Yugoslavia, and the High Commissions of India and Tanzania. I thank also *The Washington Post* and *The Guardian* for their help, Mr Wole Soyinka and Heinemann Educational Books Ltd to reproduce the poem 'The Telephone Conversation' from *The Book of African Verse*, and Mr Michael Parkin for allowing me to reproduce his modern fable.

My thanks are due also to the Humanities Faculty of the University of Kent at Canterbury, particularly my colleagues on the Board of Studies in History, for permitting me the study leave which enabled me to write this book. To Dr Peter Brooks, whose experienced advice was always welcome, I am most grateful. To Mrs Waring and her Rutherford College secretarial team, notably Jill Gosling and Sneh Jain, who coped with the typescript, I also tender my warmest thanks.

My greatest debt, however, remains to Hilary, who sustained me throughout the production of this book. She was assisted in her task by the fact that it was written amidst the magnificent scenery and generous people of the Cooley Peninsula. It is to their combined credit that optimism prevails in the text below.

D. W. HARKNESS

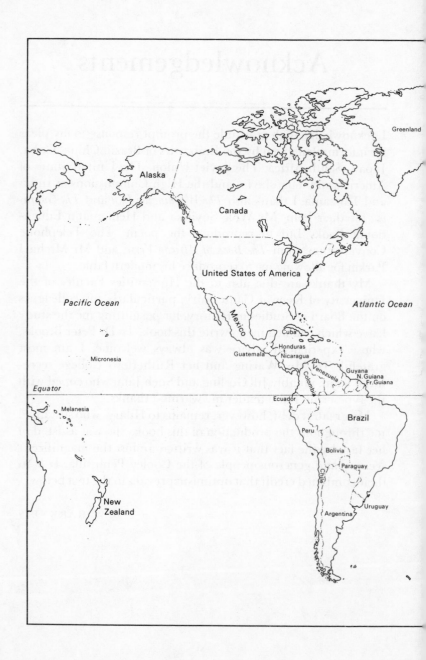

Greenland

Alaska

Canada

United States of America

Pacific Ocean

Atlantic Ocean

Mexico

Cuba

Honduras

Guatemala   Nicaragua

Micronesia

Venezuela   Guyana
N. Guiana
Fr. Guiana

Colombia

Equator

Ecuador

Melanesia

Brazil

Peru

Bolivia

Paraguay

Chile

New
Zealand

Argentina   Uruguay

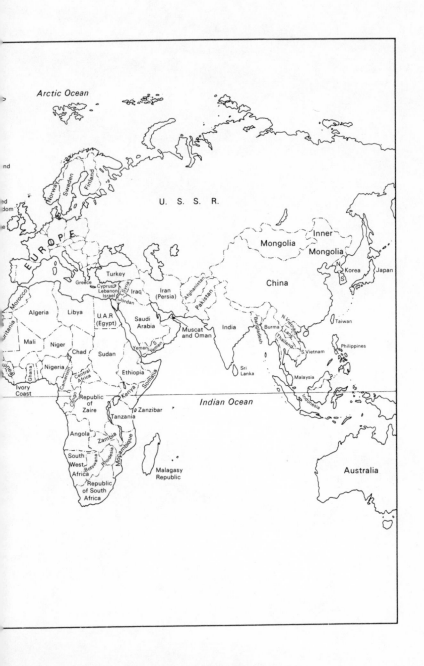

Arctic Ocean

EUROPE

Norway
Sweden
Finland

U. S. S. R.

Mongolia

Inner Mongolia

China

Korea
N
S

Japan

Greece
Turkey
Cyprus
Lebanon
Israel
Syria
Iraq
Jordan
Iran
(Persia)
Afghanistan
Pakistan

Morocco
Algeria
Libya
U.A.R
(Egypt)
Saudi
Arabia
Muscat
and Oman
Yemen
Yemen

India

Bangladesh
Burma
Laos
Thailand
N.Vietnam
S.Vietnam

Taiwan

Philippines

Mali
Niger
Chad
Sudan
Nigeria
Central
Africa
Cameroon
Ethiopia
Somalia

Mauritania

Ghana
Ivory
Coast

Sri
Lanka

Malaysia

Indonesia

Congo
Republic
of
Zaire
Kenya
Tanzania
Zanzibar

Indian Ocean

Angola
Zambia
Botswana
Rhodesia
Mozambique

South
West
Africa
Republic
of South
Africa

Malagasy
Republic

Australia

Introduction

Slowly, painfully, in this century, we have learned to regard the outbreak of war on our planet as a vital interest of all mankind: escalation is too simple, great power involvements are too complex, for us to rest easy when any conflict occurs. But we can no longer stop at this realisation. Today other phenomena, such as racial tension, pollution, and hunger, to name but three, impinge similarly on the interests of all men, whether they are aware of them or not. Ours is now a world-wide world, no longer insular or continental. Power and influence, once the monopoly of Europe, have diffused to other continents; European civilisation, while still important, is now seen in a global context side by side with other cultures. In the twentieth century a world society has emerged, and it is the purpose of *The Post-War World* to point to some of the major themes of this society as they have developed since the Second World War.

This book makes no claim to chronicle all events since 1945 (other books exist which provide that kind of outline), or to analyse these events, for they are too recent, too wrapped in secrecy, the evidence by which to judge them too incomplete. Taking continuity as well as change into account, it concentrates on broader themes: and because these themes stray into the realms of current affairs, sociology, politics and civics, in which the author claims no special expertise, many references to sources of further information and broader reading are given These are grouped at the end of each chapter to encourage the reader to follow up the issues raised and to come in the end to his own view, based on as full an understanding as possible. What this book hopes to do is to place present trends in the context at least of the recent past.

There are dangers, of course, even in so circumscribed an

enterprise. But no single view is offered, and if discussion is provoked. more informed criticism stimulated and a desire for constructive involvement roused, then the exercise will have been justified. The author's prejudices will begin to reveal themselves from the start in the very selection of chapter subjects. Here the main issues include the nuclear impact, the polarisation of power, race relations, conservation and development, the ending of European empire, nationalism and international relations. There is also a short section of appendices.

Appendix A requires no explanation, but the others do call for a brief comment. The collection of United Nations Declarations given in Appendix B is included on the assumption that many readers will be surprised at their scope and detail. They are significant because they provide the standards to which the international community aspires and which individuals in each nation can promote and uphold through knowledge and vigilance. Appendix C describes all too briefly some aspects of apartheid in South Africa. That nation, like those nations included in Chapter Five, has an individual approach to a general problem, but its solution is not one of which wider application could be recommended. We, like the South Africans themselves, must decide where we stand, so discussion cannot be left out of the look altogether. Appendix D, *2000 Words*, is included because it lends itself to endless speculation about both its tone and content, because it was abused by the Warsaw Pact countries who considered it grounds for their invasion of Czechoslovakia, and because it records, mildly, evidence of a totalitarianism in the East, the symptoms of which are by no means absent from the West.

The appendices are of course but a tiny, selected sample. They are not meant to be exclusive; simply provocative. Underlying them, as all the text, is an assumption, and it is one shared by the authors of an increasing number of books on the history of the twentieth century,[1] and by a majority of recent contributors to the distinguished BBC Reith Lecture series,[2] upon which this book has drawn heavily, that the world today is truly a single entity and a proper and logical unit of study.

Having studied themes, it remains to ask a number of questions about the priorities facing man. The simply stated but not so easily resolved problem of whether there should be bread for all before there is cake for any has long been with us, and it is still so today. But in an increasingly technical, commercial and consumer age, it must be asked as well whether things material have not advanced dangerously ahead of things cultural and spiritual, and whether they have not also advanced in dangerous disjunction in some exclusive and favoured areas of the world at the expense of others less fortunate. The need to consider how best to allocate man's energies and resources recurs in many of the thematic divisions of this book. But even more important than the quantitative factor is the qualitative. As J. K. Galbraith rightly reminds us, in a sentence to be coupled with the closing quotation on page 352: 'what counts is not the quantity of our goods but the quality of life'.[3]

David Harkness
Summer, 1973

NOTES

[1]See for example D. C. Watt, Frank Spencer and Neville Brown, *A History of the World in the Twentieth Century* (Pan, 1970); D. Thompson, *World History* (O.U.P., 1954); G. Barraclough, *An Introduction to Contemporary History* (Watts, 1964).

[2]Notably Robert Gardiner, 'A World of Peoples' (1965); Lester Pearson, 'Peace and the Family of Man' (1968); Frank Fraser Darling, 'Wilderness and Plenty' (1969). All have subsequently been published by the BBC.

[3]J. K. Galbraith, *The New Industrial State* (Penguin, 1969), p. 19.

CHAPTER ONE

The World in 1945

ONE WORLD

One world: men had been saying it for decades but in 1945 its obvious truth was brought home to the remotest corners of the globe. Not yet did men realise that their 'true nationality is mankind'[1]; but everywhere they shared depressing common experience, lay dead, or licked their wounds, and, while some mourned defeat, others counted the appalling cost of victory. A few managed to knuckle down to the task of building a future, hopefully for themselves, but, if not, at least for their children. The world at large was dazed and choked by the unsettled dust of battle, so that it was not easy to see then the implications of the six year global struggle with its terrible nuclear end. But some results were obvious enough.

Two great powers, for example, stood out clearly above the rest: America, undamaged at home, had achieved industrial and technological supremacy and had been thrust into new, world-wide responsibilities; Russia, devastated beyond even defeated Germany, nevertheless emerged in military and industrial command of Eastern Europe and beyond. The two great powers, rivals of visible potential since the late nineteenth century, had each temporarily withdrawn from world leadership after the First World War. Now they had returned, to compete, not co-operate. Wartime partnership was a mutual necessity which overlay deep interwar suspicions partly rooted in the clashing ideologies of capitalism and communism. Within months of the end of the Second World War it became clear to observers that the co-operation which had served to win victory was not going to persist to build peace. The 'one' world quickly divided into antipathetic blocs. Each believed itself to have a monopoly of freedom and virtue and each, regarding the other as its principal threat, sought first to preserve and then to extend its own system.

On the edge of these two blocs, and beyond them, other peoples reacted to the impact of a world war that had radically altered the social organisation and international framework of the old world's leading nations. In Asia, the assault on European Empire had been mounted during the war itself, and in the immediate aftermath of war new nations and new regimes continued their struggle to be born. The Middle East too was quick to show dissatisfaction with pre-existing arrangements. Africa, it seemed, had not been deeply touched. But its apparent quietude was misleading. The nationalism which had already begun there drew strength from other continents and its momentum coincided with the decline of the war-weakened imperial powers. Latin America, long dormant, stirred with a new awareness of its poverty and also of its potential. These areas, as yet uncommitted ideologically, or else unstable outposts of one system or the other, presented new challenges and new opportunities, both to the leaders of the capitalist and communist camps and to their own peoples. They also exposed another division line in our 'one' world, that between the developed and the developing* portions, a division even more pressing and crucial than that of ideology.

War has often proved a powerful accelerator of change and the world, already engaged in an unusual degree of change for half a century, had moved further in this six-year struggle than it yet knew. Some men, as at the end of the First World War, sought to return to former patterns which had secured for them comfort and order. But more were determined to build a new and better society, to salvage from the terrible losses of war something that would renew faith in humanity and give

*The terms 'developed' and 'developing' are preferred to 'developed' and 'under-developed'. 'Affluent' and 'non-affluent' might be more accurate but have not gained wide usage. What is at stake is simply relative material advance and the term 'developed' by no means implies a final stage in the process.

promise of social justice and individual fulfilment. For such there could be no looking back. The old had been found wanting and it only remained to decide on the specific means of creating the new.

WHAT SORT OF WORLD?

Most people recognised that they were living in an age of transition. But what sort of a transition was it and what sort of a world would emerge from the confusion? One answer, already assumed in this book, is that the transition was from a European-dominated world to a world of wider perspective, a world of interdependent parts if not yet undivided purposes. Even to-day, commentators are divided in their analyses. The historian Geoffrey Barraclough, however, in his *Introduction to contemporary history*[2], develops the theme that between the 1890s and the 1960s a fragmented old world gave way to a new world entity, under the impact of industrialism, population expansion and new social theory and practice. And this theme is echoed by Kenneth Boulding in his *Meaning of the twentieth century*,[3] a volume in the 'World Perspectives' series, which itself presupposes the appearance of 'one world' and the need for a 'new consciousness which can eventually lift the human race above and beyond the fear, ignorance, and isolation which beset it to-day'.[4] Boulding traces the impact of science and technology on the institutions of society and poses the stark alternatives ahead. We may create either a society of unshakable tyranny, resting upon all the knowledge which we are going to gain in social sciences, and of unspeakable corruption resting on man's enormous power over nature, especially biological nature, . . . (or) a society in which the major sources of human misery have been eliminated, a society in which there will be no war, poverty, or disease, and in which a large majority of human beings will be able to live out their lives in relative freedom from most of the ills which now oppress the major part of mankind'.[5]

The same transition in society and the choice before us have been expressed in a different way, with particular relevance to the developed, Western portion of the world, by psychologist Erich Fromm.[6] In developing his thesis, he uses an analogy of the child-parent relationship. It is a characteristic of maternal love, he observes, that it is unquestioning; it provides the child with warmth and security irrespective of his behaviour, good or bad. Paternal love is sterner, for the father's role is to educate, introduce the child to society, to reward and to punish. Paternal love must be earned; it may also be forfeited.

Fromm sees societies in matriarchal and patriarchal terms, the one breeding dependence and lack of individuality, the other, based on authority, on law, justice, discipline and work, favouring individual initiative within the established system. A healthy society requires a balance of these characteristics. Briefly, he would maintain that the developments of Protestantism and the subsequent industrial revolution have swung society too far into a paternal mould, but that the very success of the industry and capital accumulation of the nineteenth century has produced conditions which no longer favour such a society. The Western, affluent, consumer society of today, a complex and co-operative, materialistic, mass society, risks swinging too far back to a predominantly maternal mould. But if the tendency for unbalanced paternal society is towards law without justice, maternal society swamps individual development. We are again faced therefore with the job of achieving the right proportion of each. And to Fromm the necessary balance must be achieved in man himself. Man must reject mere materialism and the worship of machine production and maximum consumption, and concentrate instead on the fullest development of each individual. Let us relieve the basic material needs of mankind and then nurture the individual fulfilment of each man. Such a fulfilment can start in the West with personal self-knowledge, with selfless, outgiving love and compassion, but it must proceed to change the ownership and production of goods and forms of political life on a world scale.

In such ways have three very different contemporary observers described the nature of the contemporary world and speculated on its future. They raise questions of individual purpose and social aims in the context of an age of unprecedented demographic expansion and technical achievement and they call for new thinking and new structures, both national and international, to suit new men. To refer to their ideas is in some measure to anticipate both the immediate post-war themes, to be described below in chapter two, and a number of the specific topics dealt with in subsequent chapters. First, however, something of a factual base (this chapter) and a chronological framework of the post war era (Chapter 2 and Appendix A) must be built up, from which analysis and discussion can then proceed.

WORLD SURVEY 1945

What had the peoples of the world to face up to in 1945? What had they managed to salvage from the holocaust, and what were their hopes, their fears and their prospects? In chapter five some detailed attempts are made to follow through these questions by a closer look at the social aims and world view of selected nations. Here all that can be done is to tackle the broad issues along more or less continental lines. It will be a rapid tour but it should at least remind us of the scope of our task. Because of Europe's dominant role in the past, that continent will be examined first.

EUROPE

In 1945 Eastern Europe lay under the domination of Russia, while the West found itself increasingly dependent on America for aid and protection. Europe had been divided into 'spheres of influence' rather as in the past it had itself divided up many other parts of the world. But for Europeans, East and West, the immediate preoccupation was with simple survival. It is hard to imagine today the enormous physical destruction which most of Europe had endured. Communications and transport systems had been prime military targets, and road, rail and port installations were in ruins, with rolling stock and vehicles in scarce supply. Industrial centres had been flattened, with factories, machines, mines and housing destroyed. Agriculture had been neglected, marketing disrupted, with labour reduced and normal currency arrangements distorted. And European peoples themselves had been hard hit by this total war. Not only had civilians shared with soldiers the death, wounding and destruction; whole peoples had been transported to provide work-slaves for the Nazi war machine, so that to the bombed homeless were added many thousands of displaced persons.

The incidence of disruption was uneven, but it has been estimated that in France one fifth of the housing was destroyed, two thirds of its railway stock and half the livestock, the total losses amounting to about 45% of French wealth. Italy lost most heavily in the South, leaving its Northern industrial complex relatively unscathed, but even so one third of the country's assets were destroyed. In Germany, though devastation was particularly heavy in some cities, both agriculture and industry remained in good order; but loss of life was enormous and misery was very widespread. Holland's losses amounted to more than three times its annual national income, while Britain, which escaped much physical damage outside the large cities, suffered from lack of industrial renewal and above all from the loss of huge overseas financial assets, sold to pay the cost of the war.[7]

In general it can be noted that in 1945 and 1946 industrial production in Europe stood at only one third of its 1938 figure, while D. W. Urwin, in his *Western Europe since 1945* has concluded more specifically that:

> Of the former leading European powers, Germany had been destroyed; Italy had been revealed as having a hollow shell; Great Britain was incapable of being the prime mover of a balance of power checkboard; while France was still suffering from the military and moral collapse of 1940.[8]

The mood of the European peoples is also important in this context. Urwin has remarked on the universal feeling of exhaustion which followed the enormous drain on human as well as material resources. Amidst problems of starvation, cold and refugees, there was genuine doubt as to whether Europe was psychologically or physically capable of tackling its economic reconstruction. Stephen Spender, who wrote his *European Witness*[9] after a visit to Germany in 1945, described the feelings of isolation amongst European communities who were nevertheless sharing common discomfort and also formulating similar hopes and fears for the future. Thinking men realised the great capacity now available for creation or further destruction. Some had already begun to plan for a better Europe during the war itself.

The most interesting of those who had already formulated peace aims in detail were the various Resistance groups working to undermine Nazi control of Europe. Men of the Resistance debated the future, and, observing how ill they had been served by the traditional European nation states and the prevailing social order, tended to demand complete political, economic and social change. Their vision was sweeping and idealistic, encompassing a Europe united federally and a European society giving full expression to the dignity of the individual, full equality and real justice. Some of their inspiration was drawn from the *Report (Social Insurance and Allied Services)* produced in Britain by Lord Beveridge in 1942; some derived from communist theory. Most of their leaders were left-wing and progressive and shared a determination to cleanse Europe from the evil of Nazism and of collaboration, and many of their best ideals were expressed in the French Resistance Charter of 1944, and the wider Resistance Declaration of July in the same year. Admittedly, much of the broad vision of the Resistance perished in the urgent immediacies of survival and recovery, and in the unfortunate divisions that occurred amongst partisans, mainly between communists and non-communists. But something of their grand conception *was* realised and still persists. To quote Urwin once more:

> The rejection of the old liberal democracy with its emphasis upon political rights, ... and the acceptance of the need for a social democracy with its emphasis upon social and economic rights was forged by the experience of war and resistance.[10]

It is also true that hopes for a wider European Union did not die after the initial rejection of the first tentative plans.

Of course it was not only amongst the Resistance that blueprints were being drawn up for the future. The advancing Allies, too, looked ahead, and as they moved further and liberated more of Europe so they became preoccupied with the

actual problem of feeding and reorganising broken communities. Anticipating the creation of the United Nations Organisation, the United Nations Relief and Rehabilitation Administration (UNRRA) was established in November 1943. By
1945 it had achieved prodigies of first aid, something it was to
continue to do for another two years. And while UNRRA was
coping with immediate difficulties, particularly in East and
Central Europe, steps to facilitate long term recovery were
taken with the establishment, on 27 December 1945, of the
International Bank for Reconstruction and Development and
of the International Monetary Fund, both brain-children of
the Conference at Breton Woods, in the United States, in
1944.[11] In 1945 also, the World Food and Agriculture Organisation (FAO) was created, and then in October, from
meetings at Dumbarton Oaks, in 1944, and San Francisco
earlier in 1945, the United Nations Organisation (UNO)
emerged. Thus, to the means of coping with the problems of
survival there was added an organisation intended to preserve
peace, promote understanding, and achieve international co-
operation in broad fields of economic and social improvement.
The membership of the United Nations, even in 1945, and the
disposition of real power within it, reflected the reduced circumstances and minor significance of post-war Europe. But the
relief agencies already mentioned, as well as new, subsidiary
organisations of the United Nations, enabled Europeans to
make a start towards helping themselves back on to their feet.

As a footnote to this section, special mention must be made
of Great Britain, not only because it was in 1945, as before and
since, a European anomaly, but also because its Empire and
Commonwealth gave it important links with all other continents.

In Britain itself, the end of the war paved the way for the
election of a Labour government, the third in the country's
history but the first to hold power with an over-all Parliamentary majority. The British people, and most of all those in the
forces, wanted to dedicate their huge wartime sacrifices to the
creation of a better society at home as well as a better world
at large. Labour offered an unequivocal commitment to the

fare state ideals of the Beveridge Report, to greater social
uality and a fairer distribution of the nation's resources. In
1945 Labour Britain stood at the threshold of social transformation.

The British also emerged from the war as one of the Big
Three world powers, sharing decision-making with America
and Russia. The British Empire remained intact and Britain
enjoyed enormous moral prestige from her wartime achievements. British power, however, was an illusion. As well as its
loss of financial assets, and its war debts to America, Britain
was about to conclude new United States loan agreements
which would in future severely restrict its independence of
action. Militarily, Britain was over-stretched and the obligations of peace-keeping in Europe and Asia restricted its ability
to control its increasingly restless colonial peoples. Within two
years a Greek crisis forced the British Government to face the
facts of life of a Soviet-American bi-polar world. In the same
period the British Commonwealth of Nations, too, underwent
radical change.

By 1945 the British Commonwealth of Nations (Britain,
Canada, Australia, New Zealand, South Africa and Eire[12])
had evolved with heightened stature, out of the old British
Empire. Backed by the Indian Empire and scattered colonial
territories, it had stood alone against the Fascist Dictators at
the darkest period of the war, making that period not only
Britain's but 'the Commonwealth's finest hour'.[13]

This British Commonwealth of Nations had emerged in the
inter-war years as a partnership of states, all the Dominions
winning complete sovereignty, independent of British control,
and all choosing to continue in association through sentiment
and self-interest. The sound basis of free co-operation which
they established provided an exciting opportunity for future
extensions, a factor recognised when, in 1947, the Indian
Empire gained its independence, and both successor states,
India and Pakistan, became members. Their willingness to do
so transformed the British Commonwealth of Nations into a
largely non-white community with a potential for linking freely
peoples of all colours, creeds and continents. As this potential

moved towards realisation in the post-war decades the association shed its Anglo-centric bias and nomenclature to become simply The Commonwealth.

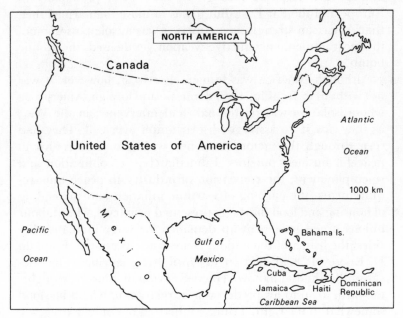

United States of America

The close of the Second World War left the United States the greatest single industrial and military power in the world. Coming late into the war and then meeting an ever increasing proportion of war requirements, American industry had benefited from initial anti-Axis purchases and then from the enormous demands of the Allied battle lines. Even five years after the war America led the world in such fields as the production of iron ore (43% world total), crude steel (45%), locomotives (60%), motor vehicles (74%), radio receivers (64%), rayon (50%) and other synthetic fibres (86%)[14]. The industrial boom did not end with the war, for high home demand, due to a wartime dearth of consumer goods, kept up production in the post-war years as industry switched over from the service of war to that of peace.

Militarily, the United States, with a population in 1945 standing between 132 million (1940 census) and 151 million (1950 census)[15], had in arms the unprecedented number of 12 million men disposed throughout the world, principally in Europe and the Far East. But it was in more than armed men that American strength lay. America was in sole possession of the most immense destructive weapon yet devised, the atomic bomb.

Although America was immensely strong, however, it was not without its troubles, both domestic and foreign. Americans, whose isolation was traditional, had intervened in the War, as they saw it, to assist good to triumph over evil. They had seen through the victory and they wished now to return to peaceful business pursuits. Immediately, demobilisation and re-employment, the conversion of industry to peace time requirements, the curbing of wartime inflation and the ending of housing and food shortages presented problems, while labour unions urged long pent-up demands for wage increases. Besides, the leader of the nation, Democratic President, Franklin D. Roosevelt, had died on 12 April 1945, leaving as his successor the almost unknown Harry S. Truman. Sincere, straightforward, loyal to his predecessor in relation to whom he stood somewhat to the right, Truman inherited not only 'a dragging war' and a 'sudden peace' but, more importantly, 'a recalcitrant Congress'[16]. Truman's elevation was unsought and unexpected; neither he, the American people, nor Congress accepted it easily, and it was two years before he could move out of the shadow of Roosevelt and adopt a.clearly defined stance of his own.

But America's new world status raised questions, the answers to which could not wait until the new President had settled down. And anyway Truman happened to have strong views on the role his country should play in the world; views reinforced by the mistakes which history showed America to have made at the end of the First World War.

Thus, while most Americans wished, as in 1918, to return to traditional normality, those prominent in the Administration, Truman at their head, saw that this time America could not retire from world responsibilities. America had a vital role to play in the rehabilitation of the war-torn world; America needed now not only to champion the United Nations Organisation, as it had previously championed the League of Nations, but to take, this time, the leading role in using and financing it. The war had unleashed forces of nationalism and communism and had also brought the threat of starvation or poverty to millions. Only America and Russia were in a position to provide aid and guidance. America could not risk forfeiting world leadership to a totalitarian, ideological rival. America, under Truman, already deeply engaged in supporting UNRRA, accepted the challenge of leading the non-communist world, and that acceptance, signified in July 1945 by the Senate's ratification of the United Nations Charter by 89 votes to 2, marked a watershed in American history.

A prosperous America, it was stated, could only be maintained in a world that was prosperous too, and free and at peace. But having made the commitment to lead, how precisely was America to act? This was the crucial question. It brought confusion at the time and has aroused bitter debate ever since.

To understand the difficulties facing Truman, we must appreciate both the novelty of the task before him and the deficiencies in his machinery for accomplishing it. America had no experience in and no tradition of world power politics. The State Department, though being overhauled, was not yet equipped, in numbers or expertise, for its new role. Dean Acheson, promoted to Under-Secretary of State in August 1945 (he was later to be Secretary from 1949–53), has described the Department as it had faced up to war in 1941:

> the Department had no ideas, plans, or methods for collecting information or dealing with the problems that this situation presented. With some brilliant exceptions, the bureaucracy was unequipped for appraisals of capability based on quantitative and technical judgements and of intentions by painstaking and exhaustive collection and correlation of intelligence.[17]

Much was achieved in a short time, but, as the war ended,

Acheson noted that, because President Roosevelt had virtually excluded his Secretary of State, Cordell Hull, from high-policy decisions during the war, the State Department's post-war planning was far removed from the practical world; was on the contrary 'theoretical and unreal'.[18] A subsequent commentator, John Spanier, has pointed to the naive idealism in foreign relations which characterised Roosevelt's wartime Administration. The American government expected post-war security 'to stem from mutual Russo-American goodwill, unsupported by any power considerations'; it anticipated a post-war 'era of good feeling' with an unsuspecting optimism characteristic of the 'utopian nature of American wartime thinking'[19].

It is part of Spanier's thesis that the Roosevelt approach was very much in accord with habitual American foreign policy. Traditionally 'the United States rarely initiates policy; the stimuli which are responsible for the formulation of American foreign policy come from beyond America's frontiers'.[20] Spanier stresses that such an attitude was natural to a nation which considered itself the repository of true democracy and universal moral values. As a result, having been provoked to action, Americans tend to embark on moral crusades – 'to make the world safe for democracy' – with a total dedication and in pursuit of the total destruction of their enemy. Such a policy based on a 'depreciation of power and [a] moralistic approach to foreign policy'[21] is ill-suited to a diplomacy designed to guard national interests without actual resort to force. It is, rather, a blunt, unsubtle instrument. In 1945 Americans had to learn to discard it and acquire finesse. But finesse takes time to acquire.

Nevertheless, American policy did begin to change in 1945. It did so in a manner which can be ascribed to a realistic reappraisal of world forces, notably Russian, or alternatively to an over-hasty swing away from optimistic idealism to pessimistic self-interest. The unsympathetic David Horowitz, exonerating Russia from blame for this change, identifies America's new, tough attitude squarely with Truman and concludes that its aggressive self-confidence resulted from the United States monopoly of nuclear power.[22] Unfortunately, many grounds for mutual Russo-American suspicion existed in the troubled and confused world of 1945 (not least in the contrary inter-pretations each Great Power placed upon such key words as 'democracy', 'freedom', and 'justice'). Spanier, chronicling both Russian and American acts of provocation, also notes a hardening American line. Though not formulated by George Kennan (see p. 54) until 1946, the new policy had begun to take shape by the close of 1945. America, capitalist champion and invincible world power, had begun to make up its mind on the real nature of communism and had started to set its course to prevent Russia from fomenting world revolution. To Kennan, Soviet communism would always be antagonistic to America, however much its short-term tactics might appear to the con-trary. Russia would exert pressure on the 'free' world with patience but with relentless persistence. Thus American policy in reply must be one of 'long-term, patient, but firm and vigilant containment of Russian expansive tendencies'.[23]

Union of Soviet Socialist Republics

If Russia, like America, emerged from the Second World War as one of the two dominant powers, her situation was very different from that of her rival. Russia expanded her territory and population as a result of the war, it is true, but no country had suffered more in the struggle:

More than twenty million Soviet people fell.
More than 70,000 towns, settlements and villages were wrecked.
The country lost nearly 30 per cent of its national wealth.[24]

This suffering and the geographical situation of Russia as well as its historical legacy of suspicion towards the West, contri-buted to the post-war psychology of the Russian leadership. That leadership of course – and here is another crucial differ-ence from the American case – was concentrated incontestably, and with continuity, in the hands of one man, Joseph Stalin.

To Stalin, the war had represented a disastrous break in his plans for consolidating socialism in Russia. It had disrupted agriculture, dislocated industry, upset concentration on ideo-logical purity. It was, in short, 'an unfortunate interruption to

the introspective development of 'socialism in one country'
which Stalin had pursued so laboriously from 1925'.[25] Now
that the war had ended, Stalin sought, successfully, to return to
the pre-war pattern. At home, coercion of the people, in the
interests of heavy industry (largely producer goods), of controlled agriculture (in state collective farms) and of party
orthodoxy, was resumed. Abroad, Stalin's aim continued to
be security, his means the co-ordination of 'Soviet diplomacy
and organised communism into one coherent instrument'.[26]

But Stalin had also to construct a balance sheet of vast losses
and gains while he adjusted Russia to its new world position
and opportunities.[27] The statistics of Russian losses, for example, are almost incomprehensible in their magnitude.

Some 8 million service personnel and 11 million civilians
died, with a disablement of a further 3 million. 25 million
people were rendered homeless, while uncounted millions
were transported around Russia as refugees from the German
advance or as workers for the war industries moved for safety
beyond the Urals.* During the war the economy was equally
devastated: production of pig iron fell by 73 per cent of the 1940
total, steel by 55 per cent, rolled steel by 61 per cent and electric
power by 44 per cent. Vital oil production at the principal
Baku oil fields was down in 1945 to half the 1940 figure, while
Russian scorched earth policies in the face of Nazi advance, and
German destruction in their turn on retreat, accounted for the
loss of factories employing 4 million persons and vast quantities
of agricultural produce. Farm output in 1945 represented 60
per cent of the 1940 crop, and housing and consumer production, already neglected before the war, suffered further
setbacks. Consumer goods were down in 1945 to two fifths of the
tiny 1940 total. The Russian people who had suffered so at the
hands of fascist aggressors would place a high premium on
security in the future, but they would not themselves readily
contemplate war as an instrument of national policy.

In the midst of this devastation it is worth noting that Russia
received some $3,000 million worth of goods from the Allies

*The total population of the U.S.S.R. in 1940 is estimated as 194.1 million. See
Harrison Salisbury (ed.), *Anatomy of the Soviet Union*, (Nelson, 1968), p. 239.

annually, and that when, in 1945, America suddenly cut off
lend-lease supplies, their value was about £1,100 million:
more than one third of the value of pre-war Russian industrial
production.[28]

It is also worth emphasising that the impact of such losses
and the terrible physical effects of war, combined with changes
of emphasis in Stalin's policy and unaccustomed contact with
the outside world, had induced sharp psychological reactions
amongst the Russian people. During the war nationalism and
patriotism had been nurtured, the tight grip of the party had
been relaxed and the Church, from 1943, had been to some
extent rehabilitated as part of a drive for unity in the face of
the enemy. By 1945 the cumulative effects of these measures,
in the harsh circumstances of the times, threatened the communist system. At the very least, Russians looked to Stalin for
some easing of life after the war.

But Stalin, alarmed at the threat posed to party control and
Marxist-Leninist orthodoxy, reverted to his own well-tried
methods of rigid authoritarian discipline. Socialism must be
preserved in its one developed homeland. That was the priority.
And a recognition of this principle is the first clue to an understanding of Soviet diplomacy at the close of the war and in the
immediate post-war period. Dazzling opportunities presented
themselves for daring initiatives in the outside world. But to
over-extend Russia there would be to risk the home base.
Stalin always had to judge between the diplomatic prize and
the domestic risk. For him consolidation at home, after the
disruption of war, took priority over all other considerations.

Nevertheless the Soviet Union did make great gains in power,
prestige and resources as a result of its wartime victories. Military success, for example, took the Red Army into most of
Eastern and Central Europe, and Stalin, claiming an extensive
sphere of influence from Bulgaria to Finland, was able to build
the protective screen he sought. Also, between 1940 and 1945,
Russia absorbed portions of Finland, Rumania, Czechoslovakia, Afghanistan and East Prussia. Russian acquisition of the
part of Poland lying beyond the 1920 'Curzon Line' was con-
ceded by the Allies at Yalta, and at the same time Russia was

granted all the Far Eastern territories lost to Japan in the war of 1904–5, as well as other valuable areas, in return for the promise of Russian help in the war against Japan. In addition Russian troops later occupied North Korea and Manchuria. Meanwhile it should be noted that Russian occupation of Eastern Germany allowed Stalin to exact considerable reparations, inadequate though these may have been to compensate for German destruction in Russia. In all, Russia added some 185,000 square miles of territory outright, containing approximately 25 million inhabitants, and gained indirect control over another 560,000 square miles with almost 100 million inhabitants.[29]

Thus Russia was enlarged, as well as exhausted and shaken, by the time the war came to an end. But while America adopted her new world role in 1945 under Truman on the death of Roosevelt, and Britain began to adjust to her reduced circumstances under Attlee after the electoral defeat of Churchill, Russia faced the future under the unbroken leadship of Stalin.

The traditional suspicions and fears that animated the

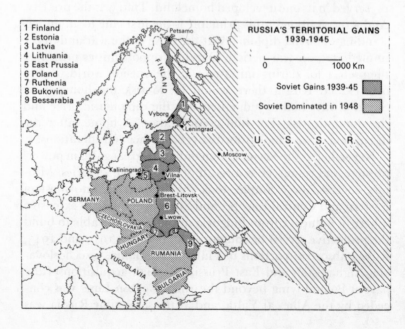

1 Finland
2 Estonia
3 Latvia
4 Lithuania
5 East Prussia
6 Poland
7 Ruthenia
8 Bukovina
9 Bessarabia

RUSSIA'S TERRITORIAL GAINS
1939-1945

0   1000 Km

Soviet Gains 1939-45

Soviet Dominated in 1948

Russian dictator have already been mentioned. Stalin sought consolidation at home and security abroad to allow that consolidation. He envisaged a new world managed by the big powers, saw the projected United Nations Organisation as a means to that end, and thought in terms of inviolable spheres of influence. His sphere was Eastern Europe. That had been agreed with Churchill in Moscow during October 1944, and confirmed at Yalta. Thus, while communism and capitalism remained incompatible, Russia would use her increased strength to build herself a communist position impregnable against capitalist wiles.

But Russia did not have atomic power. And Russia's sense of insecurity was not diminished by America's continued testing of the A-Bomb, its production of long range bombers and its acquisition of an encircling ring of air bases around Russia. Thus, as Stalin tightened the reins of the elite, ruling communist party (grown from 4 to 6 million during the war years) and set about formulating his fourth 5-Year Plan (adopted March 1946), he could look out with some satisfaction at Eastern Europe and Asia, but with less enthusiasm at the Middle East and in some alarm at America and the world of his erst-while allies. The comparative accord of the Allied Conference at Yalta in February 1945 had already given way to acrimony by the time of the Potsdam Conference of the following July, and after Hiroshima in August new tensions intruded. Russia had emerged as one of the two superpowers of the post-war world, but at the close of 1945 it stood second to America and it felt a need to stand very much on its guard.

Asia
The most populous region of the world, with an estimated 1,200 million inhabitants in 1940, out of a world total of some 2,295 million, Asia contained cultural, religious and political traditions far removed from those of Europe. The nineteenth century, however, had witnessed the increasing impact of European ideas and technology on Asia as a whole, as well as increased European Imperial control of much of South and South East Asia. Of Asian nations, it was Japan that adapted

itself most successfully to the industrial and political weapons of the West and in the first half of the twentieth century it is the history of Japan, intertwined though this is with that of China and overflowing in the Second World War to South East Asia as well, that is the most prominent.

In Japan, a combination of industrial dynamism, population pressure sharpened by the effects of the Great Depression, and imperial ambition drove the Japanese to seek markets, raw materials and outlets for their people in Manchuria and China in the 1930s. Japanese aggression antagonised both Europeans and Americans, as well as their Asian neighbours, and it was an American decision to cut off the supply of American strategic materials to Japan that led to the surprise Japanese attack on Pearl Harbour on 7 December 1941. In the next six months the Japanese were spectacularly successful in overrunning a vast area, from the Indo-Burmese border to the Solomon Islands. With these, and their conquests in China and Korea, the Japanese planned a Greater East Asia Co-Prosperity Sphere: a New Order for Asia by which Japan would develop and co-ordinate the natural resources of the area with her own industrial enterprises.

But Japanese calculations, based on the quick overthrow of Britain and Russia by Hitler, and on the willingness of the United States to come to terms, proved misguided, and from the middle of 1942 the fortunes of war slowly turned. Japan, with the miltary regime of General Tojo already discredited, was contemplating surrender when, without specific warning, the Americans dropped the world's first atomic bomb on Hiroshima on 6 August 1945. Three days later a second bomb was dropped, this time on Nagasaki, and on 14 August 1945 Japan surrendered unconditionally.

For Japan, 1945 thus brought physical ruin and the destruction of vast ambitions, leaving an economic, political and moral void. Into this void stepped the Americans, under General MacArthur, who set up new constitutional forms (1947) and began the peaceful rebuilding of the Japanese economy.

Japanese military achievements had, however, wrought profound changes throughout Asia, not least because Japanese troops were still in occupation of large areas when the surrender came. Apart from spreading confusion in China, Japan had released many colonial Asians from their European rulers and, though its own rule was no less imperial, it broke the traditions and wrecked the machinery of European control, demonstrated European weakness and stimulated the growth of national awareness and determination. Once again war had proved a great accelerator of change.

For China, huge, sprawling, proud of ancient culture, the impact of the West had proved painful, humiliating, and in the end disruptive. The pre-war national leader, Chiang Kai-Shek, and the Kuomintang Party that he inherited from the re-forming Sun Yat-Sen in 1925, were theoretically dedicated to nationalism, democracy and popular economic development, but in struggling against the strong communist movement in China and against Japanese invasion, only the first of these 'Three Principles' received much attention. During the Second World War something of a truce was reached between the Kuomintang and the Chinese Communist Party (CCP) in the interest of fighting the Japanese. But, in spite of stubborn resistence by the Chinese, it was American naval and atomic power and the threat of Russian military might that defeated Japan, leaving the Chinese mainland in political chaos.

China did not in fact suffer much physical damage during the war but communications were smashed and Party rivalries were complicated by the presence of Japanese armies and Russian and American troops and advisers. In this situation, dealing with the surrender of some 2 million Japanese troops, restoring national administration and reorganising the economy proved to be beyond the Kuomintang, which soon overreached itself in its renewed efforts to crush its communist opponents. By the end of 1945 civil war was again breaking out in China and in spite of the mediating efforts throughout 1946 of President Truman's representative, General Marshall (later U.S. Secretary of State 1947–9), negotiations between the representatives of Chiang and the communist leader, Mao Tse-tung, ultimately foundered. The last phase of the march to victory by the CCP, completed in 1949, had begun.

If China found eventual unity and modernisation under communism after the Japanese assault, South East Asia experienced no less repercussion, albeit at a more uneven pace. The 200 million people of this area, largely spread amongst Dutch, French, British, and American colonies, and stretching from the Western frontier of Burma to Eastern Indonesia, and including the Philippines, rapidly advanced their national emancipation. They did so in the wake of Japanese defeat, with the Chinese civil war in the East and Indian unrest to the West providing disturbing background music.

In Malaya alone was colonial rule successfully restored at the end of World War Two, though only, it must be added, so that local autonomy could lead steadily towards independence (achieved twelve years later in 1957). The most significant territories, however, were those formerly governed by Holland (Indonesia) and France (Indo-China). The Dutch, for economic reasons, and the French, largely for reasons of pride and prestige but also to protect French investments, were determined to reassert their authority. However as the Nazis had overrun both these countries at home, and the Japanese their territories abroad, they started from a position of weakness, while pre-war nationalist movements in Asia had grown correspondingly in strength.

In Indonesia, in 1945, the nationalist leader, Ahmed Sukarno, took his opportunity two days after the Japanese defeat to proclaim the independence of his country as the Republic of Indonesia. Sukarno had been pursuing this goal since he founded his Indonesian Nationalist Party (PNI) in 1927, and in a speech on 1 June 1945 he laid down five Principles upon which an Indonesian Republic would be founded: Faith in one God; Humanity; Nationalism; Representative Government and Social Justice.[30] Sukarno had been imprisoned by the Dutch but released by the Japanese in 1942 and given some encouragement as part of a Japanese divide-and-rule plan. The Japanese had also formed an Indonesian army, and when the Dutch decided to contest Sukarno's move, this force enabled the nationalists to provide tough opposition to the returning imperial forces.

It was not until 1949 that the Dutch gave up their attempt. They were reluctant to forego these rich territories and bitterly blamed the wartime Allies for the low priority given to Dutch re-occupation plans in 1945 (British troops eventually did take over the country but sought co-operation from the 'Republican' authorities), and for lack of support thereafter. But for the Indonesians, still lacking in unity or autonomy, 1945 presented a chance for independence that was resolutely seized.

French Indo-China comprised the three kingdoms of Cambodia, Laos and Vietnam, and here too initiatives towards independence were taken in 1945. Japan had seized control of all three regions in 1940 but as their own defeat approached they did not hesitate to encourage local nationalism. In Cambodia, Prince Norodom Sihanouk was pressed into declaring his country independent, while, in Laos, King Sisavang Vong responded to similar pressure. In Vietnam, Emperor Bao Dai also declared his country independent, under Japanese protection, but on the defeat of the Japanese he abdicated in favour of the Democratic Republic of Vietnam, proclaimed by the disciplined Viet Minh League of Ho Chi Minh.

France responded to these *faits accomplis* without enthusiasm but did recognise the 'Republic of Vietnam' as an autonomous state within the Indo-Chinese federation. France was forced to recast its colonial Empire as a result of the war and the arrangements for this were not drawn up until 1946 when a French Union was established. So far as Indo-China was concerned this allowed autonomy to the three territories within overall French protection. In Vietnam, however, the French army precipitated a showdown with Ho Chi Minh's nationalists in 1946 and the French government weakly followed its military commanders into what proved to be a costly, long-drawn-out and ultimately disastrous war. The French army was finally humiliated at Dien Bien Phu in 1954, but in 1945, before relations with French finally deteriorated, it seemed to be in the interests of both French and Vietnamese to co-operate to resist pressure in the North from Nationalist China. Nevertheless, even at that date something of what must have been the real Viet Minh feeling was expressed by Ho Chi Minh, on

2 September 1945, in a speech repudiating French claims. He spoke for many colonial peoples when he castigated European hypocrisy:

> For over eighty years the gang of French colonialists, oper-
> ating under the three colours which are supposed to stand
> for liberty, equality and fraternity, have stolen our land and
> oppressed our people ... The French have given us no
> political freedom whatever, they have instituted a barbarous
> legal code, they have opened more prisons than schools, they
> have drowned all our attempts at revolt in rivers of
> blood ... [31]

In the sub-continent of India, in 1945, the impact of neighbouring Japanese victories, the stretching of British resources
almost to breaking point, and the reputation and achievements
of Indian troops and political leaders were combining to usher
in the final act of the Indian independence struggle.

As a result of its great contribution to victory in the First
World War, India had become a somewhat anomalous member of the League of Nations, being not yet a sovereign state.
Although advances towards sovereignty were made in the
inter-war period, they were not swift enough to please Indian
nationalists who accused the British of trying to perpetuate
imperial rule by building up Hindu-Moslem divisions on the
one hand and entrenching the conservative Princes against the
progressive Indian National Congress on the other. Certainly
the legislative highlight of these years, the 1935 Government
of India Act, was open to criticism on both these charges, but
it did represent an attempt by the British to give Indians some
experience of managing their own affairs. The British were
committed to progress towards Indian independence sooner
or later. The Second World War ensured that it would be
sooner.

Wartime Indian sentiment was antagonised from the start
when the British Viceroy declared India to be at war, without
consulting the Indian leaders, and, despite the great numbers
of military recruits to the Allied cause, most Indian politicians
refused to co-operate. In efforts to win their co-operation the
British offered a number of concessions, but during the War

itself it became clear that the very real divisions in the country would allow no simple independence solution.

In 1940, the Indian Moslem leader, Mohammed Ali Jinnah, had already declared his goal of a separate Moslem state of Pakistan. Jinnah had watched Congress extend its appeal to the masses through the saintly Gandhi's emphasis of traditional Hindu virtues. Jinnah identified Congress with Hinduism and feared the economic, political and religious suppression of his people by the vast Hindu majority in a united independent state. By 1945 he had convinced Moslems sufficiently for them to demonstrate solidarity at the polls, Jinnah's Moslem League winning all thirty of the reserved Moslem seats in the Central Assembly. Congress, favouring a single independent federal India, won the bulk of the remainder, leaving the Indian political scene polarised in deadlock. Meanwhile the election of a Labour Government in Britain, in July 1945 – a Government pledged amongst other things to the granting of Indian independence – meant that immediate steps would be taken to try to resolve the deadlock. Independence came, however, with the deadlock unresolved, and the two states of India and Pakistan were born in 1947 amid scenes of horrifying communal hatred and destruction.

The Middle East

The Middle East, as an expression, has been subjected by numerous commentators to a wide range of interpretation. At its most comprehensive, however, it refers to the lands stretching from Turkey and Iran in West Asia, through the Eastern Mediterranean countries of Syria, Lebanon, Jordan and Israel (in 1945 Transjordania and Palestine, both territories having been mandated by the League of Nations to Great Britain), backed by Iraq, Saudi Arabia and the Gulf States, to Egypt and the North African states of Libya, Tunisia, Algeria and Morocco. In population these countries varied in 1945 from the largest, Turkey (19 million), Egypt (16 million) and Iran (13 million), down to Libya, Transjordania and the small Gulf Sheikdoms, numbering only thousands. It is not wise to generalise about so varied a region, but it is important

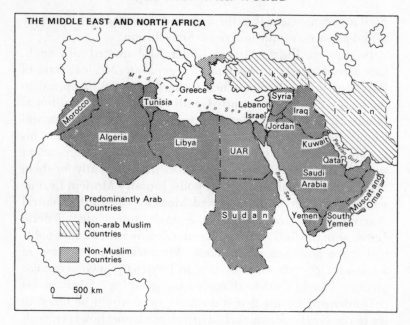

THE MIDDLE EAST AND NORTH AFRICA

Predominantly Arab
Countries

Non-arab Muslim
Countries

Non-Muslim
Countries

0   500 km

to convey something of its nature and significance at the end of
the Second World War.

The Middle East lies at the junction of Europe, Africa and
Asia. While this situation has long provided trading riches for
a few, its people have suffered in the main from poverty in a
terrain often arid and inhospitable. However, by 1945, the oil
resources of the area had begun to be tapped in earnest. Iran
and Iraq were the first to benefit, Iran going into production in
1901. Bahrein (1933) and Saudi Arabia (1936) joined in this
lucrative development between the wars. Kuwait, other Gulf
Sheikdoms, and Libya did not discover their huge deposits
until after the Second World War, but obviously the presence
of oil added great economic significance to an area already
deemed of high strategic importance by the great powers.

The Middle East, home of the Moslem faith which dominates
its religious and cultural life, had come under European political control in the nineteenth century. The most important
fact of life in the Middle East in 1945 was its continued subjection to Europe, which in this instance meant largely Britain

and France. North Africa had been one of the fiercest battle-grounds of the war, but Arab hopes of liberation from British, French and Italian control were disappointed. British influence remained paramount in Egypt and Transjordania while the French re-asserted their authority in the Maghreb and Levant, and Britain and France together replaced the defeated Italians in Libya.

Turkey remained, of course, an independent state, as was Iran (Persia), the other non-Arab Moslem nation. Both of them were subjected to severe Russian pressures in 1945, but both resisted successfully. The bulk of the Arab world, however, with the two exceptions of Saudi Arabia and Iraq, suffered at that time the indignity of some form of British or French control (Iraq, which had received full independence in 1932 after the ending of the British Mandate, had been occupied by British troops during the war, but this had been a purely wartime expedient). The majority of Arab peoples did not enjoy self-rule, and although the years since the ending of the World War have witnessed a total reversal of this situation, in response to intense Arab nationalism, there was little cause for Arab encouragement in 1945.

Nevertheless some straws were already in the wind. Arab pride and Arab hatred of foreign interference are traditional and by the end of the war were becoming more articulate. Not only a growth of national self-expression was apparent; strong pan-Arab feelings too were in evidence. In language, religion and sentiment the Arab world had long harboured yearnings for unity which had not been projected in the political sphere, largely, it was felt, because of the selfish vested interests and poor political qualities of territorial Arab leaders. Now, in 1945, an Arab League was founded by sovereign and semi-sovereign states (Egypt, Iraq, Jordan, Lebanon, Saudi Arabia, Syria and Yemen) to further common Arab interests. Its Secretariat was established in Cairo, which, because of its geographical situation, large size, and sophistication, was well situated to become the centre of Arab ambition in the post-war world. In 1945, such leadership emanated from the corrupt court of Farouk, or from the already discredited Waf'd Party. However, the fanatical Moslem Brotherhood was beginning to exploit foreign interference, the terrible social circumstances of the mass of the people, and the blatant wealth of the ruling few, in order to stimulate both Egyptian independence and wider Arab unity. The British occupying forces, conscious of the importance of the Suez Canal and of the need for stability in the Middle East, showed no inclination to relax their grip. Strategic crossroads and Western oil reserve, the Middle East was too vital an area to expose to ideological risks in the uncertain aftermath of world war. But the weapons of revolution were soon to prove more potent than either native leaders or occupying forces suspected in 1945.

Though not yet grown to contemporary significance, the Palestine problem was already the source of much difficulty by 1945, and must be mentioned here. Under British Mandate since 1920, Palestine had long been the source of inspiration to Jews, who had been encouraged to regard it as their National Home by the British Balfour Declaration of 1917. The Declaration was a response to the gathering Zionist Movement which sought to draw together once again the world's scattered Jews. But Zionist plans naturally provoked intense opposition amongst the Arab peoples, most notably the inhabitants of Palestine itself.

The whole situation was greatly complicated, both physically and emotionally, by the Second World War. Nazi policy towards the Jews, resulting in the extermination of millions and the transportation of millions of others, created both a huge refugee problem and much world sympathy towards the survivors. By 1938, steady Jewish immigration since the First World War had contributed to a total of 400,000 Jews in a Palestinian population of about 1.4 million, and although this immigration had been interrupted by the Second World War the huge increase in those wishing to settle, and the open militancy of those already there, gave the British authorities in 1945 a far from enviable task. With brutal Palestinian violence tying down 95,000 British soldiers on the spot, with Arab-Jewish terrorism in full swing, and with a background of international Jewish intrigue and much world interest, the

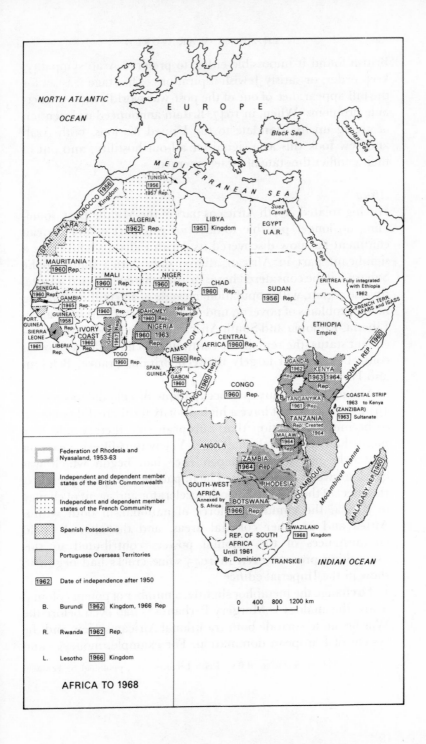

NORTH ATLANTIC OCEAN

EUROPE

Black Sea

Caspian Sea

MEDITERRANEAN SEA

SPAN. SAHARA

MOROCCO 1956 Kingdom

TUNISIA 1956 1957 Rep.

Suez Canal

ALGERIA 1962 Rep.

LIBYA 1951 Kingdom

EGYPT U.A.R.

Red Sea

MAURITANIA 1960 Rep.

MALI 1960 Rep.

NIGER 1960 Rep.

CHAD 1960 Rep.

SUDAN 1956 Rep.

ERITREA Fully integrated with Ethiopia 1962

FRENCH TERR. AFARS and ISSAS

SENEGAL 1960 Rep.

GAMBIA 1965 Rep.

GUINEA 1958 Rep.

PORT. GUINEA

SIERRA LEONE 1961

LIBERIA Rep.

VOLTA 1960 Rep.

IVORY COAST 1960 Rep.

GHANA 1957 Rep.

TOGO 1960 Rep.

DAHOMEY 1960 Rep.

1961 to Nigeria

NIGERIA 1963 Rep.

CAMEROON 1960 Rep.

SPAN. GUINEA

GABON 1960 Rep.

CONGO 1960

CONGO 1960 Rep.

CENTRAL AFRICA 1960 Rep.

ETHIOPIA Empire

SOMALI REP. 1960

UGANDA 1962 Rep.

KENYA 1963 1964 Rep.

COASTAL STRIP 1963 to Kenya (ZANZIBAR) 1963 Sultanate

R.

B.

TANGANYIKA 1961 Rep.

TANZANIA Rep. Created 1964

ANGOLA

MALAWI 1964 Rep.

ZAMBIA 1964 Rep.

RHODESIA

MOÇAMBIQUE

Moçambique Channel

MALAGASY REP. 1960

SOUTH-WEST AFRICA Annexed by S. Africa

BOTSWANA 1966 Rep.

SWAZILAND 1968 Kingdom

REP. OF SOUTH AFRICA Until 1961 Br. Dominion

L.

TRANSKEI

INDIAN OCEAN

Legend:

Federation of Rhodesia and Nyasaland, 1953-63

Independent and dependent member states of the British Commonwealth

Independent and dependent member states of the French Community

Spanish Possessions

Portuguese Overseas Territories

1962 Date of independence after 1950

B. Burundi 1962 Kingdom, 1966 Rep

R. Rwanda 1962 Rep.

L. Lesotho 1966 Kingdom

0   400   800   1200 km

AFRICA TO 1968

British found it impossible either to preserve Arab sympathy, keep order, or satisfy Jewish aspirations. The stage was set for the full appearance of one of the post-war world's most intractable problems. When, in 1947, Britain announced its intention of giving up its Mandate to the United Nations, both Arab and Jew took this as a signal for all-out hostility, and out of their conflict the state of Israel emerged.

Africa

Having treated North Africa as part of the Middle East, something no longer possible to-day (for this part of the African continent has now discovered its African identity and plays a significant part in African affairs) only Africa south of the Sahara will be considered here. In 1945 this constituted a large, diverse region, with population in excess of 200 million, sharing many problems of poverty, under-development and ignorance. Liberia, Ethiopia and South Africa alone could boast of independent status, the remainder continuing to lie under a colonial control shared out largely between Britain, France, Belgium and Portugal.

Amongst the many pre-occupations of colonial powers in 1945, Africa did not have a high priority for there did not seem to be much indication that European rule there would face more than superficial challenge. Yet within fifteen years an avalanche of African independence had begun which was quick to sweep all before it. The impact of European presence, the effect of the War, itself both accelerator and agent of change in Africa, the cumulative force of nationalism both within Africa and in other colonial areas, and the altered world circumstances of the colonial powers contributed to this astonishing process: even in 1945 some cracks had begun to show in the Imperial edifice.

To change the metaphor slightly, a number of potent colonial acids (the analogy is Margery Perham's*) had even before the War begun to corrode both traditional African society and the system of European domination. For example, money – and

*See her *Colonial Reckoning* (B.B.C. Reith Lectures 1961, published by Fontana, 1963).

the creation of a cash economy – had allowed new men to acquire wealth and had undermined old values and traditional hierarchies; while education, even more potent, not only per-mitted notions of equality and self-determination to be grasped by the tiny educated elites, but also allowed them to disseminate such ideas through newspaper and pamphlet to the broadening numbers of those able to read for themselves, and so able to pass on the word to others. Some colonial authorities, too, slowly and unevenly to be sure, did take seriously their task of 'trusteeship', as demanded by the League of Nations Mandates in 1919 and as expressed authoritatively by the British Lord Lugard in his book *The Dual Mandate*, published in 1922. Also the combined effects of European economic development – roads and railways, mines and towns (leading to large gather-ings, migration of workers and erosion of tribal structures) – as well as a limited amounted of European settlement, particul-arly in the East and South, set in motion unplanned forces difficult later to restrain.

The Second World War speeded and multiplied these forces, and added to them the experience of African troops abroad and the sight of far from elite European troops at home. The commitment of Britain and America in 1941 to an Atlantic Charter, promising that they at least would 'respect the right of all peoples to choose the form of government under which they will live', provided encouragement to emerging African leaders despite Churchill's denial that the Charter applied to colonies. The victory of the Allies, the determination of both Russia and America to end European colonialism, and the creation of a United Nations much more vigilant in promoting proper colonial development than its League predecessor had been, as well as the debilitation of the colonial powers, added to that encouragement, while Japanese victories over the same colonial powers in Asia, and the advanced nature of burgeon-ing nationalism in that continent were observed with interest. That these phenomena were matched by new anti-imperial currents in the colonial powers themselves meant that by 1945 the moment for challenging Europe in Africa was much more propitious than either ruled or ruler imagined at the time.

The world was, indeed, about to experience a form of Nationalism uniquely African. Nationalism, as conceived in Europe and as expressed in other continents, forms an important
part of the next chapter, but it must be emphasised here that
African nationalist sentiment had been expressed by an elite
few throughout the nineteenth century,[32] that it had gradually
been widening its scope in the twentieth century and that, far
from being a mere reaction to European domination, it contained a significant positive appeal of its own. African nationalists sought a synthesis of the best from the African social
and the European technical heritages. Asserting the equality
of black peoples, demanding the modernisation of often primitive economies, they sought also to make their own contribution to a wider world: a world too selfishly materialist, too
competitively chauvinist.

Africa was a continent beginning to stir in 1945. But its
broad regions, each appropriated and sub-divided by competing European powers, stood at different levels of consciousness
and development.

West Africa, stretching in a sweep of French territories from
Mauritania, on the north west coast, inland and round to
Camaroon in the south west, with British colonies reaching
northwards from the western seaboard, interspersed with more
French colonies and the one independent state of Liberia, had
the longest experience of European contact. But it was in the
British colonies that political consciousness had developed
fastest even though the imperial authorities had shown no haste
in developing and promoting it. In 1945 the British continued
their slow process of bringing Africans into the management
of their own affairs, implementing the Burns Constitution in
the Gold Coast, and the Richards Constitution in Nigeria.
Though the process of African involvement was now to be
speeded by the new British Labour Government, both these
constitutions were criticised by the African intelligentsia for
favouring the Chiefs' Councils and allowing only a tiny minority of African representatives to be directly elected. Power
anyway remained steadfastly in the hands of the colonial
governors.

French authority had been split in Africa during the war by the opposed Vichy and Free French Governments, each of which vied for colonial support. De Gaulle actually held a major conference of colonial officials at Brazzaville in 1944 and although its proposals were far from radical and no form of independence was envisaged for French territories, the Conference did recognise the right of qualified African colonials to help in formulating the constitution of post-war France. In 1945 and 1946 the French mood became less progressive, but the October 1946 Constitution did advance representative institutions in West Africa and its creation of the French Union, of France and all its overseas territories, set up separate territorial Assemblies (subject to supreme control by Parliament in Paris), and stimulated colonial political organisation. Though heavily criticised for neglecting the African masses and for grossly under-representing overseas subjects in Paris, the new arrangements, like those in British territories, provided a stepping stone for further advance.

Central Africa, with the French Equatorial provinces in the north, the Belgian Congo in the middle and the British Rhodesias and Nyasaland in the south, was the meeting ground of all European imperialisms. Apart from its own experience, it touched on its borders the Italians to the north, the Portuguese to the east and west, and to the south the white South Africans. Largely underpopulated, except for the Western edge, it had some rich mineral deposits (notably copper in the Congo and Northern Rhodesia), and areas of white settlement in the Congo, the Rhodesias and Nyasaland.

The British, striving unsuccessfully to balance black and settler interests in the Rhodesias, while supervising the feudal calm of Nyasaland, established in 1945 a Central African Council to co-ordinate services for all three regions. But settler opposition mounted below the surface. The Belgians, with a more paternalistic policy for the Congo, had concentrated on building a sound economic base; the State, the Church and the large Companies co-operating successfully. But they neglected political institutions and in the face of political progress elsewhere African demands in the Congo were soon to be mounted. The French Equatorial Provinces had strongly resembled the Belgian Congo prior to the war, for in both there were vast, backward areas subject to strong company influence, under metropolitan-controlled administration. But the unexpected support of these areas for de Gaulle during the war and their full participation in the Brazzaville Conference took them on the same development path as French West African colonies, in this respect leaving the Congo behind.

During the War the Belgian and French territories swung to the support of the British Colonies, in spite of, or because of, Nazi control of their metropolitan governments. The political issues at stake in the war were forced into prominence, stretching African horizons and awareness, while the economic needs of the Allies had a similar impact on the development of the resources and towns of the region. In spite of this the territories remained politically and socially backward, so that in 1945 no immediate challenge to colonial authority was mounted. Nevertheless that challenge had in fact been brought much nearer by the war.

East Africa, apart from the ancient and independent Ethiopia in the north and the offshore French colony of Madagascar, was British controlled. It is a region of contrasts in climate, geography, resources and peoples. It too was deeply affected by a war which saw British-Italian conflict in the North (resulting in Italian defeat and the restoration of the Ethiopian monarch, Haile Selassie, in 1941) and an influx of transit troops to Nairobi. Many of these latter returned to settle at the end of the war, adding more whites to an area already containing significant European, Arab and Indian communities, and further exacerbating race relations. Indeed the issue of land, the fundamental resource in Africa, was to prove a powerful stimulus to East African endeavour in the post-war years. Concentrated in Kenya, European farmers had appropriated 16,000 square miles [33] of the best arable land and the resentment aroused by this affected all East Africa.

As in Central Africa, the British tried during the war to facilitate co-operation in Kenya, Uganda and Tanganyika by creating common institutions. When Labour came to power in Britain equal unofficial representation on a central Legislative Assembly was proposed for Africans, Asians and Europeans (December, 1945), despite the gross disparity in numbers between the three groups. But even this was too much for the Kenyan settlers who prevailed upon the British Government to backpeddle (1947), an ominous sign of entrenched attitudes boding ill for the future. Even so, constitutional advances were made under the Labour Government, too slow and too cautious perhaps, but progress nonetheless. Growing urbanisation, commercial development, racial tension and the creation of avenues of political progress, enabled East Africa by 1945 to approach the self-conscious, nationalist stage.

In the South the dominant influence was that of the Union of South Africa, a British Dominion but one under predominantly Afrikaner political sway since 1924. South Africa, more dynamic, richer and with a greater proportion of white settlers (nearly twenty per cent of the total population) than Portuguese Angola to the West, British protected Bechuanaland to the north and Portuguese Mozambique to the east, had evolved the most sophisticated system of settler domination in the entire continent.

In 1939 Premier Hertzog's motion for neutrality in the war had only been defeated through an amendment by Deputy Premier Smuts, and South African commitment to the Allied cause was followed by rebellion. This increased the conflict between settlers of British and Boer stock and added nothing to the wellbeing of the African population. The war stimulated the European-owned economy but drove Africans further into the web of urban and mining development and away from tribe and land. Outnumbered by so many black Africans, the dominant European class had already argued its way into an autocratic control which sought justification in segregation and notions of 'separate development'. By 1945 that basic dichotomy of post-war South Africa, between fearful racial prejudice and the insistant labour demands of the economy, had been created. Ideologically, white South Africans could claim that the black and white communities must develop apart at their different levels; economically white prosperity demanded the continued presence of a massive black labour force.

So much for Africa on the ground: who were the new men of 1945 and what were their aims? As it happens, from both the territories of the two dominant imperial powers, Britain and France, African leaders met in 1945 to plan and co-ordinate their actions. Idealistic, proud, black, educated, able, they determined to win for Africa and Africans the equality and dignity that was their due. But they were not yet strong, not yet united, not yet noticed.

At Manchester, late in 1945, British West Africans gathered more or less at the same time that their French equivalents were participating in the Paris Constituent Assembly. The Manchester meeting was the fifth Pan-African Congress in a series dating from the 1919 Peace Conference. Organised by Kwame Nkrumah, future leader of Ghana, George Padmore, West Indian ex-communist, and Jomo Kenyatta, later Kenya's first President, it was chaired by the veteran American negro, W. E. B. DuBois, and attended by Nnamdi Azikiwe, Nigeria's Ibo spokesman, and by other future leaders. These widely drawn enthusiasts discussed the Atlantic Charter and Roosevelt's Four Freedoms (see chapter 4, p. 173 below) as the basis of the independent societies they wished to build in Africa. They also formulated nationalism and Pan-Africanism as tools with which to attack colonialism.

In Paris the energies of such men as Leopold Senghor and Lamine Gueye from Senegal, Felix Houphouet-Boigny of the Ivory Coast, and Fily Dabo Sissoko from Mali, were more directed towards the achievement of equal partnership with France in the French Union, and equal status for their fellow countrymen with Frenchmen, than towards territorial nationhood. But in Paris and in Manchester, Africans in 1945 were articulating their demands with new force and solid argument. Africa had been put into gear by the war and was ready to drive for equality and independence. The post-war world – confused, exhausted, but still embattled – was, unknown to Africans, both less able to resist their claims and more sympathetic towards their realisation.

Latin America

Central and South America, with the islands of the Caribbean, had a population of some 140 million by the end of the Second World War. Largely Spanish-speaking, except in Brazil, where the language is Portuguese, and in the peripheral British and French West Indies, the area as a whole had shared a turbulent and bloody history. The continental territories, which had escaped from Spanish and Portuguese dominion early in the nineteenth century, had not proved ready for popular constitutional development. Instead, a patchwork of dictatorial *caudillos* (military tyrants), who established themselves after the independence struggles, and civilian oligarchies had imposed themselves on largely ignorant and primitive peoples. War, *coups d'etat* and revolutions had followed, to the detriment alike of social, economic, and political development. Less gloomy exceptions to this general rule were, in the nineteenth century, Chile, Argentina and Brazil, and in addition, in the twentieth century, Mexico and Uruguay, but in 1945 an observer would have been justified, in view of past violence and present unrest, in concluding that it was to the future that Latin Americans would have to look for their Golden Age.

Certainly, Latin America had great potential, both in human and natural resources. But in the development field the two World Wars of the twentieth century and the Great Depression from 1929–31 had exposed both the existing weaknesses of Latin American economies and their future perils. For too long individual countries had been dependent upon a few export items, usually minerals or agricultural produce, to trade with more developed markets whose financiers controlled production and price. Latin America was painfully short of capital so that, as the nineteenth century gave way to the twentieth and British finance gave way to North American, the United States consolidated its hold. President Monroe had proclaimed his country's concern for the region as early as 1823, when he warned Europeans not to interfere there. Now Washington and Wall Street established a position of dominance which offered to Latin America the possibility of economic progress but only at the price of dependence on United States favour.

World War One, which interfered with normal patterns of
trade, both import and export, had revealed economic weakness and stimulated a measure of industrialisation. But the
Great Depression, devastating Latin American economies by
then more heavily dependent on the United States, had generated new forces of social discontent. Now the Second World
War had increased enormously the pressures for both economic
and social change and provoked much political self-examination.

In the political sphere, Latin American intellectuals had
already responded to the democratic aims of the First World
War Allies and to the ideology of the triumphant Bolsheviks.
Now, Second World War opposition to Fascist Dictatorship
in Europe (all the Latin American Republics had declared
war on Hitler's Germany, though Argentina, the last one to
act, had done so only in March 1945) stimulated a greater
urge for democratic practice at home. As the war ended, the
problems of peaceful political change, constitutional safeguards
and general governmental stability had been added to the
serious search for diversification and growth in economies
throughout Latin America.

As in other developing regions of the world, the war had
quickened the pulse, accelerated development, brought new
pressures and left a new blance of forces. The cumulative
effect of these, economically, politically and socially were unpredictable in 1945. But there were some guides to change.
In several countries, demands for a radical break with the past
were mounted, presaging a more widespread expectation in
the years immediately ahead.

In Brazil, for example, by far the largest country with some
46 million people, with a more stable tradition and better
equipped with sophisticated services than most, the dictatorial
regime of President Vargas was replaced in 1945 by a democratic system. Argentina, most developed socially, with the
largest middle class in Latin America (40 per cent of its 15
million inhabitants) was on the eve of a decade of rule by Juan
Peron. Though ruthless and authoritarian, Peron came to

power in 1946 with the support of the largely urban working
class population and promised social reform.

In Venezuela, a country of some 4 million people in 1945, a
coup by junior officers over threw the ruling Generals and instituted a democratic civilian regime. In Guatemala, a traditional
Central American 'banana republic' with a 3 million population, pressures of war and the presence of many American
troops had stimulated intellectual opposition to the corrupt,
degrading rule of a typical *caudillo* strong man, Jorge Ubico,
in 1944. After a short interregnum, a social democrat, ex-
schoolteacher, J. J. Arévalo, emerged as President in 1945 and
began to implement progressive economic and social reforms.
Education, housing and national integration were first to benefit. Bolivia too experienced powerful change during the war.
Most turbulent of all South American lands, this tin and agriculture Republic of about 3 million inhabitants, experienced
between 1943 and 1946 something of the reforming zeal of
Professor Paz Estenserro. His National Revolutionary Party,
formed in 1940, shared power during these years and gave
some foretaste of the social revolution it was to carry out during
its period of power after 1951.

Something of the motivation of the reformers in all these
countries, and of others yet stirring, was nationalism, born of
poverty, resentment and emulation of those emerging Asian
nations which had been more closely involved in fighting the
war. True, there was to be a reaction against democratic systems – too often inefficient and weak – later in the postwar
period, but this reaction itself was to prove but one swing of a
yet uncertain pendulum. Poverty amidst potential plenty, reform vitiated by inexperienced democracy and the highest
population increase anywhere (3 per cent per annum overall),
and a nationalism partly reacting against continued domination by the United States, were the obvious characteristics of
post-war Latin America. An area as yet unsuccessful in its
search for stability, it had been prodded by the war into
critical self-examination. By 1945 its leading representatives
had begun to acquire a new confidence and determination.

UNITED NATIONS

PREAMBLE TO THE UNITED CHARTER
The Preamble to the United Nations Charter expresses the ideals and the common aims of all the peoples whose governments joined together to form the United Nations. It says:
We the peoples of the United Nations determined
TO SAVE succeeding generations from the scourge of war, which twice in our lifetime has brought untold sorrow to mankind, and
   TO REAFFIRM faith in fundamental human rights, in the dignity and worth of the human person, in the equal rights of men and women and of nations large and small,and
   TO ESTABLISH conditions under which justice and respect for the obligations arising from treaties and other sources of international law can be maintained, and
   TO PROMOTE social progress and better standards of life in larger freedom,
And for these ends
   TO PRACTICE tolerance and live together in peace with one another as good neighbors, and
   TO UNITE our strength to maintain international peace and security, and
   TO ENSURE, by the acceptance of principles and the institution of methods, that armed force shall not be used, save in the common interest, and
   TO EMPLOY international machinery for the promotion of the economic and social advancement of all peoples,
Have resolved to combine our efforts to accomplish these aims....
Accordingly, our respective governments, through representatives assembled in the city of San Francisco, who have exhibited their full powers found to be in good and due form, have agreed to the present Charter of the United Nations and do hereby establish an international organization to be known as the United Nations.

PURPOSES AND PRINCIPLES

The purposes of the United Nations are:
TO MAINTAIN international peace and security;
   TO DEVELOP friendly relations among nations;
   TO COOPERATE internationally in solving international economic, social, cultural, and humanitarian problems and in promoting respect for human rights and fundamental freedoms;
   TO BE A CENTRE for harmonizing the actions of nations in attaining these common ends.
The United Nations acts in accordance with these principles:
It is based on the sovereign equality of all its members.
   All members are to fulfill in good faith their Charter obligations.
   They are to settle their international disputes by peaceful means and without endangering peace, security and justice.
   They are to refrain in their international relations from the threat or use of force against other states.
   They are to give the United Nations every assistance in any action it takes in accordance with the Charter, and not to assist states against which preventive or enforcement action is being taken.
   The United Nations is to ensure that states which are not members act in accordance with these principles in so far as is necessary to maintain international peace and security.
   Nothing in the Charter is to authorize the United Nations to intervene in matters which are purely the national concern of any state.

THE DISPOSITION OF POWER

The reality of power in 1945 reposed in America and Russia, each with vast natural resources, industrial development, man-power and military forces. For the moment America held the sharpest cutting edge, with its monopoly of the atomic bomb. Had it not been for this, then the advantage would probably have been Russia's, with its dominant strategic position in Europe and Asia, and its preponderance of conventional weap-ons. But while the two Great Power rivals jockeyed for pos-ition, using the techniques of ideology as well as finance and force, they and the rest of the world had to face up to a number of pressing problems. How were post-war international relat-ions to be organised? How could the resources of the world best be harnessed to rebuild after the destruction of war, and developed to feed a rapidly expanding population? And how were the peoples of the globe to come to terms with the dawning nuclear age? One possible answer to all these questions lay with the United Nations Organisation.

Projected by the Allies from as early as 1941, the United Nations Organisation came into effect on 24 October 1945. Earlier in the year its Charter had been refined at a two month meeting at San Francisco, and then signed there on 26 June by the representatives of fifty states (Poland, not represented at San Francisco, signed later to become one of the original fifty-one founder members). Full appreciation of the purpose, structure and extent of the new Organisation would require more space than is available here. Suffice it to state that the devisers of the Charter were not blind optimists. They hoped for co-operation in peace but recognised that only by Great Power agreement could major world issues be solved. So they vested final power in the Security Council, assigning five of its eleven seats permanently to the United States, Russia, Britain, France and Nationalist China. The remaining six seats would be filled by election in the General Assembly on the Council's recommendation (for a two year term).*

Designed to prevent all war, the United Nations assumed

*See p. 344 for later expansion of seats.

THE UNITED NATIONS SYSTEM

The United Nations

The Specialised Agencies and IAEA

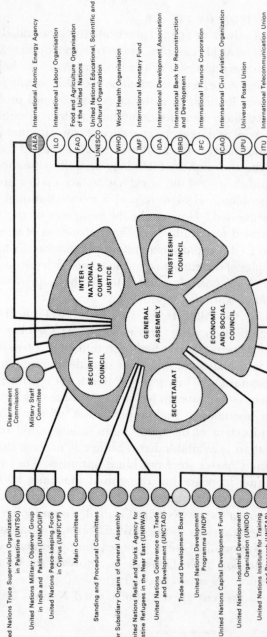

United Nations Truce Supervision Organization in Palestine (UNTSO)

United Nations Military Observer Group in India and Pakistan (UNMOGIP)

United Nations Peace-keeping Force in Cyprus (UNFICYP)

Main Committees

Standing and Procedural Committees

Other Subsidiary Organs of General Assembly

United Nations Relief and Works Agency for Palestine Refugees in the Near East (UNRWA)

United Nations Conference on Trade and Development (UNCTAD)

Trade and Development Board

United Nations Development Programme (UNDP)

United Nations Capital Development Fund

United Nations Industrial Development Organization (UNIDO)

United Nations Institute for Training and Research (UNITAR)

United Nations Children's Fund (UNICEF)

United Nations High Commissioner for Refugees (UNHCR)

Joint United Nations - FAO World Food Programme

Disarmament Commission

Military Staff Committee

INTER-NATIONAL COURT OF JUSTICE

TRUSTEESHIP COUNCIL

SECURITY COUNCIL

GENERAL ASSEMBLY

ECONOMIC AND SOCIAL COUNCIL

SECRETARIAT

Regional Economic Commissions

Functional Commissions

Sessional, Standing and Ad Hoc Committees

IAEA — International Atomic Energy Agency

ILO — International Labour Organisation

FAO — Food and Agriculture Organisation of the United Nations

UNESCO — United Nations Educational, Scientific and Cultural Organization

WHO — World Health Organisation

IMF — International Monetary Fund

IDA — International Development Association

IBRD — International Bank for Reconstruction and Development

IFC — International Finance Corporation

ICAO — International Civil Aviation Organization

UPU — Universal Postal Union

ITU — International Telecommunication Union

WMO — World Meteorological Organization

IMCO — Inter-Governmental Maritime Consultative Organization

GATT — General Agreement on Tariffs and Trade

the widest brief, setting out to remove the sources of conflict by furthering international social, cultural and educational development as well as tackling the vast problems of world hunger and disease. It declared at the beginning its determination to uphold human rights, to care for those in special need (for example refugees), to promote aid to developing lands and to foster the independence of colonial peoples.

The first session of the United Nations met in London on 10 January 1946 and it is interesting that even there, before the great flood of new Asian and African members, European nations found themselves in a minority. As well as Russia and Britain, both with interests beyond Europe, eight other European countries attended. They were heavily outnumbered by the Latin American and Middle Eastern States, the United States, the British Dominions, Liberia and Ethiopia. It was also significant that the Soviet bloc appeared in a minority position, so that the ideological balance at the United Nations favoured the West.

Composed of individual sovereign states, the United Nations Organisation was designed, unlike its League predecessor, to be something more than the sum of its parts. It was charged with preserving peace and building a better world through the development of both resources and peoples, and its Charter tried to invest it with the authority to fulfil those tasks. Soon, too, an attempt was made to make the United Nations the repository of the new and terrifying nuclear knowledge.

The atomic bomb had originated in British wartime research (conducted by British and European refugee scientists who were fearful that Hitler might succeed before them, and co-ordinated by the Maud Committee). Once America joined the war the British decided to contribute their expertise in order to utilise American resources, and atomic energy development for war and peace continued thereafter as a joint enterprise. Increasingly, however, the project came under American military direction until, by mid-1943, Britain no longer had any controlling voice.

The resulting United States monopoly, and the decision, unusual in scientific circles, to keep secret the details of this

whole area of research, presented the world with terrible possibilities after the power and horror of the nuclear bomb had
become evident at Hiroshima. In the post-war world of Soviet-
American rivalry, America's wartime decision to exclude its
Russian ally had particular repercussions and led to deep
divisions amongst America's scientists as well as amongst its
military and political leaders.

Perhaps traditional suspicions and Stalin's undisguised
determination to build a shield for himself in Eastern Europe
made America reluctant to put so formidable an additional
weapon in Russian hands. But as the war ended the fact had
to be faced that a continued U.S. monopoly might provoke
Russia to a new arms race that could in turn lead to the destruction of mankind. Making such a forecast in September 1945,
U.S. Secretary for War, H. L. Stimson, recommended that
America, entirely on its own initiative, should invite immediate
Russian co-operation in nuclear development so that together
the two nations could harness atomic energy for peace. He
saw the future of Soviet American relations hingeing on this
issue.

President Truman, however, decided eventually to pursue
a different policy, and in November 1945, America, Britain
and Canada, announcing their joint nuclear co-operation,
called for the establishment of a United Nations Commission
to control atomic development. When in 1946 the United
States did present a plan to the United Nations (the Baruch
Plan) it broke down on the issue of the safeguards deemed
necessary to prevent secret military research by individual
nations. The Russians were unable to accept proposals which
would have vested in the United Nations not only the development of atomic energy but also inspection and control mechan-
isms not subject to Security Council veto. In the United Nations
Russia could always be outvoted and Stalin preferred to pursue
his own researches rather than put Russia at the mercy of an
American-dominated agency.

Thus the United Nations was relieved of a potentially thorny
responsibility, at the cost of the sort of nuclear arms race against
which Stimson had warned. Paradoxically, however, once

Russia had achieved nuclear parity (A-bomb 1949; H-bomb 1953), the caution engendered by the potential outcome of any nuclear war provided a greater inducement to peace than the United Nations itself had been able to devise.

The United Nations began in 1945 with cautious optimism. In the years ahead it survived much criticism, succeeding in expanding its authority and achievements, particularly at the level of its specialised agencies such as UNESCO, WHO, ILO. But it could not, in the nature of things, resolve the major problems of world power. No collective-security machine could succeed while its component nations were determined above all else to preserve their national sovereignty, especially when the two most powerful of them represented opposite opinions on many major issues.

Russia and America, regrettably, regarded the United Nations as an extension of their own diplomatic weaponry, a means of furthering their own policies. It was left to the smaller nations to create a climate of opinion to curb Great Power excesses. But the basic problem exists today as it did in 1945. The equilibrium resulting from Soviet-American power balance (and this has really dated from 1945) has given the world a breathing space. But should the nations use this to work for an accepted standard of international behaviour, with a means of restricting those who for one reason or another step beyond that standard – should they, in other words, work towards a form of world authority with the power of enforcing its will – or should they place their hopes in an unregulated world, of greater communications and fuller public debate of world issues, wherein the separate nations, freeing themselves from their division into blocs and camps, would exercise mature judgement and temper their national interests in the wider interest of mankind? One such decision or another must be reached. What is certain is that the post-war era demands that the nations place greater emphasis upon humanity than upon nationality, for an awareness of common humanity, after all, is the vital factor in realising the 'oneness' of the contemporary world.

48   THE POST-WAR WORLD

IN CONCLUSION, 1945

Dean Acheson, American Secretary of State 1949-53, has entitled his autobiography of the post-war years *Present at the Creation*. He compares the aftermath of the Second World War with the events described in the first chapter of Genesis. That tells of the creation of 'a world out of chaos'. The task facing America's leaders, as Acheson saw it, was scarcely less formidable: 'to create half a world, a free half, out of the same material without blowing the whole to pieces in the process'.[34]

In spite of its special pleading, this analysis does give something of the novelty, scale and atmosphere of events in 1945. The world's leaders conferred to achieve present order and future security. But the slate had not been wiped clean, and Great Power interpretations of both the present and the future were contradictory. The world's peoples watched, some clearly with bated breath and agonised apprehension, others scarcely aroused, being preoccupied with more immediate interests, with food, or employment, or national sovereignty. Stalin, Truman and Attlee, de Gaulle and Chiang Kai-shek stood in the limelight; Mao Tse-tung, Sukarno, Adenauer, Nehru, Ho Chi Minh, and many others not yet emerged from the shadows, occupied the wings. Nationalism, discredited in its European birthplace, coiled itself to spring out in other continents; technology poised itself to reach for the moon; communism and capitalism braced themselves for icy confrontation. In 1945 our present world, newly equipped for massive development or total destruction, but still incapable of organising wayward humanity to fit new national theories, with old problems in new forms, and new problems undreamt of, assumed its modern shape. Some of its contours are described in the next chapter.

NOTES
[1]Robert Gardiner, *A World of People* (BBC, 1965) p. 91.
[2]G. Barraclough, *An Introduction to Contemporary History* (Watts, 1964).
[3]K. Boulding, *The Meaning of the Twentieth Century* (Allen & Unwin, 1965).

[4]*Ibid.*, from the Introduction by Ruth Nanda Anshen, p. ix.

[5]*Ibid.*, pp 22–3.

[6]See, for example, Erich Fromm, *The Sane Society* (Routledge & kegan Paul, 1956); *The Art of Loving* (Allen & Unwin, 1957).

[7]The British had, indeed, incurred a debt of £4,198 million. See T. A. Neale, *Democracy & Responsibility* (Macmillan, 1969), p. 283.

[8]D. W. Urwin, *Western Europe Since 1945* (Longmans, 1968) p. x. I am indebted to this book for much of the information in this section.

[9]S. Spender, *European Witness* (Hamish Hamilton, 1946).

[10]D. W. Urwin, *op. cit.*, pp. 25–6.

[11]For an American account of these events see Dean Acheson, *Present At The Creation*, (Hamish Hamilton, 1970), Chapter 10.

[12]The Irish Free State, made a Dominion in 1921, became known as Eire in 1937. Eire remained neutral during the Second World War in protest against the continued partition of Ireland. For the Irish contribution to the evolution of the Commonwealth see D. W. Harkness, *The Restless Dominion: The Irish Free State and the British Commonwealth of Nations, 1921–31* (Macmillan, 1969).

[13]P. N. S. Mansergh, *The Commonwealth Experience* (Weidenfeld & Nicolson, 1969), p. 285.

[14]C. Ware, K. M. Panikkar & L. M. Romein (eds), *The Twentieth Century* (Allen & Unwin, 1966), i, p. 27.

[15]Both figures to nearest million. For U.S. statistics I have found helpful Dan Golenpaul (ed.), *Information Please Almanac* (1968 edition).

[16]R. B. Nye and J. E. Morpurgo, *The Growth of the U.S.A.* (Penguin, 1955), p. 694.

[17]Dean Acheson, *op. cit.*, p. 16.

[18]*Ibid.*, p. 88.

[19]John Spanier, *American Foreign Policy since World War II* (Praeger, NY, 3rd ed., 1965). pp. 18–19.

[20]*Ibid.*, p. 15.

[21]*Ibid.*, p. 16.

[22]David Horowitz, *From Yalta to Vietnam* (Penguin, 1967). See for example pp. 31–2 and 57–60.

[23]G. F. Kennan, *American Diplomacy 1990–50* (Mentor, New York, 1951). See also D. Horowitz, *op. cit.*, pp. 59–60.

[24]*High Points on the Road* (Moscow, n.d.), p. 35.

[25]J. P. Nettl, *The Soviet Achievement* (Thames& Hudson, 1967), p. 176.

[26]*Ibid*.

[27]I have relied on R. W. Pethybridge, *A History of Post-War Russia* (Allen & Unwin 1966), Chapter 1, for this section.

[28]J. P. Nettl, *op. cit.*, p. 192. See also D. Horowitz, *op. cit.*, p. 28, for greater detail of Nazi destruction and looting of occupied Russia. Horowitz (p. 42) also records Stalin's annoyance at the abrupt way in which lend-lease was terminated, pointing out the difficulty caused to a country with a planned economy.

[29]H. Gatzke, *The Present in Perspective* (Murray, 1966), p. 112. See also Map 1 on p. oo above.

[30]Bruce Grant, *Indonesia* (Penguin, 1967), p. 29.

[31]Quoted in Jean Lacouture, *Ho Chi Minh* (Penguin, 1969), p. 97.

[32]See for example Henry S. Wilson (ed.), *West African Nationalism* (Macmillan, 1970).

[33]J. Hatch, *A History of Post-War Africa* (Methuen, 1967), p. 125.

[34]Dean Acheson, *op. cit.*, p. xvii.

CHAPTER TWO

The World since 1945

It is the object of this book to clarify some of the general trends and fundamental concerns of the post-war world, and in the chapters that follow the consequences of rapid population rise, the spread of industrialism and urbanisation, and in their wake the growth of increasingly collectivist States, the changing pattern of international relations in the nuclear era, and the cumulative impact on the earth's natural resources of industrial waste and human despoliation, will be discussed. Something, too, will be said about the emergence of a dividing line between the poor coloured peoples of the world and the affluent white nations, and about the revolt of the dispossessed and the young against the privileged and the established.

In this chapter the approach will be more limited in area, the subject matter being confined to three phenomena of the last quarter century which lend themselves to historical treatment. The first of these is chosen with the deliberate intention of providing a narrative thread of international political and military affairs from 1945 to 1970. Combined with the statistical material in Appendix A, 'Cold War and Co-existence' provides the historical context inside which the remaining concerns of the book are treated. Other events, perhaps of more lasting significance, have taken place while the Soviet-American power struggle has held the foreground, but it is this struggle that has preoccupied the world's leading statesmen. Largely centred upon Europe and Asia, it has affected all the world, other nations being lined up as allies or competed for as such by both major powers. In this way most of the international crises that provide the punctuation marks of the post-war story will come under scrutiny.

COLD WAR AND CO-EXISTENCE

Historians and commentators do not agree on the precise beginning or duration of the period of intense Soviet-American hostility known as the Cold War. Nor do they agree when they try to apportion blame for the deterioration of relations between the two major partners of the successful anti-Hitler Alliance. So far as the latter is concerned, indeed, it is probably fruitless to try. As one Sovietologist has observed of the two protagonists, 'both were the prisoners of their knowledge, experience and ideology'.[1] America and Russia had come by different roads to a similar greatness but the legacy of history and the suspicions and dangers of the present hour undermined co-operation once the immediate bond of opposition to Hitler had been dissolved by victory.

From Washington, Truman saw Stalin, paranoid dictator of a communism sworn to the overthrow of capitalism, consolidating his grip on Eastern Europe in a manner which scarcely seemed to accord with the wartime agreements of Yalta and Potsdam. In Moscow, Stalin remembered the hostile intervention of the capitalist powers in Russia at the end of the First World War, and viewed with alarm continued American development of the atomic bomb and the establishment of American bases around Russia's perimeter. The ambiguous language of Yalta and the very different world perspectives from the Kremlin and the White House served only to exacerbate strain and tension.

With a stable balance of power and the arrival of the nuclear bomb, however, both sides took care not to take up extreme positions. Hot war was avoided, but a cold hostility built up in which many of the conditions of war prevailed: propaganda branding the 'enemy' as evil and raising the home flag of righteousness; lack of contact or sympathy; competition for allies; feverish research and development of weapons of destruction. Even so, relations did not cool at once. A short transition period occurred, from late 1945 to early 1947, before Soviet-American relations sank visibly below zero.

1945–47

At the Yalta Conference in February 1945, Roosevelt, Stalin and Churchill planned the post-war occupation of Germany, arranged Russian involvement in the war against Japan, and agreed to support a United Nations Organisation to promote peace and security after the war. The Conference was fairly cordial, the several parties reasonably accommodating. At The Potsdam Conference, from 17 July to 2 August 1945, the atmosphere was less amicable. Germany had already surrendered. Stalin, and to a lesser extent Truman and Attlee (who replaced Churchill during the Conference), had already started to think more in terms of national interest rather than Allied success. To some commentators, the Cold War was already beginning.

It is probably true, however, that American policy had a number of adjustments to make yet, before its traditional optimism and its new faith in international co-operation faded. Russia had no such faith, suspected the West, and sought to consolidate its gains and repair its losses. In pursuing its interests with single-minded intransigence, it confirmed, or provoked, the Western hostility in which it believed. Points of irritation soon emerged; differences of interpretation of hasty wartime agreements, conflicting solutions to new problems and then the chain of action and reaction as each felt disadvantaged by the other's moves. Both Russia and America were feeling their way in this period and mutual clumsiness in new roles added ample grounds for mutual antagonism to the already existing confrontation of two rival great powers.

American critics of Russia complained because Stalin, thinking above all in terms of 'spheres of influence', went his own way in Eastern Europe. Stalin's interpretation of 'free' choice of government in Poland, his determination on the Oder-Neisse line as Poland's frontier, his domination of Finland, Bulgaria, Hungary and Rumania, and his subjugation

of Eastern Germany, disappointed the West. Slow Russian
withdrawal from Iran in 1946 and Russian demands for a share
in the control of the Turkish Straits indicated expansionist
intentions, with grave repercussions for both Middle East and
Mediterranean. Russian obstructionism over the Peace
Treaties, from July 1946 to March 1947, further soured the
international atmosphere.

American foreign policy altered accordingly. In 1944,
Cordell Hull, American Secretary of State, was busy planning
a post-war utopia on theoretical lines which assumed co-
operation through international machinery. By 1946, Secretary
of State Burns, still seeking to create a strong United Nations
Organisation, had formulated a policy of 'firmness and
patience' in the face of Russian intransigence. He believed that
America had shown a willingness for friendship, had been re-
buffed, and must now indicate that it would not yield to threats
or compromise in the interests of quick solutions. Already
Winston Churchill had warned America at Fulton, Missouri,
that the only language understood by Russians was the language of strength, and that America and the British Commonwealth must oppose powerful Russian expansionism by equally
powerful resistance. This view was taken further by George
Kennan, appointed in 1946 Director of the Policy Planning
Staff at the State Department. Bringing together a deep knowledge of Russian history and close observation of the Russian
leadership, he concluded that Communist Russia was basically
and constantly hostile to the capitalist world, that it would seek
every opportunity to harass and undermine that world, and
that America, the capitalist world's champion, must base its
own actions on 'policies no less steady in their purpose, and
no less variegated and resourceful in their application, than
those of the Soviet Union itself'.[2] By March 1947 the time
seemed ripe for America to take the initiative in this new policy
of 'containment'.

Meanwhile, of course, critics of America were not without
plenty to support their point of view. The very dropping of the
atom bomb on Hiroshima could be interpreted as an unnecessary act more designed to frustrate Russia than defeat
Japan. The purpose of the bomb, it was argued, was to end the

Japanese war before Russia was ready to invade, and thus qualify for the territories agreed at Yalta as its price for breaking the 1940 Japanese-Soviet Non-Aggression Pact. Certainly the Russians had not been taken into America's confidence. The continued development of the bomb, before any proposals for sharing nuclear knowledge, provided further evidence of American anti-Soviet hostility.

Western concern for the peoples of Eastern Europe was looked upon as hypocritical interference in Russia's sphere of interest by Stalin, who also found cause for suspicion in capitalist reluctance to exact reparations from Germany. And the American administration itself was divided over its own policies, some officials being afraid of promoting Russian hostility by apparent aggressiveness and by interference along Russia's borders. As Russia watched the establishment of American bases, from Western Germany to Japan, and listened to aggressive Western language, its alarm and obstinacy grew. But Russia, so heavily devastated by the war, was in no position to push America to extremes, while America, almost paralysed by its own nuclear power, still fumbled for an agreed policy. In fact a form of military stalemate had already occurred, even if few realised it at the time. America simply could not use its atomic bombs unless subjected to direct attack; and no nation could contemplate such an action. Later, when Russia acquired nuclear parity, and research began to be directed towards ever more sophisticated delivery and warning systems, it had already become too late to contemplate the actual use of nuclear weapons. But this is to look ahead. In the meantime the cold war had several phases to run.

1947–49

The occasion for the public inauguration of the new, tougher American policy was a crisis in Greece in 1947. There the British had assumed responsibility for supervising a return to normality after the war, and by 1947 a combination of civil war in Greece and economic crisis in Britain together ensured that the British were no longer able to uphold a corrupt but elected Greek Government in the face of communist insurgents, supported from Bulgaria, Albania and Yugoslavia. In February the British informed the Americans that they would not be able to continue their commitment after the end of March. With an early appreciation of the 'domino theory', President Truman decided to act to prevent Greece falling to the communists, with the subsequent collapse of the Eastern Mediterranean and beyond. On 12 March, Truman asked Congress for 400 million dollars (250 million for Greece, 150 million for Turkey) to 'support free peoples who are resisting attempted subjugation by armed minorities or by outside pressure'. The 'Truman Doctrine' had been enunciated. The United States now assumed the burden of preserving the 'free' world for 'democracy'. To Soviet intransigence and singlemindedness were henceforward joined American determination and inflexibility. The Cold War had begun in earnest.

This specific rescue operation was followed by a much more imaginative and far-reaching American plan of assistance for the whole of Europe. The Marshall Plan, based on a recognition that Europe was one of America's vital interests, and announced by Secretary of State, General George Marshall, on 5 June 1947, was directed 'against hunger, poverty, desperation and chaos' all of which were growing in a Europe still ravaged and dislocated by war. It is in such conditions, of course, that communism thrives. But the American offer was not restricted to the non-communist world. All could benefit from American aid who would work out their own needs and a full recovery plan. Admittedly, by making so wide an offer, the Americans could not fail to benefit, for if Russia rejected help then her rejection would be interpreted as surly hostility, while if Russia accepted, then American aid and organisation would undermine Russian authoritarian control in Eastern Europe, and possibly even communism itself. Russia, noting this declared purpose of the 'Truman Doctrine', rejected Marshall aid and also prevented its satellites, and even Czechoslovakia, from accepting. Thus Western Europe, quickly agreeing on its needs, was the sole beneficiary of the 13,000 million dollars of enlightened self-interest expended by America in the four years from 1948. And thus too, the 'iron curtain' division of Europe was reinforced.

In 1947, Czechoslovakia had not yet come fully under Russian domination, the government of Benes and Masaryk still hoping to provide a real bridge between East and West. But in February 1948 a communist *coup* placed the Czechs squarely inside the Russian orbit and cast much gloom over an insecure Western Europe. Matters were made worse when, in June 1948, East-West dissension over Germany, simmering since 1946, boiled up into a Russian blockade of West Berlin.

Because of opposing views on reparations, and the failure to conclude a German Peace Treaty, the temporary zones of the Allied occupation of Germany, agreed at Yalta, had become semi-permanent. The Western Allies had begun to rationalise their zones, to co-ordinate their administrations and establish a common currency, which in turn led to a flow of goods into the West German shops, which proved embarrassing to the Eastern authorities. The point of maximum embarrassment was West Berlin, lying deep within the Soviet occupation zone, and the Russians consequently decided to prevent Allied road and rail access there. The Western Allies thus faced a challenge which could have resulted in a humiliating abandonment of West Berlin's two and a half million citizens and a monumental psychological defeat, which, as in the case of the Greek crisis, might have had incalculable consequences in other areas. Deciding to stand firm, however, America and Britain conducted an airlift of essential supplies into West Berlin until, on 12 May 1949, the Russians gave up their blockade. Soon after, on 21 September 1949, the Western Allies finally merged their zones into a new German Federal Republic, with its capital at Bonn. In the following months the Russians too recognised the permanence of the division line in Germany by setting up the German Democratic Republic.

The Czech coup and the Berlin blockade caused great apprehension in Western Europe and underlined its military unpreparedness. Britain and France had already signed a Defence Pact at Dunkirk in 1947 and they now instigated the Brussels Defence Treaty, in March 1948, by which Britain, France, Belgium, Holland and Luxembourg promised military co-operation in the event of war. This was expanded in turn

to incorporate American strength on 4 April 1949, when the
North Atlantic Treaty Organisation was created, adding to the
Brussels powers the United States, Canada, Denmark, Ice-
land, Italy, Norway and Portugal (Greece and Turkey joined
NATO in 1951, and in 1955 the German Federal Republic
was admitted). Just as Russia had responded to the Marshall
Plan by organising her Eastern European satellites into
Comecon (Council for Mutual Economic Assistance), in
January 1949, so in due course Russia replied to NATO by
creating amongst its allies the Warsaw Pact (1955).

In this way, by the time that the Berlin blockade ended – and
its end provided welcome relief to Western exchequers and
morale – both sides had more or less established their positions,
assured themselves of their moral rectitude and injured innocence, and built up a chicken-and-egg chronology of
virtuous action based solely on response to the aggressive
designs of the other.

1949–53

In the next phase (and it must be stressed that these phases are
very arbitrary divisions in what is in reality a single process,
here broken down into manageable portions) the front line
of the Cold War, hitherto largely confined to Europe, shifted
to other parts of the globe, principally to the Far East.

Before turning to the outbreak of the Korean War in the
summer of 1950, however, two occurrences of the autumn of
1949 should be noted. The first was the announcement by the
watchful President Truman, on 23rd September, that the
Russians had exploded an atomic device. The American
nuclear monopoly was hereby ended. The second, the triumph
of Mao Tse-tung's army and the establishment of the Peoples
Republic of China on 1st October, had a similar effect on
Russia's ideological monopoly of Communism. Already
challenged in 1948 by tiny Yugoslavia, Russia's claim to communist infallibility was now faced by a more formidable rivalry,
even though, at the time, Mao's success seemed simply to add
an even more fearsome threat to the beleaguered capitalist
West.

It was in the shadow of these events that the communist troops of North Korea penetrated South Korea on 25 July 1950. Korea, under Japanese control since 1910, had been divided, like Germany, into occupation zones at the end of the war, Russia dominating the North, America the South. Communist and conservative capitalist regimes had been set up to mirror the occupying powers, whose forces then withdrew, in late 1948 and mid-1949 respectively, after failing to agree on how to unify the country. The Americans had at one stage proposed nationwide elections to achieve union; now the North Koreans adopted a military solution of their own.

Their action was branded as aggression by the United Nations and on 7th July the Security Council established a United Nations Command to aid the South Koreans. This Command, dominated by the United States, which had already decided to intervene and whose troops in Japan were nearest to hand, was made possible by a temporary boycott of the Security Council by the Soviet Union, which consequently was not able to exercise its veto. The Russians nevertheless quickly branded American action as illegal.

For a year the conflict in Korea see-sawed up and down that unhappy peninsula, the United Nations forces first retreating, then advancing beyond the border into the North, then reversing under the weight of Red Chinese military intervention, then fighting slowly back to the 38th Parallel, the original demarcation line. By the spring of 1951 the two sides had settled down in deadlock along this line. Negotiations for a cease-fire were opened in the summer at Panmunjom, but two years of fighting, haggling and recrimination elapsed before a truce was reached on 27 July 1953.

Korea provided a focus for Cold War tensions, though America and Russia avoided direct contact and neither was prepared to commit itself fully. It was not the only theatre of operation however. The Communist Chinese consolidated their position in 1951 by over-running Tibet. In Indo-China, the unresolved conflict between France, increasingly backed by America, and the communist-nationalist rebels under Ho Chi Minh and General Giap, pursued its bloody course. This particular struggle, begun in 1946, was concluded in 1954 with an agreement partitioning Vietnam along Korean lines. France, after the humiliating defeat of Dien Bien Phu, was ready to negotiate, as were the interested Russians and Chinese as well as the North Vietnamese. Only America, under the aggressive leadership of Secretary of State John Foster Dulles, was reluctant, fearing total communist control of South East Asia.

American interest in Indo-China did not in fact end with the 1954 settlement, as is all too tragically apparent from the subsequent narrative. Nor did America slacken its efforts to build up around the world a comprehensive network of alliances against communism. A brief list of United States Treaty relationships in 1953 gives no real guide to this American military network, re-inforced as it was with numerous bases encircling Russia, but it is illuminating and interesting none the less. By 1953, regional Treaties existed with Latin America (the Organisation of American States, 1947), Europe (NATO, 1949) and Australasia (The ANZUS Pact 1951), while bilateral treaties had been conducted with the Philippines (1951), Japan (1951) and South Korea (1953). In the following year the South East Asia Treaty Organisation (SEATO) was added, and a formal treaty with Nationalist China (America also joined the Central Treaty Organisation (Cento) in 1959). The Korean War had forced America into the novel step of committing troops to battle abroad in peace time, on the assumption that American interests were threatened by the advance of communism anywhere. And this network of alliances was designed to guarantee support around the globe against Russian expansion or communist subversion. It was soon to involve America in further military actions.

Meanwhile, however, something of the intensity of the Cold War was lessened by events at the end of 1952 and during 1953. It was significant that in November 1952 Truman and the Democratic Party were defeated by a Republican Party which had sworn to end the Korean war and whose Presidential nominee was General Dwight Eisenhower. Eisenhower set out to negotiate peace and his efforts were not hindered by the death, on 5 March 1953, of Joseph Stalin. The truce signed on 27 July 1953 allowed hope of better times. The astonishing news on 12 August that Russia had exploded a hydrogen bomb, only one year after America had made this breakthrough, emphasised that the balance of power, now a balance of terror, was balanced indeed, and that real accommodation between Russia and America was necessary.

1954–62

The Cold War thus entered its next phase in hope. The stop-gap Russian Premier, Malenkov, (March 1953–February 1955), and his more assured successor, Khrushchev, talked a new language of 'peaceful co-existence': a competitive struggle for the allegiance of the world's peoples, no less than before, but now to be conducted on a scientific and economic, rather than a military and political footing. This language was actually matched by Churchill and by Eisenhower and Kennedy. But the facts of conflict were often at variance with it and in the course of these eight years the temperature of the struggle rose and fell while its battle lines extended worldwide in a bewildering number of directions, culminating in a spine-chilling Soviet-American confrontation over Cuba.

Never before had the oneness of the world been so underlined by the divisions amongst its peoples. The American and Russian blocs saw their vital interests extending everywhere; unrest in any part provided opportunity or threatened danger, and all non-aligned nations were wooed and pressured towards commitment, one way or the other. Thus it is possible to see as Cold War incidents such widely separated events as the American-backed extinction of a communist-oriented Guatemalan regime in 1954, and the Czechoslovakian arms deal to Egypt in 1955. And while something of a thaw in Soviet American relations was evidenced by the Russian willingness to conclude at last a Peace Treaty with Austria, in May 1955, and by the Geneva summit meeting between Eisenhower, Bulganin (Russian Premier and nominee of Khrushchev who officially replaced him in March 1958), Eden of Britain and Faure of France in July 1955, no progress was achieved on German

re-unification, disarmament, European security or East-West
contacts, the major issues of the time. And gloom returned in
1956 when uprisings in Poland and Hungary, (the latter
crushed by Russian troops), and an abortive attack on Egypt
and the Suez Canal by Britain and France in collusion with
Israel, revealed the underlying bloc hostilities and renewed
the aggressive rhetoric of war.

1956 demonstrated clearly the continuation of 'spheres of
influence'. Hungary reminded the world tragically that Eastern
Europe was Russia's preserve and that even after denouncing
Stalinist methods* Khrushchev was not prepared to forego
Stalin's security shield. But what of the Middle East and South
East Asia? Russia now raised tension in the former by seeking
in Egypt an Arab foothold in an area the West, though often
in conflict with Arab nationalism, sought to control. South
East Asia, however, was a more open hunting ground, in no
agreed sphere, and it was here in the years ahead that some of
the bitterest confrontation was to occur, as the 1954 Geneva
Settlement of Vietnam began to crumble under communist
pressure.

1957 brought no major international crisis, but it afforded
little relief to the capitalist camp. While Khrushchev consolidated his domestic position, Russian scientists achieved not
only the successful testing in August of an intercontinental
ballistic missile (needed for the delivery of nuclear warheads)
but also launched the first space satellite, Sputnik 1, in October,
followed by Sputnik 2 in November. Suddenly Russia had come
from behind to lead in the power battle.

Events in 1958 seemed, in consequence, to be inspired by a
new Russian confidence. Most notable in this context was
Khrushchev's announcement in November that Russia no
longer recognised Allied rights in West Berlin and that after
six months had elapsed Berlin would become a 'free city'. But
there had already been a number of incidents in the Middle
East where increasing Russian involvement in Egypt brought
American and British counter-intervention in the Lebanon

*On 24 February 1956 Khrushchev delivered an astonishing attack on Stalinism
at the 20th Congress of the Communist Party of the U.S.S.R.

and Jordan. In July an anti-Western revolution had been successful in Iraq. So, over Berlin the Allies decided to stand firm, and Russia, gratifyingly, did not pursue its policy. Instead Khrushchev opened negotiations for another 'summit' meeting.

To prepare for this, a meeting was arranged in August 1959 between Khrushchev and Eisenhower, and this took place cordially enough in the American President's retreat at Camp David, in September. Mr. Khrushchev's mood was no doubt improved by the first rocket (a Russian one) to hit the moon, and by the retirement from the U.S. Secretaryship of State of 'brinkman' John Foster Dulles. Thus 1959, a year which had begun excitingly with the overthrow of the Dictator of Cuba, Fulgencio Batista, by an obscure ex-teacher, Fidel Castro, on 1st January, ended in a more relaxed big power atmosphere. But the summit conference arranged for the spring of 1960 did not bring any increase of accord.

On 1 May 1960, an American U2 spy plane was brought down over Russia. This was denounced on 5th May by Khrushchev as 'direct provocation' and an 'aggressive act'. When the first session of the Summit Conference assembled at Paris on 16 May Khrushchev demanded an apology for this incident, cancelled Eisenhower's proposed visit to Russia, and ended the Conference before it had begun when no American apology was proferred. Khrushchev proceeded to issue dire warnings to nations harbouring American spy planes and to offer rocket protection to Castro's Cuba. In the autumn he attended the United Nations Assembly and delivered more invective. With the collapse of order in the newly independent Congo, in June, and with the subsequent adoption of Cold War stances on this issue in the United Nations and in Africa, another continent was added to the Cold War battle zones. In June also, Eisenhower was prevented from making a goodwill visit to Japan by the strength of left-wing opposition there. 1960 was therefore not an encouraging year for world amity, but there was some sign of decreasing tension when, in the autumn, on the election of John F. Kennedy as the President of the United States, Khrushchev despatched a telegram of congratulation, which also added a hope for greater East-West understanding.

Yet the years 1961 and 1962, if anything, saw an intensification of Cold War incidents, punctuated with moments of hopeful thaw. Space-competition entered a new dimension when, on 12 April 1961, Yuri Gagarin orbited the earth for Russia and became the first man in space. An American, Commander Alan Shepard, entered space in an up-and-down rocket flight in May, but Russia retained her impressive lead with a further prolonged, orbiting flight. President Kennedy had announced impressive plans for aiding developing countries in general and Latin America in particular (The Alliance for Progress) in March 1961, but his reputation suffered a severe set-back when an American-backed invasion of Cuba was humiliatingly defeated after landing in the 'Bay of Pigs' on 17 April.

This fiasco did not prevent Kennedy from meeting Khrushchev in Vienna, on 3–4 June 1961, but they failed to reach agreement on Germany, or Disarmament. Then, after Khrushchev had again threatened Western rights in Berlin, the East German Government tackled the severe drain on its manpower through defection to the West by erecting on 13 August that ghastly monument to the 'sixties, the Berlin Wall. On 1 September Russia resumed nuclear testing in spite of an unofficial Soviet-United States-British moratorium since 1958. In October 1961 Russia exploded a huge 50-megaton hydrogen bomb. The United States then resumed its nuclear testing in April 1962.

1962 is memorable of course for the dramatic 'Cuban Missile Crisis' of October – November. During the year American intelligence reports had indicated Russian assistance in building Castro's defences. On 16 October, U-2 reconnaissance photographs disclosed that ground-to-ground missiles were being installed; on 22 October, Kennedy, announcing this information to the world, placed an air-sea blockade on Cuba to prevent the shipment of further offensive materials and warned Russia to remove those already there. On 28 October, Khrushchev announced that the missiles on Cuba would be withdrawn and on 20 November Kennedy lifted a blockade that had forced

the entire world to hold its breath. These are the outline facts
of the story, so compellingly told from the American side by
Robert F. Kennedy in his short book *Thirteen Days*.[3]

President Kennedy had received personal assurances from
Khrushchev that Russian assistance to Castro was purely
defensive. Now these had proved to be untrue and Kennedy
felt it essential to have a showdown with Khrushchev. It was not
that a few missiles in Cuba had increased the threat to America
or upset the existing missile ratio: Russia could attack America
from her own soil if the need should ever arise, and America
still held many more missiles than Russia. Rather it was the
political loss of face and the impact of this on America's NATO
allies that worred Kennedy. He also feared that lack of resolution here would lead inevitably to worse Russian pressure
elsewhere, particularly on Berlin. Indeed the whole Russian
plan seemed to be based on an alarming assumption that
Kennedy would always back down in the interests of preserving
peace. Perhaps Khrushchev had misjudged his man, in Vienna;
perhaps Khrushchev's bid for a prestige success in Cuba was
motivated by domestic and satellite worries in Europe. At all
events the Russian leader was bidding for high stakes – nothing
less than the tipping of the world balance of prestige and power
dramatically in Russia's favour. But he was making dangerous
miscalculations, Kennedy thought, of the sort that might
involve the world in destruction if they were not instantly
exposed and countered. So the American President checked
his armaments, bided his time until his forces could be alerted,
and then issued his warming.

There followed great tension as a number of Russian vessels
steamed towards Cuba. Then Khrushchev sent two letters,
first suggesting withdrawal if America would guarantee not to
attack Cuba, but then adding some confusing afterthoughts
about the ending of American bases in Turkey. Kennedy
agreed not to attack Cuba but insisted on immediate Russian
withdrawal without any reciprocal action, though he hinted
that American bases in Turkey were no longer needed and
would shortly be terminated. On 28 October, the thirteenth
day of the crisis, Khrushchev accepted the situation and

recalled his missiles. The most direct Soviet-American confrontation of the Cold War had ended.

Kennedy, resisting American pressure for much tougher action, had exercised enough diplomacy in the crisis to avoid forcing Khrushchev into a corner. And he was careful not to follow up his success with boasting propaganda. But to at least one critic the crisis posed an ominous warning to the world of its own nuclear future: 'a future dominated by the immense gap between man's revolutionary technicological means, and his traditional, limited, political and ethical outlook'.[4] Nevertheless it went a long way towards clearing the freezing fog of the Cold War and ushering in a welcome thaw. To many commentators, indeed, the Cuban Missile Crisis marks the end of the Cold War.

1963–70

Statesmanship seemed to have triumphed in the face of nuclear holocaust and the world breathed a little easier after Cuba. The establishment of a 'hot line' telephone link between Washington and Moscow, designed to reduce tension, was agreed on 20 June 1963 and opened on 30 August 1963, while on 25 July, Russia, America and Britain signed a Nuclear Test Ban Treaty prohibiting all nuclear tests except those conducted underground. But though a more peaceful (if equally competitive) co-existence set in between Russia and the United States, the following years were not without tension and the two superpowers still often found themselves at serious odds. Ominously for both Russia and America, communist China also began to assume Great Power status, condemning as it did so both United States imperialist aggression and Russian Marxist perversions and inadequacies. Indeed the Sino-Soviet quarrel, simmering from the late fifties, boiled over after the Cuban Crisis, which afforded the Chinese the opportunity of criticising Khrushchev's weakness and his renewed commitment to 'peaceful co-existence'. Other central features of the Cold War in this period also stemmed from the later fifties, including the terrible tragedy of Vietnam, with the huge escalation, under successive Presidents, of American commitment there, and also the emergence of a 'Third World' group of nations mostly ex-colonial and anxious to avoid alignment with either commun-ism or capitalism.

Chronologically, the years from 1962 have had their share of drama. In 1963 President Kennedy was assassinated, in Dallas, Texas, on 22 November. He was automatically suc-ceeded by Lyndon Johnson, who was elected to the Presidency in his own right a year later. During that year Khrushchev was unceremoniously but bloodlessly deposed, the Kremlin announcement being delivered on 15 October 1964. The two pillars of his power were split, his Premiership passing to Kosygin, and his position as First Secretary of the Communist Party of the U.S.S.R. to Brezhnev. The following day Com-munist China conducted its first atomic explosion.

In 1965 the United States conducted in the Dominican Republic its third major post-war intervention in a neighbour-ing sovereign state (after Guatemala 1954 and Cuba 1961). This time American troops invaded and established a right-wing conservative, pro-American dictatorship.

United States-Soviet competition in space continued, with Russia gaining most of the spectacular 'firsts', particularly in 1966 with rockets soft-landing on the moon and striking Venus, though America caught the imagination of the world by putting the first men on the moon, Neil Armstrong and Ed Aldrin, on 20 July 1969. It was noticeable as the sixties advanced, how-ever, that the monolithic nature of both Eastern and Western blocs was disappearing. The most obvious Eastern division lay between Moscow and Peking, but some of Russia's European satellites were asserting themselves also. In the West, De Gaulle's France defied American leadership, and even within America itself dissent and protest grew. Meanwhile the con-tinuing war in Vietnam provided a constant barrier to Ameri-can-Soviet rapprochement, until the shock of Russia's invasion of Czechoselovakia, on the night of 20–21 August 1968 – an example of naked aggression against the legal Czech govern-ment and purely in the interests of the invading powers – sent a sickening shiver around the world and further reduced the possibility of East-West understanding. Russia stood con-

demned by a world which was deeply sympathetic to the self-
disciplined and dignified Czechs, but which was made all too
conscious of its inability to aid them as their hopeful 'socialism
with a human face' was brutally murdered.

World anger had also risen over the fighting in Vietnam.
America had assumed the protection of S.E. Asian, non-communist states after the Geneva Agreements of 1954, believing
that without help, these states must inevitably fall 'like a row
of dominoes' to communist pressure. Already in 1950 American
fear of communism had led to American support of the French
colonial regime, in spite of a general American commitment
to anti-colonialism. In the years after 1954 both North and
South Vietnam failed to implement the Geneva Agreements
and America stepped up, slowly but steadily, its support of the
South Vietnamese regime. In 1955 the Americans assumed
responsibility for training the South Vietnamese Army. From
1957, communist guerillas began to attack installations in
South Vietnam, and they increased their activities in 1960, the
year that the South Vietnamese National Liberation Front
(NLF) was formed. President Eisenhower responded in that
year by raising the number of American military advisers from
327 to 685.

The corrupt regime of Ngo Dinh Diem in Saigon was on the
point of collapse by the end of 1961, however, and the Americans were forced to prop it up against the communists by
raising their military personnel to four thousand (Feb. 1962).
This was not enough to avoid Diem's downfall, which occurred
in November 1963, to be followed by more right-wing regimes.
At the end of 1964 America announced the active aggression
of North Vietnam and their own determination to resist it.
The United States had responded to naval incidents in the
Gulf of Tonkin, in August, by bombing North Vietnamese
bases, and President Johnson had used the affair to acquire
from Congress power 'to take all necessary measures to repel
any armed attack against the forces of the United States and
to prevent further aggression'. On the basis of this power ('the
Tonkin resolution of Congress') the number of American forces
in Vietnam were increased ever more rapidly.

Early in 1965 American combat troops were first committed
to Vietnam, 100,000 men being rushed in during the summer;
then as the South Vietnamese regime proved unequal to the
struggle, the Americans also embarked on a policy of selective
bombing in North Vietnam. American troops were still theoretically deployed in support of the army of South Vietnam, but
this strategy was reversed in the autumn of 1966, when the
latter was assigned the role of pacification, leaving major combat to the Americans. By the end of 1967 the American military
strength had increased to half a million men, equipped with
the most sophisticated weaponry, transport and logistical support and backed by total air superiority. Explosive and napalm
bombing and aerial defoliation of suspected guerilla areas had
begun to reach fearsome proportions.

Step by step the United States government responded to
military advice promising an end to the war if only that extra
commitment required to break resistance was made. In 1970
the same enthusiasm for 'peace with honour' led President
Nixon to authorise his troops to enter Cambodian territory in
pursuit of Viet Cong base-camps there. Yet the problems of
South Vietnamese stability and social development, let alone
North Vietnamese military commitment, seemed no nearer to
solution. For what purpose therefore had the Americans embarked upon, sustained and expanded so unrewarding a
struggle?

The plain official answer is that America was helping the
free people of South Vietnam to resist aggression from the
North. This, and the wider implications of American commitment were spelled out fairly typically by President Johnson
on 28 July 1965:

Most of the non-Communist nations of Asia cannot, by
themselves and alone, resist the growing might and grasping
ambition of Asian communism. Our power, therefore, is a
vital shield. If we are driven from the field in Vietnam, then
no nation can ever again have the same confidence in American promise, or in American protection. In each land the
forces of independence would be considerably weakened.
And an Asia so threatened by Communist domination would
imperil the security of the United States itself.

We did not choose to be guardians at the gate, but there is no one else.

Nor would surrender in Vietnam bring peace. We learned from Hitler at Munich that success only feeds the appetite of aggression. The battle would be renewed in one country and then another, bringing with it perhaps even larger and crueller conflict.

Moreover, we are in Vietnam to fulfil one of the most solemn pledges of the American nation. Three Presidents – President Eisenhower, President Kennedy and your present President over 11 years, have committed themselves and have promised to help and defend this small and valiant nation.[5]

A different analysis of the issues involved might be presented by anti-American observers around the world but the words of a leading public figure in America itself, the passionately patriotic Democratic Senator from Arkansas, and Chairman of the Senate Foreign Relations Committee, William Fulbright, no less, may be the more significant because of their origin. Senator Fulbright has written in *The Arrogance of Power* – a book the apposite title of which reaches to the source of America's post-war dilemma – the following substantially different answer:

Why are the Americans fighting in Vietnam? For much the same reason, I think, that we intervened militarily in Guatemala in 1954, in Cuba in 1961, and in the Dominican Republic in 1965. In Asia as in Latin America we have given our opposition to communism priority over our sympathy for nationalism because we have regarded communism as a kind of absolute evil, as a totally pernicious doctrine which deprives the people subjected to it of freedom, dignity, happiness and the hope of ever acquiring them....

The view of communism as an evil philosophy is a distorting prism through which we see projections of our own minds rather than what is actually there. Looking through the prism, we see the Viet Cong who cut the throats of village chiefs as savage murderers but American flyers who incinerate unseen women and children with napalm as valiant fighters for freedom; we see Viet Cong defections as the rejection of communism but the much greater number of defections from the Saigon Army as expressions of a simple desire to return to the farm; we see the puritan discipline of life in Hanoi as enslavement but the chaos and corruption of life in Saigon as liberty; we see Ho Chi Minh as a hated tyrant but Nguyen Cao Ky as the defender of freedom; we see the Viet Cong as Hanoi's puppet and Hanoi as China's puppet but we see the Saigon government as America's staunch ally; finally we see China, with no troops in South Vietnam, as the real aggressor while we, with hundreds of thousands of men, are resisting foreign intervention.[6]

This description of a distorting prism serves, I believe, as the best explanation for the whole course of the Cold War, not merely the particular struggle in Vietnam, though it is not to be denied that much clear, hard-headed realism has also been involved by both communists and capitalists determined to preserve their vested interests. Communism, by very definition, regards capitalism as evil, rapacious, essentially aggressive. Capitalist imperialism, Communists argue, has been the cause of war in the modern world and because it recognises in communism its chief opponent it must in its own interest seek to destroy communism. The record of the capitalist powers from the establishment of Bolshevik control in Russia bears out this analysis, so Communists must be both vigilant in the present and active in the future to seize opportunities to weaken capitalism and hasten its inevitable destruction.

But capitalists, (rather like the forces of the *ancien régime* viewing the American and French Revolutions of the eighteenth century) have only to read official communist policy-statements to be made aware of the threat to their own existence. The early Bolsheviks looked to world revolution to overthrow capitalism, and communists since have made no secret of their determination to promote this end. Thus each side, believing itself to embody real freedom, and holding that the other personifies evil and represents the major threat to its own survival, adopts a firm, belligerent stance.

Summary
With this in mind what retrospective judgements can be made on the first quarter-century of the Cold War? America's declared purpose during this period has been to contain com-

munist aggression, exemplified first and most visibly by Russia and the Red Army in Eastern Europe, but later seen to be embodied equally by Communist China in Asia. Yet containment of aggression has taken many unpalatable forms, and fear of a communism deemed to be undemocratic has led America to prop up many unsavoury regimes, in Europe and the Middle East as well as in Latin America, whose only virtue can have been their anti-communism. Right-wing dictatorships, from Spain to Guatamala, from the Dominican Republic to Turkey, and from Saudi Arabia to South Korea, to name but some, have enjoyed the bounty of American dollars, military equipment and 'counter-insurgency' advice. Even so respected a figure as Arnold Toynbee was led to conclude sadly, in 1961, that America had become 'the leader of a world-wide anti-revolutionary movement in defence of vested interests'.[7]

America, which had decided that Russian communist expansion must be curtailed above all else, did not observe that communism had ceased to be a mere Russian tool by 1948, took no heed of the independent communism of Yugoslavia and of China, and increasingly identified all revolutions designed to change the lot of the world's poor as communist revolutions and therefore to be opposed. Bad initial diagnosis, worse confounded by the distorting prism, has resulted in a contemporary denial of the outstanding characteristics of historic America. As David Horowitz has concluded bitterly:

> When America set out on her post-war path to contain revolution throughout the world, and threw her immense power and influence into the balance against the rising movement for social justice among the poverty-stricken two-thirds of the world's population, the first victims of her deed were the very ideals for a better world – liberty, equality and self-determination – which she herself, in her infancy, had done so much to foster.[8]

It would be idle to pretend however that the basic incompatibility of communism with capitalism, which underpins America's strategy, does not exist. Russia, since 1945, and China, increasingly since 1949, have both worked assiduously to destroy capitalism, China with specific venom against its

American champion as a result of the immense damage done
to China by America's policy since the war. Indeed Chinese
rage against America was partly behind the Sino-Soviet split,
for the Chinese would not tolerate the notion of peaceful co-
existence with America. Thus, in spite of the emergence of
'polycentrism' – the breaking down of the monolithic Eastern
and Western blocs into several centres of authority – fierce
rivalry continues and is likely to do so until, in Khrushchev's
phrase, 'shrimps learn to whistle'.

The competition in arms development, in international aid-
giving, and in space research, which has gained in tempo
between America and Russia since the end of the Second
World War, has now been fully augmented by Communist
Chinese participation. From the rifles of South East Asia in
the 1950's, to the cotton mills and guerilla tacticians of Africa
in the 1960s, on to the Chincom earth satellites of the 70s,
China has expended at least some of its resources to hasten the
downfall of international capitalist imperialism and heighten
the prestige of international communism. Today, as much as
ever, bloc competition is 'global in scope; military, political,
economic, social, and ideological in means; and total in aim'.[9]

Newly significant, however, is the nature of the internal
struggle being waged, equally in all camps, between progress-
ives and reactionaries, often between young and old, usually
between satisfied authorities and insistent peoples urging social
change. Here perhaps exists a world-wide but undogmatic
demand for social justice and a more equal distribution of the
world's resources; an impatience equally disposed against
rigid communism and greedy capitalism. Nowhere is it more
relevant than in the emergent nations struggling to form a
Third World.

THE END OF EMPIRE AND THE EMERGENCE OF
THE THIRD WORLD
The forces which led to the emancipation of European colonies,
particularly those in Africa, have already been referred to in
Chapter One (e.g. pp. 32–3). The European presence amongst
technically less advanced peoples both generated opposition

and created the tools by which that opposition was able eventually to triumph. European colonial administrations were built up to rule and exploit both already existing and, more often, newly created territorial units. European education, ideas and technical expertise then spurred colonial aspirations and showed the way to their attainment. As an Indian historian summed up the process recently:

> All over the world, nationalist leaders have been formed out of government subordinates, men who put their working hours to good use in studying the mechanics of power, and devoted their leisure to studying the obstacles barring their own promotion.[10]

European development of communications and towns broke traditional barriers and facilitated the evolution of new mass movements, which in turn demanded an end to European hegemony. The Europeans in India and in Africa gave to the inhabitants of India and Africa their first knowledge of themselves as Indians or as Africans. The scale of awareness, the pace of development, the quality of life on the continents of Asia and Africa were altered by the dynamism of Europe. But then Europe divided against itself, in murderous, uncontained, world-embracing wars, and the European powers left themselves unable any longer to hold down the rich and varied peoples whom they had temporarily ruled and permanently affected.

The end of European Empire, a largely post-war phenomenon, had, then, ancient origins, was inbuilt from the start even, though it had approached with increasing momentum in the years between the two world wars of this century. But how was it that European Empire had occurred in the first place? What is the explanation of European imperialism and what do we mean by such associated terms as 'colonialism' and 'neo-colonialism'?

The simplest way of describing that phase in the world's history in which Europeans overflowed into the neighbouring continents is in terms of physical energy and technical superiority. Empire is as old as man. Aggressive and militarily advanced peoples have throughout history subjugated, colonised and governed those unable to resist them. The modern European example began in an age-old tradition of adventure, lust after riches, personal and national glory, and even the desire to spread the gospel of religion or civilisation. By the start of the twentieth century a great deal of the world had surrendered to European domination, and the riches which Europeans acquired from their control had helped to advance European development and technical skills. The process of control had built up slowly over the centuries but there had been an acceleration of conquest in the last quarter of the nineteenth century that seemed to mark a new stage in Europe's domination of the world. European influence was extended in Asia, and though China resisted partition, it was opened up to European trade; Europe penetrated the Americas, for although that rebellious daughter nation of Europe, the United States, had warned off a re-conquest of Latin America, nevertheless European investment established a considerable degree of European influence; and Africa, more vulnerable, was overwhelmed and almost totally carved up by the predatory European nations

One way or another, power in the world thus passed into European hands. Much of the territory of the globe had been conquered and was being administered by Europeans; much of the rest was in a position of clientage to European capital. Indeed it was the advanced nature of industrial development and capital accumulation in Europe, so far ahead of the other portions of the world, that led Marx, and later Lenin, to explain European imperialism solely in terms of the capitalist process.

To Lenin, who wrote the most refined Marxist explanation of imperialism, in 1916,[11] this phenomenon was but a stage in the development of capitalism itself; an inevitable but, as it happened, the final stage. Large capitalist firms and monopoly combines, unable to keep up their level of profits at home, were forced to manipulate their governments to acquire new territories abroad, less developed territories, where, for a time, profit on investment would be high, raw materials would be available and goods would be sold, all in a stable context of

European control. In the end, of course, development in these
territories would exhaust profit opportunities, and as no new
territories would exist, the capitalist process would collapse.

Though the technical arguments used to substantiate this
theory of imperialism are complicated, it did seem to provide
a single explanation for modern European expansion. No matter what was claimed, argued Lenin, imperialism was a stage
in a capitalist economic process designed to perpetuate a system
which exploited not only its home citizens but also its colonial
peoples in the interests of the tiny minority who owned the
factories and great financial combines of Europe. Although it
was appealingly comprehensive, however, Lenin's explanation
did not fit the actual circumstances of even the most advanced
of the imperialist powers, Great Britain. Lenin's 'Monopoly
capital' had not developed in Britain at the time of the greatest
expansion of British territory, and his analysis had even less
validity, in terms of its timing and content, when applied to
such powers as France, Holland or Portugal.

Nevertheless if, to Marxists, 'imperialism is the monopoly
stage of capitalism' – a word, that is, which describes a phase
in a historical, economic process – it has a very different meaning to most non-Marxists. For them the word 'imperialism' is
used to describe all those incidents of the extension of European
rule which have occurred around the globe; which have
occurred, furthermore, for a wide variety of reasons and in a
wide variety of circumstances. Today, most of those who reject
the Marxist theory would also deny the existence of any single
replacement theory. Few would deny that economic motives –
the pursuit of private gain as well as national wealth – have
ranked high amongst the incentives for imperial acquisition.
But the private desire of colonial officials for personal glory or
adventure, the determination of colonial communities to
expand, whether their metropolitan governments approved or
not, have been stimuli from the periphery of Empire, just as the
search for naval bases, colonial counters for the European game
of diplomacy or hope of profitable markets and materials, have
been amongst the ambitions of imperial governments at the
centre of Empire. French military conquest in the Western

Sudan dragged a reluctant home government after it; successive British officials in India extended the territory of the Raj
without authorisation from London; the collapse of native
government in Egypt brought Britain and France into direct
administration to protect their investments; fear of foreign
exclusiveness prompted British, French, German, and Portuguese acquisition in Africa in the 1880's in an orgy of pre-
emptive xenophobia. The record of imperialism is infinitely
varied and there can be no single explanation to suit all circumstances. This can be further demonstrated by an examination of European activities in the territories so acquired.
Nigeria, for example, was fenced off from foreign encroachment
by a Britain anxious not to see more areas closed to free trade.
Britain had no policy of active development for Nigeria. During
sixty years of British rule only haphazard exploitation of
resources occurred and the development of administration and
communications had more or less to depend on the colony
paying its own way. The Dutch East Indies or the Belgian
Congo, on the other hand, might serve as examples of territories purposefully developed to the benefit of the metropolitan economy; while Great Britain's treatment of the West
Indies, or India, or for that matter Ireland, might illustrate
the subordination of colonial to metropolitan interests, if not
actual examples of concerted exploitation.

Imperialism – historically an accumulation of incidents –
can be defined in political terms as 'the rule of people by other
people for other people'. Springing from European technical
superiority, it carried with it an understandable if less excusable
assumption also of European cultural superiority. This latter
aspect has caused damage to indigenous traditions and confusion to indigenous peoples, and its modern legacy is as
apparent as the parallel legacy of distorted development in the
economic sphere. European arrogance and Euro-centric
policies together account for the evil reputation of imperialism,
even though a long list of benefits to indigenous communities
flowing from the imperial process can be compiled.

Controversial in explanation and analysis, imperialism was
still very much a fact of life at the end of the Second World War,

and has since been a much used stick with which Communists
in particular have sought to belabour their capitalist opponents.
But imperialism is also used today to describe the Russian
consolidation of Eastern Europe and the subjection of satellite
countries to Russian economic and diplomatic needs. The
modern imperialisms of the Red Army and the rouble, as well
as of the Green Berets and the dollar, have given new lease of
life to an old term formerly applied to the power of Western
Europe. But what of colonialism and neo-colonialism?

In the ancient tradition of Empire, colonialism ought to refer
to that most powerful spur to expansion, the necessity of finding
room for surplus population by settlement abroad. But it has
to be admitted that in modern parlance 'colonialism' and
'imperialism' have commonly been confused and interchanged.
Most conveniently, 'colonialism' can be used to describe the
system by which imperial authority has been planted and
preserved on the ground; that is in the 'colony'. This usage
also allows Marxists to use colonialism to describe the
individual incidents, or expressions, of the imperialist stage of
capitalism. The word is perhaps only worth examination
because of its more insidious modern mutation 'neo-
colonialism'.

'Neo-colonialism' has a contemporary relevance full of Cold
War significance. The term is used to describe the manipulation
of the economies of nominally independent states – usually
young, ex-colonial, underdeveloped states – by rich manufacturing nations. Or, as Kwame Nkrumah, former President
of Ghana, has put it: 'The essence of neo-colonialism is that
the State which is subject to it, is in theory independent and
has all the outward trappings of international sovereignty.
In reality its economic system and thus its policy is directed
from outside'.[12] It can refer to continued domination by the
former imperial power – for example, France or Great Britain
in West Africa – or the domination by a new master, such as the
United States, whose grip of 'independent' economies, far from
being confined to the new nations of Asia and Africa, extends
also from Latin America to Canada and into Europe. Neo-
colonialism has become a Cold War term of abuse, particularly

in relation to nations aspiring to avoid alignment with either of
the two Great Power blocs, for economic penetration has often
frustrated that aspiration, or so at least it has seemed. Thus
Cold War charge and counter-charge has been mounted, as
Russian influence has predominated in Cuba or Egypt, and
America has gained advantage in Indonesia or Guinea. In a
world of increasing interdependence of alliances, blocs and
trading groups, it has been extremely difficult for new, often
unbalanced and ill-equipped economies to withstand pressure
from the developed nations which are usually able to control
international price agreements and can in any event dictate
terms from strength. Short of capital for development, short
of technical expertise and often in need of planning experience,
the new nations have fallen prey to outside 'neo-colonialist'
influence. The term reflects the real sources of power in the
world, the prevailing tension and mistrust, and the inability of
'civilised' man to put first his human obligation to 'feed the
hungry, clothe the naked'. Neo-colonialism, pronounced by
Nkrumah to be 'the last stage of imperialism', resembles more
the practice of indirect domination that obtained in those
areas of the 19th century world which were stable and pliant
enough not to require European conquest and colonial
administration. There is little promise in it of finality, or of
better things to come, so long as the affluent, developed
countries continue to put their own affluent development at
the head of their priority list.

But enough of terminology; how has the process of decolonisation since 1945 worked out in practice? And if neo-
colonialist accusations are true, and there should in consequence be a question mark added to the expression 'end of
Empire', what are the implications for that group of countries
endeavouring to constitute themselves as a Third World, free
from outside manipulation?

In the quarter century since the end of the war some sixty
countries with a combined population of 1,250 million people,
one third of mankind, have been freed from direct colonial rule
in Asia, Africa and the Caribbean. The process has been a two-
sided one of decreasing imperial power and rising colonial

strength in not always even proportions. The initiative was first seized in Asia, where the independence of the Philippines in 1946 was the prelude to a rapid withdrawal of European powers. India and Pakistan followed in 1947, Burma and Ceylon in 1948, Indonesia in 1949 and then Indo-China in 1945, to mark out a notable decade of Asian political emancipation.

Meanwhile Libya, placed under the United Nations after the defeat of Italy, became the first African colonial territory to gain independence, in December 1951. Egypt came to terms with Britain in 1954 and the Sudan, Tunisia and Morocco attained independence in 1956. With the independence of Ghana, the first emancipated colony south of the Sahara, in 1957, the 'African decade' was firmly launched. Major territories such as the former Belgian Congo and Nigeria became independent in 1960, as did the bulk of French West and Central African colonies, while the important East African States of Tanganyika, Uganda and Kenya achieved their independence in 1961, 1962 and 1963 respectively. In Central Africa, Zambia followed in 1964. In the Caribbean, in 1962, an abortive 4-year experiment in Federation failed, and the British West Indian islands began to attain sovereignty, with Jamaica and Trinidad & Tobago leading the way in that year.

Decolonisation has thus been astonishingly quick and comprehensive, with virtually all peoples aspiring to independence gaining their objective, apart from the large, sparsely populated East and West African colonies of Portugal. Europe, already seeking to adjust to its inferior status in the world, had thus also to adjust to the loss of colonial lands which, though in some cases profitable, supplying materials, markets and employment, in others had proved to be but a drain on metropolitan resources. Dean Acheson's remark about the British post-war imperial position might therefore be given general application: not just Britain but Europe had 'lost an Empire and not yet found a role'. The European imperial powers have had to meet their new circumstances in a variety of ways. Portugal alone of these nations avoided the loss of its Empire. It is perhaps significant that Portugal was also alone in not being involved in the Second World War, and that its territories were protected from hostilities, partly through the 1943 Azores Agreement with Great Britain. Angola and Mozambique, the two major units, are largely agricultural, thinly populated and backward in political development. And although an independence war is being waged in each, the determination of the Portuguese to develop and defend the territories has not slackened in the last quarter century. A law passed in 1951 to incorporate the overseas territories into the Portuguese state is symptomatic of this determination and Portugal has resolutely resisted all attempts by the United Nations to call it to account for its colonial policy.

The Netherlands had early to adjust to the loss of its valuable East Indian colonies, unwilling though it was, as Japanese expansion in the East and German occupation at home broke both the tradition of rule and the power to recover it. In contrast, Belgium retained control of its huge Congo territory and continued its policy of *paternalisme*, by which economic and commercial activity were developed but African political advance was ignored. A rushed attempt to bring the Congo somewhat into line with political evolution elsewhere in Africa was begun in 1955 when the Governor-General announced that paternalism would be replaced by partnership. This led in 1957 to a limited form of local government and, after riots in 1959, to the sudden agreement of the Belgians to independence in 1960. Considerable chaos followed, with the former rulers endeavouring without much success to rescue something of their large colonial mining investments.

France and Britain had, of course, to make the greatest readjustments of all. France had been particularly hard hit by German occupation and by the split of authority between the home Vichy government and the Free French government in exile. After the liberation of France both the metropolitan country and its oversea territories required new constitutional forms, but the French Union, established in 1946 with the Constitution of the Fourth Republic, did not grant or even envisage independence for the colonies. Instead they were to become participants with France in the management of the

Union. Revolts, and the inability of the Paris Government to control its military commanders, changed the situation. First, in Indo-China relations deteriorated into all-out nationalist war which ended in 1954 with the independence of Vietnam, Cambodia and Laos. Then, in that same fateful year, revolt broke out in Algeria, and a bloody conflict ensued which again ended in defeat for France when Algeria became independent, in 1962.

Meanwhile, the Fourth Republic had fallen in 1958. The Fifth Republic re-organised the oversea territories into the French Community, which soon matured into a group of independent republics associating with France as well as residual island units scattered around the world. Under de Gaulle, the Fifth Republic thus adjusted to the colonial aspirations of the post-war world. However, partly due to legislation in 1956 (The *Loi Cadre* or 'Enabling Law') which emphasized territorial rather than regional (federal) development, a number of the independent units which France guided to independence were ill-equipped economically to stand on their own feet. They were thus to a large degree still dependent on French support and while this raises neo-colonialist charges, it has eased both the economic and psychological adjustment of the French.

Something has already been written of the emergence of the British Commonwealth of Nations and its transition after 1947 into a world-wide partnership of free peoples. Burma did not take up the option of membership, in 1948, nor did the somewhat ambiguously colonial Sudan upon gaining independence in 1956. In 1949 Eire departed to become the Republic of Ireland, but in the same year the Commonwealth took the decision in principle to permit members to enjoy republican status. When in 1961 South Africa sought to continue membership as a republic, such opposition to its racist domestic policies was voiced that it did not proceed with its request to remain in the association. The departure of South Africa was then viewed as an important stage in the development of a truly multi-racial Commonwealth. Subsequently, as territory after territory has attained independence, the Commonwealth ranks have swelled to include free peoples from all continents, of all creeds and at all stages of development. The Commonwealth, to the disappointment of some British 'die hards', has since proved very far from being 'the British Empire under a new name'; rather its existence has posed an exciting challenge to at least a few British, and a greater number of other Commonwealth statesmen. With traditional links and a shared understanding of administration and law (after all, as John Strachey wrote, 'To know a no-ball from a googly, and a point of order from a supplementary question are genuinely to have something in common'[13]), the Commonwealth has the potential to give a lead in international co-operation across all barriers. While it remains in being it provides the best hope for bridging the widening gulfs between white and coloured and between rich and poor peoples.

European weakness and loss of will to rule was one side of a dual process, the other being the growing force of colonial nationalism described in the next section. But if the European powers had to resign themselves to loss of direct control over many colonial areas, how have the emergent nations fared in their search for personal dignity, national progress and a better world? Something of the answer to these questions may be found by examining their attempt to creat a viable, non-aligned Third World, distinct from the worlds of Russian communism and American capitalism. Later, in Chapter five, some of the individual hopes and attainments of these nations will be discussed, but how, together, and in association with a few older, but also under-developed countries, have they managed collectively?

Poverty has been one of the strongest driving forces as well as one of the most notable characteristics of the Third World nations. But as well as being poor these nations have sought to be uncommitted, and this has meant, almost without exception, that they have been non-communist. They have also been non-European. Largely ex-colonial, the nations of this self-conscious but not always consistent or easily recognisable group, have included such ancient states as Afghanistan, Iran and Ethiopia. They have organised into regional groups such

as the Arab League (1945) and the Organisation of African
Unity (1963), but some other basic identitities of interest have
led to attempted common action at the United Nations and
to sporadic international conferences. They have tried, without
conspicuous success, to formulate common policy and action to
reject bloc domination on the one hand and to promote their
own development on the other. They have condemned surviving colonialism, sought international aid, and publicised
their crying human needs while exposing the trivial expenditure and waste of the affluent nations.

With many of the cards of survival stacked against them,
the Third World nations have tried to stick together; but, it
has to be admitted, they have also had to compete against
each other for such limited aid as has been available. Even
within their common poverty there exists sufficient variety to
cause jealousy, rivalry and outright hostility. And their differences have been highlighted rather than resolved through
such major gatherings as the Afro-Asian Conference at
Bandung in 1955, and the differently oriented Non-alignment
Conferences at Belgrade, in 1961, Cairo in 1964, and Lusaka
in 1970. Nevertheless, these Conferences have given tangible
expression to an otherwise nebulous grouping and deserve
more attention than was accorded them by the Western press
at the times of their meeting.

The 1955 Conference, at Bandung in Indonesia, was convened by the 'Colombo powers' of India, Pakistan, Burma,
Ceylon and Indonesia, and attended by 24 other countries,
including China, the Philippines, Thailand, Japan, Egypt,
Turkey, Algeria, Libya, Ethiopia, Gold Coast and Sudan.
The Conference deliberately cutacross ideology and alignment
in an attempt to promote Afro-Asian solidarity against colonialism. It was an important gathering which marked the
arrival of Communist China as a force in international affairs.
The Conference excluded Russia, in spite of Russia's claim to
be part-Asian, classifying it instead as a European, white,
wealthy nation. A new 'Bandung spirit' of Afro-Asian co-
operation was hailed, but in the ensuing years Sino-Soviet
rivalry and Cold War competition disrupted this hopeful

accord.* An attempted second conference at Algiers, in 1965, had to be postponed and when it did at last meet, in 1969, it ended in fiasco. Meanwhile an unofficial offshoot of Bandung – the Afro-Asian Peoples Solidarity Organisation, which included Russia – held conferences in 1957, 1960, 1963 and 1966. Although under communist direction the main result of these conferences was to provide a forum for the intensifying Sino-Soviet hostility.

Nevertheless, contacts established at Bandung survived and multiplied. And the obvious prestige of the non-aligned nations present at Bandung was partly responsible for the initiatives leading to separate Non-alignment Conferences in subsequent years. The conferences at Belgrade and Cairo, in 1961 and 1964, were 'Bandungs without China' with the addition of Yugoslavia and Cuba. It is notable that, whereas twenty five nations attended at Belgrade, there were forty-seven** present at Cairo.

Both these Non-alignment Conferences owed something to the cold war tensions of the time at which they were held, but they were both at pains also to hammer out policy, and to clarify the principles underlying their world outlook.

The 1961 'Conference of Non-Aligned Nations' met in an atmosphere of general world anxiety. The collapse of the summit conference in Paris in May 1960, and the Berlin crisis, the resumption of nuclear testing and the indefinite suspension of disarmament talks which followed, brought dismay and consternation to the uncommitted nations. The two cold war blocs stood, as Raymond Aron has remarked, 'like two goats face to face on a narrow bridge, each as incapable of moving

---

*For a text of the final communique of the Conference, see C. P. Romulo, *The Meaning of Bandung* (U. of N. Carolina Press, 1956), pp. 92–102.

**Afghanistan†, Angola, Algeria†, Burma†, Burundi, Cambodia†, Cameroun, Ceylon†, Congo-Brazzaville†, Central African Republic, Cuba†, Dahomey, Ethiopia†, Ghana†, India†, Indonesia†, Iraq†, Jordan, Kenya, Kuwait, Laos, Lebanon†, Liberia, Libya, Malawi, Mali†, Mauretania, Morocco†, Nepal†, Nigeria, Saudi Arabia†, Senegal, Sierra Leone, Somalia†, Sudan†, Syria, Tanzania, Togo, Tunisia†, Uganda, U.A.R.†, Yemen†, Yugoslavia†, and Zambia. Ten countries sent observers: Argentina, Bolivia‡, Brazil‡, Chile‡, Finland, Jamaica, Mexico‡, Trinidad & Tobago, Uruguay‡, and Venezuela‡. [†also at Belgrade (plus Cyprus), ‡observers at Belgrade (plus Ecuador)]

forward as the other'.[14] It was up to the nations outside these
blocs to take the initiative for peace, so they met to make their
views known to the world with all the weight of their combined
assent. The Foreign Ministries of these countries felt, rightly,
that the Great Powers were tending to conduct world affairs
on the basis of might being right, with little inhibition about
ignoring the wishes of smaller nations, and with scant regard
to the precious sovereignty which many of these same nations
had just won. They realised, too, that the intensity of rivalry
between the Great Powers, expressed as it was in military
alliances and an arms race, posed a real threat of renewed
world war. They also observed the sharpening of economic
inequalities in the world. Partly to co-ordinate their efforts
at the United Nations, and partly to give what might be
termed a highly interested bystander's commonsense analysis,
they thus met and spoke out on behalf of a non-alignment that
was not just passively anti-bloc, but rather a positive expression
of the basic ideals of the United Nations.

Peace, reduction of tension, anti-colonialism (particularly
relevant with the Congolese cauldron bubbling still) were the
particular themes of 1961. In 1962 an Economic Conference
for developing countries was held at Cairo, and in 1964, also
at Cairo, the Second Non-aligned Conference met. It did so
in an atmosphere more congenial to its pre-occupations, for a
hundred nations had by then put their signatures to the 1963
Soviet-American nuclear test ban treaty. The Cairo Conference
issued a 'Programme for Peace and International Co-operation' and spelled out in detail the platform of non-alignment.
The underlying principles of this platform were later listed by
the Yugoslav Dr. Ranko Petkovic as: respect for sovereignty
and territorial integrity; equality of nations; non-aggression;
non-interference in the internal affairs of other countries; self-
determination; peaceful settlement of disputes; active international co-operation; and non-participation in military alliances of Great Powers.[15]

Unexceptionable, high-minded and hopeful, these principles
have yet had little attention in the years following Cairo. Already, before that gathering, India and Indonesia had quar-

relled, and the emergence of a bombastic China into the world of 'peaceful co-existence' had brought a further deterioration in international dealings. The very timing of the Cairo meeting, in relation to the proposed Second Afro-Asian Conference, had been the source of unfraternal manoeuvrings between India, China and Pakistan, while the subsequent dissension over membership, once Algiers had finally been nominated as the venue, prevented the 'Second Bandung' from taking place in 1965 at all, the fall of the Ben Bella regime in Algeria merely providing a face-saving excuse.

In 1970, from 8–10 September, a third Summit Conference of Non-aligned Nations took place at Lusaka, Zambia. At its close, the fifty-five participants bravely issued the 'Lusaka Declaration on Peace, Independence, Co-operation and Democratisation of International Relations', expressing concisely the non-aligned vision of the world, and commenting, in six resolutions, upon *apartheid* in South Africa, the continued existence of Portuguese Colonies, the situation in Zimbabwe (Rhodesia), the conflict in Indochina, the decolonisation process, and the Middle East. There was much high political thinking but little evidence of practical economic co-operation, that mutual co-operation which both President Kaunda of Zambia and President Nyerere of Tanzania had strongly advocated as the best means of development without alignment.

Frustratingly for the non-aligned, real power, both economic and military, remained with the developed countries of the two worlds of communism and capitalism. Third World weakness and necessity was not capable of resisting neo-colonialist penetration and cold war blandishments. The Western camp in particular has been able, by 'aid' tactics and military connivance, to enforce its own conception of non-alignment, requiring a narrow restriction of relations with communist countries but allowing wide freedom to deal with Western nations. As the 1960s entered their second half, a comment by Dr. Conor Cruise O'Brien revealed something of the stark truth lying behind those hopeful declarations of the minor nations – coloured, poor and apparently non-aligned – of the Third World. 'Instead of thinking of a non-aligned Third World', wrote Dr. O'Brien, 'it would be more realistic to think in terms of a world-wide capitalist economy of which the supposedly non-aligned countries form an integral part, and, considered as whole, a profitable part'. To O'Brien, the real problem facing the 'non-aligned' world remained its own advancement of social justice and welfare, and this would necessitate 'disciplined, revolutionary, political movements which are likely to be of communist type'.[16] This view is also the view of the greatest advocate from the Third World itself, Frantz Fanon.

Fanon's writing deliberately tears us away from cosy notions of a 'partnership for progress' between developed and developing nations, always conceived, of course, on terms and at a pace that suited the former. Fanon's analysis of the colonial situation is harsh, his language brutal, his description of 'real' and 'false' independence unsparing. His call to action is violent and uncompromising, and his writings have troubled the conscience and the comfort of the West and have inspired the oppressed in many continents, not least those of Black America searching for civil rights.

Frantz Fanon, a French West Indian negro, born in Martinique in 1925, was trained as a doctor in France and took up employment as a psychiatrist in Algeria in 1953 just as the revolution was about to break out there. Before his death from leukemia in 1961 he had completely identified himself with the struggle of the Algerian people and had written extensively of his experiences and observations. His classic denunciation of, and call to action against, colonialism, *Les Damnés de la Terre* (translated into English as *The Wretched of the Earth*) was published a month before his death.

Colonialism, to Fanon, was a violent outrage, a white rape of the defenceless non-white. It was achieved by military violence and maintained by oppressive force, racial, cultural and economic, as well as legal and physical. The colonial situation was starkly black and white, with evil and good, ruled and ruler, identified at opposite ends of the spectrum. Settler arrogance kept alive the colonial will to gain independence, but independence, once achieved, too often brought no real change.

For independence was too often accomplished by a native elite, which was educated to imperial standards, and which was in fact a middle class minority without creative ability, that simply wished to take over, not change completely, the existing system. Mere imitators of the Western middle class, these elites became cyphers of the West, mere intermediaries of Western capitalism, setting up their country 'as the brothel of Europe'.[17] Too often they allowed their country to degenerate into one-man rule with a dictator whose sole purpose was to 'become general president of that company of profiteers impatient for their returns, which constitutes the bourgoisie'.[18]

For Fanon, real independence lay only in revolution; violent, purifying revolution, drawing on the strength of the simple, rural communities, led by an enlightened vanguard, and exemplifying true national purpose. Here his plan was general, his language emotional; but his call to action was loud and clear. It was the mass of people, with whom the artist and the political leader must identify, who would constitute and would recreate the nation, who would bring the nation to its true independence.

Fanon occupies a high place in the pantheon of Third World heroes. Here, he is the forerunner of Che Guevara, would-be liberator of Latin America, in his reliance upon the peasant class (as Mao Tse-tung too had relied). Fanon presented a contrast to the non-violent, spiritual, Gandhi, who desired to achieve for Indians a personal sanctity, making them worthy of independence. Yet Fanon, like Gandhi, gave individual fulfilment top priority before national efficiency. Fanon, whose castigation of selfish ruling elites is mirrored in the Caribbean novels of V. S. Naipaul (e.g. *The Mimic Men*) and in such satirical works as Chinua Achebe's *Man of the People*, describing post-independence Nigeria, was spared the experience of office which, for Nkrumah and Nehru, so compromised their earlier radicalism, though he drew some of his insights from their failures.

Fanon wrote for 'millions of men who have been skilfully injected with fear, inferiority complexes, trepidation, servility, despair, abasement'.[19] His works provide a dazzling insight into the psychology of the colonised. His case, polemical, over-stated, dramatised though it may be, is as rousing a call to action to those still suffering colonial rule as was the *Communist Manifesto* of Marx and Engels to the oppressed proletariat of Europe a century before. But when Fanon talks of man's inhumanity to man, it is of white man's inhumanity to black man. His voice is the voice of the black poor, the black suffering, the black dispossessed.

Dispossession: this is Fanon's key to the continuing claims of the developing world. For it is not sufficient for the imperial power to pull out its administrators and soldiers and proclaim 'independence'. To Fanon, contemporary European opulence is derived from 'slavery and from the piratical robbery of the fruit of the natives soil and subsoil'[20] in the past. The West has kept the colonised in subjection for centuries and must now actively rehabilitate them. But Fanon also demands that the 'wretched of the earth' rise up themselves to claim their just share of the earthly kingdom.

Disillusioned and frustrated, the peoples of the Third World may yet respond to the rhetoric of Fanon, perhaps along the practical models supplied by Guevara and Mao Tse-tung. Their governments may continue to pay international court to the high ideals of non-alignment, but they do so uneasily astride domestic social volcanoes. Poverty and inequality demand direct and positive action at home, and so far there are few more which, like the government of President Nyerere of Tanzania, have the courage and insight to pursue such action.

Meanwhile, as Fanon's broad denunications of false independence await response in Asia and the Americas as well as in Africa and the Caribbean, we must observe that he placed precise confidence in the nation state as the means through which true independence would be achieved. Fanon's 'nation' may not be synonymous with the historic nation state of Europe, but in emphasising its role Fanon did identify with one of the most powerful inspirations of the post-war world. Nationalism, it seemed to Europeans in 1945, had run its course, outlived its usefulness. But its powerful resurgence throughout the continents of Asia and Africa in the following years requires us now to examine it. A vital part of the decolonisation story, nationalism retains an ambiguous place in the modern world, held to be both the source of much good and of great evil.

NATIONALISM

'The foremost ideology of the modern world',[21] Nationalism has appeared to oppressed peoples of many ages as a shining vision of hope; but if it has presented a beautiful vision, it has turned out to have in practice, as Yeats poetically recalled, a 'terrible beauty'.[22] It has been a two-edged sword, creative but also destructive, promoting aggressive divisiveness in international relations, though also proving, at times, a powerful engine of national, social and economic advance. What, then, is to be made of this phenomenon, and how can it be understood?

Nationalism is, of course, rooted in the idea of nation, itself by no means an easy concept, for, as soon as an attempt is made to list the essential characteristics of a nation, it becomes clear that there seem to exist nations which lack some, or nearly all such characteristics. A nation should, for its own benefit, have a common language, a common religion, a natural geographical unit, a common historical development, with common traditions, values and culture. But such an ideal has rarely existed, and definitions of nation must remain general. In the last resort a nation is simply a people which feels itself to be a nation, or, as Julian Huxley has despairingly put it, a nation is 'a society united by a common error as to its origin and a common aversion to its neighbours'![23] G. W. Keeton, whose definition of 'state' is also useful, defines nation more fully as:

> a community of persons linked either by their historical development, common speech, or common social customs, or several of these criteria, in such a way that such persons would still tend to cohere even if separated under different governments.

Of the state, Keeton has this to offer:

> [A state is] an association of human beings, whose numbers are at least considerable, united with the appearance of

permanence, for political ends, for the achievement of which
certain governmental institutions have been evolved.[24]

These definitions are valuable because they make a clear
distinction between nation and state. A nation need not be
political in organisation but can be divided amongst a number
of States, for example the Somali, German, Korean or Kurdish
nations of today, or the Polish, and Italian nations of the recent
past. On the other hand, a state may be composed of a number
of nations, like contemporary Switzerland, India and Nigeria,
or the Union of Soviet Socialist Republics.

It is also true of course, that nation and state can be co-
terminous. Indeed we might go on from this to define nationalism in its simplest form as an attempt of a nation also to
become (or remain) a state. In doing so, however, we would
have to observe that the nation state is a phenomenon of
European origin, and that it grew up over long periods of time,
very long in the case of Britain and France, for example, though
more quickly in the case of Germany, Italy and Hungary.
These 'historic' nationalisms have provided models towards
which others have aspired in the twentieth century but it must
be admitted at once that outside Europe nationalism has
developed in very different circumstances and with widely
varying results.

In Europe, nationalism enjoyed its heyday in the nineteenth century, its triumphant culmination coming a little later
at the close of the First World War, when, in 1919, the Great
Powers sought to implement those principles of self-determination so idealistically enunciated the year before by President
Wilson of America. National self-determination in 1919
encountered real difficulties in Europe, however, for many
peoples were hopelessly admixed with others, and no amount
of juggling could make the physical map conform to neat
national boundaries. Besides, even self-determination was seen
to require tempering by international organisations to which
all nations would belong and which would assist in removing
national irritations and frictions.

National self-determination and international co-operation
were the harmonious ideal. Their complementary nature

accorded with the desires of such distinguished, historic
national figures as the Italian Romantic Mazzini and the
French Socialist Jaurès. Such men had not proclaimed
nationalism as an end in itself. The nation was but the proper
unit of world development. As Mazzini put it, nations were
instruments in the orchestra of mankind. To Jaurès, the nation
was a facet of the diamond, that was the world, an integral part
which helped the whole to sparkle more brightly. To both, the
nation had first to be secured so that it could begin to play its
wider world role. Modern nationalism, unfortunately, has
sometimes moved at a pace that has left such lofty ideals far
behind.

Partly this has been due to the artificial nature of the
nationalism which, having travelled in the baggage of European imperialism, took root in the soil of Asia and Africa.
Despite nineteenth century nationalist beginnings in India and
in other parts of Asia and Africa, Afro-Asian nationalism is
largely a contemporary phenomenon which has presented
strange paradoxes. For one thing it has preceded the nation.
Nationalist leaders in Asia and Africa have often had to appeal
to a 'nation' in the mythical past or in the hopeful future in
order to cement tribes and peoples inside the unreal units
created by European imperial powers without regard to
geographic, linguistic, ethnological or cultural realities. These
territories have been yielded up largely in the post-war era to
those articulate elites who, like the Bolshevik elite in Russia in
1917, have claimed to speak for the broad masses not yet
conscious of their destiny. Such men have needed nationalism,
with all its identification of the individual with the community,
which is the nation, to have any hope at all of survival.

Much tragedy has resulted, however, from the fact that
many of the colonial territories were ill-suited for adaptation
to the European model. (The scale of European tragedy, too,
exemplified by the fascist, racialist nationalism-run-riot of
Nazi Germany which, like so much modern nationalism, was
based on grievance, must not be overlooked. The Nazis raised
the nation state to the highest end of man and in the process
committed vile excesses against humanity). The trouble with

imported ideas of nationalism is that they have taken insufficient account of local social and 'national' patterns. Arnold
Toynbee has eloquently denounced the trail of 'persecution,
eviction and massacre' that has ensued where 'national states'
were:

> not part and parcel of an indigenous social system but were
> an exotic institution which was deliberately imported from
> the West, not because it had been found by experimentation
> to be suitable to the local conditions of these non-Western
> worlds, but simply because the West's political power had
> given the West's political institutions an irrational yet
> irresistable prestige in non-Western eyes.[25]

The fact that in much of Asia, for example, nationalities are not
compact but rather interwoven 'like a shot-silk robe',[26] conforming not to natural boundaries but to occupations and
trades, has hardly militated towards successful adaptation.

The nation state was part of a total European culture, and
non-Europeans who sought to reject that culture but to adopt
merely some of its techniques, found that the chosen technology
and institutions inevitably acted to transform their own
societies. For example, European medicine increased populations beyond the ability of ancient structures to cope, and
European notions of nationalism disrupted communities living
in harmony, generating xenophobia and intolerance on an
unprecedented scale. Certainly, nations such as India or
Nigeria could not claim to be 'natural' in the European sense,
being creations of the will and the reason rather than of nature
or history, and they have had to struggle continuously to retain
their being. But for all this, and despite all the post-war feeling
in Europe that nationalism had outlived its usefulness, a
single glance at nationalism outside Europe will convince us
of its surging strength and popular appeal. Nationalism bound
together the grievances and aspirations of colonised peoples
throughout Asia and Africa and reversed the established
imperialism of Europe. It put the glory of the nation's future
before the all too prevalent squalor of the native's present.
Admittedly, in doing so, it raised many dangerous hopes and
sometimes required a total commitment that was reminiscent

of the all-embracing nationalism of the Nazis. Nevertheless its popularity rested on firm foundations, for in the stress and turmoil of independence and departing imperialism, nationalism gave the reassurance of a new life of fulfilment, dignity and purpose. The enation was being born (or reborn). Every citizen could now hope for equality in the service of this new divinity.

In Asia, nationalism had been gathering force since the beginning of the twentieth century. In both China and Japan attempts had first been made to exclude European influence, then to come to terms with it through the adoption of selected European technology. China, vast and crumbling, did not succeed in achieving singleminded unity until the Communist triumph of 1949; Japan successfully adapted itself earlier. Embracing European techniques and the concept of nationalism, Japan not only defeated Imperial Russia in 1905, but proceeded to an imperialist expansion of its own in the 1930s. Defeat in World War 2 and American occupation in turn stimulated a new, economic direction for Japanese energy and inventiveness. By the 1970s Japan proved able to take its place as the world's third most dynamic industrial nation.*

Both China and Japan achieved their modern statehood without succumbing to conquest, but most Asian nationalism was primarily a reaction against foreign occupation. Thus, in India, the Indian National Congress, founded in 1885 partly through British initiative, grew in the twentieth century to spearhead national consciousness, arouse the Indian masses, and win independence. But the emancipation from British rule of the Indian sub-continent in 1947 was achieved in the name, first of all, of an Indian nation that did not exist. This was evidenced immediately by the split along religious lines into the successor states of India and Pakistan. But even the India that remained, populous, linguistically and ethnologically divided, hardly resembled a nation. Appeals were certainly made to Mother India, Hinduism, and to experiences derived from two centuries of subjection to Britain. But it is doubtful if the villagers of Bengal, the Punjab, Maharashtra or Madras were aware of themselves primarily as Indians.

*See Chapter 5.

The point is worth making because it is the Indian model rather than the European that is relevant to much of modern Asia and Africa. The overseas unit of European imperialism first won independence, and then its leaders sought to weld diverse peoples and tribes into a nation, using every device of communication, stressing unity to achieve material progress, and often relying on external danger to emphasise the need for internal solidarity. These former imperial units vary in size, from the millions of India (and Nigeria) downwards. They are burdened with artificially drawn boundaries and many contradictions of geography, history and culture. But in spite of this there is no real reason why Indian (or Nigerian) nationalism should not succeed in creating a nation, given time. Common experience does lead to that awareness of difference from others that is the ultimate definition of a nation. Scotsmen, Welshmen and Englishmen will no doubt bear out this contention, so far as Britain is concerned.

In Asia, apart from the paradox of the nation state preceeding the nation, there occurred the paradox of nation states dividing larger groups with at least some claim to nationhood. The Malays, for example, found themselves scattered amongst a number of states on the post-war Asian map. But this factor is even more strongly in evidence when the Middle East is examined. There, Egyptian, Syrian, Iraqi, Jordanian, Libyan, Tunisian, Algerian and Moroccan nationalist movements split what had been claimed as a single nationalism of the Arab people. Islamic and Arabic-speaking, the Arabs have a strong homogeneity, on the face of it, and a self-conscious tradition as well. An Islamic Conference in Jerusalem in 1931, for example, proclaimed Pan-Arabism in unequivocal terms:

1. The Arab lands are a complete and indivisible whole...

2. All efforts in every Arab country are to be directed towards the single goal of their complete independence, in their entirety and unified.[27]

But in practice Arab leaders have been more notable for their differences, and such dramatic post-war exceptions as the

United Arab Republic of Egypt and Syria survived for only 'three-and-a-half years of endless troubles'.[28] Nevertheless Pan-Arabism, like Pan-Africanism south of the Sahara, remains the inspiration of many emotional idealists as well as of rational nationalists who see the possibility of emancipation from Eastern and Western finance only in terms of economic units which are sufficiently large to stand on their own feet and to command world respect by their own achievements.

Reference to African nationalism introduces another variation on the nationalist theme that demands explanation. For although some of the claims of African nationalists have been more grandiose than exact, the peculiar history of Africa and the African people, not least the terrible trauma of slavery, has produced powerful attempts not only to bring political emancipation from European rule, and to achieve unity in independence for all Africans, but also to rehabilitate the negro race in its own eyes and in the eyes of a falsely 'superior' world. African intellectuals have sought to exalt the concept of '*négritude*', to define the unique 'African personality'; and to propagate an 'African socialism' based on traditional aspects of co-operative living and decision-making, in their attempts to exorcise that 'inferiority complex' referred to by Fanon, to weld disparate tribal units into viable modern nations, and to emphasise the contribution which Africa can make to the contemporary world.

Nkrumah's Ghana, independent in 1957, led the way in propagating socialism as the only method of bringing a better standard of life to all sections of the community, and followed successive Pan-African Congresses in urging co-operation beyond colonial frontiers. In its Constitution of 1950, Nkrumah's Convention Peoples Party had included amongst its aims a determination 'to establish a socialist state in which all men and women shall have equal opportunity and where there shall be no capital [ist] exploitation', and a desire 'to support the demand for a West African federation and of Pan-Africanism by promoting unity of action among the peoples of Africa and of African descent'.[29] 'Ghana's independence is meaningless without the independence of the whole of Africa,'

Nkrumah added, as the nation's flag was run up in 1957; and although subsequently the execution of his ideals left much to be desired, he never ceased to urge them vehemently. Although attempted federations of former colonial territories have been disappointing on the whole, and although disagreements between governments, and entrenchment of vested interests, political as well as economic, have proceeded apace, the creation of the Organisation of African Unity in 1963 does bear witness to a continuing Pan-African ideal.

The numerous Black African states, which have appeared since 1957, illustrate a narrower nationalism that is nevertheless distinctly African. Formed in the crucible of anti-colonialism, and fiercely perpetuating the anti-colonialist spirit in an endeavour to retain fragile unity inside colonial boundaries, these States have exemplified nationalism that cannot be understood in mere European terms. Anti-racialist, modernising, self-conscious, this nationalism has been termed by Professor James Coleman:

> Broadly a consciousness of belonging to a nation (existent or in the realm of aspiration) or a nationality, and a desire as manifest in sentiment and activity, to secure or maintain its welfare, prosperity, and integrity, and to maximise its political autonomy.[30]

Julius Nyerere pointed to the dangers awaiting triumphant African nationalism, however, when he protested in 1957 that 'we do not seek freedom so that our people may remain in poverty and ignorance or revert to primitive savagery'.[31] Too many new States gained their 'freedom' inadequately equipped with the skilled personnel and economic resources to maintain and develop it. In this respect the dilemma of new African states was symptomatic of many of the ex-colonial nations to emerge in the post-war period. Commentators, usually drawn from the former imperial powers, have been prone to ask whether African peoples had not been over-hasty in demanding independence before they were ready for it. But the evidence, however studded with post-independence upheavals, would rather indicate that only by assuming independence can a people ever qualify to manage it. The problem of neo-

colonialism may have been acute: democracy as defined in
Europe may have given way in state after state to elite corruption or military *coup*. But the process of learning by experience
is as necessary and useful to Africa and Asia as it was in the
past to Europe. Africans, themselves acutely aware of the
'Balkanisation' of their continent and of the Cold War economic rivalry being fought out there, remain determined to
achieve their own salvation. They will assert their right, in the
words of Tom Mboya of Kenya, to be 'neither pro-West nor
pro-Russian' but 'pro-African'. And this they must achieve
their own way.

In the cultural field the negro peoples have not agreed any
more readily than in the political. Though Aimé Césaire,
French West Indian negro, or Léophold Senghor, the
Senegalese scholar-President, might develop their separate
paeans in praise of *négritude*, others have been ready to point out
that the very proclamation of *négritude* is itself an admission of
inferiority: a tiger, after all, in the words of Nigerian play-
wright Wole Soyinka, does not need to go about proclaiming its
'tigritude'! Nevertheless, modern academic research in arche-
ology and history has uncovered a rich and varied African past
that has helped to restore to Africans a belief in themselves;
a belief as well backed by the quality of new Africa's leading
novelists and poets as by such statesmen as Nyerere and
Kaunda. And Wole Soyinka, no less than the apostles of
négritude, has sought from the African tradition and the
techniques of Europe a synthesis of the best which can produce
an expression of modern nationhood that is still uniquely
African.

Turning now, finally, to nationalism in Latin America,
one of the fundamental questions of nationalism is raised:
where lies the nation? Given the existence of states, distinct
entities with a long common experience, who is entitled to
speak for them? Is it the military junta monopolising government? Is it the wealthy, cultivated, traditional oligarchy?
Or could it be the suppressed mass of the people, the illiterate
downtrodden, peasant majority of all too many of the Latin
American lands? This question has also relevance to the

African elites of today. For the Latin American precedent, as well as 'Balkanisation', haunts the morrow of the African continent. In Latin America, time, which for too long stood still, stands still no longer. A dedicated few have already declared in favour of the masses and hoisted the banner of social and economic liberation from 'illegitimate', unrepresentative governments, as 'foreign' to their people as the earlier *conquistadors*. Perhaps it is twisting the concept of nationalism to refer to the imminent social revolution in Latin America in terms of the silent nations speaking out at last to claim their emancipation. But Fidel Castro and Che Guevara have shown one way. And when the undogmatic experiment of Eduardo Frei's Chile seemed slow to bear fruit, the Chilean people turned voluntarily to the Marxist Salvador Allende. Others will surely be drawn by the Cuban example.

So much, then, for the nationalism that has swept and is sweeping around the post-war, non-European world. What validity has it as a concept and where does it fit into the Great Power world of interdependent economies and ideological blocs? Certainly the answers to the latter question will incorporate much of the discussions already voiced in relation to the Third World, neo-colonialism and the Cold War. For the nationalist desire exists in no vacuum but in the world of nations, sometimes co-operating, sometimes competing, amongst which power is so unevenly distributed. Can small nations continue to survive in this world? Tentatively, perhaps, the answer can be in the affirmative. Despite the lesson of Czechoslovakia – for the Czechs seem to have been fated to betrayal and to dependence upon great neighbours by virtue of their geographical position – the near-monopoly of power in the hands of the two Great Powers is not incompatible with the continuing existence of small nations. It is partly in the interests of the Great Powers themselves; it is also a fact of modern life that military conquest and annexation is not as effective as in former times. The emergence of the guerrilla has given a warning universally applicable. Nationalism, which idealizes the nation state, can never of course be valid as an end in itself. Nations, like individuals in society, have to discipline themselves in the interests of the world community. 'My nation right or wrong' was never an honourable sentiment. National virtue reposes in adherence to the laws of humanity, and national sovereignty must be tempered by international welfare. The organs of international welfare do now exist and it is in their support that the interests of nations truly lie.

Nationalism, however, is no concrete concept, for if there is one lesson that the study of nationalism drives home it is that each manifestation, like each manifestation of imperialism, requires careful historical examination. In each case its circumstances and form will be different. But there is one strange paradox of this paradoxical concept that remains to be stated, and this is not only highly contemporary but in some ways summarises much of what is contained in this chapter of historical outlines. It relates to the two great supranational ideologies of our time, capitalism and communism.

For capitalism and communism are both in theory ideologies that dispense with nationalism altogether: the one promising to free mankind by a process of 'enlightened self-interest rising above mercantilist repression and hostility and building a world of good neighbours';[32] the other embodying a classless vision of international solidarity, with working men of the world at last united. Yet our peculiar misfortune, resulting from the development of the one in the United States and the other in Russia, has been this final paradox stated succintly by Barbara Ward:

> Nationalism conquered both the American thesis and the Russian antithesis of the universalist faith. The two great federated experiments, based upon a revolutionary concept of the destiny of all mankind, have ended in counterpoint, as the two most powerful nation-states in history.[33]

It is a timely observation. For the historic 'manifest destiny' of Americans and the preoccupation of Russians with 'socialism in one country' might serve as present warning that nationalism is no mean concept. It exists still in each of the Great Power rivals, America and Russia, and it is their nationalism, above all, that must be directed into the channels of international order if world peace is to be secured.

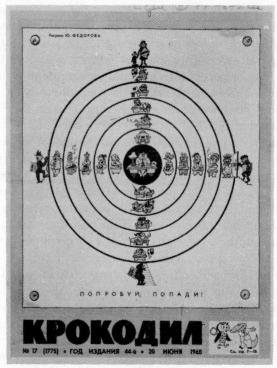

'*Krokodil*' attack on over-centralization

NOTES

[1]J. P. Nettl, *op. cit.*, p. 186.

[2]G. F. Kennan, *op. cit.*, p. 99.

[3]Robert F. Kennedy, *Thirteen Days* (Pan, 1960).

[4]D. Horowitz, *op. cit.*, p. 389.

[5]Reprinted in *Why Vietnam* (U. S. Information Service, 1965).

[6]J. William Fulbright, *The Arrogance of Power* (Penguin, 1970), pp. 107–8.

[7]A. Toynbee, *America and the World Revolution* (1961), quoted in D. Horowitz, *op. cit.*, p. 15.

[8]D. Horowitz, *op. cit.*, p. 426.

[9]John Spanier, *op. cit.*, p. 264.

[10]Anil Seal, *The Emergence of Indian Nationalism* (Cambridge University Press, 1968), p. 116.

[11]V. I. Lenin, *Imperialism, the Highest Stage of Capitalism* (1916:

republished Moscow, n.d.).

[12] K. Nkrumah, *Neo-Colonialism: the Last Stage of Imperialism* (Nelson, 1965), p. ix.

[13] J. Strachey, *The End of Empire* (Gollancz, 1961), p. 250.

[14] R. Aron, *Peace and War* (Weidenfeld and Nicolson, 1966), p. 506.

[15] Ranko Petkovic, 'Non-alignment in the contemporary world' in *Studies*, No. 26 (Belgrade, 1968), pp. 29–36.

[16] C. C. O'Brien, 'Epilogue: Illusions and Realities of Non-Alignment' in J. W. Burton (ed.), *Non-Alignment* (Deutsch, 1966), p. 131–33.

[17] F. Fanon, *The Wretched of the Earth* (Penguin, 1967), p. 123.

[18] *Ibid.*, p. 123.

[19] D. Caute, *Fanon* (Fontana, 1967), p. 7.

[20] *Ibid.*, p. 66.

[21] K. R. Minogue, *Nationalism* (Methuen, 1969), p. 8.

[22] W. B. Yeats, 'Easter 1916' in W. B. Yeats, *Selected Poetry* (Macmillan, 1965), p. 95.

[23] Julian Huxley, *'Race' in Europe* (O.U.P., 1939), p. 7.

[24] G. W. Keeton, *The Elementary Principles of Jurisprudence* (Pitman (2 ed), 1949), p. 30.

[25] Arnold Toynbee, *The World and the West* (BBc Reith Lectures, 1952, published by O.U.P., 1953), pp. 70–71.

[26] *Ibid.*, p. 73.

[27] *Survey of International Affairs*, 1934, p. 107. Quoted in A. Cobban, *The Nation State and National Self-determination* (Collins, 1970), p.229.

[28] President Nasser's words, according to Peter Mansfield, *Nasser's Egypt* (Penguin, 1969), p. 61.

[29] Constitution of C.P.P., 1950: 'Ideology & Organisation'. Quoted in D. Apter, *Ghana in Transition*, pp. 203–4.

[30] J. S. Coleman, *Nigeria: Background to Nationalism*, p. 425. (Also quoted in C. Legum, 'The Phenomenon of Nationalism in Africa' in James L. Henderson (ed.), *Since 1945*, p. 181.)

[31] Quoted in Ware, *op. cit.*, ii, p. 1042.

[32] Barbara Ward, *Nationalism and Ideology* (Hamish Hamilton, 1967), pp. 60–61.

[33] *Ibid.*, p. 99.

CHAPTER THREE

The World's Natural Resources

A) HUMAN

'A world of peoples' was the title chosen by Robert Gardiner for his BBC Reith Lecture series in 1965. He was at pains to give to his hearers a proper perspective view of the world, one that emphasised its common humanity, the Brotherhood of Man. In the spirit of those lectures, this opening section on the world's resources is devoted to the world's primary natural resource, its people. It is the skill, husbandry and industry of the world's peoples alone that will turn the world's other resources to good account, or failing in that attempt, will destroy the world entirely.

The destructive device, if the latter course is taken, may be either nuclear or demographic: a sudden, suicidal atomic war, or a more relentless but no less suicidal expansion of population beyond the means available to sustain it. It is with the latter that this chapter is partly concerned, for the pressing weight of increasing numbers presents a danger to all men unless man's other creative capacities can be fostered and developed apace. The creative capacities of all men will be needed, and these are unlikely to be harnessed if the world which Robert Gardiner described and deplored is perpetuated; the world of racial antipathies and of confrontation between the rich few and the poverty-stricken many. First, then, the development of the human animal will be examined.

Man

Man is a relative newcomer to this planet. Life has existed on earth for six hundred million years, but man arrived a mere million to half a million years ago. And it took man until about ten thousand years ago to acquire the techniques of a settled farming existence, a stage that was necessary before anything that could now be called civilised could be reached.

Civilisation, however differently it is defined, usually implies the existence of cities, the coming together of peoples into a close community, with the social organisation, specialisation of labour and advancement of skills that this permits. The earliest civilisations were found in separate regions of the world, where soil, water and climate were particularly favourable. The first was the civilisation that flourished in Mesopotamia between the two great Middle Eastern rivers, the Tigris and the Euphrates, and in the 'fertile crescent' leading round to Egypt. Dating from around 7,500 years B.C., this civilisation had influenced life over much of Europe, North Africa and the Middle East by the year 2000 B.C. Meanwhile another civilisation had flourished nearby in Egypt, in the Nile valley and delta. At first in two kingdoms of Upper and Lower Egypt, this Egyptian civilisation was united under one king around 3250 B.C.

Civilisation also flourished in the regions of Mexico and Peru, and from 2000–1000 B.C. in northern India and China. In all of these areas, while much of the rest of the territories of man remained at a primitive Stone Age level, the art of living together under law in compact communities was developed, and methods of government and of waging war expanded. Pottery, metal, the wheel and writing were discovered and harnessed to the greater comfort and convenience of man. In the Middle East, Egyptian supremacy was succeeded by that of the Assyrians, then the Persians, whose wars with the Greeks and eventual defeat by the Macedonian conqueror Alexander, in the fourth century B.C., bring us to relatively modern times.

Man, in separate centres, bounded by deserts, oceans, and mountains, thus pushed forward, slowly but at a gradually increased pace, the development of his skills and of his under-

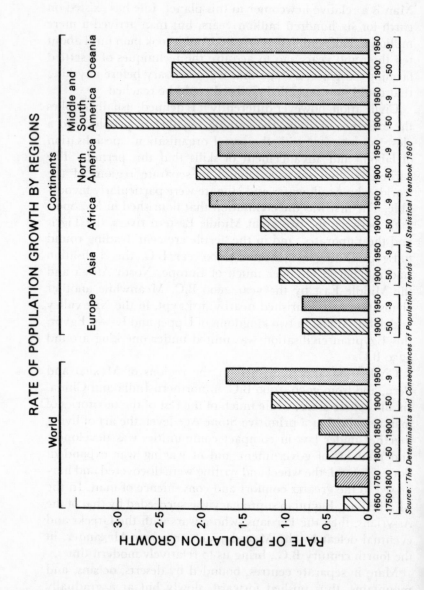

RATE OF POPULATION GROWTH BY REGIONS

Source: 'The Determinants and Consequences of Population Trends' UN Statistical Yearbook 1960

standing of the world in which he found himself. The separate
centres were still, in truth, 'worlds of their own', and side by
side with them there existed pockets of primitive Stone Age
men, hunting, fishing or literally grubbing a harsh living from
the soil. The earth's resources were scarcely tapped, and the
earth's population was correspondingly sparse. No figures
exist, of course, but it is estimated that by the beginning of the
Christian era, the total population of the world was about
250 million. Some indication of the scale and perspective of
this figure can be gained by viewing the estimates for subsequent dates, and the more accurate and astonishing figures
for this century.

By 1650, it is estimated, the 250 million people of the time
of Christ had doubled to 500 million. In 1850 there were
approximately 1200 million people and by 1900 this reached
1500 million, in effect a trebling of the population of the world
in 250 years. But by 1950 the figure had reached 2,500 million;
already we have passed 3,000 million; and if present rates
of population increase are maintained it is projected that the
total for the end of this century could reach 6,500 million. 'If
present population rates are maintained' is the key phrase
here, but even if, somehow, that rate is slowed the implications
for the quality of life of those endeavouring to win a livelihood
on earth in the future are enormous. The accompanying table
shows the rate of population growth over the world as a whole,
and region by region. It is the rate of acceleration that is significant. Between 1850–1900 the world increase was 6 per cent
per annum. Between 1900–1950 this had risen to .9 per cent
per annum. But from 1951–5 this overall figure rose to 1.6
per annum, with regional variation ranging from under 1 per
cent in Europe to over 3 per cent in Southern America. The
world increase has since risen to 1.9% per annum, between
1960 and 1968, and shows no sign of slackening. This is what is
called the population explosion, or the demographic revolution, and it constitutes one of the major problems of the mid-
twentieth century. But it is a problem further complicated by
factors of economics and of race.

Modern Man

Modern man is still predominantly rural and peasant, but he is everywhere coming increasingly under the influence of industrialism, and in many areas the agricultural sector of the economy no longer predominates. Beginning in the nineteenth century, the rapid expansion of industry and the concurrent growth in urban living has, like its associated population growth, accelerated ever faster in the twentieth century. Scientific, technological and industrial advances have in large part led to population growth, and have given to modern man new dimensions of power and control over many of the natural resources of the earth and the natural hazards of life. They have resulted in vast population movements: migrations to new lands overseas as well as from the countryside to the towns.

England led the world in progressive urbanisation. The census of 1851 was the first to record more than half of the population in urban areas (today over 80 per cent live in towns). Other countries followed. By 1900 eleven cities existed in the world with a population of over 1 million. By 1950 there were 63. From half to two-thirds of the population of Western Europe, the United States and Australia were urban dwellers by mid-century, and even outside towns, road and rail systems, electricity, radio and television had begun to transform the life of hitherto isolated rural communities.

In the first developed countries – in Europe and North America – the process of industrialisation led on to mass production and mass consumption that have spread wealth widely and produced high standards of living for almost entire populations. Industry, with its demands for materials and markets, has led internationally to the creation of a world economy, drawing peoples and the interests of countries all over the globe ever more tightly together: nationally it has required increasing expansion of the activity of governments to regulate and guide its complex production and distribution sectors. Industrial expansion, like population growth, has achieved a momentum, a cumulative, self-generating drive that has accelerated growth at an ever-increasing pace. In material terms, man's progress in the last hundred years has been revolutionary indeed.

But the process of industrial development has been no more evenly spread than that of population increase. It has remained concentrated in those areas where it first developed, with Great Britain, Western and Central Europe, Russia and the United States being joined, by mid-century, only by Japan, Czechoslovakia, Canada, Australia, Poland, India and Argentina on a significant scale. And even in the last three of these countries agriculture has continued to employ more than half of the labour force. In the rest of the world, the agricultural sector has remained even more pronounced, 60 per cent or more in most South American and East European countries, at least 75 per cent in much of Asia and North Africa, and over 90 per cent in the rest of Africa outside the white population of the southern tip.

The point of including these brief statistics, which properly belong to the second half of this chapter, is to emphasise one of the fundamental features of the population explosion of the contemporary world. This phenomenon, which has been made possible primarily because of the scientific and technical achievements of the developed lands – notably in medical advances leading to the reduction of premature mortality – has occurred most dramatically in developing lands least able to support such growth with material resources.

The developed areas, slowly building up their industrial, largely urban, societies, have adjusted over a long period of time to a new way of life, to new levels of leisure and education that scientific and technical progress have made possible. The social and cultural impact of these new forces has been immense, and the process of readjustment has often been tough, marred by great hardship for many people, but it has been comparatively gradual. And in Europe at least, cultural attitudes towards both work and the material world have helped to promote a view of society that is essentially scientific in its outlook. Furthermore, in developed areas, partly because urbanisation tends to reduce fertility, and more because economically advanced peoples tend more readily to adopt

methods of family planning, developed countries have reduced
their birth rates considerably.

Very few of these factors have characterised the experience
of the less developed majority areas of the world. There has
been no real industrialisation to make an impact on the economy or culture of the people, and societies have preserved many
of their old attitudes, while adopting, under enlightened government initiative, many of the advances of medicine and
hygiene made available by the developed world. The result
is a dramatic reduction in the number of deaths in infancy and
from diseases such as malaria, without any change in traditional practices (which have often been based on the assumption of high mortality) designed to perpetuate the family by
bringing as many children as possible into the world. Nor has
there been sufficient change in economic capacity.

By the middle of the twentieth century, just when many of
these developing lands were gaining independence and hoping
to embark upon ambitious schemes of industrialisation, the
increase in population presented grave problems – pressure
on land, movement to already overcrowded towns, immense
housing shortages, demands for education, chronic unemployment, frustration and despair – problems so urgent and
demanding as to prohibit the raising of living standards. In
Latin America to take but one such area, the estimated
annual population growth in the period 1950–5 was 2.4 per
cent per annum as compared with 1.9 per cent before the war.
Brazil, for example, had a population of about 17 million in
1900. By 1920 this had almost doubled, to 30 million; by 1960
it had more than doubled again to reach 70 million. Thus the
problem of providing for new citizens at existing low standards,
let alone of improving these standards for all those clamouring
for a share of the good things of life, has been almost insuper-
able. A health official from Venezuela, one of the richer countries of Latin America, has put the problem graphically and
in words that are only too apposite to the developing lands not
only of Latin America, but also of Asia and Africa:

> Our successful campaign to reduce infant mortality has
> given us more problems. If we do not have adequate food

supplies at reasonable prices and an understanding of nutrition, the babies we save may sicken or die of malnutrition before they reach school age; when they reach school age, there will not be enough schools, unless we can greatly expand our educational facilities; if they lack schools, they may become juvenile delinquents and present us with still other needs for services; if they reach working age without sufficient training, they will not earn enough to give their own children a good home – even if we manage to get enough housing built; and whether they will find jobs at all will depend on the rate at which we can expand our industry and improve our agriculture, and find the capital resources with which to do so. Unless we can move forward on all fronts at the same time, the saving of lives only puts us further behind.[1]

How can such countries cope without some measure of birth control to correspond with the dramatic increase in control over premature death? Even social revolution and a redistribution of existing wealth will hardly be sufficient unless the numbers being born to share that wealth are reduced. It is true that programmes of family planning and birth control are being undertaken in some African and Asian countries, in the face of ancient, contrary traditions. The population explosion is an unprecedented problem for mankind and calls for unprecedented action. But the action cannot simply be left to the developing areas, nor confined to mere restriction of births. The population explosion, linked as it is to the underdeveloped economies of largely non-white nations, is a fundamental, human problem and it calls for the combined resources of humanity.

But, regrettably, almost incredibly, humanity does not seem to be aware of its obligations. Somehow, humanity has failed to grasp the fact of its essential oneness; has concocted notions of race, given way to prejudices, and channelled selfishness and hatred along the divisive lines of colour. Within nations and between nations an age-old but comparatively minor human deficiency has begun to assume major world significance. Colour prejudice and racial discrimination, emotional and irrational as they both are, pose one of the keenest challenges to the modern, supposedly scientific and rational world. Two quotations from the 1960's convey something of the scale of this problem confronting man in his relation to man. The first comes from Colin Legum, one of the foremost authorities on contemporary Africa:

> On the political level we have to grapple with the problems of Negro people uprooted from Africa and planted in Western societies, as well as with those of people of European stock planted in African soil. There is a much wider problem, too: that the end of the Age of Imperialism finds the world divided between mainly rich white nations and almost entirely non-white poor nations.
> Our ability to meet these challenges is severely crippled. by deep-seated and complex colour prejudices that are age-old.[2]

The second is from Robert Gardiner, with whom we began this chapter, and it takes up Colin Legum's final point:

> The peoples of the world are trapped in a vicious circle composed of notions of superiority and inferiority, of suspicion, misconceptions, preconceptions, frustrations and insecurity. Above all there is fear. It is fear that sets the racial moods, and if we are to break the vicious circle we must concentrate our assault upon these racial fears in all their forms. Hatred and intolerance are not innate in peoples; they are the children of fear, as fear is the child of ignorance.[3]

The task facing our generation is the construction of a 'World of Peoples who are free and equal in their opportunities to exercise their abilities'[4], and it is an urgent task. But its beginning, as Robert Gardiner implies, is knowledge: knowledge of the common ancestry of man, of the spread of mankind, of the impact of industrialism, and urbanisation, and of the modern population explosion, and, most pressingly, of the fallacies behind racism.

Homo sapiens

Our human species, *Homo sapiens*, has through the isolation of some groups and through the operation of the process of natural selection in a variety of climates, produced a number of type-variations or 'races' which can be differentiated by distinctive common physical characteristics. The word 'race' is in inverted commas because it is not a definite, scientific word of precise meaning but rather a useful label of classification which has historically been used in a much wider sense than merely to describe the divisions of man (e.g. a race of dandies, poets, nobles; the human race, the feathered race; the race of Abraham, the race of Beelzebub). When it is used to describe human groupings, it is often used misleadingly, for no sharp lines divide the 'races' and there is probably no such thing as a 'pure' race. Where the word is used scientifically it has a biological meaning, referring to the physical characteristics of groups which are genetically determined; physical characteristics such as stature, colour of skin, hair, shape of head, nose and lips etc, which are the consequence of heredity.

In spite of much common usage, distinctions of mere colour are insufficient, and terms such as 'white' and 'coloured' races or black (negroid), white (caucasoid) and yellow (mongoloid) are gross over-simplifications. More precise divisions, based on the criteria listed above, but still containing wide varieties of type within each, can be reduced to five in number: *Euripiform*, ranging in distribution from Northern Europe to North Africa, North West India and Japan; *Mongoloform*, ranging from Asia to Polynesia, the Arctic and South America; *Negriform*, distributed throughout Africa and areas of South East Asia; *Khoisaniform*, confined to South West Africa and central parts of mainland Tanganyika; and *Australiform*, confined to central and South India and Ceylon and Australia. But such a compressed statement can only begin to hint at the variety of subdivisions within the main groups, and all that can definitely be said in addition here is that the present populations of Europe, America, Africa and Asia are hybrid in the extreme.[5]

Such a statement will be of little interest of course to those who will declare that the colour of a man's skin is all one needs to know in order to decide upon his mental ability, social habits and sexual prowess! People who feel this way probably stand outside rational argument anyway, victims of colour prejudice which, however understandable it may be in some

cases, is always, like any prejudice, to be deplored and combatted. Prejudice, based on skin pigmentation, or some other
physical feature, is, however, all too common, and irrational
though it may be it has very strong forces operating behind it.

   Groups of people, particularly groups with distinct characteristics, have always been liable to generalise about those who
differ from them in any obvious way, whether their generalisation is in terms of fear, contempt, hatred or even admiration.
But prejudice against foreigners or strangers is particularly
liable to develop in those groups who feel themselves insecure
or under some sort of threat. Unfortunately *colour prejudice*
seems to have behind it not only a bitter historical legacy of
'white' conquest, 'non-white' subjugation and 'black' slavery,
but also an extraordinarily deep, and universally consistent
colour symbolism. This symbolism associates white with such
admirable phenomena as: 'joy, light, innocence, triumph,
divine power, purity, happiness, gaiety, peace, chastity,
modesty, truth, delicacy and femininity', and black with: 'woe,
gloom, darkness, dread, death, terror, horror, wickedness,
curse, mourning, mortification, error, annihilation, strength,
deep quiet, defilement and despair'.[6] Historical memories and
symbolic associations thus add considerable weight to prejudices all too easily acquired. They also help to produce what
is often the next stage after prejudice; discrimination.

   It is important to distinguish between colour prejudice and
racial discrimination. Colour prejudice is a state of mind;
racial discrimination translates prejudice into action; action
that deprives individuals or groups of work, or housing, or
services or basic civic rights, on mere grounds of race (usually
of mere colour). Racial discrimination can be employed by
entire societies whereby those of a superior social, economic
or political status perpetuate their position. It can thus be the
reaction of individuals or groups to situations in which they
find themselves threatened, for example by a new wave of
foreign immigrants competing for jobs or housing; or it can
becaome an integral part of a society in which the relationships
of conqueror and conquered are retained, such as in modern
South Africa or ancient India.

These examples give some hint of the causes of racial discrimination; the symbolism of fear, the past history of conquest, the bitter legacy of slavery. A hierarchy of 'races' has been publicised throughout the world for centuries, with the fairest skin at the top and the darkest at the bottom. In China, girls with the whitest skin were traditionally sought as the most desirable brides; in India the caste system reflected the fair skin of the conquerors from the north who established their rule over earlier, darker inhabitants; in the West Indies, in Brazil and the United States, no matter what was decreed from time to time to the contrary, white remained synonymous with the best, with every subtle gradation of colour being used to favour the lighter skin, until today, at last, in indignant rejection of humiliation and degradation, the darker militants of African descent have begun to blazon out the unique beauty of their blackness.

In contemporary terms, racial discrimination has often been simply the first irrational response of insecure men in the face of the unfamiliar at a time of change, but in so far as it has been an historical problem, racial discrimination has been perpetuated by the fostering of separate racial communities side by side in mutual ignorance. Usually because the dominant group has wished to preserve its 'purity' and position, contacts have been strictly limited and formalised. But the immense extension of communications throughout the modern world, the impact of mass media, the availability of cheap transportation and the movement of peoples, has resulted in new assaults on traditional structures based on simple accidents of history, colour or 'race'. World-wide, the demand has become one for equality of opportunity, for an end to privilege, and for justice based on the needs of humanity rather than on the protection of property. The result of this demand has been turmoil, both in societies long composed of more than one race, and in societies newly experiencing the presence of other races. As colours and cultures clash with new frequency, but with all too little evidence of new understanding, the question for many lands becomes an urgent one. Will the meeting of different peoples result in a contented multi-racial society; in an agreed withdrawal to separation; or in a bitter and desperate struggle for domination?[7]

The issue is almost universal. In the Americas, the Caribbean, and in parts of Asia, Europe and Africa, official government commitments have been made to the concept of multiracialism. But how are the world's peoples facing up to the challenge which this concept presents (posed above by Colin Legum)? And how aware are they of the new dimensions of the problem?

In America, North and South, and in the Caribbean, the racial situation was vitiated from the start by slavery, that grotesque trade in humanity which transported millions to servitude beyond the seas and disposed of countless thousands by brutality, overcrowding and disease on the 'middle passage' to the plantation lands. Slavery was abolished in the British West Indies in 1833 and in the United States in 1865, as the Civil War was being waged. In South America legislation followed more slowly and slavery was not outlawed in Brazil until 1888. But no new heaven of emancipation anywhere replaced the conditions of slavery. Human attitudes changed more slowly on farms and in the cities than did legislation in parliaments. Men continued to preserve privilege, power or perverted self-esteem, by supposing the less fortunate; while the values, attitudes and social effects of servitude long outlived the institution of slavery.

In the United States it was one thing for the Thirteenth Amendment to declare: 'Neither slavery nor involuntary servitude, except as a punishment for crime whereof the party shall have been duly convicted, shall exist within the United States, or any place subject to their jurisdiction', but quite another for the negro to acquire the normal rights of citizenship. To the shame of white Americans, prepared to pose as the champions of democratic, free-enterprise capitalism in our post-war world, their own society still permits great injustice and the denial of civil rights to vast numbers of their non-white fellow citizens. Back in 1896 the United States Supreme Court ruled that the provision of 'separate but equal' educational facilities for coloured Americans was in accord with the

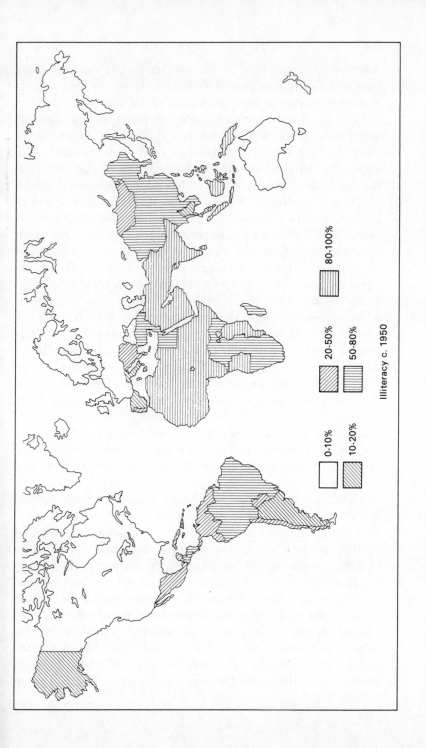

Illiteracy c. 1950

0-10%

10-20%

20-50%

50-80%

80-100%

American Constitution. It was not until 1954 that the same
Supreme Court was prevailed upon to recognise that segregation could never provide genuinely 'equal' facilities.

The 1954 decision was a historic step along the way towards
integration of the negro American citizen into American society. And it has been succeeded by a volume of humanitarian
legislation designed to uphold that equality of man of which
the American Declaration of Independence was so early and
eloquent a statement. But it remains true that the relation of
man to man, in the Northern cities no less than the Southern
States, is still soured by enduring colour prejudice. Gathering
in momentum, from the humble dedication of the negroes of
Montgomery, boycotting segregated buses from December
1955 to June 1966, and the eloquent leadership of Martin
Luther King, who sought equality through the discipline of
non-violence, through the harrassment of Klu Klux Klan
murder and the brutality and injustice of so much of the mis-
named machinery of law, to the strident demands of Black
Muslims calling for a separate negro polity, and Black Pan-
thers invoking the anti-colonialist rhetoric of Frantz Fanon,
the civil rights struggle has more and more dominated the
domestic American scene. Violence, hatred and bloodshed, stark black and white confrontation, have turned, in
ever more areas, the American dream of a land of equality of
opportunity into a nightmare of discrimination, tension and
terror.

The Caribbean islands and South America provide further
evidence that it is not legal enactments but human attitudes
that matter most; and human attitudes cannot be changed
with the stroke of a pen. Thus a Jamaican[8] could write bitterly
in 1962, the year of full Jamaican independence, of the persist-
ing legacy of slavery: the poverty, irresponsibility and cultural
confusion that have so long survived emancipation; the aping
of all things white that has stunted the development of the
bulk of citizens. In the Caribbean, with the exception of Cuba,
'black' and 'white' denote not so much skin colours as attitudes,[9] and in conditions where poverty and unemployment
prevail, the antagonism between communities, Negro, Indian

and Chinese as well as White, remain unresolved, a source of potential calamity.

Unfortunately there is no more evidence of successful multi-racial harmony in Latin America, an area which traditionally has appeared to lack colour consciousness. Even there, where intermarriage has created a large population of intermediate colour, the economic structure reflects continued white domin-ation, while the social structure perpetuates equally a white superiority and a negro inferiority.

In Europe, Great Britain has assumed something of the characteristics of the Americas, largely since 1948, as successive waves of ex-colonial subjects, many of them from the West Indies, have created sizeable immigrant communities in a num-ber of industrial centres. Where housing and work opportun-ities have become scarce, the British people have proved no more immune than other peoples from prejudice. In an effort to limit the numbers of immigrants to a rate capable of absorp-tion, the British Labour Government found it necessary to introduce an Immigration Act in 1966. Already the authorities had been warned by race riots, in London and Nottingham in 1958, of what might happen in apparently tolerant and easy-going Britain; already the previous Conservative Government had introduced immigration control by work voucher in 1961; and already racialism had begun to influence politics, notably at Smethwick in the 1964 General election.

Yet coloured immigrants, like Irish immigrants before them, had been encouraged by labour-hungry industry to come to Britain. Now coloured immigrants, like Irish immigrants be-fore them, were finding on arrival in significant numbers, that neighbours, landladies and job-competitors reacted violently to their presence. But coloured immigrants, unlike the Irish before them, could be distinguished easily, generation after generation, by their mere appearance, and the first, prejudiced labels could be attached time and time again by anyone with a grievance – a health, housing, employment or imagined griev-ance – or simply by delinquents in search of a target. Britain, proud imperial land which had set out to bring the benefits of Anglo-Saxon administration, law and religion to the 'lesser

breeds' around the globe, in the nineteenth century, was discovering in the twentieth that it was no more able to ensure
coloured equality at home than it had been in the past in its
oversea territories.

Britain is of course, a small, crowded island, and it does
make sense to limit the numbers coming to it in search of work.
And it would be wrong to think in terms of a population dominated by racial hostilities, for there are many who welcome the
economic, cultural and social contribution that modern immigrants have added to a British nation traditionally enriched
by successive immigrations over many centuries (Normans,
Huguenots, Irish to list but three), and who recognise the continuing obligation of Britain to-day towards people who contributed so much to Britain's former greatness. The 1965 Race
Relations Act reflects the desire of such people to establish a
legal framework favouring justice and prohibiting discriminat-
ory practices. But the facts of immigrant-native contact emphasise that harmonious multi-racial communities are unlikely
to develop spontaneously. Such communities demand constant
hard work, education, direct communication, sympathy and
understanding, before the mutual benefits of harmonious co-
operation can be made evident.

In Britain, as in America, it is worth noting how successive
governments have had to respond to potentially explosive
situations with action designed to reassure white, affluent
citizens that their future is not under threat; extra educational
expenditure, community relations officials, job training, urban
renewal and a host of devices have been employed to coddle the
susceptibilities of already privileged white citizens. But still the
process of white adjustment to a coloured presence in equality
has proved slow and difficult. Can white communities be
surprised, then, that the same racial tensions and difficulties
provide explosive issues in poorer nations of Asia and Africa?

In Asia, for example, the presence of large, dynamic Chinese
communities in more easy-going nations has led to many outbreaks of race conflict. Malaya, hopefully harmonious, exploded in May 1969. Indonesia has undergone sustained anti-
Chinese convulsions; Cambodia has shown hostility of a very
bloody kind against its minority of Vietnamese citizens. In

India, the Hindu religion built a caste system that was in effect a hierarchy of colour, and accompanied it with a belief in the paramount duty of acceptance. There too religious prejudice and discrimination between Hindus and Moslems paralleled those of colour in other lands, giving rise to even more bloody communal murders and riots. But communal strife in the Indian sub-continent (its religious counterpart may be seen only too tragically in contemporary Northern Ireland) has resulted from the same, side-by-side existence of communities living in ignorance of one another that has so often characterised communities of different colour in all continents. Fear, grounded in ignorance, has been the cause of violence the world over.

China, more homogeneous internally, has traditionally reacted arrogantly and with hostility to foreigners, be they 'pink devils' or 'black devils'. But the Chinese have been sensible, since the Communist success in 1949, of the real conflicts of the world between coloured and white peoples, and have done much to heighten coloured awareness and stir coloured revolt against that white-dominated *status quo* which tends to deny coloured peoples the fruits of life beyond subsistence.

Bolshevik Russia, early the champion of non-whites striving to break free of the domination of capitalist imperialism, and itself composed of many peoples, has increasingly in the last decades itself succumbed to prejudice and discrimination of the most emotional kind. This has been tragically evident in the arena from which prejudice ought to be most remote – the universities. The nineteen sixties have witnessed a succession of racial outbursts against students of African origin, for example in Moscow University in 1963 and at Baku in 1964. But such outbreaks pale into insignificance beside the increasing virulence of anti-Chinese hostility, since 1962, often expressed in the crudest racialist terms.

In Africa, Kenneth Kaunda's courageous, multi-racial ideal in Zambia is frequently threatened by the self-regard of white mining communities, while in the Sudan and in Nigeria men of Arab stock have come into open conflict with Negro sections of their nations. In Rwanda, the Bahutu turned upon their former Batutsi rulers in 1963, admittedly in the panic of invasion, in what was an attempt at genocide. In East Africa, real efforts have been made to create harmonious societies to include Indian and British immigrant minorities, but poverty and natural demands for Africanisation pose a continuous threat, and the deportation from Uganda and to a lesser extent from Kenya of Asians who have failed to take up citizenship has further raised racial temperatures.

In South Africa a different approach has been adopted by the dominant white population. Multi-racialism has been dismissed as a myth and official policy has been directed towards the 'separate development' of the racial groups which compose the nation. Whites, blacks, coloureds and Asians, the argument runs, should be allowed to develop at their natural pace along their own lines. It is an argument currently being echoed from the opposite pole of Black Power enthusiasm, in America, but however realistic it might be in regard to the human weaknesses which bedevil attempts at multiracialism, it has not proved possible to implement honestly in practice.

Perhaps this is inevitable when its control is vested entirely in a white community as jealous in regard to its economic privileges as it is nervous in regard to its cultural purity. *Apartheid* in practice means white power, black servitude; it means the abominable grading of men according to skin colour; it means the uprooting of non-white families, the perpetuation of the ignorance which communities have of one another. *Apartheid* reduces individuals to stereotyped generalities. It ignores the absolute interdependence of South Africa's communities and its enforcement machinery constitutes one of the world's greatest affronts to human dignity. Furthermore, the existence and survival of an *apartheid* South Africa exacerbates every area of colour tension in the world and provides a measuring rod by which the battle lines of colour conflict can be drawn. For the nations that are not against South Africa must be for it. And the nations which invest in, trade with and offer support to, South Africa cannot be at the same time friends of Black peoples. And of course the nations which deal so willingly with white South Africa (however reluctant some of their sportsmen may be to compete against white South African sportsmen) are largely the affluent white nations of Europe and North America.*

'Battle lines of colour conflict': must it really come to this? And will the lines also form the boundary between affluence and poverty? The prospect is a real one. The second half of this chapter will emphasise only too clearly the division of the world between the 1000 million affluent whites and the 2,500 million others who live in want. And want is no mere shortage of money; it is shortage of life itself and of all the things which go to make life worthwhile. The coloured millions who are always in hunger are usually ill also, can expect to live only half as long as their white brethren, are unlikely to be able to read, can never know security, can never hope to develop their talents. Figures of *per capita* income from country to country can give only the roughest guide to average actual wealth, but it emerges from the crude income satistics of the world that it is the white nations alone that stand above the 'frontier of wealth'[10], that alone can hold out to their citizens the general possibility of fulfilment. Figures of expectation of life give an altogether more accurate and telling picture of the relative wealth and poverty of nations. There is little room here for complacency.

Which is it to be then: races, distinguished by shades of colour and marked off similarly on graphs of wealth and life, standing opposite in two great hostile camps, the one risking the loss of so much, the other with nothing at all to lose; or a harmonious world of peoples, conscious of their real inter-dependence, striving together to extend equality of oppor-tunity world-wide? The gloomy world tour conducted above gives little ground for optimism. Racialism is universal, and modern communications – particularly transistor radio, but also television, press and travel – remove that isolation and ignorance which once made injustice and exploitation easy and profitable. Now the poor know of their poverty, and equ-ally of the luxury of the rich: the coloured poor; the white rich. Can nothing be done?

*For a more detailed account of South Africa's domestic policy see Appendix C.

TELEPHONE CONVERSATION

The price seemed reasonable, location
Indifferent. The landlady swore she
    lived
Off premises. Nothing remained.
But self-confession. 'Madam,' I
    warned,
'I hate a wasted journey — I am
    African.'
Silence. Silenced translation of
Pressurized good breeding. Voice,
    when it came,
Lipstick coated long gold-rolled
Cigarette holder dipped.
Caught I was, fully.
'HOW DARK?'. .I had not mis-
    heard. . . Carry on
'Are you light
Or VERY DARK?'
Button B. Button A. Stench
Of rancid breath of public-hide-and-
    speak.
Red booth. Red pillar box. Red
    double-tiered
Omnibus squelching tar. It WAS
    real! Shamed
By ill-mannered silence surrender
Pushed dumbfoundment to beg sim-
    plification
Considerate she was, varying the
    emphasis—
'ARE YOU DARK OR VERY
    LIGHT?' Revelation came
'You mean — like brown or milk
    chocolate?'

Her assent was clinical, crushing in
    its light
Impersonality. Rapidly, wavelength
    adjusted
I chose, 'West African sepia' — and
    as an afterthought
'Down in my passport.' Silence for
    spectroscopic
Flight of fancy till truthfulness clang-
    ed her accent
Hard on the mouthpiece. 'WHAT'S
    THAT?' conceding
'DON'T KNOW WHAT THAT
    IS.' 'Like brunette.'
'THAT'S DARK ISN'T IT?'
    'NOT altogether.
Facially I am brunette but, madam,
    you should see
The rest of me. Palm of my hand,
    soles of my feet
Are a peroxide blonde. Friction
    caused—
Foolishly — madam — by sitting
    down has turned
My bottom raven black —
O, one moment, madam!'—sensing
Her receiver rearing on the thunder-
    clap
About my ears—'Madam,' I pleaded,
    'Wouldn't you rather
See for yourself?'

Wole Soyinka

Humanity
Much is being done. In the first place, the world of states
gathered in the United Nations Organisation has done much
to set the goals; to define standards of humanity and to foster
adherence to these standards ever more widely. The United
Nations has been able to build on the foundations laid by the
League of Nations, particularly upon the codes of behaviour
drawn up by its subsidiary, the International Labour Organisation. The Universal Declaration of Human Rights,* adopted
by the United Nations in 1948, is a notable advance on anything achieved by the League. In 1919, a tentative Japanese
request for a recognition of the equality of all races was rejected,
largely through the energetic opposition of the Prime Minister
of Australia. But in 1948, after the horrors of Nazi racism, and
in accord with the spirit of the 1941 Atlantic Charter of
Churchill and Roosevelt, the members of the United Nations
declared majestically that:

> All human beings are born free and equal in dignity and
> rights. They are endowed with reason and conscience and
> should act towards one another in a spirit of brotherhood.

They then prefaced their list of basic rights by a specific
statement of universality:

> Everyone is entitled to all the rights and freedoms set forth
> in this declaration, without distinction of any kind, such as
> race, colour, sex, language, religion, political or other status.

Empty words, all too often, but this Declaration provides
the standard towards which all can aim and by which all will
be judged. Increasingly, the wrongs suffered by individuals
are becoming the concern of men of conscience everywhere.
Amnesty International seeks to publicise the cause of every
prisoner of conscience, everywhere, to expose brutality, to
pursue justice. Disaster anywhere, whether it be in Yugoslavia,
Rumania, Peru or Nigeria, whether it be the result of earth-
quake, flood, famine or folly, has become the concern of all
peoples. Awareness of individual tragedy stirs the human
heart. Awareness of the greater tragedy that is existence for so

*See Appendix B(i).

many must in time produce a similar result; and awareness of the unity and interdependence of all who live on our planet, awareness, that is, of the sheer self-interest of assistance from the rich to the poverty-stricken, must follow. Transition is the distinguishing feature of our age in almost every quarter, and transition to a citizenship of mankind may be one of the more hopeful prospects of change.

There is a long way to go. The United Nations Commission on Human Rights continues to point to shortcomings and recommend action. And because nations so obviously have fallen short of the standards of 1948, the United Nations has since adopted a resolution more specifically directed at race antagonism. The preamble of the United Nations Declaration on the Elemination of all forms of Racial Discrimination (1963) summarises the aspiration of men of reason from all races; its articles lay down a programme necessary for the security as well as the harmony of the world:

Text of the Resolution

The General Assembly,

Considering that the Charter of the United Nations is based on the principles of the dignity and equality of all human beings and seeks, among other basic objectives, to achieve international co-operation in promoting and encouraging respect for human rights and fundamental freedoms for all without distinction as to race, sex, language or religion,

Considering that the Universal Declaration of Human Rights proclaims that all human beings are born free and equal in dignity and rights and that everyone is entitled to all the rights and freedoms set out in the Declaration, without distinction of any kind, in particular as to race, colour or national origin,

Considering that the Universal Declaration of Human Rights proclaims further that all are equal before the law and are entitled without any discrimination to equal protection of the law and that all are entitled to equal protection against any discrimination and against any incitement to such discrimination,

Considering that the United Nations has condemned colonialism and all practices of segregation and discrimination associated therewith, and that the Declaration on the granting of independence to colonial countries and peoples proclaims in particular the necessity of bringing colonialism to a speedy and unconditional end,

Considering that any doctrine of racial differentiation or superiority is scientifically false, morally condemnable, socially unjust and dangerous, and that there is no justification for racial discrimination either in theory or in practice,

Taking into account the other resolutions adopted by the General Assembly and the international instruments adopted by the specialised agencies, in particular the International Labour Organisation and the United Nations Educational, Scientific and Cultural Organisation, in the field of discrimination,

Taking into account the fact that, although international action and efforts in a number of countries have made it possible to achieve progress in that field, discrimination based on race, colour or ethnic origin in certain areas of the world none the less continues to give cause for serious concern,

Alarmed by the manifestations of racial discrimination still in evidence in some areas of the world, some of which are imposed by certain Governments by means of legislative, administrative or other measures, in the form, inter alia, of apartheid, segregation and separation, as well as by the promotion and dissemination of doctrines of racial superiority and expansionism in certain areas,

Convinced that all forms of racial discrimination and, still more so, governmental policies based on the prejudice of racial superiority or on racial hatred, besides constituting a violation of fundamental human rights, tend to jeopardize friendly relations among peoples, co-operation between nations and international peace and security,

Convinced also that racial discrimination harms not only those who are its objects but also those who practise it,

Convinced further that the building of a world society free from all forms of racial segregation and discrimination, factors which create hatred and division among men, is one of the fundamental objectives of the United Nations,

1. Solemnly affirms the necessity of speedily eliminating racial discrimination throughout the world, in all its forms

and manifestations, and of securing understanding of and respect for the dignity of the human person;

2. Solemnly affirms the necessity of adopting national and international measures to that end, including teaching, education and information, in order to secure the universal and effective recognition and observance of the principles set forth below;

3. Proclaims this Declaration:

Article 1

Discrimination between human beings on the grounds of race, colour or ethnic origin is an offence to human dignity and shall be condemned as a denial of the principles of the Charter of the United Nations, as a violation of the human rights and fundamental freedoms proclaimed in the Universal Declaration of Human Rights, as an obstacle to friendly and peaceful relations among nations and as fact capable of disturbing peace and security among peoples.[11]

The international community properly sets the standard. Individual states have the responsibility of conforming and individual citizens the obligation of vigilence.

Amongst individual states, those with an imperial past and those with a multi-racial composition must have particular responsibilities. The process of decolonisation tends to generate racial antagonism, as subject people focus opposition against their imperial governors: hatred roused on one side is easily matched by resentful hostility on the other; both attitudes may last a good deal longer than the initial struggle unless positive steps are taken, and taken by and large by the ex-imperial power. That power must recognise that old agreements may have to be adjusted, that concessions for mining, oil or trade may require renegotiation on terms of equality rather than along the old lines of dictation from strength; and loans and financial aid must be granted on especially favourable terms, rather than on the rates prevailing amongst the already developed nations. Only thus can ex-colonies progress at all, economically, and self-respect and dignity grow, and grounds for antagonism lessen.

Inside multi-racial states, more than mere education will be needed to achieve harmony, though education can certainly help. A legal framework promoting accord and penalising discrimination (perhaps along the lines of the British Race Relations Act) may be necessary to make better standards of behaviour the accepted norm. But prejudice must also be tackled by preventing the circumstances that give rise to it, and this will require an assault on social insecurities as well as the involvement of all races in community effort. In the past the prejudice of men against female suffrage has been seen to respond to practical experience, toleration following the discovery that the vital interests of men were not threatened by voting women, and that, on the contrary, the equality of women enriched the whole community, men included. So may race prejudices respond to experience, with equally fruitful results.

The individual citizen can do so much to create the right atmosphere in his country. He may influence it towards hate, suspicion and prejudice or more constructively, in the direction of understanding, sympathy and equality. He can expose examples of injustice, demand conformity to the United Nations Declarations, adopt a personal standard of colour-blind behaviour. He can reject racial stereotypes and treat all individuals as fellow men, subject to the same emotions, endowed with the same strengths and weaknesses as himself.

The beginning of hope lies in awareness of the problem. But the magnitude of the task must also be appreciated. Racial antagonism is 'as old as human greed, the fears and hatreds of inequality, the distrust of difference, the arrogance of strength'.[12] And the task of removing it is not only human and political; it is also economic and cultural.

B) MATERIAL

The physical, climatic and economic characteristics of the earth vary enormously and have asserted a powerful influence on man's development. But if in the past men and continents have developed separately, evolving their different cultures, harnessing or failing to harness the resources at their disposal, today the existence of one world argues a different, more unified experience. Certainly nations and peoples will wish to preserve their cultural distinctiveness, but they will need also to conduct as a matter of urgency a more rational appraisal of the earth's material resources and the means whereby they are utilised and exchanged, and to adopt a much greater degree of planned co-ordination. What is at stake can be appreciated by observing the disposition around the globe of the various resources valuable to man, in particular food, metal and energy; by glimpsing something of the nature of economic development and world trading practice; by exposing both the sources of wealth and the existence of hunger, poverty and ignorance, the relationship between the rich and the poor nations, and, not least, man's corrosive impact on the environment in which he lives.

Food, Metal and Power
The easiest way of indicating the extraordinary imbalance of resources in the world is by such statistical tables as the annual tonnage of steel produced by individual nations, the amount of cement used, the total volume of electricity generated or the *per capita* consumption of calories. But statistics give little impression of actual human conditions and conceal in their average amounts the wide differences existing even within single territories. Statistics can indicate the widening gap between the developed and developing nations, can reveal diet deficiencies, incidence of diseases, or income disparities, and can provide convincing evidence of disturbing trends of populations and living standards. But they seldom reveal that other rich-poor gap which is so prevalent in the developing lands – the gap between the standards of town and country – and, because they reduce human conditions to abstractions and arithmetical averages, they too seldom succeed in moving their readers to action.

Statistical tables are an essential tool, a short cut to the understanding of many complex problems, but they must be treated with caution and in this context supplemented with further details of history, geography, tradition and taboo. Above all they must be approached by Europeans with a conscious effort to shake off their 'Eurocentric' assumptions.

It is tempting to judge others from one's own technical and cultural stand-point, to assume similar nutritional, educational or constructional requirements for people in vastly different circumstances and surroundings. Each table, each nation, demands to be put in its proper context. And part of this context concerns the level of human skills available to utilise the resources under discussion.

With all these cautionary observations in mind, world agricultural resources, the distribution of basic foodstuffs, will first be looked at. Here, as in every other commodity, comparisons will constantly be drawn between the developed and developing world. After all, in the matter of food, it is regrettably true that while the developed third of the world's people can afford to worry about what they eat, the remaining two thirds must worry about whether they will eat at all. Two thirds of the world's people will go to bed hungry each night, will seldom know a 'square meal', and many of them will suffer the disease and debilitation that go with malnutrition. This is our starting point.

For the fact of food distribution throughout the world is that there exists a surplus beyond requirements in a number of highly developed nations where the proportion of population in agriculture is, paradoxically, low, but their individual output correspondingly high. In developing nations, all with a predominently agricultural economy but much of it at a subsistence level, hunger is the norm. Ignorance and social custom hold back production and proper utilisation of existing resources, as well as preventing the introduction of new crops and methods. Thus, while the United States farmer of a century ago could produce enough to feed himself and four others, and can today feed himself and twenty-five others, the farmer of some developing lands cannot even guarantee all-year-round subsistence for himself, let alone his wife and family or those in the towns who depend upon him to create a surplus.

Climate, soil and water are of course major factors dictating the type of basic cereals grown in different regions, but good husbandry, the careful application of irrigation, fertilisers, and crop rotation, for example, have combined to produce much

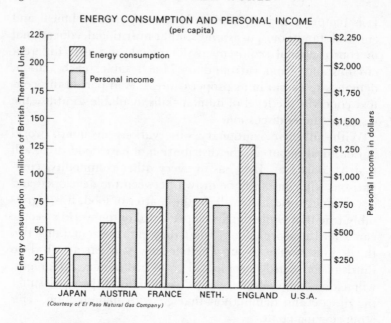

ENERGY CONSUMPTION AND PERSONAL INCOME
(per capita)

(Courtesy of El Paso Natural Gas Company)

higher yields per acre in many developed countries. Cereals supply man with 97% of his food (measured in calories) and the two major world examples are wheat and rice, the former being produced predominantly in Europe, North America, the Argentine and Australia, the latter in Asia (in Monsoon Asia the words for rice and food are the same). Rye, oats and barley too are grown extensively in Europe and North America, with barley also being grown in the Near and Far East. Maize (sweet corn) is extensively cultivated in North America and in Southern Europe and also in Africa and the Far East. In Africa and Asia, grain sorghums are the staple food, along with millet, and these rank next to wheat and rice as the most widely used of the world's cereal foods.

Vegetables – the potato, manioc (cassava), the sweet potato and the yam are also staple crops – and fruit (bananas and dates having vital importance in the Caribbean and Middle East respectively), sugar, cacao, tea and coffee, are other agricultural products, unequally distributed around the globe, which are of major significance to man's bodily needs and to world trade. The production of meat for consumption – largely beef, pork and mutton – and also poultry and fish, again are vitally important, but it is noticable with all of these that there is a narrow concentration of consumption. The vast proportion of the people of the world do not enjoy a varied diet, being forced to rely on a single staple. Outside the thirty-odd developed countries, even where bellies are filled it is often with mere starch which does little more than remove the feeling of hunger: swollen limbs, resourcelessness, lassitude, and early deaths continue to predominate. Man must eat, but two thirds of mankind are, in the words of Arthur Hopcraft, 'born to hunger'.[13]

Developed and developing: the evidence may be most visible in terms of hunger and malnutrition, but the criteria separating the one from the other will be most often expressed in terms of industrialisation as the means of creating and sustaining wealth and further development. Here the distribution of the world's metal resources ought to be significant. For since men moved away from stone tools, the Ages of his development have been distinguished by his use of metals; from Bronze through Iron to Aluminium. But here too a paradox of deposits and development exists. Although the developing lands contain a disproportionate share of the world's mineral resources, it was the developed countries which, by their timely development, acquired the extracting and manufacturing techniques. These in turn enabled them to develop further so that they are today in a position to purchase their raw materials cheaply and sell their finished products dear.

Iron-ore, which has been processed by man for the last four thousand years, remains the most plentiful, widely distributed and widely used metal, accounting for 90% of world metal tonnage. But although deposits are widely distributed, iron mining is not, and processing and the manufacture of steel is confined to even fewer centres, because of the need for development capital, technological skill, cheaply available power and assured markets.

The story of non-ferrous metals is different, in so far as they are scarcer; but while many of the principal sources of output of such vital examples as copper, lead, zinc, tin and aluminium, are found in the developing world, the centres of consumption are, as before, in the developed countries. World reserves of leading non-ferrous metals are far from inexhaustible and may not suffice present usage for more than twenty or thirty years. Demand soars, particularly for aluminium, and more and more the developed countries are becoming dependent for supplies upon foreign resources.

Metal production and consumption is one indicator of industrial development, and something of the world imbalance can be realised by the estimated total value of the production and usage of all metals (and also construction materials such as sand and gravel). For the year 1960, out of a total figure of 13,000 million dollars for this purpose, the United States alone accounted for 7,000 million dollars, leaving 6,000 million for the rest of the world put together.

The world's energy production and consumption once again reflects the powerful position already achieved by the developed countries, and the burden of backwardness bearing upon those struggling to develop. The availability of cheap energy was crucial in their early days for the developed countries, and it remains the key factor in the future development of a world economy. In the developed nations, as the table indicates, man has come a long way from reliance merely on his own muscle power. In the most advanced country, the United States, more than forty per cent of the world's vast output of mechanical energy is consumed, and forty per cent of the world's oil production, 30 per cent of the world's harnessed water power, and 25 per cent of its coal. All developed countries consume millions of thermal units of energy and the demand steadily rises; in the sixties world fuel needs rose by 70 per cent. They are expected to double in the fifteen years between 1970-1985. Meanwhile, the developing lands rely largely on the muscle of man and beast, but desperately need to harness and utilise other forms of power.

Coal and oil have served man in the past and with natural gas (the other major fossil fuel) must continue to meet much of the world's future needs, even though hydro-electric and nuclear power are being brought increasingly into service. For the latter, shortages of vital materials, technical difficulties, and problems of waste disposal will restrict development. Solar energy gives hope of future use but is of low intensity and will be confined to areas of high annual sunshine.

Fuel supplies, like those of non-ferrous metals, are far from being unlimited, and here too it behoves the nations of the world to use their resources efficiently. Although today fuel is readily available and cheap, such a situation can hardly survive the anticipated demand for energy over the next fifteen to twenty years.

The Developed World

Food, metal and energy must continue to dominate man's search for material progress. Meanwhile, the concentration of energy and productive capacity in the few developed countries of Europe, North America, Russia, Japan, Australia and New Zealand is such as to render the world highly unbalanced. Inside the developed sector, competition between the capitalist and communist camps creates dangerous tensions, and, along with a common absorption in the complexities of modern industrial development, distracts from the urgent world problem of meeting the desperate requirements of the remaining two thirds of mankind. The rich nations contain less than one third of the world's population but produce and consume more than two thirds of the world's goods. And because their output is rising faster than their population, they can look forward to ever larger *per capita* incomes.

It is so easy for the advanced minority to take for granted its comfortable conditions: the high level of literacy, the range of social services, health and welfare organisations and amenities for learning and recreation; the regulation of working conditions, high earnings and the ever-increasing proportion of leisure time; the growing level of nutrition, health and life expectancy. All these factors, which promote the security and permit the fulfilment of the individual, are virtually unknown to the mass of people in developing lands, as also are the complex administrative machines of central and local government,

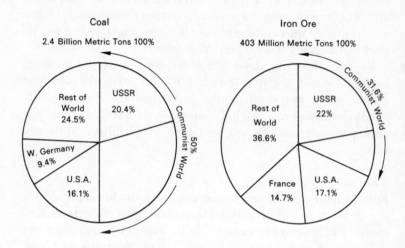

Coal

2.4 Billion Metric Tons 100%

- Rest of World 24.5%
- USSR 20.4%
- W. Germany 9.4%
- U.S.A. 16.1%
- 50% Communist World

Iron Ore

403 Million Metric Tons 100%

- Rest of World 36.6%
- USSR 22%
- France 14.7%
- U.S.A. 17.1%
- 31.6% Communist World

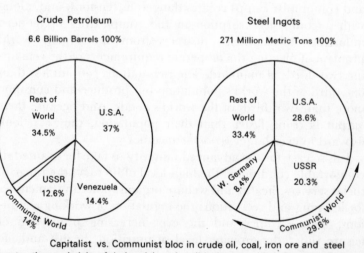

Crude Petroleum

6.6 Billion Barrels 100%

- Rest of World 34.5%
- U.S.A. 37%
- USSR 12.6%
- Venezuela 14.4%
- 14% Communist World

Steel Ingots

271 Million Metric Tons 100%

- Rest of World 33.4%
- U.S.A. 28.6%
- W. Germany 8.4%
- USSR 20.3%
- 29.6% Communist World

Capitalist vs. Communist bloc in crude oil, coal, iron ore and steel ingots, the yardsticks of industrial and political power (after Elmer W. Pehrson) the wide range of commercial services which support the productive engineering sector, and the sophisticated transport and freight networks.

The developed countries have established the means whereby their citizens may live abundantly. Their economies have 'taken off' along the road of self-generating development. Technical innovations and scientific discoveries broaden the horizons of convenience and affluence at an accelerating pace. Ever-accelerating, but also of ever-increasing complexity: this is the problem. For the electronic world of computerised automation or satellite telecommunications is a world of stupendous financial and technological demands. Size becomes vital to both research and development and to market outlets; the smaller developed countries draw closer in order to harness their combined wagons to the rising star of modern industrial growth. The developed nations recognise their interdependence as they push forward with enthusiasm both the frontiers of knowledge and their own already high living standards.

They also begin to recognise a number of very real problems. The Western governments in particular have had to assume increasingly the task of managing the level of public demand for goods so that the nation's whole resources can be fully utilised, without the waste of unemployment or periodic recessions. Prices too require management, to be steadied at a competitive level, and this necessitates agreement on social aims between governments, workers and employers. Proper development of services is also needed to ensure that education and research are adequate to requirements; international standards must be ensured through the stimulus of foreign competition. All these activities require increasing government intervention into the affairs of the nation and place added emphasis on the need for central planning, contrary though this may appear to be to the spirit of a free market economy. Planning, however, brings with it a new range of problems. What is to be included in planning; and what should be centralised in government hands, what left to the decision of private firms and individuals?

Advanced economies have become so complicated and so

delicate. Western democratic electorates are fearful of every cool breeze lest it weaken their prosperity. The experts who nurse the economy are accorded popular esteem, but their diagnoses are watched with anxious incomprehension. For the complexity of modern industrial society defies common under-standing. And those democratic electorates (which lacked the desire to govern subject peoples far beyond the borders of their nations, as the age of Empire came to a close) have not yet begun to look beyond the health of their own national econ-omies when required to hold to account their national govern-ments and 'experts'. As yet, the bulk of citizens, even in the advanced countries, lack an awareness of the interdependence of their own nations, let alone of the indivisible interests today of *all* the world's peoples. How then can they be expected to sanction 'aid' to nations less well off? Indeed, why should they, amidst their own pressing difficulties, syphon off even a tiny percentage of their wealth to help those whose folly or ignorance is presumed to have found its own reward further down the ladder?

Ignorance of economics, however, must not continue to fog the issues of humanity. And these urgent issues must bring before long an outline appreciation at least of economic interest and obligation, and a realisation that for the benefit of all men, all the world's resources must be controlled and co-ordinated.

The Developing World
For, as it happens, in the developing lands there is a race between a growing population and the provision of food which the former seems likely to win. There is a shortage of develop-ment capital and of technological skill and there is often, too, a backlog of ignorance and disease, and a culture pattern that stubbornly resists change. What is the way ahead for such countries? Must they try to emulate the capitalist development of the nineteenth century, or can the expertise of the twentieth century provide them with short cuts? And must they advance by their own efforts alone, or can the developed nations give them assistance with finance, technology and skilled men? Such questions cannot for ever await an answer, yet in the

developed nations even the alert few cannot agree on their reply.

Some see the struggling nations of Asia, Africa and Latin America solely in European development terms, their future lying in a step by step pursuit of the pattern of European progress. Short of capital, these countries have a surplus of labour. Such capital as is available for investment must be used wisely to achieve the maximum effect in creating employment, which will in turn increase national production and provide more capital. The stages of development, therefore, must be first of all to concentrate on industries which require little capital and harness a lot of labour (i.e. labour-intensive industry); agricultural processing and textiles are a good example of this kind of industry. Secondly, as time advances and labour surplus is drawn into 'primitive' industry, and basic industrial skills are acquired, the country can move on to more 'capital intensive' industry, light engineering and consumer goods. Later still, industrial maturity will permit the production of machinery and large-scale engineering, the sort of industry that generates real development, creating as it does a demand for subsidiary industry and services and, more importantly, greater profits and capital surpluses to promote more employment and consequently more purchasing power and demand for more production amongst the people. At this stage the country can even afford to purchase some of its foodstuffs abroad as well as the consumer goods that it cannot easily manufacture at home.

This is the model of development pursued by various capitalist countries in the nineteenth century and by Japan in the early twentieth, though all advocates of such a policy today envisage a much more active role for government in the developing lands than was the case in nineteenth century Europe The policy involves a slow build-up and a slow increase in living standards; perhaps too slow. For the trouble today is that in most developing countries the population explosion, and the consequent need to feed, house and educate ever increasing numbers, runs away with the small surplus of capital which would otherwise be available for development. Expectation of

improvement has been aroused, knowledge of affluence elsewhere has been imparted, but, for people often newly independent, things either do not improve at all or else so
imperceptibly as to be scarcely noticeable. The brutalising conditions of development transition, which were features of many
pre-democratic nineteenth century European nations, are not
easily accepted in the one-man-one-vote circumstances of the
twentieth century. But the mass of people remain caught in a
vicious circle of rising population, unemployment, poverty and
ignorance.

Socialists, viewing the achievements of Russia in the past
and China in the present, deny that this imitation of capitalism,
doomed to failure anyway, need be adopted. Central planning,
the proper ordering of priorities and the harnessing of the
nation's total resources can produce results, at first slowly, but
then with gathering and startling momentum. The argument
is advanced that, no matter how little the nation is able to
invest, this should be invested in the sort of production that
will increase further the investment potential. Even if at first
there is a conflict between a quick expansion of employment
and the nation's economic growth, the latter must be pursued,
for within a short time it will yield greater employment and
consumption than would otherwise be possible.

The immediate priority, therefore, must be to produce
capital goods – machines and materials for construction – which
alone can bring rapid expansion and the means to construct and
equip future factories and power plants. Of course attention
must be paid to the production of *some* consumer goods and to
the provision of *some* social services, but the point is made that
discipline and hardship in the early stages will be repaid by the
certainty of future benefit. From the unplanned imitation of
capitalism, the argument runs, hardship will eventually be
overwhelming and the consequent misery will lead nowhere at
all. But planned and disciplined growth leads to the promised
land of national prosperity and individual fulfilment. Thus
Kwame Nkrumah could quote in self-justification, after the
failure of his regime in Ghana, a letter of encouragement he
received even before Ghana received its independence:

I say to you publicly and frankly: the burden of suffering that must be borne, impose it upon *one* generation! Do not with the false kindness of the missionaries and businessmen, drag out this agony for another five hundred years: ......be merciful by being stern! ...

There will be no way to avoid a degree of suffering, of trial, of tribulation; suffering comes to all people, but you have within your power the means to make this suffering of your people meaningful, to redeem whatever stresses and strains may come.[14]

That Nkrumah failed in his attempts to build a socialist Ghana in one generation can be explained, in his own eyes anyway, by the inadequacy of the human material used for so great a task (a factor with which all theoreticians of every New Jerusalem must perforce reckon). To him the principles of his actions remain sound.

The U.S.S.R., which succeeded in dragging a backward peasant land into industrial greatness, did have some advantages of skill and scale to aid it, and did even so find it necessary to resort to methods of brutal terror only justifiable, if at all, in terms of the future generations who could benefit from the death and terrorising of their peasant forefathers. Humanity can be moved to action by hope and by fear, by promise of reward or pressure of the lash or the gun. Countries in a hurry have in the past pessimistically relied more on the latter than the former.

China, even more peasant, even more populous than Russia, also transformed itself and did so in terms that seem even more relevant to the developing countries, most of which agree that their only hope is industrialisation, but lack the required know-how and organisation to achieve it. Chinese regimentation has been obvious. Chinese setbacks have leaked out, despite general secrecy, but Chinese progress has impressed visitors, and China has begun to disburse rather than receive technical and financial assistance. China's increasing population does not appear to be starving, does appear to pursue national progress and does rejoice at the restoration of China's greatness amongst the nations of the world. Again, though it must be observed that China is unique, culturally and physically different from

Latin America or Africa, China's real and relevant achievement is largely self-produced (in spite of some valuable Soviet assistance in the 1950's), while the very mistakes and fluctuations in China's policy have rendered the Chinese more approachable. China has shown what resolute sacrifice and rigid planning can achieve, and if individual liberty has suffered, in the eyes of Western commentators, it must be enquired just what form of individual liberty existed before, or can exist for any man oppressed by famine, poverty and ignorance, in a corrupt and divided society?

China had, of course, the scale of greatness, and in this the fragmented ex-colonies of Africa and Latin America cannot compete. They can, however, think more in terms of regional co-operation. And they can order their own priorities in the light of their own potential resources and skills. Here, getting down to the details of, for example, the needs of individual African states, broad theorising encounters many shocks. Ghana, though small, was better educated and with greater financial reserves than many African states which have succeeded it to independence, but its troubled history since 1957 is instructive. For many others the problems to be faced do not seem to lend themselves to socialist or capitalist models: backwardness, disunity, illiteracy, poverty, debilitating disease and hostile social customs present difficulties as formidable to central planning, always supposing the planners can be found, as to the development of an expanding free-enterprise economy.

It is not surprising therefore that some observers have argued against industrialisation and for the development of agriculture and the promotion of rural life, with educational policies devoted to practical more than to academic learning. Let the African uniqueness survive in the countryside of Africa, they beg, though they would also, naturally, wish for Africans the benefits of medicine and hygiene, agricultural and veterinary skill and, urgently, family planning to prevent the overwhelming tide of new births from drowning all hope of betterment for those already seeking higher standards.

Capitalist emulation, socialist planning, indigenous development based on a synthesis of native tradition and modern technology: the recommendations are alluring in theory, difficult and demanding in practice. But the important fact remains that the widely shared and terrible problem of development does not exist in a vacuum. It lives in the world of international trade and international organisation, and alongside rich, developed nations with skills and techniques and financial resources which *can* be applied to the unique difficulties of a Brazil or a Guinea, an Egypt or an India, a Tanzania or a Guatamala. Though the success of developing countries must inevitably depend on their own efforts, the developed nations have it within their power to help. Self-sufficiency is an outdated ideal, and no nations of the world are more dependent on the products and skills of others than the most highly developed. The world really *is* one and it is within the interest of all that the rewards of life should be accessible to men the world over. True, wealth must continue to be created before it can be distributed equitably: industry and initiative must continue to be encouraged in the present centres of development, in Europe and North America, as a high priority. But these centres have the obligation as well as the means to promote wealth elsewhere, by advice, by involvement and by a degree of self-sacrifice.

Trade and Aid
It is in the field of international trade and development and through the international instruments of economic and technical assistance that much can be done immediately to reduce the magnitude of the problems facing the developing nations. Charity is not asked for, nor has it proved of lasting utility where it has been given. Rather, what must be disbursed by the developed nations is help to the developing to help themselves; help to create wealth on the one hand, and help to participate in international trade on favourable terms, on the other.

In both areas of assistance the United Nations has taken a lead by establishing machinery and recommending policy. The 1944 Bretton Woods Conference brought into being the International Bank for Reconstruction and Development (World

Bank), to which was affiliated in 1960 the International
Development Association (I.D.A.), founded specifically to
supply loans to developing countries (most of which had not
gained independence at the time the World Bank was created).
Orthodox in its lending policy, the World Bank has made
considerable funds available to governments at fixed rates for
development, and has endeavoured also to build advisory
machinery to ensure that its money makes a real development
contribution. In particular, the Bank has encouraged such
schemes as electricity generation and distribution, and also
transportation which together have accounted for about two
thirds of its loans; and industrial development and agriculture,
water supply and education which have also received significant support. Usually loans have been assigned to particular
projects, though some departures from this have been made, for
example, a 'programme' loan to India in 1964 to assist commercial vehicle production. The World Bank also helps to
provide expert advice for planning, undertakes the training of
economic officials and serves to arbitrate in international
financial disputes. Another of its affiliates, the International
Finance Corporation, channels investment to private-enter-
prise concerns and plays a major role in establishing industrial
development finance companies in developing countries.

The United Nations also established, in 1950, the Expanded
Programme for Technical Assistance (UNEPTA) which sends
experts at the request of governments to solve technical and
economic problems and to train officials. UNEPTA associates
with other United Nations subsidiaries such as the World
Health Organisation and UNESCO, contributing its own
funds in addition to the regular budgets of these bodies. As well,
a U.N. Special Fund was established in 1959 which works
closely with the above bodies and devotes itself to financing
resource surveys, research, vocational and technical training
and experimental pilot schemes.

The immense work done by United Nations subsidiaries,
financed jointly by those participating and by the non-
Communist members of the UN, is only hinted at in the list
above. They do emphasise the variety of ways in which the

developed countries can be of service to the developing, and they also serve as a guide to individual developed countries which undertake their own programmes of assistance.

In the field of international trade, the United Nations first of all established in 1948 the General Agreement on Tariffs and Trade (GATT), which was designed to promote the growth of international trade through the removal of obstacles. A multilateral treaty, since adhered to by many developing countries, GATT lists the maximum tariff rates that each adherent nation applies to the products of others and provides a code of principles and rules of international trade. By so doing it has won acceptance of the notion of international trading principles and has provided a forum for the discussion of the trading policies of individual nations and their impact upon others. However, major criticism of GATT has been levelled by the developing nations, for although it has removed many restrictions and reduced pre-existing disorder, the terms of the newly established order have favoured the developed lands at the expense of the developing. It was to meet this criticism that the United Nations Trade and Development Conferences (UNCTAD) were inaugurated in 1964.

The 1964 UNCTAD meeting was partly inspired by the trade paradox resulting from much of the assistance already given to developing countries. These countries had been encouraged to industrialise, and the developed world had contributed both finance and machinery as assistance. But once under way, the fledgeling industries found themselves up against protective tariffs and quotas by which the developed countries sheltered their own industries. This is only part of the problem of the developing countries, which also found that the trend of prices for primary produce, their main exports, was to reduce, while that of manufactured goods was to rise. In these highly adverse international trading circumstances, created by the developed lands, the developing nations called UNCTAD into being.

Its purpose, according to U.N. Secretary General U Thant, was to seek 'active and positive measures to encourage the export trade of developing countries both in primary products and in manufactures, and to deal with any movements of the terms of trade against them'.[15] But its achievements were disappointing. Although important decisions were taken and a new Trade and Development Board was set up, on which the developing countries had a majority, and a host of resolutions were passed on preference, commodity agreements and aid, too little application of the new principles followed in practice.

Dr. Raul Predisch, the Argentinian Secretary-General of the Conference, had drawn up in advance a detailed list of suggestions, couched in vigorous terms, calling for developed country discrimination in favour of the products of developing nations. The trade balance of the latter was adverse, their modest progress in jeopardy. Only active measures – greater access to developed countries' markets, encouragement of developing industries and periodic conferences and reviews – could prevent the gap between the rich and the poor nations from growing wider and wider.

It was noticed at the Conference how well the 77 developing countries attending stood together to support Dr. Predisch. Predictably, the developed countries were more reticent. The Western nations preferred to support GATT, (and in 1965 they did endeavour to introduce some of the UNCTAD recommendations into that Agreement); the Soviet bloc supported the developing countries and attacked GATT to which it did not belong, but, as Western trade accounted for some 70% of developing countries' trade, as against 6% to the communist bloc (the remainder being among the developing countries themselves), the attitude of the Western nations was more significant.

The 1964 UNCTAD was useful for clearing the air and demonstrating the difficulty of the problems facing the developing countries. It also received a request that the developed nations devote 1% of their Gross National Product (GNP) to aid developing countries in the future, a commitment that was actually made at a second UNCTAD meeting in Delhi, in January 1968. (This was subsequently supported in depth by the Report of the Pearson Commission on International Development, published in September 1969.)[16]

But the facts of international trade remain gloomy from the point of view of the developing nations. They find themselves losing more from the declining terms of trade and the remission of profits and dividends and the repayment of loans than they are gaining from aid and new investments. Though investments from the capitalist world are eagerly seized to finance development schemes, interest payments are often a real strain before the developments become productive. One commentator has shown that between 1950 and 1965, although U.S. investments in developed countries were higher than in developing countries, the return from all investments in developing countries was much greater. In order to attract such investments developing lands have had to outbid developed countries by offering higher interest returns. It is thus estimated that by 1979 virtually all the money now reaching the developing countries from both government and private sources will be required to meet the current interest charges and pay instalments on past borrowing. Thus, by offering investment opportunities to citizens and companies of the rich nations it is the developing countries who are aiding the developed countries and not the other way round.[17]

It is this process that has reminded a number of observers of Lewis Carroll's Walrus who showed such fine sensibility as he first encouraged, and then with the Carpenter consumed, the hopeful young oysters assembled at his feet:

'I weep for you', the Walrus said;
'I deeply sympathize'.
With sobs and tears he sorted out
Those of the largest size,
Holding his pocket handkerchief
Before his streaming eyes.[18]

The leading industrial powers lament the sad fate of the developing countries; they will even help to fatten them up, but only in order to eat them. And while some of the satisfied rich might say, righteously, that their money is hard earned and deserves to earn proper interest, it should also be pointed out that the present wealth of developed lands is partly based upon the past exploitation of the resources of under-developed territories. A clear obligation exists to put something back whence so much has been taken.

Some of the explanation of the existing upside-down state of affairs, of the lack of assistance and of the 'worsening terms of trade', lies in the difficulties which developed countries, for all their high standard of living, are themselves experiencing. Balance of payments crises and chronic currency problems have combined to preoccupy developed lands with their own affairs and to persuade them to drop or reduce their programmes of development aid. Other reasons stem from the very different understandings which prevail in the developed nations as to what 'aid' really is, and from that still prevailing, self-satisfied feeling amongst some Western nations that in the last resort only the rules of supply and demand can uphold international trade: that a dual system, whereby special preferences would be given to the developing nations, would undermine the successful, developed nations to the disadvantage of all.

Certainly there are difficulties in establishing what are 'fair prices' for raw materials. If producing countries supply too much tin, or rubber, or cocoa, or coffee, or sugar for the rest of the world to consume, then prices will fall: and the situation is not helped by the inability of such commodity producers to agree on quotas or to stick to the agreements they have managed to make. It is also difficult for Western governments to fix prices and agree quotas when most Western trade is not done by governments but by private companies. Nevertheless, the fact remains that countries such as Ghana and Malaya, which have made heroic efforts to increase production of their staple exports, have found that they have in the end earned less foreign exchange, not more. Thus, for example, Ghana raised its cocoa exports from 227,000 long tons in 1954 to 590,000 long tons in 1965. But a fall in the world price of cocoa over the same period meant that, whereas the 1954 crop earned £85$\frac{1}{2}$ m, the more than doubled 1965 crop earned only £77 m. Similarly, Malaya increased its rubber exports between 1960 and 1961 by 4%, but the revenue realised fell by 35%. And such countries can with some justification point to the changes in internal policy of developed nations which have at times contributed to the fall in demand for their products: taxes, tariffs and restricted quotas being some examples of such changes.

Developed countries would help to meet these difficulties if they could replace the stop-go cycle of their own economies with steady expansion, and developing countries might improve things if they could combine to fix commodity prices on the international market, though admittedly such agreements act against the efficient producer and can be complicated by the development of synthetic substitutes in the industrial nations. Lack of success in both these directions leaves the old pattern of trade to operate as before in the interests of those already developed. As is so often the case, the opportunities for improvement seem to be with those already in possession of abundance.

If international trade is proving intractable, international aid ought to be more susceptible to reason. But what is aid and what are its objectives?

Something of the assistance given by the United Nations special agencies has already been mentioned, and in its purest terms this is aid: grants of money to meet carefully worked out programmes which will in turn create revenue, employment and production; long-term loans without interest for similar purposes; the supply of advisers and instructors; the financing of surveys and pilot improvement schemes in agriculture or health; the training of nationals from developing countries abroad or the provision of training facilities in their own lands. In such ways the United Nations agencies, supported by the Western nations and by the developing countries themselves, encourage development. But these agencies were slow to develop and have never channelled more than a small proportion of total world aid. The Western nations, and to a lesser extent the Communist bloc, have disbursed the bulk of all aid. They might agree that they generally have political motives in doing so, but they do not agree upon what actually constitutes 'aid', being inclined at times to include normal investments and loans at commercial interest rates. Nor are they agreed on the principles of aid-giving, some donors tying their 'aid' to the purchase of their own goods, thus confusing aid with com-

mercial policy both in their own eyes and in the eyes of
recipients; others confine much of their 'aid' to military equipment.

As the rich/poor gap widens, clearly there is a case not only
for more aid but for more assurance that aid is being as effectively used as possible. Aid should have clear development
objectives on the assumption, apart from considerations of
humanity, that the removal of poverty and hardship will
contribute to a more stable world. But the fact of wasted aid
and counter-productive competition in aid between different
donors is at present all too noticeable, and government economists and private fund-raising organisations alike are
increasingly concerned to see both closer international co-
ordination of aid and closer donor supervision.

In the recipient countries, moves to end the tying of aid to
donor products is welcomed, as this allows greater freedom to
pursue what are felt to be the most pressing development
priorities with the most suitable equipment (and recipient
nations can get advice on both priorities and equipment
from such bodies as the O.E.C.D.'s Development Assistance
Committee, set up initially in 1960 as the Development Assistance Group). Recipient nations will also welcome moves to
increase aid funds and the lengthening of loan repayment
periods and any success that the donor countries might achieve
in removing international restrictions on their currencies, i.e.
increasing 'liquidity'. But they will have more reservations
about the desire for donors to supervise the administration of
aid in the field. Suggestions have been made to increase the role
of the Development Assistance Committee as a co-ordinator of
regional aid schemes, and even as an adjudicator of aid
priorities on a world scale. These suggestions are seen by
developing countries as attempts to undermine their independence; and the desires of donor nations to administer their
aid, and to co-ordinate the aid schemes of all aid givers in a
particular territory, are viewed with even greater suspicion.
Here the sensitivity to neo-colonialism is genuine; the danger
presented to economic sovereignty real. But for the corruption
and inefficiency which has in the past too often led to waste and

Newmont Mining's Interests

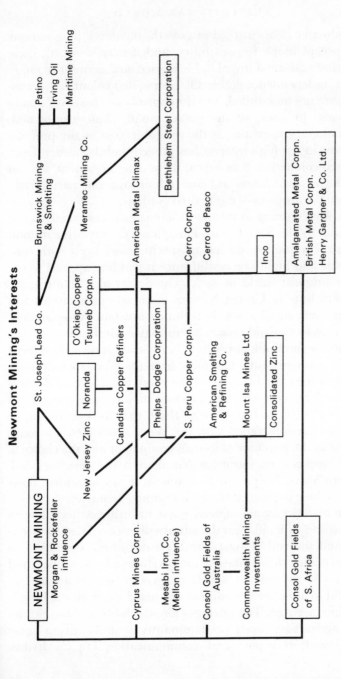

Chart of wide interests of Newmont Mining Corporation (formed Delaware, USA in 1921). Taken from K. Nkrumah, *Neo-colonisation. the last stage of imperialism* (Nelson, 1965) p.169, it shows the complexity of the large capitalist corporations.

unproductive debts instead of growth, the developing nations must accept much responsibility, and it may be worth their accepting realistic if unpalatable advice now in order to enjoy proper independence later. Of course neo-colonialist accusations are not unfounded, and the control exercised over young economies by some of the great, usually American-owned, international companies, is discreditable, just as the practice of borrowing at high interest has proved unduly burdensome. But neo-colonialist fear strengthens the argument for an increase in *multi-lateral* aid and administration, particularly through the auspices of the United Nations.

It is worth noting at this point some of the characteristics of aid given by the Soviet bloc. Though never very large in total amount, communist aid has in specific cases been both considerable and highly successful since it was first applied to the non-communist world in 1954. The Soviet bloc countries do not contribute to United Nations financial organisations and only in a very small way to its technical assistance programmes, preferring to give aid on a bilateral basis. Most of this aid has been in the form of loans, which in the early days were offered at a lower interest rate than those from the West, though this is no longer the case. Like that of the West, Soviet bloc aid serves a political purpose and tends to find its way to major neutral countries (such as India) or to those that for one reason or another have quarrelled with the West. All Soviet bloc loans are tied to the purchase of its own equipment and the choice of equipment is even more limited than is the case for 'tied' Western loans. No private investment, it can be added, flows from the bloc to projects in the developing countries.

The actual volume of Soviet aid has always been low in comparison with aid from the admittedly richer West. Between 1950 and the end of 1964, the West disbursed some $51,000 million net in official bilateral aid (excluding U.N. support and investment as well as aid from private organisations), as opposed to about $2,400 million disbursed aid from the bloc,[19] (starting in 1954). The purposes for which Soviet bloc aid has been given have been predominantly manufacturing (over 50%), with transport and communication (14%), hydro-electric power development (12%), irrigation and reclamation (10%) and agriculture (3%) accounting for most of the rest.[20]

Originally having something of a Cold War competitiveness about it, Soviet bloc aid has been further stimulated by the Sino-Soviet split. The Chinese, so much poorer in developed resources, have gained a measure of success in the acceptance of their views partly through concentrating their aid on a limited number of countries, notably in East and Central Africa, and partly through offering technical advice and entire projects rather than loans, for example, the Dar es Salaam Friendship Textile Mill, or the more ambitious Tanzam Railway. The Chinese, stressing the relevance of their own experience as a developing country, have pushed hard for militant revolution as the key to the achievement of communism, which they feel alone can bring an acceptable level of material advancement and true social justice based on equality. The Russians, wealthier and more absorbed in their own technical progress, have been more inclined to allow conditions conducive to Marxist control to develop in their own good time. For although there is no doubt that the Russians wish to see general living standards rise, and to assist the developing countries to escape the clutches of 'capitalist imperialism', they are also convinced that history is on their side: for if living standards are raised through Western aid then the capitalist process will be developed nearer to the point where orthodox Marxist revolution can occur; and if living standards do not rise, then misery will hasten a revolution which communists will probably dominate.

To talk blandly of general concepts of aid, its methods and its justification, in Cold War competitive terms, or in terms of donor self-interest, moral obligation, or mere expediency, however, is to risk losing sight of the actual battlefront conditions of the war against hunger and poverty. These conditions are encountered in full in the field where, for example, small agricultural teams of the Freedom from Hunger Campaign build pilot schemes in Tanzania, or well-digging groups from War on Want bore away in India, or medical units supported by Oxfam, or Caritas, or by the large number of other private foundations as well as by United Nations agencies and bilateral aid projects from East and West, operate in the face of natural disaster and ignorance all over the globe. Vividly recounted by Arthur Hopcraft, in *Born to Hunger*,[21] a book which describes expert teamwork amongst primitive tribes in desert Africa, education and health policies in remote Brazil, and malnutrition and birth control campaigns in teeming village India, these front line conditions are also the common experience of hundreds of youth volunteers who have gone, partly in the last decades, from the developed to the developing lands.

Mostly these young volunteers have brought with them professional and technical skills, though in some cases they have had to offer only their concern and enthusiasm and the higher level of education and administrative ability that is the privilege of developed peoples. Long-term voluntary service (usually two years) has provided one of the most vital requirements of developing countries; skills at middle level. For it cannot be too strongly emphasised that underdevelopment, though an economic phenomenon too, is primarily human. It is at bottom the people who lack the ability, the education, the experience to bring their countries forward. And the harnessing of much youthful idealism and talent from the developed countries has proved far more productive than the employment of a few highly qualified, well paid experts who have so often in practice been remote from the people they were sent to serve, and have found themselves underemployed in the field of their expertise.

Young, dedicated and enthusiastic, the multitude of Overseas Volunteers and Peace Corps members have proved invaluable. In 1967 there were some 20,000 of them in a hundred countries and territories. More than half were engaged in education, helping particularly to staff specialist posts and to enable the so-necessary expansion of learning that is one of the most urgent investments in developing lands. Community development, agriculture and medicine have also attracted significant numbers of volunteers, for a majority of volunteers are graduates with professional and technical training to give. But skilled craftsmen and tradesmen have also served in large numbers, imparting such industrial skills as lathe operating, motor vehicle maintenance, joinery – anything that is needed.

The international youth volunteer is not merely a phenomenon of the 'sixties, for many served in the inter-war years in work camps for short-term projects. But a great number of new organisations with more ambitious aims blossomed in the late fifties and early sixties. The British Voluntary Service Overseas (1958) and the New Zealand Voluntary Service Abroad (1959) were amongst those preceeding the American Peace Corps (1961), but the scale and organisation of the American project caught the imagination of the world and stimulated many European governments and organisations to follow suit and support similar ventures. Finally UNESCO stepped in to supply a Co-ordinating Committee for International Voluntary Service (CoCo) to advise on the placement and preparation of volunteers.

Skill and leadership have been the paramount requirements, and volunteers have been called upon to exercise a wide range of both in an extraordinary variety of circumstances, some rugged in the extreme. Although the majority have found themselves working in schools, others have met more esoteric demands:

A British volunteer made plastic legs for lepers; another tended to 3,000 sick or about-to-be-sick coffee trees, and a third improved mangrove swamp oyster cultivation in Sierra Leone. The German Development Service sent a beekeeper to Latin America and a pottery instructor to Afghanistan. The European Working Group sent a bush pilot to Kenya...A Danish International Co-operation engineer helped plan the expansion of Accra's electricity supply... Peace Corps volunteers have: planted figworts and opened a refuse disposal system in Ecuador; helped supervise the construction of 300 miles of road in Tanzania; quelled an epidermic of cerebral malaria among children in Togo; and restored endangered art treasures in India.[22]

But the benefit has not been one way only. Individual

volunteers have gained an understanding of other peoples and cultures and have had the personal reward of making a real contribution to societies in the process of creation. They have also brought back to their own countries a new conception of what life is like for the bulk of the world's peoples, and have continued to make their contribution simply by disseminating this knowledge amongst their own peoples.

The experience of volunteers, added to that of international economists, agronomists, traders, civil servants and politicians, may increase the pace of the slowly dawning consciousness, amongst peoples of developed countries, of the interdependence of all peoples. Within individual modern nations a majority now recognises the truth of the economic importance of equal educational opportunity for all, for no country can any longer afford not to develop the potential skills of all its people. What has to be recognised is that this is a *world* truth as well as a national one. And the world need to utilise the brainpower and technical and artistic skills of all the world's peoples is mirrored by the world need to develop world foodstuffs to feed the growing world population, and harness world raw material, fuel and power resources to raise world standards of living.

But impassioned statements of the urgent needs of economic and cultural man beg many questions about the means of satisfying them. How can developed and developing nations agree on the formulation and implementation of plans for a better world when so many unresolved issues remain within both categories of country? Within single nations, arguments rage over the proper relation of man to society: theoretical political schemes, based on the co-operative sharing of the risks and rewards of social endeavour, confront opposite schemes based on a belief in competitiveness as the necessary spur of selfish humanity towards productive activity; conservative preferences for security conflict with the progressive urge for change; the short-term interests of particular groups perpetually clash with what are held to be the long-term interests of society as a whole. All of these national problems require resolution the world over. But man's proper relation to society must be agreed not only with reference to his local community but to the world community.

The conflicting ideologies of communism and capitalism address themselves to this problem on a world scale and to their rival panaceas the next chapter will be devoted. Meanwhile some equally fundamental points remain to be made about the material context in which the ideological debate takes place. What sort of a physical world will be left for man to dwell harmoniously in once his social conflicts have been resolved? Is there not a real danger that before men learn to live in peace, they will have reduced the living earth as we know it now to a sterile and polluted shell? (The 's' may be omitted with equal relevance.)

The Environment

Man and his relation to the total world in which he lives is part of the concern of ecology, the science of the living environment, and many ecologists whose job is to study each organism in relation to its whole enviroment, in relation to other organisms of different species, and to those of its own kind, have begun to make forecasts rivalling those of the demographers in gloominess. Devoting their energy to assessing the cumulative impact of man on earth, since he lit the first fire to the present nuclear-explosive times, they have become acutely aware of the extent to which man's destruction of nature is depleting his present and endangering his future. At least one eminent ecologist, Frank Fraser Darling, identifies two major problems facing the world, both central to the global 'ecosystem' (the naturally balanced world habitat): the first is the population explosion to which we have already alluded and to which we will return briefly; the second is environmental pollution.

In his moving 1969 Reith Lectures (so moving and so apocalyptic that one commentator referred to them as the Wreath Lectures), Frank Fraser Darling pulled no punches. 'Population and pollution are the two great problems of our age' he proclaimed, pointing out that 'pollution is a function of population increase though it need not necessarily be so. Most pollution comes from getting rid of wastes at the least possible cost'.[23] We are not, he maintained, 'prepared to pay the price of our technology, the cost of cleaning up after ourselves'.[24] And he came to a decisive judgement:

> As a world problem, pollution and population pressure are partners, spectral and sinister. The question is whether they are going to shrink our lives to a condition of life in death, or whether we look outward and proclaim that we live in a beautiful world in which we believe and which we intend to maintain.[25]

Frank Fraser Darling's lectures were delivered as a preface to European Conservation Year, 1970. Entitled *Wilderness and Plenty*, they brought, to the British public at least, a sense of the urgent need for conservation on a world scale. Wilderness and plenty are not contrasting alternatives to Fraser Darling, but complementary prerequisites of a balanced world, the natural wilderness playing a vital part in the scheme of nature, e.g. cleaning, converting and restoring the air that man pollutes. Conservation he presented not as a matter of sentimental concern over nature, but of the sheer survival of life, human as well as other forms. The key words of his address, apart from 'conservation' itself, were 'preservation', 'rehabilitation' and 'dereliction', but before turning to look more closely at them, we must be aware of the scale of man's corrosive impact on the physical world: a world of which, in spite of his egotistical delusions of lordship, man is but a component part.

Most of man's real destruction has followed the Industrial Revolution, but since he ceased to hunt for food, like other animals, his methods of living have taken cumulative toll. The fires that first warmed man and later burned forest land for grazing began the erosion of one of nature's most valuable assets; then the overgrazing practised by primitive herdsmen reduced many fertile areas to desert; the extraction of metal for man's use accelerated the consumption of forest resources, while destructive war laid waste his fragile civilisations and cultivated lands.

With the technical advances and the increase in population which accompanied the Industrial Revolution came a new dimension of environmental pollution. Industrial and human waste turned rivers into sewers, upsetting the natural balance of life; coal and iron mining scarred the landscape and piled high barren heaps of slag; brick, gravel and cement works despoiled more and more land, while the new factory chimneys belched tons of sulphur dioxide upon a defenceless country-side; buildings on an unprecedented scale upset natural drainage systems, waterlogging new areas. Today, technical advances have launched detergents, pesticides and fertilisers into the environment with devastating side-effects on the natural habitat; lakes into which polluted rivers flow have become sterile, all life but algae gone; the debilitating water-born disease of schistosomiasis has multiplied with improved irrigation schemes in developing lands; the atmosphere of industrial cities in advanced countries has become choked with the cumulative weight of carbon monoxide from the internal combustion engine.

Frank Fraser Darling was emphatic about the increase of carbon dioxide in the atmosphere. The danger derives partic-ularly from the extending consumption of fossil fuels, notably oil and coal, and from man's careless interference with the natural carbon dioxide cycle. Vegetation, particularly forest wilderness, in the natural order of things removes carbon dioxide from the atmosphere by the photosynthetic activity of the leaves, turning it into wood on the one hand and giving out oxygen in exchange. The forest wilderness, so generous a partner of man (for it willingly spared a reasonable proportion of its trees for ships or shelter), has been so abused in the past that it can no longer cope with the job of conversion; and the oceans, which also soak up carbon dioxide, cannot cope with it, either. 'The activities of industrial and technological man in our day are adding carbon dioxide and also injuring the capacity of the biosphere to redress the balance.'[26]

But the carbon dioxide problem, so much less dramatic on the surface than that outrage of pollution, radio-active fall-out from the nuclear bomb, does not end there. The oceans are gradually being warmed by the increasing concentration of carbon dioxide in the air. Eventually they will begin to melt the polar ice caps: eventually, not in our time. But what is our responsibility to those future generations of men and animals faced with rising waters and shrinking productive land? Can we really wash our hands and say that posterity must look after itself? The answer must be no. For if in the past man's assault on the natural hand that fed him was conducted in ignorance, man is now ignorant no longer. He knows just what he is doing to his environment and to the balance of the natural community of which he is a part. That he continues to pillage and make desolate is due solely to his worship of short-term efficiency and his subjection of ecology to economics. The quality of life is lost sight of amongst the target quantities of industry. Far too little is attempted, at far too slow a pace, to curtail the erosion of the environment, let alone to reverse the cumulative damaging processes. To quote Fraser Darling directly once more, 'Folk and family are forgotten in some figment called gross national product, expressed in dollars or pounds sterling'. The problem is now world-wide and it has become acute enough to press on our own lives and upon those of our children. Of global concern, it demands a unified global response, and soon, before irreversible damage spreads too far. Time, as Gordon Rattray Taylor reminds us, is short:

> The fact is, we are just beginning to press up against the limits of the earth's capacity. The realisation has dawned that earth is a spaceship with strictly limited resources. These resources must in the long run be recycled either by nature or by man. Just as the astronaut's urine is purified to provide drinking water and just as his expired air is regenerated to be breathed anew, so all the earth's resources must be recycled sooner or later. But the margins are getting smaller. All we have is a narrow band of usable atmosphere no more than seven miles high, a thin crust of land only one-eighth of the surface of which is really suitable for people to live on, and a limited supply of drinkable water which we continually re-use. These resources are tied together in a complex set of transactions. We heedlessly intervene in these transactions.[27]

All over the world the challenge is being realised by the few and the first steps are being taken, tentatively as yet, to meet it. Governments and private bodies are addressing themselves to 'conservation', 'preservation', 'rehabilitation' and a reduction of 'dereliction'. In the ecological sphere, conservation means so much more than mere 'preservation' – the maintenance of avenues of trees, of unspoiled areas of coastline or of historic buildings – valuable though this contribution to conservation is. Conservation itself is total in its concern, assuming responsibility for the persistence and survival of entire habitats; 'conservation isn't just the importance of nature and all that, but a concern with the human being and his habitat, a concern for the survival of the human species on the planet from the environmental viewpoint'[28]. It assumes a responsibility for the future as well as addressing itself to the problems of the present.

And 'rehabilitation' is the most encouraging of the achievements of conservationists: the rescuing of 'dead' lakes and rivers, for example, achieved through legislation preventing the indiscriminate dumping of industrial or urban effluent, the reclamation of 'desert' through controlled irrigation and planting, the renovation of slag heaps and gravel pits into wooded areas or recreational amenities by thoughtful treatment. Rehabilitation and the prevention of further erosion can be ensured by society insisting upon the adoption of the simple ethic of making those responsible tidy up after their work is done. One suggestion for river-polluting industry is that it should be required by law to draw its clean water downstream from its waste disposal pipes; cement and brick producers might equally be required to devote some of their profits to restoring the landscapes they have scarred. In such ways can dereliction be reduced if not entirely avoided. For dereliction, in contrast to productive and valuable wilderness, is an ecological disaster, 'an ecosystem set back to beyond its pioneer stage with little hope of return';[29] dereliction is landscape devastated by pollution, by the high explosives of war or the steady pressure of machines, effluent or bad husbandry. In tiny, populous Britain, ten acres per day, on estimate, were being added in 1969 to the already existing quarter of a million acres of dereliction,[30] and the increasing demands for more roads, more houses and more urban amenities continue to erode further the areas of productive land and natural landscape.

In Britain such bodies as Nature Conservancy, the National Trust, the Forestry Commission, and the Countryside Commission have concerned themselves actively with conservation as a vital component of national wellbeing, and similar bodies have grown to prominence in countries throughout the world. In America, National Parks and Wild Life Refuges are assisted by American Nature Conservancy to protect existing eco-systems for survival and study; in Russia action to preserve threatened species has been combined with the yield of crops useful to man, a thoughtful marriage of sentiment and material interest; in Africa even impoverished new governments have sought to maintain existing national parks and to extend preservation of the uniquely rich and varied wild-life stocks of their continent.

But isolated preservation will not suffice. Conservation on a world scale to meet a world problem is required. Once more the unity of the planet is emphasised by the urgent need for international co-operation. A truly global problem urges a unified global response. The International Biological Programme has already been established in recognition of the fact that isolated, unco-ordinated action can be no more effective in this field than in the fields of food, mineral and energy production discussed earlier. The International Union for the Conservation of Nature, formed in 1948, has thrown itself into the struggle by offering its services as a clearing house and thermometer of world needs – 'from Tropic to Arctic, from the deep ocean to the sea shore'.[31]

Clearly, too, the whole process of international development must be geared to a global scheme of conservation. Mass spraying of insecticides, blinkered extension of disease-carrying irrigation, hydro-electric power schemes in one nation that seriously threaten the fertility of others – all can have repercussions stretching beyond the intentions of localised planning. Development there must surely be but co-ordination must ensure that it is development free of despoliation, and free too, many ecologists and economists would add, of the mere purpose of keeping abreast of population increase.

Rather, man's population increase must be controlled to allow the environment of man to be conserved. Population explosion, the twin of the pollution problem, inevitably re-enters the discussion. Ecologists no less than economic planners are appalled at the irresponsible rate of human reproduction. But while the economist warns of collapsing living standards, lack of economic growth, and the menace of famine, the ecologist is equally concerned with the squalor and stress of overcrowding and its impact on social behaviour. Over-crowding soon diminishes the physical environment as well as the human prospects. How then can the principles of the Declaration of Human Rights, that children born healthy have a right to life and that as adults they should be able to express their potential both for themselves and for the community, be upheld? The cancerous circumstances of uncontained urban growth, where population is increasing explosively, deny any possibility of the fulfilment of such principles.

The inescapable conclusion is that man cannot any longer postpone a thorough examination of his relation to nature and his place in the natural community. If in the past he has enjoyed living off the capital of the world's resources, feeling no corresponding responsibility towards them, man must now realise the necessity of his living as an integral part of the world's resources, with the special, technical role of servicing nature's requirements. Man should act towards his environ-ment 'as if posterity stretched into infinitude and by thus acting...make this more possible'.[32] His attitude must accord more closely with the view of the American ecologist, Aldo Leopold:

> That land is a community is the basic concept of ecology, but that land is to be loved and respected is an extension of ethics. We abuse land because we regard it as a commodity belonging to us. When we see land as a community to which we belong, we may begin to use it with love and respect.[33]

It is of course all very fine for Western exponents of conserva-tion to tell the world, which the West has so defiled in the past, that now and in the future care must be taken to put back as well as take out. Are not Western instructions to the developing peoples to restrict their families a subtle form of genocide? And are not Western attempts to restrict pollution and dereliction merely devices to prevent the developing nations from harnessing industry to win equality? The burden of the past is heavy; the evolution of Western Society has not been a simple story of unfolding technical progress or enlightened human charity! The responsibility of the West for conservation as well as development on a world scale remains after the age of Western imperial domination has ended.

In the introduction to this book one of the fundamental questions posed concerned that point in history which mankind has reached; where have we got to, where are we now? The short answer of the ecologist is that we have got into a mess; that we are wallowing in our own industrial excreta. It is as bad as that and we will sink further unless we become very quickly aware and very actively concerned. What is the use of worshipping material progress and maximum industrial efficiency of we blight our spiritual stature through the continued violation of our environment? It is a certain truth that a man reared without beauty, and away from the cycle of nature, its change, its flow, its infinite complexity and variety, is a stunted man; but stunting will be merely the first of the consequences of not caring. Ecologists state plainly the simple alternatives facing everyone if man continues carelessly to foul his global nest; either an explosive choking, or a no more pleasant, slow but certain withering. Frank Fraser Darling recommends to mankind instead the immediate 'therapy of the green leaf',[26] a simpler, happier prescription, but one on offer for a limited period only.

NOTES

[1] D'Espiritu Santos Mendoza, quoted in Ware, *op. cit.*, i, pp. 516–7.
[2] Colin Legum, 'Colour: the Age-Old Conflict' in *The Observer*, 10 March 1968.
[3] Robert Gardiner, *op. cit.*, p. 51.
[4] *Ibid.*, p. 10.

[5] See Anthony H. Richmond, *The Colour Problem* (Penguin, 1961), p. 16.

[6] Colin Legum, *op. cit.*

[7] For one outspoken answer to this question see Ronald Segal, *The Race War* (Cape, 1966).

[8] Katrin Norris, *Jamaica: the Search for an Identity* (O.U.P., 1962).

[9] Philip Mason, introduction to Katrin Norris, *op. cit.*, p.v.

[10] See Barbara Ward, *The Rich Nations and the Poor Nations* (Norton, New York, 1962).

[11] *U. N. Declaration on the Elimination of All Forms of Racial Discrimination.* (See also Appendix B (ii).)

[12] R. Segal, *op. cit.*, p. 9.

[13] Arthur Hopcraft, *Born to Hunger* (Pan, 1968).

[14] Richard Wright to Kwame Nkrumah, quoted in K. Nkrumah, *Dark Days in Ghana* (Lawrence and Wishart, 1968), p. 6.

[15] Quoted in H. J. P. Arnold, *Aid for Development* (Bodley Head, 1966), p. 213.

[16] Report of Commission on international development, Chairman Lester B. Pearson. Published as *Partners in Development* (Praeger, New York, 1969; Pall Mall, 1970).

[17] Pierre Jalée, *The Third World in the World Economy* (Monthly Review Press, New York, 1969).

[18] Lewis Carroll, *Through the Looking Glass* (Macmillan, 1910 ed.), p. 72.

[19] Arnold, *op. cit.*, p. 220.

[20] *Ibid.*, p. 166.

[21] A. Hopcraft, *op. cit.*

[22] A. Gillette, *One Million Volunteers* (Penguin, 1968), p. 187.

[23] F. F. Darling, 'Wilderness and Plenty' in *The Listener*, 27 November 1969, p. 724. [The lectures have since been published as *Wilderness and Plenty* (B.B.C., 1970).]

[24] *Ibid.*

[25] *Ibid.*, p. 726.

[26] *Ibid.*, 4 December 1969, p. 783.

[27] G. R. Taylor, *The Doomsday Book* (Thames & Hudson, 1970) pp. 15–16.

[28] F. F. Darling, *op. cit.*, 11 December 1969, p. 819.

[29] *Ibid.*, 20 November 1969, p. 694.
[30] See John Barr, *Derelict Britain* (Penguin, 1969).
[31] Frank Fraser Darling, *op. cit.*. 11 December 1969, p. 821.
[32] *Ibid.*, 18 December 1969, p. 848.
[33] Quoted *Ibid.*

CHAPTER FOUR

Man and Society

Nationalism and the nation state have already been discussed: but what of the organisation of the state, the machinery and institutions of government, the relationship between the state and the citizen; and what of the alternative ideologies and political organisations open to man in the mid-twentieth century? The origin of states and the conflicting theories formulated to justify and explain their creation and growth do not concern a book devoted to the post-war world. But even an outline statement of the capitalist and communist alternatives now before us requires a consideration of some basic principles. Unless we are clear about the ends of political association, we cannot begin to discuss the best ways of achieving them; and it is logical to expect that if separate societies have different views as to what the proper ends of political association are, then they are likely to formulate different means for their attainment, though it may become apparent that modern societies, East and West, differ more on the means of achieving their goals than on the goals themselves. This chapter will concern itself with both ends and means.

POLITICAL ORGANISATION
Ends
Man is the basic unit of politics, and although this is an obvious truism it is worth beginning with a statement of it before general theories of the state or society obscure its truth. Man, individual and unique, is the fundamental component of all human association, and when the great issues of survival of

communities, of freedom, of rights, of sacrifice, of change, of progress, of centralised organisation and planning arise, it is essential to keep this small, unique individual in mind. To fail to do so is to risk the loss by society of the very humanity which should be its primary concern.

Man is a social animal. Man alone on a desert island may be as free as imagination can conceive of, but what sort of freedom is this in reality? There may be no irritating legal restrictions on his movements, no boundary to what he calls his own, no limitations imposed upon his will; but even if he has not to spend all his time merely surviving, he will hardly enjoy any of the freedoms that are truly prized by men, the freedoms born of companionship and association with others. Man cannot live alone. Yet as soon as men come into contact with one another they have to curb something of their theoretical 'freedom' in order to enjoy that higher social freedom that alone is worth having. They must agree to accept the limiting rules of social behaviour; they must restrain their freedom in order to enjoy companionship and all the benefit of goods, services and culture that this entails, and yet they must contrive to remain as far as possible free to develop their own talents and follow the promptings of their own reason. It is the delicate balancing of freedom and restraint that politics is all about. Man cannot live alone; all men differ; all are liable to want their own way, to impose their will upon others. Once man associates in order to meet the deep need for companionship, political organisation is needed to solve the problems created by his tendency towards conflict with other men.

The first goal of political organisation will be to ensure for all members of the community security of life. No man can be permitted to take the life of another for his own private purposes. This goal is likely to be agreed by all to be of fundamental importance. Other goals, which may be subjected to different ordering by different communities, must include the regulation of social conduct, that is the establishment of a general level of conduct between man and man, which will be formulated into a code of criminal law; the settlement of differences honestly or dishonestly arrived at between man and man, which will be achieved through a code of civil law; provision for the development of the skills and talents of each man, through education and training; the nurturing of the health of the community and the provision of facilities for communication and for the creation and distribution of wealth. And, as important as these internal ends, the protection of the community from external aggression.

It is only through society organised to achieve security and prosperity that man can enjoy real freedom. But freedom itself remains a concept difficult to define and very widely interpreted. Social freedom may be less important than economic freedom, or may only be possible given a certain level of economic development. Individual freedom has often to be curbed in the interests of society, but different communities will hold contrary views as to the primary importance of the individual or of society, and this will influence the area of freedom open to the individual member. It is through the variety of attempts to resolve the difficulties posed by freedom versus restraint, and by the proper ordering of social, political and economic freedoms, that the themes of the post-war world already discussed – the Cold War, nationalism, pollution, population explosion, racial antagonism and the division between rich and poor – receive proper perspective. An attempt must be made to clarify this situation.

The condition of perfect freedom exists when man is not prevented from doing what he wants to do, and not forced to do what he does not want to do.[1] Yet clearly perfect freedom cannot exist in society; restraints on individual freedoms are necessary if the conditions are to be created in which any freedom at all is possible. Thus without traffic regulations it would not be possible to-day for man to drive anywhere. Restraint of freedom to drive on any portion of the road in any direction and at any speed is essential if the freedom to drive safely from A to B is to exist at all. Society has evolved rules controlling such matters as the use of firearms, dangerous drugs, and toxic fluids, or the transportation of poisonous gases, unstable explosives and atomic waste, all limiting the freedom of some in the interests of the security of all. Man in western society is permitted only one wife; soon the number of children he may father may also be limited. A man may wish to chop down rural trees, play the trumpet at midnight in his suburden garden, put his children to work as soon as they are able to walk, shop naked in the High St.; or take similar freedoms of greater or lesser gravity, but although such freedoms may be in the past have been permitted they are unlikely to be sanctioned now, for they infringe the environment, the peace, the prevailing sense of right or decency or morality of others, and ultimately corrode the society from which the individual himself derives his other freedoms.

Freedom reposes where restraint is absent, and even the most authoritarian societies usually permit some freedoms – freedom to choose one's occupation or marriage partner, for example. Just as freedom for a social animal can only arise through the subjection of some individual freedoms to the needs of society, so a Christian might define freedom as the service of God ('Whom to serve is perfect freedom'); while a Marxist might claim that the only freedom is the freedom to be useful to society, or to serve the Party. The area free from restraint in which the individual moves varies from society to society and from era to era within one society; the amount of freedom an individual requires also will vary from individual to individual, many desiring, many rejecting the responsibility for decision-making that freedom implies. To a large extent man will be conditioned by the society in which he is reared, its social conventions as well as its legal rules; he will not feel conscious that his liberty is being unduly restricted if he tailors his desires to fit what is acceptable. But what is the right balance of freedom and restraint? What should be acceptable behaviour in a civilised society? It is for each community to decide for itself the proper answers to these questions, though no doubt each will add to the ends of political organisation listed above the maximum amount of individual freedom compatible with the continued life of the community. How will this be organised?

Means
If the basic unit of political association is man, the principal

unit of political organisation is the state. It is the state which will embody the legal codes, the means of enforcing them and of altering them. Social man needs rules of behaviour, and the state is 'a people organised for law within a definite territory'. The state is the regulator of power, determines how and by whom power is exercised, decrees the balance between freedom and restraint for its citizens. It is designed to eliminate the necessity of resorting to force in everyday affairs and to promote the well-being of its citizens, or as the United States representatives to the Commission for Human Rights put it: 'The state is created by the people, for the promotion of their welfare and the protection of their mutual rights. Everyone has the right to a fair and equal opportunity to advance his own physical, economic, spiritual and cultural well-being, and to share the benefits of civilisation. It is the duty of the state, in accordance with the maximum use of its resources, and with regard for the the liberties of the individual, to promote this purpose by legislation or by other appropriate means'.[2]

Yet it has to be admitted that the creation of a state carries with it dangers. If the state embodies power which is its means of maintaining law, power can easily become an end in itself to be used by the few against the many; only by constant vigilance can liberty be sustained.[3] Even the best of states are ambivalent in this respect: on the one hand the state is always the instrument by which certain people or groups dominate others; on the other hand it is also the means by which the desired order is maintained and by which the individual citizens are integrated into the main body of society. In any state, therefore, there will exist a certain tension between rulers and ruled, though ideally there will also be present a common respect for the order which the state maintains, to the benefit of all.

Here the form of the state and the institutions which it employs may be relevant. The form which the state takes may be monarchical or republican, its expression democratic or authoritarian; it may follow a capitalist or communist ideology. Each form will define differently the proper relations between the individual and the state. But within this broad framework the institutions of each state are likely to be similar; a legislature which will have the function of making the law of the land; an executive (for example a trained civil service) charged with the administration of that law, and a judiciary to uphold and interpret the law in practice. How the institutions might function in theoretical models of the two main contending alternative forms of state in the contemporary world, liberal democratic capitalism and totalitarian communism, will be dealt with below in this chapter, while some variations in practice will be discussed in the following chapter. But first it is worthwhile considering briefly the general concepts of law, justice and human rights.

The law which any state enacts and upholds merely expresses 'the current dominant sense of right'; furthermore the 'dominant sense of right' belongs to that 'will in society which has known how to make itself effective'.[4] It does not have to reflect the will of the majority of the citizens, but only of those who have learned how to control the machinery of state. Thus it has been possible for the law to value personal property more highly than life itself; to condemn a starving man to death for stealing a rich farmer's hen. It is necessary to distinguish, therefore, between law and justice. Ideally, the law should be just; but in practice what is believed to be just changes (even though it is possible to believe in a natural law and an ideal standard of justice that coincide and never alter). Justice reflects the values held by a particular society, at a particular moment in time, and history records a continuing search for justice, declared and defined for all men, that is yet far from being fulfilled. Nevertheless, the belief in an objective standard of justice, timeless and universal, is useful in pushing forward the national and international frontiers of 'good' society. Upon the belief in this 'ideal' justice, the attempt to secure basic human rights is founded.

What are considered to be the basic rights of the individual in society may well be one of the best tests by which that society is judged, along with its record in upholding them. The definition and maintenance of human rights are, after all, what political organisation is in theory all about, bringing us back to the beginning of this chapter. The United Nations Charter

of Human Rights provides a standard from which many
nations to-day fall short; the list of basic human rights which
follows will, therefore, serve as a reference by which we may
judge the theoretical models outlined below, and indeed the
society in which we ourselves live.*

Human Rights
The notion of human rights, based on theories of natural
justice and the equality of man, is also founded on the belief
that freedom is of the essence of man; that personal freedom
for each individual human being is essential, alike to the
development of that individual and to the enrichment of
society. Human Rights have been embodied in written
constitutions in varying degrees of detail, most notably in the
documents of the American and French Revolutions. But it is
worth recording that the evolution of complex democracies
since the eighteenth century has shifted the emphasis forward
from rights based on natural humanity to civil liberties based
upon the right of the individual to participate in political
activities, and further, in the most developed nations, to those
human 'freedoms' gained through government, such as freedom from destitution.[5]

The history of human rights is expressed in the 1949 United
Nations Declaration, a compilation of all three forms of rights:
the oldest body of rights which were designed to protect the
individual *against* government, to preserve his individuality;
then that body of rights designed to permit him to participate
in government, to assert his individuality; finally those rights
that flow only *through* government, to develop his individuality.
Elaborated at slightly greater length below, these varied rights
are best summarised in President Roosevelt's proclamation, on
6 January 1942, of the 'four freedoms' which formed the basis
of Allied war aims in the Second World War: freedom of speech
and expression; freedom of worship; freedom from want; and
freedom from fear.

*A sentence in *The Observer*, 26 October 1970, commenting on the Churches'
Working Party on violence in Southern Africa, made this interesting reference to the
Republic of South Africa: 'The list of human rights in the Charter is a list of what
Africans may not do in South Africa'.

Human rights will have meaning only in the context of a society which can uphold them, in conditions, that is, of settled order. But given stability and peace, a civilised society should aim to guarantee its citizens freedom from arbitrary arrest, imprisonment or execution (that is, without following the prescribed legal processes of charge, trial and sentence); freedom to acquire and hold personal property; freedom to speak, write for publication, meet publicly, form associations for peaceful ends, and make contracts for all legal purposes; freedom to vote, be elected and hold public offices; freedom from economic insecurity and exploitation; the right to free education and if possible to housing, employment, medical care and other social facilities, so that body and mind may develop to their fullest capacity.[6]

THE DEMOCRATIC STATE

The conflicting interpretations of the word democracy which obtain in the communist and non-communist worlds make it difficult to find general characteristics of democratic states which can be applied to both camps. Clearly both will start with a concern for popular sovereignty (*demos* 'people'; *kratos* 'power', being the Greek origins of the word); and both will place a primary emphasis on the good of the common people. The liberal democratic tradition of Western Europe and North America, in which the concern for individual human rights arose, stresses choice of political programmes and peaceful change of government through free electoral procedures, along with basic individual freedoms, while the communist tradition of democracy regards as more fundamental the ownership of the means of production by the state and central planning to promote national wealth, believing that only by subordinating every interest and activity to the state can it be ensured that the common good takes precedence over private interests. The two systems diverge, the one preferring a system of government 'designed to enable a pluralistic society to change itself through the free interplay of its component parts', the other a government which 'will lead the society to the goal of communism'.[7] For this reason we will look at the aims and institutions of the liberal democratic state and the soviet, or peoples democratic, state separately.

The liberal democratic state of the capitalist world
Liberal democracies of the West European and North American tradition have stated their belief in the primacy of the individual citizen and have sought to guarantee to that citizen the rights due to him because of his humanity and his membership of a regime resting on popular sovereignty. 'What concerns all should be approved by all'; 'there should be no taxation without representation'; 'community decisions must be subject to majority approval'; these have been the arguments of liberal democrats, the last being a practical solution to the first, acceptable when its practicality is approved by all. Politics in the liberal democratic state is essentially personal, so that the 'goodness of a State is largely proportional to the scope given to individual responsibility, to the widespread development of a civic sense, to the opportunities given to the ordinary man'[8]. This sense of the importance of the individual also implies a particular responsibility of the state in respect of justice. Justice can never be established by injustice to any one citizen; though thousands may be pleased by an injustice to one individual, that individual must be respected; no individual (or group) may be sacrificed by the community on behalf of ends in which he (or it) will not share. However imperfect the practice of the liberal democratic state, it must always strive to uphold the principle of justice thus conceived. Further, it is only by defending the primacy of the individual in the community that liberal democracy can be true to itself. By guaranteeing the fewest possible restrictions on the development and creative self-expression of all the individuals that compose it, liberal democracy nourishes itself and fulfils its purpose. It cannot act otherwise without betraying its *raison d'etre*.

Holding that a primary regard for the individual is the best means of sustaining the community will imply a number of the political commitments of liberal democracy: its machinery must encompass as well as possible an equality of rights and of opportunities for all; must permit the expression of differences of opinion; must embody toleration and concede the possibility of change. Its political institutions will deal with internal order and the conduct of foreign affairs; with justice and with the raising and the allocation of state expenditure. To-day this expenditure will be considerable in advanced societies, both to enable the state to regulate its complex industrial, commercial and financial sectors and to provide the range of educational and welfare services which such societies require and expect. Just how state expenditure is raised, how much and to what ends, will vary from state to state, but for the liberal democratic state its fundamental concern for individual initiative will never be more crucial than in this sphere. As always it will be encumbent on the state to achieve the right balance between individual and community needs. The community has continuity and resources beyond the individual; the individual is the indispensible source of initiative and agent of action, the subject and object of common measures. The state will wish to avoid too much stifling social control, and, equally, too much unconnected individual effort. Its principle of action will be based upon the knowledge that democracy was built up by the spontaneous initiatives of individuals and groups, so that what can be left to their continued care should not be undertaken by the state. The state should only assume responsibility for matters which are beyond the capacity of private individual or group action or which clearly must be the monopoly of the state.

These considerations may lead to the justification of capitalism as a method of ordering society. In its simplest form, capitalism places complete reliance on the individual citizen. Man, the only rational animal, must exercise his intelligence in order to live. He must be as free as possible to do so; he must have the right to support his life by his own efforts and to dispose of the fruits of his efforts, for only thus can initiative and inventiveness flourish. Conceding the right to dispose of the fruits of individual effort implies a fundamental belief in the right to own property. The holding of private property, the operation of self-interest, the free play of individual minds for personal reward are held to be the engines of progress, of innovation and of prosperity, and the society which allows these engines fullest operation will be the most soundly based and become the richest in every respect.

Here the defender of capitalism will draw sharp contrast between capitalist society's reliance upon individual rights and those collective societies which place more emphasis on the community; will contrast a belief in man as 'a sovereign individual who owns his person, his mind, his life, his work and its products' with the contrary view of man as 'the property of the tribe (the state, the society, the collective) that may dispose of him in any way it pleases, that may dictate his convictions, prescribe the course of his life, control his work and expropriate his products'[9]. To such a defender, capitalism has a proud historical record as the outstanding agent of advancement of the frontiers of learning and material development. Its key is the recognition of man's right to pursue his own good.

So extreme an atomistic view of society, so marked a belief in self-interest as the motivator of man is not commonly held in modern liberal democracy (to its imminent peril, the worried defender would argue). Such a view would reduce the operation of the state to a minimum, (holding that such defects as can be detected in the operation of capitalism in the past (e.g. slumps) ought to be laid not at the door of capitalism but at that of government interference with the free operation of capitalism). However, as they have evolved, the populous, industrial societies of to-day have brought ever greater increases in the role even of the liberal democratic state, the institutions of which now extend far beyond the political sphere into the economic and the social. It is worth looking at these institutions and why they have grown; at how liberal democracies have operated in practice.

Direct democracy, by which all members of the community participate in the decisions affecting its well being, an ideal supposedly realised in the small city states of ancient Greece, in which citizens could gather in the market square to vote upon the business of the day (the majority view prevailing), is no longer possible in the densely populated and complex modern state. Indirect democracy, by which the citizens elect representatives to participate in decision-making on their behalf, has evolved as the best practical alternative. In the liberal democratic state, representative government will imply a legislature elected by and responsible to the people, and an executive subject to popular control: but the form of the legislature is likely to be determined by the particular electoral machinery employed.

In organising a representative system, it will be necessary to define the electorate (for example, all adults over a certain age – 18 or 21 are commonly used – who are not disqualified by any agreed impediment, such as insanity or criminal conviction) and the number of votes each may have (usually one each). The size of the constituencies (the units into which the total population will be divided for purposes of electing representatives) and the frequency at which elections will be held must also be determined. Then the machinery of election must be created and this can be of crucial importance in deciding the number of parties represented in the legislature, the stability of government, and the degree to which individual citizens feel that their personal views are in fact represented.

There is a variety of electoral methods operating in liberal democracies, indicating the difficulty and importance attaching to this aspect of the democratic process. The methods fall into two main categories, each open to a range of criticisms. One category involves constituencies roughly equal in population, each returning a single member. This member may be chosen, as in Britain, by a simple majority (that is the candidate with the most votes) or by an absolute majority (that is fifty per cent of the votes cast plus at least one); in the latter case more than one ballot may be necessary, with some device for eliminating the weakest candidates, before any one candidate obtains an absolute majority. Or the system known as the single transferable vote may be employed, whereby the voter indicates the order of his preference for all the candidates, so that if his top choices are eliminated, his lower choices can be included in a recount.

The other category of electoral machinery involves multi-member constituencies, usually employing a system of proportional representation (P.R.). Even within P.R. there can be variations in the method of allocating seats, but in each case the voter will have as many votes as there are seats in the constituency. In a three-seat constituency the voter will have three votes and those candidates may be elected who gain the most votes, though more often an elaborate quota system will be operated.

Under one such system, favouring broadly organised parties, the quota is the number of valid votes cast divided by the number of seats in the ballot. Each elector has as many votes as there are seats and may cast them for a particular party list (supposing the party has put up candidates for all the seats), or may select from all the candidates listed. Once the votes have been counted and the quota determined, the procedure for establishing the successful candidates is carried out in three stages. First, any candidate gaining an absolute majority of the votes cast is elected; second, the average vote gained by each party list is divided by the quota and the party wins that number of seats; third, if any seats remain, these are given to the list with the highest average, if any candidates are left on it unelected, or the next highest, until the seats are filled. A simple example might be as follows:

Three member seat
90,000 valid votes.   Quota 30,000
Votes cast as follows:

Party & Candidate	Votes
A 1	46,000
B 1	20,000
B 2	10,000
C	6,000
A 2	4,000
D	2,000
A 3	1,500
B 3	500

Stage 1   A 1 elected

Stage 2   Party A total vote   51,500 divided by 30,000 = 1
                  B total vote   30,500   ,,   ,,   ,,   = 1

Seats go therefore to A 1 & 2 and B 1.

An even more complicated, and perhaps fairer system (that employed in the Republic of Ireland) determines the quota by dividing the number of valid votes cast by the number of seats plus one, and adding on one to the total. Thus under this system using the same example as above, the quota would be arrived at as follows: 90,000 valid votes divided by 3 plus one give 22,500 and adding one gives a quota of 22,501. (Clearly only 3 candidates can achieve this total, a fourth candidate, mustering all remaining votes could only reach 22,497). The voter again has three votes but, as this system incorporates the transferable vote, he is asked to number his candidates in order of his preference.

Reverting to the voting returns in the example, it is clear that candidate A1 has gained not only the quota, but also a surplus above that figure of 23,499. His huge surplus will therefore be distributed proportionately in accordance with the second preference vote of all those who voted for him. That is, all 46,000 votes will be examined and the 23,499 surplus votes will be distributed in proportion to the second preferences stated on all 46,000 votes. This may well give enough votes for, shall we say, candidate C (a popular local non-party figure, perhaps) to gain the quota, his six thousand first preference votes needing only 16,501 of candidate A1's redistributed second preferences (leaving 6,998 of these to be placed elsewhere). If the remaining 6,998 of A1's surplus do not raise a third candidate to the quota, then the lowest candidate (B3) is eliminated and his second preference votes are redistributed (or his third preference if the second preference vote is cast for candidate A1 or C already elected). The process of elimination is carried on from the bottom until the third seat is filled. An actual example, taken from the 1967 Irish local government elections, is given in order to make things clearer. Here, it will be noted, no candidate reached the quota at the first count, so redistribution of votes occurred only through elimination from the bottom. The procedure is highly complex. It requires time and patience to complete the post-poll counting and calculating, but it is nevertheless easy to operate by the voter.

Louth County Council Elections June 1967.

Carlingford Area

First Count

Seats	3	Thomas Elmore (Fine Gael)...548
Candidates	7	Bernard Rafferty (Fianna Fail) 484
Electorate	3,737	Patrick J. O'Hare (Fine Gael)..469
Total Poll	2,824	Seamus McArdle (Fianna Fail)458
Spoiled votes	31	Arthur McKevitt (Labour) ...370
Quota	699	John Savage (Fine Gael)......321
		Seamus Rafferty
		(Cumann na Poblachta)....125

Second Count
(S. Rafferty's
elimination)
Elmore (17)......565
B. Rafferty (12)...513
McArdle (30).....488
O'Hare (11)......480
McKevitt (30)....400
Savage (13)......334

Third Count
(Savage's elimination)
O'Hare (162)...............642
Elmore (70)................635
B. Rafferty (25).............538
McArdle (23)...............511
McKevitt (38)..............438

Fourth Count
(McKevitt's elimination)
O'Hare (186) (Elected) ..828
Elmore (74) (Elected) ...709
Rafferty (60)...........598
McArdle (38)...........549

Rafferty was elected on the next count
Fine Gael 2; Fianna Fail 1.[10]

The purpose of these elaborate electoral devices is to give the widest possible representation of opinion in Parliament. Multi-member constituencies and P. R. favour, in practice, a greater number of parties than single-member, simple majority systems. In this respect the latter can be held to be less in accord with democratic theory, particularly as in many cases the single member elected may not represent the majority of electors in the constituency, and in some cases a party winning overall power may not have the support of an absolute majority of citizens in the state – (an extreme example might be a constituency of 100,000 where three parties contended and the winning candidate scored a mere 34,000. If there were a hundred constituencies in the state and all were fought in the same way with the same result, one party could emerge with all the seats but with little more than a third of the votes. This is scarcely imaginable, but less extreme results have often occurred in Britain, where a clear majority of seats has been obtained by a party lacking an absolute majority of votes.) It is a feature of the single-member method that a two-party system tends to emerge. Not only this, but it also appears that these parties will tend more and more to approximate to each other. The alternative platforms the two parties offer will grow more similar as they compete to attract the widest possible public support. Broad, middle-of-the-road policies will emerge and the individual voter may be left wondering how to differentiate between them. Nevertheless it is also a feature of this system that stable government results. One party will tend to gain a majority in the legislature and will thus be in a position to implement during its term of office the measures presented to the electorate before the election.

On the other hand, the system designed to give fuller expression to democratic theory, allowing minority groups a chance of representation, and encouraging the existence of numerous small parties, tends in practice to defeat the democratic purpose it is designed to serve. A number of small parties, none with a clear majority, may emerge, so that a coalition government must be formed. Too often, however, coalitions are formed on the basis of some hybrid platform acceptable to all its member parties (often the lowest common denominator of those platforms submitted to the electorate) but one which has not in fact been submitted to, let alone approved by, any of the electors. Coalitions are often unstable and their breakdown and reassembly during the life of Parliament may be achieved in secret conclave without reference to the voter and may lead him to despair of and eventually reject the democratic process (the experience of many European countries in the 1920s and 30s).

Here, then is a paradox of democratic politics. The system of single-member constituencies, on the face of it less democratic than that of multi-member constituencies, may in practice conform more closely to the best that can be achieved under a society striving to make modern industrial life comply with democratic principles. While the theoretically more democratic multi-member system may in practice lead to autocracy through chaos. It is a lesson only too widely applicable to human affairs, showing that it pays to beware of theoretical solutions which ignore the vagaries of human behaviour.

If the electoral machinery is crucial to the democratic process, and to the number and even type of political parties, it is the parties that are the most obvious distinguishing features of liberal democracies. Voluntary organisations, generally but by no means always national in scope, composed of people broadly agreed on desirable policies, political parties strive to capture the legislative and executive organs of the state through popular election. In the modern state, few individuals will gain election without party organisation behind them. In the representative government system, it is the national party, with its branches spread throughout the constituencies, that is more likely to decide upon those candidates who stand at the polls with some hope of success; and it is from the successful candidates of the party winning a majority of seats that the government will be formed. Parties have become integral components of the parliamentary structure in liberal democratic states, with clear roles to play both in power and in opposition. Whether the system of election results in two parties or in a multitude of parties, their presence in competition for electoral support on the basis of issues freely discussed remains 'the prime essential of the liberal democratic state'.[11] The political parties involve the individual in the democratic process, provide him with choice and offer him the means of peaceful political change, which is the hallmark of a civilised community.

It is worth adding, however, that many other ways exist of giving voice to public opinion in liberal democracies. Trade Unions provide one significant example, but professional bodies, chambers of commerce, and a host of voluntary organisations concerning themselves with noise abatement, cruelty to animals or sexual equality will give publicity to particular viewpoints, seek broad support, expose problems, or lobby parliament. Such bodies will provide expressions of view and a measure of public concern in patterns other than the arbitrary geographical divisions of constituencies. By provoking discussion, airing alternatives and endeavouring to indicate the extent of concern, they play a vital part in a process designed primarily to reflect popular wishes in the conduct of government. An increasingly employed addition to the tools at the disposal of such bodies is the public opinion poll which, if unreliable as a guide to the political intentions of the electorate, may nevertheless gauge public opinion on specific, easily understood matters.

Parliament lies at the centre of the liberal democratic state, the source of authority, the repository of sovereignty. Its purposes, 'justice and order, external relations and defence,' and 'the fiscal allocation of the national resources for the common good'[12] have already been discussed. Its form may be that of a single chamber elected on a universal franchise, with a Head of State elected by that chamber (or alternatively also directly elected by universal franchise, or even hereditary as in Britain); there may be in addition a second chamber which may be directly elected, or may be nominated from the first, directly elected chamber, or a combination of direct election and nomination, or it may even be hereditary, or part hereditary, part appointed, part *ex officio*, as the British House of

Lords. However composed, the second chamber (often called a senate) will normally act as an experienced and more leisurely watchdog upon the activities of the larger, busier, fully representative chamber.

In some countries there will exist machinery by which the electorate may try to ensure its control over parliament in between the periodic elections fixed by law. To this end such devices as the Popular Initiative, whereby a given number of citizens (sometimes the figure of 50,000 is used) can propose constitutional amendments or even specific laws, and the Right of Recall, whereby a representative can be recalled if he is deemed unsatisfactory, have been incorporated into some constitutions. The devices of plebiscite and referendum may also be employed, for example to sanction a new constitution in the case of a plebiscite, or to review particular items of legislation of especial importance in the case of a referendum. But while these latter may be desirable democratic tools, they can be initiated by the government and are liable to abuse by authority through biased presentation or through inadequate explanation of alternatives.

Parliament itself, designed to debate public issues, to determine action and to see to its implementation, will be burdened increasingly in modern industrial society with complex, technical legislation. It will probably adopt such procedures, as the use of expert committees, to deal with this mounting problem. It will utilise increasingly the advice of the expert bureaucracy which modern states have, without exception, built up to assist the process of government, though as it does this it will be aware that one of its own prime functions is to control and keep open to public scrutiny the activities of that same bureaucracy.

In describing the general features of modern liberal democracies in practice, rather than simply outlining theoretical possibilities, it must be observed that in all cases there has been a remarkable expansion of bureaucratic administration, as governments have assumed more and more responsibilities for public utilities, welfare services, industrial supervision, financial regulation and a host of other tasks. It is in this sphere that the most spectacular institutional changes have occurred, as will be amplified in the economic and social sections below.

The national civil service or bureaucracy has altered in numbers (in Britain for example 18,000 employees in 1855 had grown to 700,000 by 1955; in the U.S.A. 200,000 in 1900 had become 2,000,000 by 1950) and in character. In many cases, states have established autonomous or semi-autonomous corporations to handle specific projects or services and these in turn have developed their own burgeoning bureaucracies (e.g. in Britain, BOAC is an example of the first; the Coal Board of the second). Devolution of central government responsibilities to municipal or local government bodies is common, providing closer contact between the citizen and the administration. But here too the complexity and cost of services has tended to increase the size of local government units and the tendency for local government administration to grow apace is also evident.

From a preoccupation with the drawing up of political legislation on broad policies, bureaucracies have thus had to cope with ever-widening responsibilities for regulating society and for operating government services. These functions have entailed a great deal not only of rule-making but of rule interpretation by the administration, adding a considerable quasi-judicial function to its traditional role. Administrative law, formulated and interpreted not by judges but by civil service departments, has become a major feature of the advanced democracies, covering many everyday matters, from income tax, town planning regulations and building standards, to labour relations and public health and social insurance instructions. The danger of abuse of these extensive bureaucratic powers has been recognised and attempts in some countries have been made to counter it by establishing appeal procedures, whereby the general public may challenge bureaucratic decisions; by the appointment of officials (such as an ombudsman) charged solely with investigating complaints; and by periodic reviews of the operation of administrative law by members of the judiciary.

The judiciary has continued to bear the responsibility for regulating the relationships among individuals and corporations on the basis of civil law, of safeguarding society and the state through the application of the criminal law, and, not least in the complexities of contemporary administration as indicated above, protecting the citizen from the state and ensuring him the rights for which he is eligible.

A judiciary independent of the whim of government has proved to be a major bulwark of liberal democracy, even though at times it has constituted a conservative force, putting a break on desired social changes. By upholding the due processes of law it has maintained that framework of security for the citizen which is so rightly prized by democrats everywhere but which is so noticeably absent in arbitrary and autocratic regimes.

The growth of economic institutions in liberal democratic states reflects the increasingly technical and complicated nature of industrial organisation and urbanised living, the need for regulation and supervision and, increasingly, the necessity for governments to take direct control of public services too important to be left in private hands, or services vital to public well-being which cannot be run at a profit (such as defence establishments, or, in a different category, such things as railway networks to outlying or depopulated communities both as a benefit to those communities and as a provision against future need, for instance, in time of war or emergency).

Early evidence in modern times of government intervention in the economic sphere may be found in the factory legislation passed in the nineteenth century to protect workers from exploitation and to set standards of safety. Although the essence of capitalism is competitive profit-seeking in a free market operated by the interaction of supply and demand, certain trends in the twentieth century development of capitalist economies have forced governments increasingly to intervene, first to protect worker, investor and consumer, thus providing a framework for the conduct of the economic activity, and then to uphold the national economy in the face of threatened collapse or severe oscillations from boom to slump.

Perhaps the most notable trend in capitalist economies has been that towards mass-production and consumption, leading in turn to the emergence of large, dominating corporations. The ability of these corporations to establish the price structure of their products and to maintain these prices by limiting or expanding output according to demand, reducing or increasing their labour force rather than their prices, has interfered with the hitherto free market and forced governments to act. And intervention has also been made acutely necessary by periodic threats of large-scale unemployment and depression, or racing inflation, sufficient to jeopardise the stability of society.

The free-enterprise market of simpler days having become distorted by the practices of large companies, governments have not hesitated to redress the balance (thus reducing free operation further) by manipulating taxation rates and controlling the level of public works programmes, social security payments, bank rates, hire purchase regulations and the numbers and conditions of government employees, so stimulating or repressing the 'free' market as required.

Governments then, have found it necessary to interfere in the competitive, capitalist market with financial measures, as well as to intervene in the regulation of trade and industry. And although all this activity has been in theory deplored in a society dedicated to free-enterprise and individual initiative, it has been accepted as necessary in practice because the community has found itself under threat from uncontrolled economic forces, and rightly has taken the initative to bring these forces within the supervision, and where necessary the direction, of the state. As one commentator has observed, 'free enterprise in the free market has both proved its extreme efficiency as a producer of goods and also its need to be balanced, supplemented and supported by a measure of external public direction'. The pursuit of profits has been of necessity 'set in the wider context of maintaining steady demand and hence steady employment in the whole community'.[13]

In another broad, economic sphere, that of advanced planning, liberal democratic governments have also sought to cope with the complexities of industrialism and the needs of modern society. The free, competitive market had proved dynamic and productive, but, as we have seen, it began to become menacing once its mechanism had been distorted. The market had led to the creation of great wealth, but also unprecedented disparities in the distribution of that wealth, with widespread poverty surrounding pockets of great riches. Such a condition accorded ill with notions of democratic equality, and one way in which governments have acted to even out, if not remove, inequalities of wealth, has been by the deliberate use of progressive taxation, thus reducing the incomes of the rich and making it impossible to accumulate great quantities of capital in individual hands. In recent years, however, planning has been extended in a number of liberal democracies to cover a much broader range of activities. Planning has begun to involve, as the post-war British Chancellor of the Exchequer, Sir Stafford Cripps, remarked: 'the laying-out of all national resources in the national interest to a nationally desirable end, and the organisation of the necessary methods, by the use of all the means that the people in a democratic society are prepared to give to the government'. Planning, as another British Minister, Herbert Morrison, remarked at that same time, requires a positive commitment to five stages of action: 'making up one's mind to plan, getting the necessary facts, devising alternative plans, choosing between these and deciding what is to be planned and what is to be left unplanned, and finally carrying out the plans, and adjusting and devising so that things happen in the right way and at the right places and at the right time'.[14] And planning on this scale implies an increasingly active and involved government.

Of course these planning remarks were made by British Labour Ministers at a time of great scarcity, when the British people were perhaps more inclined to agree that limited resources might best be divided according to prearranged principles. But it is true that even in normal times, liberal democracies are turning to some measure at least of government economic planning in order to provide the essential conditions inside which the fullest possible measure of free enterprise can operate. Policies of wages and prices have been devised to enable industrialists to plan ahead to win valuable export markets; policies of support for areas where unemploy-

ment is high, due to the death of out-dated industries, have
been implemented to encourage new employment and retrain
workers with the necessary new skills; overall plans to utilise in
the optimum manner the nation's power and its resources, or
to harness its waters or to modernise its communications, have
been recognised as essential by numerous democratic communities traditionally suspicious of the role of government in
economic matters. Just as the individual has had to learn to
curb his freedom in the interest of social living, so the free-
enterprise capitalist has had to adjust to at least some measure
of government planning. Believing that poverty is unnecessary
and that techniques are now available for overcoming it,
liberal democratic states have increasingly deemed it their
duty to adopt these techniques. Such states will, however,
endeavour to combine planning with the protection of the
conditions of free-enterprise. They will stake their future on
liberating their citizens from fear and want in harmony with
the values of free-expression and free-enterprise, and not at the
the expense of these values.

In the economic sphere, the instruments and institutions of
the state have been both negative and positive; for the protection of citizens from exploitation, evil conditions, want and
unemployment on the one hand, and for the promotion of
prosperity, the harnessing of resources, the injection of capital,
the provision and maintenance of full employment on the other.
The major remaining field of activity, the social field, may be
looked at in the same way. The state will take measures to
regulate against bad housing, poor town planning or specul-
ative building, against unhygienic handling of food and drink,
against wanton pollution of the atmosphere and erosion of the
environment; on the other hand it can promote new town
development schemes, establish standards and training in
design, provide health facilities – mass x-ray or inoculation
programmes or free medicine and hospitalisation – and it can
increase recreational and leisure facilities, whether in terms of
urban sportsgrounds or rural parklands.

In the social sphere, the liberal democratic state will undertake such of these tasks as it feels to be beyond the capability of.

private or voluntary enterprise. One of the commonest provisions in this category is free education, the state setting up
primary, secondary and University schemes in many countries
to ensure that no child with ability should be prevented from
fulfilling his potential through lack of money or facilities.
Exhibiting a concern for the development of the individual in
so doing, the state will also be realising its own purpose of
developing to the full all the talents which the community
itself needs to sustain and increase its level of welfare.

While education is almost a separate and universal category,
such items as housing or medical welfare, or unemployment or
sickness insurance, old age pensions and other social security
benefits may be stimulated by the particular conditions of each
state; housing may be built by the state after a period of war
has created needs too large for private enterprise to meet;
children's allowances may be paid when a falling birth rate
threatens the level of population renewal upon which the state
depends.

Though once again, in theory, provisions of this nature might
contradict an ethic of sink-or-swim, competitive free enterprise, the conditions of industrialism, in which individuals are
subject to forces far beyond their control (such as factory shut-
downs, industrial accidents, slum clearance schemes, housing
shortages, chronic sickness, and a host of others) has persuaded
society by and large that it is right to make provision for some
redistribution of the wealth of those enjoying normal good
fortune to those temporarily or permanently afflicted. It is
through the operation of state social services on a fair and
equitable basis, rather than through the haphazard operation
of private chairty, that this provision can best be implemented.

Even passionate advocates of the liberal democratic state
admit to defects in its practical operation, and many stringent
criticisms have been mounted (though the fact that these can
be openly promulgated and discussed within the state is one of
the virtues of liberal democracy). Some of the shortcomings,
contradictions and compromises with theory will be apparent
from what has already been said above. Practice has not

matched the high ideals, though it is perhaps a necessary feature of human society that it should engage perpetually in striving after more perfect forms.

Free-enterprise, claim the critics, turns out in practice to be mere freedom for the strong and wealthy. Whatever the theory, it seems that 'money makes money', that those with wealth start with an extra advantage, and that in any case large sums of capital are needed to undertake many forms of enterprise, from starting a newspaper to manufacturing an invention. Even those who recognise the inequality of individual skills and can accept an unequal distribution of wealth as natural, provided there are no great extremes, would be happier if somehow money could be earned more directly in accordance with the social utility of the job done; if the brain surgeons, the export managers, the sculptors, the pop singers, the factory janitors, the electronics engineers, the lorry drivers, the stock-exchange or property speculators, could, through some formula, be remunerated in direct proportion to the value to the community of the service they render. Supply and demand seems too rough a yardstick, too subject to distortion in pricing labour, as in pricing goods.

More fundamental is the criticism that contemporary industrial society is simply not compatible with democratic processes. 'Government of the people, by the people, for the people' can no longer obtain; it is not possible for the people to understand and share in the complexities of government and decision-making. As only the skilled managers are capable of controlling industry, so only skilled politicians can hope to manage politics. Politicians and political parties have become professionalised, their activities minority activities; elections have become simply an invitation to the people to endorse one or other political platform drawn up by a political elite. The mass of the people have lost any power to initiate, are left with no active participation in the affairs of their state, and merely perform the function of spectators who may support rival political teams. The size and complexity of the modern state reduces liberal democracy to 'the rule of the politicians'; it becomes a system 'in which individuals acquire power to decide by means of a competitive struggle for the people's vote'.[15]

Other trends are equally lamented. Some astute economic observers feel that liberal democratic society has become dominated by the great corporations. These stimulate consumption not by reducing prices or offering value for money but by their commanding positions in the economy and by sheer pressure of advertising, convincing more and more people that they need to buy more and more goods of less and less real worth or utility. The search for profits from the production of consumer goods reduces cultural development to a minimum; the dominance of advertising in the mass media, particularly newspapers, tends towards the 'cretinisation'[16] of the populace, just when modern techniques should be enabling these media to diffuse real culture universally. The need to sell to a mass readership or audience requires that no one's opinions be offended, that everything be coated in sugar. Romantic myths are fostered. The importance of sporting occasions is exaggerated. With a few honourable exceptions (and here the British people are served outstandingly by the B.B.C.) the policy of 'pleasing the customer' is followed so that, although there may be some variety of papers, periodicals or T. V. channels, this variety is rendered meaningless when all, to a large degree subject to the same pressures, are operating at the same low level.

This has led some to wonder if even the most private freedoms exist any longer. What is the point of freedom of expression if the freedom to think is scarcely permitted by the assaults of the commercially controlled mass media? Some pessimists have even been led to believe that man does not really want freedom, that in the main he would rather be led, without the responsibility of exercising choice and making difficult decisions. Will not the mass media trends, combined with the very real difficulty for the ordinary man of getting anything like enough information upon which to base his decisions, simply confirm this pessimistic view?

The danger is certainly there. But it is recognised. It is combatted by any extension of education that encourages the individual critically to appraise his society. And the current unrest and widespread dissatisfaction with the operation of the present machinery of liberal democracy would seem to indicate that so pessimistic a view is not justified. What is just as dangerous, however, at least in the eyes of those who believe that, for all its faults, liberal democracy offers man his best hope of achieving a just society, is that, in their dissatisfaction with the present machinery, current youthful critics might be led too far: to a rejection of liberal democracy altogether instead of a determination to made the machinery conform more closely to liberal democratic ideals.

Ideological opponents of liberal democracy will, of course, endure no such heart-searching or anxiety. To communists, Marxists or socialists, to try to improve capitalism is to try to perfect the imperfectible. Founded on a false premise it cannot be built into a valid system.

To the socialist, with his own special view of the historical development of man, capitalism is seen as a stage along the road towards the final good society, socialism.* Capitalism, it is argued, is the penultimate stage in man's development. Productive and dynamic, at least in its early years, it is nonetheless evil, based on exploitation and the encouragement of human vice, upon struggle rather than co-operation. Inconsistent and tending towards worse and worse inequalities, it must inevitably destroy itself. Socialists, aware of the movement of history, can hasten the destruction of capitalism and prepare the ground for the new order that will succeed it.

Such critics will point out that capitalist society is essentially divided into two classes, those owning the factories and other means of production, along with the means also of distributing goods, and the rest, the vast majority, who must work, who must sell their labour in order to live and who are never paid the value of what they have to give. Capitalist society is therefore

*Communists and Social Democrats have quarrelled in their terminology to such an extent that some confusion remains. Russians since Lenin have distinguished between capitalism, socialism and communism, socialism being seen as an 'intermediate stage between capitalism and communism'. But to social democrats and other believers in socialism, socialism has usually meant what the Russian communists call communism, that is, the final stage of development. (see next section).

one of class antagonism, for the interests of the capitalists and the worker are opposite; and in the competitive struggle of individuals and classes, all the vices, condemned alike by relgion and philosophy, flourish: avarice, self-interest, cut-throat competition; at the expense of fellowship, harmony and community welfare.

In capitalist society, based on private ownership, the exploitation of the worker and the management of affairs by the wealthy minority, the state is defined simply as the means by which the few dominate the many. The state is the legal system, the law courts and police force and the armed services which not only support the capitalist property owners, but also, in doing so, prevent the majority from realising their potential, from obtaining their just reward. The capitalist state is simply a means of oppression, and to call it democratic is ludicrous: its economic and social inequalities conform more to plutocracy; its much vaunted toleration is mere hypocrisy, for it does not operate to abolish economic privilege. Because of its emphasis on egotism, on greed, on personal profit and therefore on friction and division in society, capitalist 'democracy' is riddled with contradictions: poverty in the midst of plenty; material wellbeing accompanied by spiritual loneliness; continuous unemployment. Worse still, on the international plane, capitalists competing for markets (plus the crucial position in capitalist economies of their armaments industries) inevitably bring about wars. In short, the economic realities of capitalist society no longer conform to the declared aims of capitalist, free-enterprise theory, and the political realities are equally divorced from democratic theory: the people being unable to participate because the electoral machinery, the party organisation and the prevalence of administrative law effectively combine to isolate power from the people.

It is natural that opponents of the capitalist system should condemn harshly its present shortcomings and hail its future collapse, seeking to show that no amount of tinkering with the engine of state will do, that only a completely new machine will suffice. But there is another quarter whence criticism comes, and it is criticism less easy for the capitalist mass media to condemn. For this criticism does not emanate from opponents easily discredited as communist, or more damningly 'Stalinist'. It comes rather from peoples struggling to adopt and adapt what is best from the capitalist system and to achieve for themselves the high theoretical ideals set by capitalist liberal democracies. This criticism, from the developing countries (and we will note that it is applied to the communist countries too), dwells mercilessly on the divorce of liberal democratic theory from capitalist practice; and in the world of nations it asks for some extension of the ironing out of gross inequalities of wealth (undertaken within advanced capitalist democracies) to the wider world community. If capitalists wish to deny the charges of communists, let them demonstrate their idealism, their repugnance of exploitation, their concern for freedom of expression, their determination to destroy fear and want, by devoting their resources to the areas where such ideals have most room to operate. Let them help build in the Third World the conditions under which liberal democratic capitalism can operate.

The liberal democracy of the capitalist world receives, then, its fair measure of criticism as it seeks to adjust to the technological complexities of the industrial and urban mass age. It is criticised not only according to the standards of ideological opponents endeavouring to posit a contrary system of society, but also and perhaps most damningly, according to its own standards and values, from which it falls short. But how well do its opponents measure up to *their* ideals? What are the objectives of the soviet democracies of the communist world and how well have they been achieved in practice?

The Soviet or peoples' democratic state of the communist world
Exponents of communism see their society essentially as one based upon 'public ownership of the means of production, a planned economy, and freedom from exploitation'.[17]

Believing with Karl Marx that the method by which a society produces and distributes its goods determines all other aspects of that society (its politics and its culture), they have made it their first task to put right their basic economic arrangements. Just as private ownership of the means of production and distribution lead to the exploitation of the many by the few, to greed and selfish competition, so the abolition of private ownership and its replacement by social ownership ends exploitation, encourages social virtues instead of private vices, and creates a co-operating community able to plan and allocate its resources according to the dictates of reason, and to multiply the fruits of common endeavour to the benefit of all.

Marx, seen as the first man fully to analyse capitalism and to lay bare the processes of history, was the first also to construct a scientific revolutionary strategy and to project the true vision of a new and better order. The key to capitalism, as indeed of all historical phases, Marx pointed out, is class struggle; in this case the conflict is between a proletariat or working class, growing everlarger and everpoorer in comparison with the ever-diminishing class of capitalist owners, the exploiters, gathering into their hands ever more of the wealth of society. Historical development has flowed from a series of such conflicts, as new forms of production, new discoveries, new inventions, new methods, have rendered the existing social order untenable (thus for example, an agricultural, feudal society gave way to an industrial, capitalist society). Historical development has always been determined by economic relationships (lord/serf, land-owner/tenant, employer/worker) from which political and social relationships have followed.

But if capitalism represents a struggle between two classes, happily it represents the last such confrontation in history. For the very disproportion of numbers between these classes, and the tendency for the wealth gap between them to grow, will result, finally, in the proletariat becoming aware of its position and revolting against it. Politically conscious for the first time, equipped with the truths of Marxism, the proletariat will turn society upside down and subsequently eliminate the old, oppressive capitalist class. For a while, until the old order is eliminated, the proletariat will exercise a dictatorship of the many over the few. It will pursue socialism. Soon there will no longer be more than one class, consequently there can be no further conflict, and the fact of social ownership of production and the end of exploitation will release all men for the service of the community and the full development of their potential as individuals. The socialist system 'based upon the common ownership and democratic control of the means and instruments for producing and distributing wealth, by and in the interest of the whole community',[18] will begin a new and final phase of history. Such a system will contain no conflicts, no contradictions. An integrated community without wasteful competition it 'can have no other aim than progressively to increase the material and cultural well-being of the population as a whole'.[19]

Thus, though emphasis is laid upon the community, upon the common good through common ownership, the end sought is the development of each and every individual – intellectually, culturally, aesthetically. The classless society – a society which presupposes abundance (flowing from unrestricted, unhampered common effort), as well as a new moral order (humanity outward looking, co-operative, freed from the pressures and vices of egotistical competitiveness) – will be 'an association in which the free development of each is the condition for the free development of all'.[20] Or as one contemporary Marxist thinker has expressed the ideal for which he strives:

> The ultimate end of all our actions and all our battles as militant communists is to make *every* man a man, that is to say a creator, a centre of historical initiative and of creation on the economic and political plane, on the plane, too, of culture and love, on the spiritual plane.[21]

The communist ideal is, therefore, both an emphatic rejection of capitalism and a powerful expression of faith in a new social order. It denies the possibility of improving capitalism, that evil system dominated by the selfish few, beset with industrial anarchy, so wasteful through self-cancelling competitive efforts, so distorted economically by the need to marshall resources towards what is profitable rather than what is socially desirable, so warped morally by the starving of cultural development in the interest of material pursuits. Communism looks forward to a new man, social man, emancipated, released through the proper ordering of the means of production, permitting total planning of work and resources, of amenity and environment, directed to meet social needs, not private whims.

In classless society, the property-based legal systems and the forces of law and order, which composed the capitalist state, will wither away; service will replace self; the material wealth raised will be the means to a higher end, the provision of freedom to all men equally, to devote the major part of their energies to those pastimes, artistic and scientific, that distinguish man from the animals. Communist society will remove the barriers between man and man, rich and poor, professional and labourer; between town and country; between nation and nation.

Such a society was not forecast in detail by Marx, whose blueprint was of the march of history towards the classless society rather than of that society itself. But its outline form emerges from the hints he gave, hints that were incorporated most engagingly, if in somewhat pastoral, Utopian form, by William Morris. His classic tale, *News from Nowhere**, first published in 1888, has served to inspire many generations to rise above the mere, mundane materialism of the societies in which they have found themselves.

Communists do not expect the dominant capitalist class to yield its power willingly. They anticipate victory nonetheless, for the forces of history are moving inevitably towards the realisation of communism. Communists meanwhile will work unstintingly to spread the good news, to enlighten working men everywhere of their true position, and to hold before them a modern earthly vision; a vision so much in contrast to the blind and violent struggles preoccupying the many peoples of the world, to the gain of a mere few; a vision of men and nations striding together in harmony towards the enrichment and

*There have been many recent reprints of this work, notably by Penguin Books (William Morris: *Selected Writings and Designs*, ed. A. Briggs) and by Lawrence & Wishart (William Morris: *Three Works*, ed. A.L. Morton).

fulfilment of all. Such is the faith of communism. What is its practice?

Here of course we encounter a difficulty far more acute than any facing an analysis of liberal democracy in practice. Liberal democratic ideals may be clear, liberal democratic practice confused and disappointing. But at least there are liberal democratic states operating, however inadequately. In contrast, there is as yet no practical implementation of the communist vision, even though the theorists of Soviet Russia and the Peoples Democracies of Eastern Europe, and the Peoples Republic of China might argue that they at least are on the right road. The socialism of these countries is not so much grounded in Marxism, as upon Lenin's version of Marxism and upon a subsequent variety of interpretations to suit circumstances far removed from those foreseen by Marx. The institutions of the soviet or peoples democratic state spring, not from the overthrow of the capitalist few by the vast majority of workers, but from the opportunist seizure of power by tiny communist parties in the name of the proletarian majority. Instead of a 'dictatorship of the proletariat', overwhelming and shortlived (ending when the former ruling clique has been eliminated) there has occurred a dictatorship of the Communist Party. Dedicated to the achievement of communist ideals, the Communist Party has been prevented by internal and external forces from getting speedy results. Critics argue that the achievement of communism has been rendered impossible already by the unorthodox course pursued since the isolated success of Bolshevism in Russia in 1917 and the subsequent conquests of the Red Army in Eastern Europe and of the People's Liberation Army in China. At any event, a bureaucracy and a state apparatus has grown up in communist countries that shows as yet little sign of 'withering away', and excesses have been committed, and personal power has been exercised, in ways that accord ill with the Marxist vision. Defence can be made for these expediencies, to be sure, and we will come to these in due course. But first, how have the communist countries set about imposing communism from above, rather than expanding it from below? What institutions

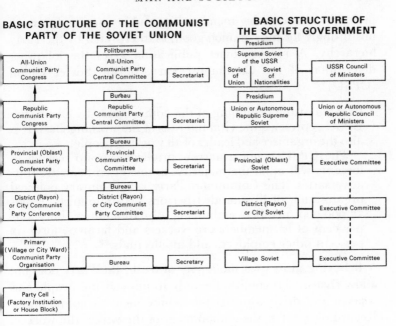

BASIC STRUCTURE OF THE COMMUNIST PARTY OF THE SOVIET UNION

BASIC STRUCTURE OF THE SOVIET GOVERNMENT

have they established to generate a new social man, now that they have ended the primary evil of private ownership of the means of production and distribution?

The Soviet Union, because of its pioneering experience and dominating position, must serve as the principal model for this section, and in the Soviet Union, as in other socialist states, the role of the Communist Party is crucial to the operation of society, in its political, economic and social aspects.

Though the most significant organs of state are economic, political power resides firmly in the hands of the Party, the sole repository of the true faith, and all major decisions stem ultimately from the deliberations of this elite political organisation. The structure of the Party is democratic and it mirrors the democratic political structure of the state (see diagram), guiding political decisions according to Party orthodoxy. The Party itself remains a minority (from 1–4 per cent of the population of communist countries) rigorous in its selection of the ablest and best-qualified members of society, who must be skilled in Marxist-Leninist thought, serve a probationary

period before receiving membership, and be prepared to work
unstintingly for the common good, as interpreted by the Party
hierarchy. A recent Soviet publication gives the following
description of the Communist Party of the Soviet Union
(CPSU):

> Created at the beginning of the 20th century by Lenin, the
> CPSU represents the vital interests of the working class. It is
> also the organiser and leader of all working people.
>
> The CPSU is not a narrow privileged group seeking to
> force its will upon the majority, as one often hears from its
> adversaries. The Communist Party is a voluntary political
> organisation of like-minded persons – Communists. It has
> 12,900,000 members embracing all nationalities. Fifty-four
> per cent of its members are workers and farmers, forty-six
> per cent other employees and intellectuals.[22]

Believing in its own monopoly of truth, the Party does not
allow rivals, who could serve only to mislead the people and
weaken the drive towards the achievement of communism.
Regarding itself as the embodiment of the will of the workers
and peasants, the Party seeks by constant discussion and
vigilance both to guide public opinion and to give expression to
that opinion, from the grass roots factory or farming community
to the highest organs of state (and here it may be noted that
supreme state power lies in the all-Union Party Congress
with the Central Committee's leading members (Politbureau)
acting as permanent executives).

The Party employs rigorous censorship to prevent the
gullible falling prey to error, controls contact with the non-
communist world, restricting travel and information. It also
regards the electoral process in a very different light from that
of the liberal democracy. Party members having been chosen as
representatives, the voting public will be asked simply to
endorse or reject the list of candidates put up by the party.
Inside the Party, candidates and delegates to higher conferences are chosen by election (though the higher unit might
remove an individual deemed unworthy of his responsibilities).
Party membership is a prerequisite of holding significant
government jobs and key positions in industry. It is the Party,

therefore, that gives to the communist state its monolithic quality:

> Identifying itself thus with the people, the Party claimed complete and all-embracing authority – in laying down domestic and foreign policies, determining the correctness of theories, planning and directing political strategy, leading, guiding and overseeing every organ of the state.[23]

The diagram of Russian government bodies indicates the chain of institutions rising to the Supreme Soviet of the USSR, the highest organ of state power. This body alone consists of '698 workers and farmers, 154 workers in science, culture and art, 320 managers of Soviet establishments and enterprises, and 289 Party, trade union and Young Communist League workers'. Behind it stretch 'more than two million deputies who represent the interests of all sections of society . . regularly elected to the Soviets of Working Peoples Deputies at all levels'.[24] A similar chain of organisation exists in the Peoples' Democracies. There too, as in Russia, a similar need to control political and economic activity from the centre, to ensure orthodoxy and maintain conformity with central planning, has resulted in the creation of a huge bureaucratic organisation. Over-centralisation, and the stultifying effect of bureaucracy have, indeed, become major problems. Conceived as a single great enterprise, all-inclusive and highly organised, the communist state has developed an administrative structure that has inevitably increased to enormous dimensions as urban and industrial developments have rendered society more and more complex. Lenin's principle of 'democratic centralism', while allowing for opinion to filter up from the bottom, tended to concentrate decision-making at the top and accentuated the possibility of dictatorship. It has also strangled initiative on the spot and has threatened to bring down the whole state edifice under a massive weight of paperwork.

The communist, single-enterprise state has as its central organ the state planning agency, which will be responsible for setting the production goals and determining the operational requirements of every economic and social unit; factory, collective farm, school or hospital. Planning, refined into five-year schedules in Russia since 1928, involves both the working out of the total requirements of the whole state, setting targets, dovetailing production down to the last detail, and the supervision of the plan in operation. The task is enormous, some would say superhuman, and, as always, it is the communist party which acts as its spearhead and watchdog: 'At the centre the Presidium of the Central Committee of the Communist Party and the party congresses established or accepted the goals. Party organs down to the factory and trade-union level assumed responsibility for watching and stimulating the execution of the plans'.[25]

The total resources of the nation are conscripted to the task of transforming and modernising society, for only through the attainment of material abundance can individual freedom occur and expand.

Thus, not only does the state take over industry but also the land, organising farm workers into state collective farms and applying the techniques of industrial management and production to larger, more rational, agricultural units.* However the removal of private property in the means of production and of the free market conditions of supply and demand do not end 'the problems of the administration and co-ordination of enterprise, of relating cost to return, of securing supply and of co-ordinating the volume and flow of production so that the output of myriads of products would be in balance and the output of a piece of machinery would not be held up for lack of a screw or switch or other necessary part'.[26] In theory to plan makes good sense, eliminating unnecessary competition and harnessing all production to the achievement of desired ends. In practice errors which occur in planning are carried through the entire economy with grossly exaggerated consequences. Gradually, however, the tools of planning, of correction and readjustment, have become more developed, and over-centralisation has begun to give way, at

*Poland & Yugoslavia have not pursued collectivisation of agriculture in practice; wisely, it has been observed, for the policy has not been notably successful in operation elsewhere. See R. D. & B. A. Laird, *Soviet Communism and Agrarian Revolution* (Penguin, 1970).

least in part, to decentralisation and the delegation of responsibility to regional and production unit managers.

Apart from the developing techniques of planning, such as statistical recording and forecasting, and apart from the processes of negotiation up and down the national, regional and local chains of production, the planners are able to employ a variety of devices to stimulate output and achieve preordained goals. Central control of the organs of the state by the Party allows a formidable array of incentives and sanctions directed at individual workers, of propaganda drives and of public agitation towards particular sectors to be harnessed to the success of the Plan.

Piece-rates and pay-incentives, publicity and prestige for those (Stakhanovites) exceeding production norms, the priority award of better housing, holiday trips and other privileges are amongst the inducements incorporated into the labour code for workers, sanctions very often being the reverse of these, or dismissal, public obloquy, compulsory drafting into labour gangs, or worse – for the idle worker might be deemed guilty of industrial sabotage, of undermining production totals and disobeying state instructions, thus qualifying for the attention of the security police. On a higher level, managerial promotion or retention of jobs, will depend on fulfilment of quotas allotted in the Plan; car or house perquisites might add to the incentive.

Posters exhorting effort, upholding the conscientious worker, damning (with blanks to be filled in with local names) the idle, the drunkard, the absentee, and the full weight of the mass media, press, radio and television, can be mobilised to condition the people and to develop their social consciousness. In the Soviet Union the agitation and propaganda section of the Central Committee Secretariat (Agitprop) holds the final authority over all editors and broadcasting producers; can select what news is to be published, and arrange the circulation of topical matters; and in more recent times has provoked discussion of projected matters to ascertain public opinion. The operation of the censor is seen to be crucial to the whole structure of education and information, restricting the latter

to that held to be desirable, limiting discussion, and retaining
public argument within the bounds of party orthodoxy.

To these techniques the weight of the trade unions has been
added, their role in a socialist society, after a period of ambiguity, having been determined in favour of service to the
state. Originally seen as defending the interests of the workers
vis-à-vis the state, they have been made responsible, in Russia
since 1930, 'for stimulating their members to reach production
goals, organising shock brigades and otherwise sustaining a
high level of worker effort, discipline, competence and conformity to party policy and programme'.[27]

Nevertheless, the planners still have to wrestle with the
financing of expansion programmes and all the social and
commercial services necessary to support growth in industry
and agriculture. Capital has to be created. In Russia this has
been achieved through restraining consumption, by encouraging saving and by levying a turn-over tax on all goods
at the point where they change hands. Resources were
devoted to industrial expansion, with little attention given
initially to the consumer comforts of life, until a strong industrial base had been established. But problems of efficiency
remained, for without the test of profitability in reflection of
public demand, manufacturing industry lacked any real
measure of success. Managers might meet their norms, but
how realistic were these, and how reliable therefore as a test?
Gradually, communist planners have learned to introduce
profitability, public demand and managerial initiative into
their centralised system, with rents and interest charged on
state loans and plant, and other devices normally associated
with capitalist society, in an attempt to bring Marxist practice
into conformity with modern industrial society. As the successful establishment of the industrial base has been accomplished,
the problems of meeting the consumer needs of a tired and
deserving populace have become ever more formidable;
impossible for a single organisation at the centre of so huge and
complex a state.

Decentralisation and the operation of public preference
alone is able to fill in the infinitely varied details of the centrally

structured outline Plan. Thus, whereas before the planners might have set the target for the production, say, of shoes (quality less important than quantity), now individual factories will decide, on their own initiative, upon the range and quality and amount of each type within broad guide-lines according to the public taste.* They will show a profit or a loss upon the plant and materials at their disposal according to how efficiently they produce and how accurately they gauge public demand. Some of the profit will be distributed to managers and workers in the form of wages or extra housing, social or welfare benefits; losses will incur disfavour and perhaps be set against future profit earnings.

Faith in planning persists, in spite of past failures and present complexities, for the logic of planning, and the need somehow to order the allocation of resources and services for the common good, remains. It is simply the techniques of planning that change, to meet the complexities of modern society.

The Plan will, of course, include the allocation of resources for education, resources which will be seen in part as investment in the skills and abilities required to fulfil all the other parts of the Plan. Economic, social, political, or all three according to viewpoint, education requires a high priority, not only because of its value to the development and enjoyment of the individual, but because the state needs well-qualified citizens. It will therefore tend to be specialised and weighted according to the needs of the state – such as engineering, medicine, machine-operating or aeronautical draughtsmanship – and graduates and school-leavers may be required to take up specific posts, initially, in return for the free training they have received. Science tends to be emphasised over arts. Ideological grounding is not neglected, between a fifth and a tenth of school time being devoted to political education, that is, instruction and examination in Marxist-Leninist theory. As the 1968 Moscow publication *Man in society*, by Eduard Rosental, puts it (p. 76):

*The problem, even in so simple an instance, can be appreciated by asking a few questions. Do you, for example, prefer quality shoes, lasting four years, at £6 per pair, or to buy each year cheaper shoes, perhaps more fashionable, at £2? Do you like suede, or leather, slip-ons or lace ups? Will you take the shoddy boots that happen to be all that are in stock, or will you wait until the shoes you want are produced?

The Communist Party attaches immense significance to the correct upbringing of the younger generation. The Theses of the CPSU Central Committee state: 'Socialist ideology is called upon to shape correct realistic ideas about the character of the problems being tackled and the ways leading to communism; to disclose continuity in the development of Soviet society; to show the connection between lofty ideals and people's everyday activities including handling current practical tasks and overcoming difficulties; to affirm the unity of word and deed, of thought and action'.

The law in the communist state may also be classed as political or social, being used 'as an instrument of both administration and education'.[28] The proper ordering of economic conditions, according to Marxist theory, will eventually remove most of the circumstances of capitalist society which give rise to crime. In the meantime, before communism is achieved, the emphasis is placed upon re-education, with further measures to supplement where required. Where the state feels that coercion rather than persuasion is needed to move the people towards the desired goals, then clearly the courts function as organs of the state. And one of the advantages of totalitarian power is that extreme measures can be taken speedily to eliminate dangerous individuals or groups deemed threatening to the existence of the state.

Theoretical Communism has been heavily criticised and questioned. There has also been criticism of what has been done in Russia since 1917 and in the more recently established communist states. This latter criticism has been voiced within and without the movement, by troubled comrades as well as by former sympathisers and outright opponents, and has ranged from criticism designed to correct minor faults, to wholesale onslaughts exposing inherent, fundamental defects. But the difficulty of weighing these criticisms is a real one. By what measure should communist states be judged? By the standards of liberal democracy or by the high ideals of communism itself? According to material statistics or by some scale of human development? Or by measurement against similar capitalist countries over a similar time-span, inexact though the comparison of like with unlike must be?

Again, in criticising Russia's ruthless, centralised authoritarianism and disregard for individual life in the pursuit of national economic expansion, we must recall that these are traditional to Russian government. Distinction must therefore be made between the Russian and the communist aspects of the Soviet experience. Nevertheless, it remains true that under Stalin there were excesses committed, and brutalities endured, which no regime could take pride in, and which, indeed, have been repudiated since by Stalin's successors. How symptomatic of monolithic communism in general is this terrible phase likely to prove? Or, taking a more extreme view, have the present communist states any real claim to call themselves communist? Certainly there are some who would point out that Russian conditions in 1917 were pre-capitalist, and quite un-ripe for communist revolution; that what has been built by Lenin and Stalin is essentially a capitalist edifice: state-capitalist, to be sure, rather than private; run by a state bureaucracy rather than a capitalist class, but capitalist nonetheless, with wage labour, oligarchical rule and the mere 'trappings' of democracy.

More sympathetic are those who point out that the Soviet Russian state was born in war and endured further civil war and foreign intervention before it had a chance even to establish itself; that within two decades it was once more plunged into the most ruinous war in history, which was in turn followed by a climate of hostility and danger that forced continued heavy investment in military strength; that during this short time revolutionary change was taking place, as the old proprietor class was eliminated and the old agricultural economy was transformed into one of the most powerful and industrialised of the modern world. And, it might be added, the process continues. The historic Russian Revolution, that created the first socialist society, is as yet an 'Unfinished Revolution',[29] still with much to change, much to achieve, before communism is finally realised.

No final judgement can be reached here. It is fair to point out that at least one commentator has observed that there is so far no evidence that the new man, destined to emerge emancipated from capitalist exploitation, has yet appeared in the communist states;[30] perhaps because as yet the individual is even more heavily hemmed in by bureaucratic communist planners than is his liberal democratic counterpart by capitalist bosses. On the other hand, another recent observer has remarked that the modern Russian is highly skilled, extremely well educated, and if not a fanatical communist, is certainly a convinced socialist who believes that the system works, and works, what is more, without slumps and unemployment.[31]

The Russian people may be very conscious of the imperfections of their society, particularly in the distribution and sale of goods (in retail shopping and restaurants above all); and they may be deeply disturbed by the implications of de-Stalinisation,[32] a process which has shown them how their own history has been falsified but which has not given them the true story, or answered the multitude of questions raised by Khrushchev's denunciation of the former dictator in whose service he himself had risen to prominence; but they are proud of their obvious achievements. They look forward to a new burst of change whereby their democracy might be wrested from the bureaucracy which has so rigidly retained control since the beginning. Life may still be dull and hard; but it is a good deal less dull and hard than recently and there is much to look forward to. By comparison with the land of terror and dread of a mere decade and a half ago, Russia to-day seems free indeed.

It remains for the hostile, the disillusioned, the ideological opponents to scorn both the faith and the practice of communism. To some the very notion of the 'common good' is repugnant as a starting point, because once such a concept is placed above individual good it inevitably becomes the good of some over the good of others. Always some must be in the position of determining the 'common good' and they will be the real tyrants among men, as the history of Soviet Russia abundantly shows. In a totalitarian system, every issue to some degree bears upon the 'common good', which is susceptible of only one interpretation. This will be decided by the ruling clique and no opposition will be tolerated, for alternative viewpoints not only distract from the pursuit of the desired end; they also challenge the authority of the rulers themselves. As this cannot be permitted, dissenters have to be eliminated.

And does not communist society, for all its lofty ideals, quickly incorporate the very evils of capitalism it set out to extirpate? In place of brotherhood and equality there has arisen a 'new class'[33] of ruling bureaucrats; communists, having rested power from their enemies, have simply proceeded 'to scrabble for it among themselves'; communists, instead of abolishing war, have used their power to enslave other, smaller nations; communists, in their obstinate pursuit of an imaginary society of changed men, have instead themselves become utterly perverted by the violence and inhumanity of the methods they have employed.[34] Duplicity abroad, censorship of information and restriction of debate at home have not proved the proper tools for the liberation and perfection of the human spirit. And, it might be added, the Communist Party elite has proved no more adept in practice at handling the technical problems of government than has its counterparts elsewhere.

And why do communists pretend so? Why do they insist upon claiming to represent the values of liberal democracy, while denying this claim to liberal democrats, with a confusion of motes and beams and rainbow-hued self-glorification that is utterly incredible? Why cannot they admit that they have made mistakes, caused immense suffering, been at times untrue to themselves, and say in honesty that there have been good explanations for most of their actions, that circumstances have been against them and that in spite of everything they have achieved much and will go on to achieve more? To continue clamping down upon freedom of expression is to stultify art, stifle initiative; to insist that Marxist dogma admits of only one interpretation, when already a variety of revisions have been accepted, is to expose to ridicule the whole system; to suppress the past history of the Soviet state is to leave in a limbo of uncertainty and indecision those most anxious to uphold its way of life.

Truly the attempt to promote the operation of reason among men, of co-operation and combined effort for common goals, has been fraught with many falsehoods, and much horror. It remains full of contradictions and unresolved tensions. So far, at this early stage at least, man has not proved himself worthy of the ideal.

Liberal Democratic Socialism

It may be apparent from the description of liberal democratic capitalism and soviet communism in action that, whatever their ideologies might indicate to the contrary, both systems are showing trends towards a convergence of practice, at least in the advanced industrial countries. This theme has been developed with particular force by J. K. Galbraith, Professor of Economics at Harvard, notably in his study of *The New Industrial State*.[35] He is, however, by no means alone in his assertions, and it might be rewarding to examine first his analysis of advanced industrial trends and then the similar conclusions of Maurice Duverger, of the Paris University Institute of Political Studies.

It has been observed above how the liberal democratic state has been forced more and more to interfere in the 'free market' of supply and demand in order to counter the distortions of that market effected by the big industrial corporations; how the liberal democratic state has been forced to employ the techniques of central planning; and how significant the role of the public sector has become under capitalism. And we have also seen that in the soviet system there has been a tendency towards decentralisation, towards increased autonomy for the large corporations, and towards some reintroduction of monetary incentives and profit-making. Professor Galbraith takes these observations further, ascribes these tendencies to the inherent needs of the industrial system, irrespective of ideology, and warns that the convergence of all advanced industrial systems carries with it grave dangers as well as exciting opportunities.

It is the sheer technical complexity of modern industry that is fundamental. The need for highly skilled manpower, for huge sums of capital to be committed for long periods of research and development before the finished product can be manufactured, the need for so much forward planning, not only of design and production, but of quantities, prices and disposal, and the consequent necessity of substantial organisations, all these are common to the vital sectors of the modern industrial state, East or West. Neither in soviet society, nor in capitalist society, can the large corporation brook interference from outside. Technical experts, forming the management group, are the only people with the particular knowledge required to make decisions, to make them in good time, to correct them as experience dictates; accountability to some government planning board or Party official can only impair efficiency, slow up the decision-making process, keep plants idle and targets unfulfilled. Increasingly, the necessity for autonomy is being realised and implemented in practice, even though within soviet society some of the planning function, something of the production targets and pricing limits, may be retained in the hands of government, with, of course, the continuing proclamation of full social authority over the enterprise. Corporation autonomy and new incentives, the measurement of efficiency through profits, and financing techniques borrowed from capitalism, do not indicate any return by communists to the free market. Far from it: as Professor Galbraith shows, the advanced capitalist countries have, equally with the advanced communist countries, outgrown the market. It can no longer suffice for either today.

In capitalist society, too, it is the big corporation, with its needs of planning, specialisation and organisation, that has made the biggest inroads into the market. But government activity (in the U.S.A. now accounting for between one fifth and one quarter of all economic activity) has played its essential part. National defence was the widely accepted pioneer of this government activity, its requirements being recognised early on as beyond the scope of private enterprise. In America, space exploration has pushed government involvement further, and many corporations now find themselves dependent on government funds for military or space contracts, for the underwriting

of their research and development and for the provision of the
huge sums of capital normally required. Governments in most
of the capitalist world have followed the insights of J. M. Keynes
(expounded in the nineteen-thirties) into ever more extensive
attempts to regulate their economies, to control the availability
of money and credit, and to influence prices and wages, both
to secure full employment and to counter inflation or
depression. There also remains a considerable area of government spending – roads, welfare, health, education being some
of the most obvious – which swells the public sector and enables
the government to plan and manage the economy in accordance with the requirements of the industrial system.

Isaac Deutscher, commenting on Galbraith's 1966 Reith
Lectures, and listing 'the supremacy of the managerial
elements; the divorce of management from ownership; the
continuous concentration of industrial power and the extension
of the scales of its operation; the withering away of *laissez faire*
and of the market; the growing economic role of the State; and,
consequently, the inescapable necessity of planning, which is
needed not only to prevent slumps and depressions, but to
maintain normal social efficiency',[36] as the characteristics of
modern America, takes care to point out that these are manifestations of 'the socialisation of the productive forces'[37]
predicted by Marx. Thus, when Galbraith asserts that 'the
imperatives of technology and organisation, not the images of
ideology, are what determine the shape of economic activity'
and points to the 'broad convergence'[38] of the two industrial
systems, it can fairly be assumed that the point of convergence
lies within the perimeter of socialism rather than capitalism.
The two ideologies, starting from opposite poles, draw together
and meet, not half-way but nearer to the pole of socialism.

Though there remain great differences between the leading
ideologically opposed nations, America and Russia, both are
subject to 'the imperatives of industrialisation ... This for both
means planning ... planning in all cases means setting aside the
market mechanism in favour of the control of prices and
individual economic behaviour'.[39] Somewhat cynically, perhaps, Professor Galbraith summarises his observations thus:

Convergence begins with modern large-scale production, with heavy requirements of capital, sophisticated technology and, as a prime consequence, elaborate organisation. These require control of prices and, so far as possible, of what is bought at those prices. This is to say that planning must replace the market. In the Soviet-type economies, the control of prices is a function of the state. The management of demand (eased by the knowledge that their people will mostly want what Americans and Western Europeans already have) is partly by according preference to the alert and early-rising who are first to the store; partly, as in the case of houseroom, by direct allocation to the recipient; and partly, as in the case of automobiles, by making patience (as well as political position or need) a test of eligibility. With us this management is accomplished less formally by the corporations, their advertising agencies, salesmen, dealers and retailers. But these, obviously, are differences in method rather than purpose. Large-scale industrialism requires, in both cases, that the market and consumer sovereignty be extensively superseded.[40]

All this implies the primacy of economic factors in the organisation of modern society, and has profound implications for both government and individual. Liberty, as we have already observed in connection with road traffic, may have to submit to some degree of organisation if chaos is to be avoided. But at what point does the organisation of liberty become tyranny? Professor Galbraith by no means recommends the system he analyses. He points out the very real erosion of individual liberty that it entails. The 'technostructure' (the technical management organisation) looks like sweeping all before it. Though the modern industrial system may well produce the goods that man desires, it may also tend to bend man to its own needs. Man will have to conform to the plan in the interests of efficiency, of optimum output: 'the system requires both in production and consumption, that individuality be suppressed';[41] furthermore, capital must be invested first in what the system wants, social needs receiving what is left over, if anything. East and West will be perverted in equal measure: 'capitalism without control by the capitalist will be matched. . . by socialism without control by the society'.[42]

Kenneth Galbraith, Professor of Economics, warns of the dangers to political man from the complex industrial machine that economic man has created. Maurice Duverger, Professor of Politics, reveals political man already adapting to many of the new economic forces. Like Professor Galbraith, he is convinced of convergence; like Professor Galbraith he is ultimately optimistic that the new industrial machine will in the end produce men capable of subjecting it to the needs of mankind.

Professor Duverger summarises the capitalist evolution towards socialism in the following stages:

> (1) technical development makes organisation of the whole economy possible: (2) this overall organisation is more effective than the approximate adjustments which result from free competition; (3) it cannot be put into effect in a capitalist system; (4) capitalism loses its efficacy as a means of satisfying individual and social needs as a whole; (5) it is therefore tending to disappear, in favour of a system of planned production, the corollary of which is that the owners of firms will lose their power of making fundamental decisions (volume of investment; trend of production).[43]

Recognising that planning can lead to mistakes, Professor Duverger believes that we may anticipate a gradual perfection of planning machinery. Condemning Stalinism, he points out that 'Stalin strengthened capitalism by making socialism identical with totalitarianism'. He looks towards a steady liberalisation, however, and in analysing modern practice in East and West he draws together wider evidence of convergence.

He notes that 'both western and Marxist thinkers agree on the main factor, that technical development is the primary cause of the evolution in the social structures'[44] which lead to political disagreement or harmony. Both capitalist and communist societies are clearly putting their trust in the achievement of their own harmonious future through an abundance of material goods. Both, admittedly, approach from opposite directions, the one feeling that material plenty will produce a harmonious society, the other that a harmonious society will lead to material plenty. Professor Duverger, in all truth, cannot believe that a harmonious, integrated society lies within man's capability, but he is convinced if it ever is to come, socialism is on the sounder footing in emphasising as a prerequisite a changed human nature: 'Only the substitution of altruism for egoism, of the common good for personal interest, as the fundamental motive of human actions, can bring about a fully integrated society.... It is quite certain however, that these aims will never be achieved...if private interest continues to be the mainspring of man's activity.'[45]

In practice, Professor Duverger feels, the leaderships of West and East are alike in underestimating the influence of ordinary values and ideals as inspirations to political action: such influence in fact becomes more important as release from the prime material necessities allows man to think for the first time. He also observes that:

> Khrushchev's programmes for Communism in the 1980s show a striking resemblance to descriptions of 'the American way of life' coming from the other side of the Atlantic. The western picture of a comfortable and depoliticized affluent society is very close to Soviet pictures of the higher phase of Communism and the decline of the state. Both show the same excessive optimism. To sum up, though western and Marxist thinkers do not share the same overall view of politics, yet they no longer imagine totally different worlds with no point of contact....The USSR and the People's Democracies will never become capitalist, while the USA and western Europe will never become Communist, but both sides seem to be moving towards Socialism in different ways: through liberalisation in the East, and through socialisation in the West.[46]

Not that the end result will be a grey uniformity achieved at last on common middle ground: Professor Duverger believes that the difference in starting point will prevent that: 'The very fact that the Marxists began by creating a socialist framework and then liberalised it, while western countries began by political democracy and are now grafting socialism on to it, is enough to prevent East and West from ultimately developing the same type of regime'.[47]

But will not Professor Galbraith's 'new industrial system' in the end triumph even over such remaining differences, forcing all men in industrial countries to fit the requirements of an essentially similar machine? Professor Galbraith himself believes this is not an inevitable outcome. He believes that the system requires for its own operation men of the highest intelligence educated to the highest pitch. Such men, once they are aware of what is at stake, and once they have developed a full sense of social responsibility, will, hopefully, see beyond the industrial system, 'reject its monopoly of social purpose'[48] and lead us to a better ordering of our resources, nurturing aesthetic values, the arts, the environment, and man himself, rather than mere material production. Professor Duverger's conclusion is remarkably similar: 'the demands for technical development make it necessary for many people to be given a high level of culture, which encourages a spirit of comparison and a critical outlook, that is, the idea of liberty'.[49] Furthermore, industrialism makes material well-being possible; the desire for material well being cannot be stifled; and 'the desire for liberty is inseparable from the desire for well-being.[50]

Both Professors Galbraith and Duverger would seem, then, to have in common a belief in co-operation and planning, combined with a lively awareness of man's need for liberty of thought and freedom of expression; faith in a democratic community of educated, socially conscious citizens, genuinely able to hold to account the industrial producer of abundance, having both the vision and the capability to allocate the resources of common effort to the satisfaction of individual needs.

But both men are fully conscious of how rarified such a vision is, only conceivable at all to that fortunate third of the world's peoples who have attained sophisticated indus-trialisation. How relevant can their vision be to the other two-thirds whose concern is with subsistence rather than with abundance?

THE WORLD COMMUNITY
Professor Duverger for one believes that the Afro-Asian world, too, must decide for democratic socialism, that the best hope

for its peoples would be such a decision now, without detouring through capitalism or communism, though he has no illusions about the chances of liberty flourishing amidst poverty. 'Afro-Asian Socialism will necessarily be authoritarian',[51] he feels, for so much has to be done and conditions do not favour the democratic process. The most brutal way, however, may not be the best, and the greater the degree of civil liberty now, the easier will be the achievement of democratic socialism later. The choice is important. How the Afro-Asian world conducts itself will have great bearing upon the developed world of Cold War rivalries, will harden or soften attitudes in Moscow and Washington. Once more the world is seen as a single community. It is futile to assault the problems of mere fragments of that community, for the problems are in fact universal and only a total approach makes sense.

We are thus driven back to the fundamental difference between those nations which are rich and industrialised, and the majority that are not. Professors Duverger and Galbraith are alike in their conviction that a world so constituted can only be a disordered world. It seems to follow that the obligation to iron out the extreme differences remains with the wealthy; communist, capitalist or democratic socialist. Can they really hope to hold out like rich 'oases lost in the desert, islands against whose coasts beat angry seas'? To try to do so would be 'to repeat the error committed by the bourgeoisie in the nineteenth century in their attitude to the working class'.[52] What is needed is something more of that realisation, enunciated even before the nineteenth century by the philosopher Immanuel Kant, that reverberations from a violation of law and right in one place are felt in all others; that world peace and brotherhood can be realised ultimately only when it is the world community that receives our foremost attention.

We are forced back to the arguments of economic and social writer Barbara Ward, whose straightforward and unequivocal condemnation of nationalism in general and national selfishness of the affluent in particular were noted at the end of chapter three. She has chosen to indict both

communism and capitalism for their failure, above all others to
live up to the 'post-national' character of their ideologies.
In her devastating outline of the development of capitalism,
whose forces were democracy and the free market, mobilising
savings and technology and automatic progress, and which
promised to free all men by a process of 'enlightened self-
interest rising above mercantilist repression and hostitlity and
building a world of good neighbours',[53] she shows that the
young American nation had become the greatest embodiment
of this process. Originally free from nationalist history,
Americans had determined at the outset to uphold the rights
applicable to all men everywhere. Yet they had since succumbed to narrow nationalism and were now dedicated to no
more than 'the American way of life'. Equally, Russians had
diverted the internationalist aims of communism, building up
an unprecedented national bureaucracy and projecting
Russian interests at the expense of the world-wide vision of
Marx. Fatefully, and it is worth repeating her words, 'the two
great federated experiments based upon a revolutionary concept of the destiny of all mankind, have ended, in counter-
point, as the two most powerful nation states in history'.[54] It is
not good enough. The world must do better than this. The
nation state is not sufficient as a centre of loyalty. Necessity
demands a carefully balanced global society and it is time
our horizons were widened to encompass the need and our
energies directed to realise the goal.

The logic of one world, would, after all, appear to demand
one government. If a single form of social order, democratic
socialism, obtains, with national units, as well as individuals,
recognising the limitations and obligations of their citizenship
in the wider community, outward looking, co-operative, not
xenophobic and competitive, then there is yet hope. Just as
petty competing princes, barons and chieftains were replaced
by national rulers in the past, so petty competing nations must
give way to a world authority in the future, a loosely federated
authority, perhaps, made up of many and varied local units,
with strong loyalties and diverse traditions, but with enough of
a sense of their common humanity, and their fellow citizenship

of a precarious planet, to allow global planning for the production and distribution of those commodities necessary for life and for individual development the world over.

In the meantime, inside the individual national pieces of the world jigsaw, men and governments will continue to grope their way towards the satisfaction of the needs of those citizens to whom they are responsible, or for whom they have responsibility. It is essential that they give thought also to perfecting their·piece of the jigsaw so that it may eventually fit smoothly into a harmonious whole.

There follows on attempt to see how some at least are approaching their twin task, national and international. This attempt can neither be comprehensive nor elaborate in detail, but can perhaps point out the contemporary experiences of a few; experiences of possible relevance to all.

Krokodil comments on bureaucracy

NOTES

[1] R. H. Soltau, *An Introduction to Politics* (Longmans, 1951), p.127.

[2] Quoted in Soltau, *op. cit.*, p. 46.

[3] Or as Lincoln put it: 'The price of liberty is eternal vigilance'.

[4] Soltau, *op. cit.*, p. 85.

[5] See C. J. Friedrich, *An Introduction to Political Theory* (Harper and Row, 1967), Chapter 1.

[6] See R. H. Soltau, *op. cit.*, p. 135.

[7] C. Ware, *op. cit.*, ii, p. 821.

[8] Soltau, *op. cit.*, p. 4.

[9] Ayn Rand, *Capitalism: the Unknown Ideal* (Signet, New York, 1967), p. 18.

[10] *Dundalk Democrat*, 1 July 1967.

[11] C. Ware, *op. cit.*, ii, p. 799.

[12] R. H. Soltau, *op. cit.*, p. 256 (The final phrase he attributes to C. E. Merriam).

[13] B. Ward, *Nationalism & Ideology*, pp. 73–4.

[14] Both quoted in Soltau, *op. cit.*, p. 273.

[15] J. A. Schumpeter, *Capitalism, Socialism & Democracy*, quoted in A. C. Macintyre, 'Recent Political Thought' in D. Thomson (ed.), *Political Ideals* (Penguin, 1969), p. 186.

[16] See M. Duverger, *The Idea of Politics* (Methuen, 1966), pp. 129–32, and also p. 227.

[17] Ware, *op. cit.*, ii, p. 820.

[18] The socialist system, as defined in 1904 by the Socialist Party of Great Britain. See *The Case for Socialism* (SPGB, 1962), p. 47.

[19] Brian Simon, 'The Present Predicament' in *The Challenge of Marxism* (Lawrence and Wishart, 1963), p. 42.

[20] K. Marx & F. Engels, *The Communist Manifesto* (1848). These are the last words of section II 'Proletarians and Communists'. The centenary edition, introduced by H. Laski (Allen & Unwin, 1948), is recommended. (ref. on p. 146).

[21] Roger Garaudy, *Marxism in the Twentieth Century* (Collins, 1970), p. 146.

[22] *High points on the road* (Moscow, n.d.), p. 44.

[23] Ware, *op. cit.*, ii, p. 813.

[24] *High points on the road, op. cit.*, p. 43.

[25]Ware, *op. cit.*, ii, p. 703.

[26]*Ibid.*, p. 701.   [27]*Ibid.*, p. 764.   [28]*Ibid.*, p. 817

[29]See Isaac Deutscher, *The Unfinished Revolution: Russia 1917–67* (O.U.P., 1967).

[30]J. Grimmond: see interesting series in *Guardian*, November 1966.

[31]A. Werth, *Russia: Hopes and Fears* (Penguin, 1969), p. 14.

[32]Isaac Deutcher's final lecture 'conclusions and prospects' in his *Unfinished Revolution, op. cit.*, raises a number of interesting points in this connection.

[33]See M. Djilas, *The New Class* (Thames & Hudson, 1957).

[34]M. Djilas, *The Unperfect Society* (Methuen, 1969), pp. 10–11. Disillusion is no more vividly expressed than in *The God that Failed*, ed. R. H. Crossman (Hamish Hamilton, 1950), in which 6 former communist enthusiasts write of their experience and loss of faith.

[35]J. K. Galbraith, *The New Industrial State* (Hamish Hamilton, 1967; Penguin, 1969). (See also his *The Affluent Society* (Penguin, 1962). References below are from the Penguin edition.

[36]Deutscher, *op. cit.*, p. 109.

[37]*Ibid.*, p. 112.

[38]J. K. Galbraith, *The New Industrial State*, p. 18.

[39]*Ibid.*, p. 335.   [40]*Ibid.*, p. 390–1.   [41]*Ibid.*, p. 325.

[42]*Ibid.*, p. 106.

[43]Maurice Duverger, *The Idea of Politics*, p. 226.

[44]*Ibid.*, p. 221.   [45]*Ibid.*, p. 206.   [46]*Ibid.*, p. 222.   [47]*Ibid.*, p. 231.

[48]J. K. Galbraith, *op. cit.*, p. 400.

[49]M. Duverger, *op. cit.*, p. 223.

[50]*Ibid.*

[51]Duverger, *op. cit.*, 224.

[52]*Ibid.*, p. 209.

[53]B. Ward, *op. cit.*, pp. 60–1.

[54]*Ibid.*, p. 99.

CHAPTER FIVE

National Aims and
Viewpoints

Varying as they do in the emphasis they place upon the domestic and international aspects of their activity, all nations contribute in one way or another to the richness, variety and level of well-being of the world community. Though we may have been slow to realise this in the past, the interests of this community require that none of the lessons and experiences of the national groups of mankind are wasted. Failures and mistakes as well as successes can instruct. And if the world community is to form itself into an ordered, self-regulating association, accepting the limitations and obligations. of responsible, active membership in the interests of common survival and common development, then the sooner attention is paid to the signposts and warnings of national experience the better.

The attempt below to pick out some of these signposts and warnings is necessarily brief and highly selective. The selection given is based on considerations of geography and ideology, and upon what seems to be of universal validity, or at least of general applicability, from amongst the separate national experiences. Where possible, recent declarations of national policy have been used as a basis of discussion, and the order in which the nations are presented is largely dictated by the need for cross-reference, so that, although much has already been said about the United States and the Soviet Union, it will be most useful to begin with some additional comment on both of the leading, pioneer nations of capitalism and communism. Each has been certain of the universal validity of its ideology and each does in fact merit treatment in some measure according to its own estimation of itself.

The United States of America

In regard to the United States, some account has already been given of its world-wide opposition to communism and of its domestic commitment to capitalism. Some of the contradictions inherent in American foreign policy, which purports to defend democracy through the support of dictatorship, have already been described, while those features of modern industrial society enumerated by Galbraith are clearly most advanced in the United States. But what has not been stressed is that America, despite being the richest and most technically advanced nation, is in many ways a microcosm of the contemporary world. In America, poverty exists in the midst of wealth (admittedly this situation is reversed in most other countries), racial division, discrimination and violence abound, and pollution, like technology, has been carried further than elsewhere. America is unlike most of the rest of the world in having the resources to combat these all too prevalent evils: consequently the degree to which resources are in fact matched up to evils will be a powerful factor in the judgement of America accorded by the rest of the world community.

America is aware of its priorities. Any Presidential Address or State of the Union Message spells out the defects of the present as well as the dreams for the future. In January 1970, President Nixon was most concerned with change, with new emphasis on national unity and spiritual commitment, to make the America of the 1970s worthy of the hopes of its founders of the 1770s. Making political capital out of the failures of the 1960s – a decade of Democratic Party rule – he pointed to the unprecedented growth of crime, inflation and social unrest in America, matching its admittedly unprecedented economic growth. 'Never' he observed, 'has a nation seemed to have had more and enjoyed it less.' Peace abroad and reform at home, the stabilisation of prices so that the government might 'plan

programmes for progress', the maintenance of law and order
(with this astonishing admission about the nations' capital:
'I doubt if there are many members of this Congress who live
more than a few blocks from here who would dare leave their
cars in the Capitol garage and walk home alone tonight.'), and
above all else an emphasis upon conservation, formed the
content of his address. With these attended to, President Nixon
could look forward hopefully to the bicentenary celebrations
in 1976:

> I see an America in which we have abolished hunger,
> provided the means for every family in the nation to obtain
> a minimum income, made enormous progress in providing
> better housing, faster transportation, improved health,
> superior education.
>   I see an America in which we have checked inflation, and
> waged a winning war against crime.
>   I see an America in which we have made great strides in
> stopping the pollution of our air, cleaning up our water,
> opening up new parks, and continuing to explore in space.
>   Most important, I see an America at peace with all the
> nations of the world.[1]

The previous year, in his Inaugural Address, President
Nixon had been less specific about the future dream and the
present nightmare. He had stressed the community that is the
earth, echoing the spaceship analogy of his predecessor, quoting
Archibald MacLeish's description of a single world of 'riders on
the earth together, brothers...'[2] (President Johnson, in 1964,
had spoken of all men as 'fellow passengers on a dot of earth').[3]

Unfortunately it is not only the language of space that has
characterised the successive Presidential messages of the past
decade. President Johnson too gave voice to his vision of the
American future. He too stressed, as long ago as 1965, the
compelling need to concentrate at last upon conservation; to
achieve at last equality of rights for all American citizens
('There is no Negro problem. There is no Southern problem or
Northern problem. There is only an American problem.'[4]); he
too posited a 'national agenda'[5] (plan?) to achieve what he
had already begun to call 'the Great Society'.

The Great Society at that time, according to the political commentator Walter Lippmann, was to rest upon the 'two pillars of controlled affluence and of political consensus'. As enunciated by Johnson in May, 1964, the Great Society, of abundance and liberty for all, free from poverty and racial injustice,

> is a place where every child can find knowledge to enrich his mind and to enlarge his talents. It is a place where leisure is a welcome chance to build and reflect, not a feared cause of boredom and restlessness. It is a place where the city of man serves not only the needs of the body and the demands of commerce, but the desire for beauty and the hunger for community. It is a place where man can renew contact with nature. It is a place which honours creation for its own sake and for what it adds to the understanding of the race. It is a place where men are more concerned with the quality of their goals than the quantity of their goods. But most of all, the Great Society is not a safe harbour, a resting place, a final objective, a finished work. It is a challenge constantly renewed, beckoning us toward a destiny where the meaning of our lives matches the marvellous products of our labour.[6]

Here indeed is a vision worthy of the most powerful nation on earth, and the fact that it can be formulated there and proclaimed as the national goal must give hope to the world at large. The Great Society provides an admirable target for all the peoples of the earth. The Great Society, Johnson himself recognised, would have to be a world society, but it could start in America. Yet how elusive it has turned out to be!

One of the Great Society's most poignant phrases describes man's 'hunger for community' and this phrase was picked up with telling relevance to the American and the world condition by that great American negro leader Martin Luther King. The negro, he pointed out, and he might have been referring to coloured people everywhere, was still living his daily life 'in the basement of the Great Society'.[7] The Great Society, indeed, far from being near attainment, stood in mortal danger. The hunger for community was there, sure enough, but the prospect of chaos was more real. *Chaos or community?*: this was the choice outlined by Dr. King in a calm but ominous book in 1967. His own brutal murder in April 1968 seemed to presage, for America at least, the former rather than the latter.

Martin Luther King did not hesitate to point out the glaring conflict between the language of dreams and the reality of life; between the law of the land and the injustice of its administration; between the state of white affluence and liberty and the state of negro poverty and oppression. Martin Luther King too had a dream,* the greatest dream of all, of the brotherhood of man, of black and white man, in America and in the 'world house' in which all men dwell now in such proximity. But he had no illusions about the effort needed to win for that dream some degree of reality. America, strong on visions for the future, was crippled by divisions in the present. And the divisions were principally divisions of colour and poverty and discrimination.

The society which the non-violent negro leader described in 1967 was one of mounting backlash against 'community': violent white backlash against negro rights; conservative backlash, often no less violent, against the most obvious expressions of deviation from an idealised 'American way of life'. Students and hippies, drugtakers and drop-outs in their way often sought a scale of values superior to those imposed by an over-materialistic society dominated by the industrial machine. No less than successive Presidents they were conscious of a need for human and spiritual values, however inadequately their actions served to demonstrate or develop them. Abundance of material goods was not yet matched by an abundance of human generosity, of service or of love. And although Johnson could in 1965 adopt the great negro assurance 'we shall overcome', and speak of ending inequality, fulfilling the hope of freedom and of opening 'the city of promise to all our people', Black Panther Eldridge Cleaver had still to make a defiant ten-point plea in 1969:

*Expressed in his 'I had a dream' speech, one of the most moving pleas of 20th century oratory, delivered to almost a quarter of a million civil rights demonstrators, before the Lincoln Memorial, Washington, 28 August 1963. Some of the speech is reprinted in L. Bennett, *What manner of man* (Johnson, Chicago, 1964), p. 162.

One: We want freedom; we want power to determine the destiny of our black communities.

Two: We want full employment for our people.

Three: We want housing fit for the shelter of human beings.

Four: We want all black men to be exempt from military service.

Five: We want decent education for black people, education that teaches us the true nature of this decadent racist society and that teaches young black brothers and sisters their rightful place in society; for if they don't know their place in society and the world, they can't relate to anything else.

Six: We want an end to the robbery of black people in their own communities by white-racist businessmen.

Seven: We want an immediate end to police brutality and murder of black people.

Eight: We want all black men held in city, county, state, and federal jails to be released because they haven't had fair trials; they've been tried by all-white juries and that's like being a Jew tried in Nazi Germany.

Nine: We want black people accused of crimes to be tried by members of their peer group, a peer being one who comes from the same economic, social, religious, historical and racial community. Black people, in other words, would have to compose the jury in any trial of a black person.

Ten: We want land, we want money, we want housing, we want clothing, we want education, we want justice, we want peace.[8]

Clearly the Presidential dream had not yet been given substance. Martin Luther King's careful statistics of negro depression make this clear also[9]; for years America has progressed on the back of cheap negro labour, while the negro community has known only cheap education, cheap housing, cheap amenities. Equality now will be more costly than registration for the vote; it will mean hard cash to up-grade negro education, housing and amenities; equality will be expensive but white America must not shrink from the bill if it is to know peace and justice and decency. After all, the sacrifice will not really be great, for 'the poor can stop being poor if the rich are willing to become richer at a slower rate'.[10] A little self-sacrifice, a little self-discipline is all that is asked of white America; but the sacrifice and discipline must be conscious and willing.

With determination from the American people there is little doubt that the democratic structure of America could begin to turn the Presidential vision into reality. For the system that set out to provide government 'of the people, by the people, for the people' rests on a constitution that well provides the means for reaching this desired end. The American Constitution, balancing power between Federal and State governments, and dividing the executive, legislative and judicial functions, breathes popular participation in decision-making through every branch of authority, from village, township, city and county, to State Legislature and Federal Congress. The democratic machinery is there; only the will is sometimes lacking, and the complexity of modern industrialism sometimes baffling. Of the latter Galbraith has spoken, but his conclusion was not pessimistic.*

The accompanying charts of constitutional machinery illustrate the American democratic method. Corruption, intimidation, privilege may interfere with the ideal forms, but popular determination can triumph over these ills, as has been proved so many times in the past. What is new is the extent to which the black section of America's population has become aware of its exclusion from the normal processes, and the militancy and urgency with which it has sworn to change a *status quo* no longer acceptable. White reaction to this legitimate demand will determine the future of America; on the one hand progress and strength through integration; on the other disintegration.

Though equipped with a fine democratic structure, America has chosen to pursue a cautious course of social welfare legislation, and in this sphere lags behind what is considered normal in many developed European countries. Here the

*See p. 218.

THE PEOPLE

Choose the President
by the Electoral College
in general elections

Directly elect the
House of Representatives
and the Senate

The President appoints
Supreme Court Justices
with consent of Senate

EXECUTIVE BRANCH
THE PRESIDENT

LEGISLATIVE BRANCH
THE CONGRESS

JUDICIAL BRANCH
THE SUPREME COURT

ENFORCES THE CONSTITUTION,
THE LAWS MADE BY CONGRESS,
AND TREATIES

MAKES AND PASSES
THE LAWS

EXPLAINS THE LAWS,
INTERPRETS THE
CONSTITUTION

THE FEDERAL GOVERNMENT IS MADE UP OF THREE INTERLOCKING BRANCHES

How Federal Government and States Divide Powers

The National Constitution provides that certain government powers be

Delegated to the Federal Government

- Regulate interstate commerce
- Conduct foreign affairs
- Coin and issue money
- Establish post offices
- Make war and peace
- Maintain armed forces
- Admit new states and govern territories
- Punish crimes against the U.S.
- Grant patents and copyrights
- Make uniform laws on naturalization and bankruptcy

Reserved to the State Governments

- Authorise establishment of local governments
- Establish and supervise schools
- Provide for a state militia
- Regulate commerce within the state
- Regulate labour, industry and business within the state
- All other government powers not delegated to U.S. or specifically prohibited to the states

Shared by both Federal and State Governments

- Tax
- Borrow
- Establish courts
- Charter banks
- Promote agriculture and industry
- Protect the public health

PROHIBITED POWERS

The personal rights of citizens of the United States, as listed in the Bill of Rights (first ten Amendments to the Constitution) and in state constitutions cannot be reduced or destroyed by the Federal or the state governments.

emphasis, traditional to American society, has been placed upon individual responsibility, upon a belief that 'everyone should plan for his own security'.[11] The state has endeavoured to ensure steady employment and high wage levels, so that the individual, by savings accounts, life insurance, home purchase and property acquisition can provide for his own security and standard of living. The state has, of course, recognised that industrial society carries hazards for the individual beyond his own control – factory closures, slumps, accidents, for example – and it has made provision for old age, survivor (dependent) and disability insurance; there is also provision for job re-training, public assistance and child health, welfare and rehabilitation.

The American education system is quantitatively impressive and qualitatively uneven: it has many features of interest. Americans have always respected education and this respect has if anything increased in the twentieth century, which has released so many American children from the necessity of early employment, and permitted ever increasing numbers to continue through high school and on to further education. Extension facilities based upon state schools and universities serve to bring educational and vocational learning to the adult community. Television courses beamed into the home add further opportunities for individual advancement and enrichment. It must be emphasised that the basic high school and state university system provides free education and opportunity, although private facilities also exist. Though the level of education may not be high in terms of specialised excellence, the curriculum and extra-curricula activities together provide a broad, general education with a strong emphasis on civic responsibility, while the best schools and universities (particularly the latter) reach standards not bettered anywhere in the world.

But the most notable feature of the American education system is its lack of government control. Though there may be State guidelines, it is local initiative and local management, through local school board governors, that are the main sources of authority. This emphasises democratic participation and leads to an enormous variety of type, size and quality in high school education. There is much experiment, and there is a widely held belief in integrating school and community with most high schools fulfilling the triple task of providing a general education for all, preparing university entrants and equipping non-university school leavers with suitable courses. Thus, though there is no 'state plan' moulding facilities and opportunities to the particular national needs of the moment (so many engineers, so many chemists, for example), the system does succeed in supplying the advanced industrial economy of America to a remarkable degree.

There are also some disadvantages. Quality is often low, the high school or even junior college graduate emerging with a broad smattering of superficial knowledge, rather than a real understanding of a more limited number of subjects. And the fact that high schools are usually neighbourhood schools, serving the locality in which they are situated, has meant that poor localities have tended to suffer from poor schools, and that children from the various social levels have tended to encounter only their own kind. This has of course been acutely relevant to the negro population which has often lived in ghetto conditions and thus endured segregation and often sub-standard negro neighbourhood schools, despite Federal legislation designed to promote school integration. Bussing children from locality to locality, black children to white neighbourhoods and white to black, is hardly a satisfactory answer.

In general terms, however, the lack of central control or state planning reflects the wider American concept of democracy, of individual enterprise, initiative and liberty. This concept rejects absolutely monolithic, single – plan solutions. Because there is no single, decreed system, there can be disagreement, argument, diversity; ideas and methods can be burnished and refined in debate and competition; processes can be developed on the test-bed of practical experience and then employed or discarded as need dictates, and this applies not only to education but throughout the economy also. For all that free enterprise capitalism may encourage inequality of wealth and the worship of materialism, it also promotes a degree of drive, efficiency, and innovation unequalled else-

**COUNCIL-MANAGER PLAN
ADMINISTRATIVE ORGANISATION**

VOTERS

MAYOR

COUNCIL

CITY MANAGER

LAW
FINANCE
PARKS
STREETS
POLICE

OTHER DEPARTMENTS

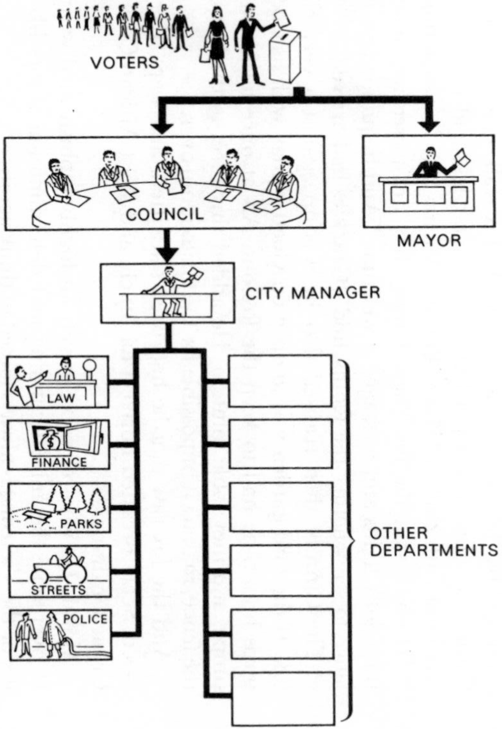

**MAYOR-COUNCIL PLAN
ADMINISTRATIVE ORGANISATION**

VOTERS

BALLOT BOX

MAYOR

CITY COUNCIL

CHIEF ADMINISTRATIVE OFFICER

STREETS
PARKS
POLICE

FINANCE
LAW
OTHER DEPT'S

OTHER DEPARTMENTS

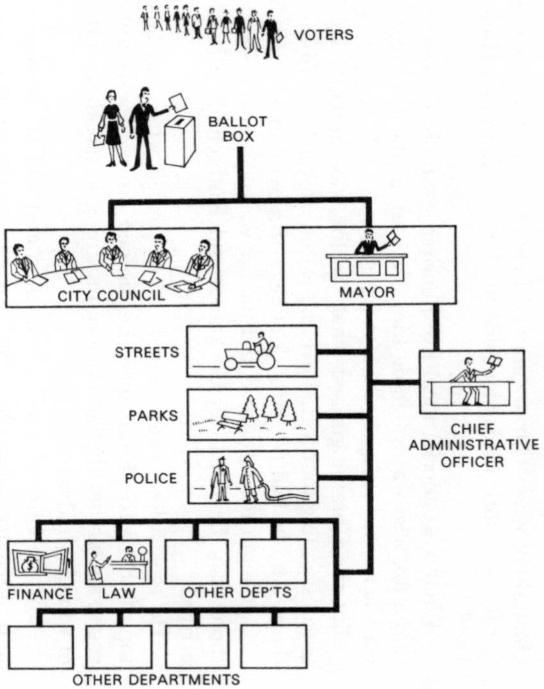

FABLE OF A FLYING FOX

Once there was a Curator named Peter Brown who was building a garden for exotic birds alongside the lake at Harewood House, near Leeds.

'What a wonderful meal five hundred exotic birds would make,' said a fox who was watching him. 'As soon as the lake freezes I will walk across the ice and gobble them up.'

But the Curator guessed what the fox was thinking. He built a fence, standing four feet above the water, 20 yards out from the lake shore. And he had two strands of electrified wire sticking out from it.

One night the lake froze and the fox walked across to see whether those tasty Leadbeater's Cockatoos and Rothschild's Grackles had arrived.

He took a long run, cleared the electrified wires and landed on top of the fence. From there he jumped down to walk among the cages, spying out the land before returning to tell all the other foxes of what he had seen.

Now the Curator was a clever man and had all the sophisticated aids of science behind him. So he fixed into the fence a device to go 'click-click-click.' He put flashing lights on top of the fence. And he left a VHF radio receiver, with amplifier, on the lakeside and tuned it to the police frequency, the only one where the noise goes on for the 24 hours.

By and by the lake froze again and the fox walked across it. Lights flashed for him, and a machine went click-click, and the night air was loud with calls of 'This is BD to Z Victor One,' or something.

'Ho-ho!' said the fox, 'how happy they are to see me, with all those jolly lights and messages of welcome.' And he jumped over the fence to see whether the Rothschild's Grackles had arrived.

The Curator then realised that he was up against a very clever fox. If the bird garden was to open on Good Friday with its stock of birds intact, he had to keep the fox out. All at once he found the simple and inevitable solution. He added three feet to the height of the fence, making it impossible for the fox to jump over.

And the fox saw that he had been outwitted, and wept over the loss of Scaly Breasted Lorikeet for lunch, and West African Crowned Crane for dinner.

Moral: He who relies exclusively on highly sophisticated weapons to overcome the animal cunning and determination of foes like the fox or the Vietcong is always forced to think again.

(by Michael Parkin, reprinted from the *Guardian* 26 March 1970) where; for all that it emphasises self-interest at the expense of community, it also develops confidence and a self-reliance that often, paradoxically, seeks satisfaction in community service or benefaction.

There is much that is American that other peoples will not wish to emulate. Affluence will be reckoned poor compensation for physical insecurity, racial tension, violence and crime and the treadmill of material acquisitiveness. Divided and destructive, America does not yet offer to the world an example of the good society let alone the Great Society. But it must be remembered that America is paying the price of outstanding achievement; the penalty of being the first to win the means to bring general affluence. America now has the means and may find the will to harness those means; may incorporate a degree of state responsibility towards the oppressed black minority, raising it to the general white level, so that the whole community can then move forward in step. And thanks not a little to the dimensions of the pollution problem, state responsibility and action are no longer seen as hostile to the American way of life. If state action alone can check the depredations of unfettered individuals or companies, then more state action there must be, while the blue sky can still be seen, while some unspoiled forests remain to be walked, while a few fish can still be caught in once-teeming rivers. If America can find its unity, recover its idealism and succeed in harnessing its industrialism to the needs of man, avoiding a subjugation of man to the needs of industrialism, then it will indeed realise its own dream, and in the process create a new objective for mankind.

The Union of Soviet Socialist Republics

Two years after the 1917 Revolution in Russia, John Reed's eye-witness account *Ten Days That Shook the World* was published, bringing to the world a vivid description of that momentous event. Since then it is no exaggeration to say that Soviet Russia has given us 'fifty years that shook the world'.* In what is now a little over half a century, the Russian people

*Harrison Salisbury, indeed, uses this title for his chapter on the history of Soviet Russia, in his 50th Anniversary volume *Anatomy of the Soviet Union, op. cit.*

have turned a largely backward agricultural country into the
world's second most formidable industrial nation. They have
welded together the diverse nationalities of the old Tsarist
Empire; they have introduced to the world the concepts of the
single Party and of national planning (from the first 5-year plan
in 1928). They have created the first nation based upon the
social ownership of production, guaranteeing work and welfare,
and moving in accordance with a concept of history and a view
of the world that is generally accepted by all citizens. They have
charted the course of socialism pragmatically, without any
blueprint, conscious that they were building for the enlighten-
ment of others. In material and social terms their achievement
has been colossal, and when the devastation of war is recalled,
truly remarkable. Thus, in July 1967, the Central Committee's
Fiftieth Anniversary *Survey* could proclaim triumphantly:

> Socialism brings the peoples of the world both social and
> national liberation; ...it does away with exploitation and
> oppression and creates instead friendships, co-operation and
> mutual aid amongst both classes and nations; instead of an
> elemental, hazardous and chaotic economy, it provides a
> planned development of the economy... Having radically
> changed the social aim of production, socialism has relieved
> the worker of all anxiety about the next day; Soviet humanity
> now knows neither fear of unemployment nor the fear of
> abject poverty...[12]

The Russians are proud of their record in industry, education
and welfare, the more so since their successes have been won
at the price of immense sacrifice and hardship. Pointing to
their successes they would confidently ask us to judge them on
these terms, and also upon the terms of socialist morality which
orders their common priorities and governs their relations, man
to man. Their example is clear for all the world to follow.

The Russians toiled hard, in often wretched circumstances,
to build the industrial base upon which their new society could
in the future be founded and defended (and the need for defence
against a hostile world must not be forgotten, ever present, ever
eating into the available resources). The central planning that
they adopted allowed the mobilisation of resources to particular

tasks, so that the maximum economic growth could be achieved, even though this had to be done at the expense of immediate comforts. The fruits of common endeavour were directed to social welfare, into schools and clinics and transport rather than to private consumption, washing machines, cars or even houses. The immense effort, requiring so many long years of hard work, was thus combined with an improving environment and sustained by a great faith in the future; and in the end many of those who toiled also reaped the harvest of a secure and increasingly comfortable society, offering their children and grandchildren a level of education, housing and consumer goods unimagined in the pre-revolutionary days.

And yet, in spite of all the effort of the Soviet people, serious mistakes were made by their leaders and their system itself has produced much inefficiency and waste. Communism, as interpreted by the Russians, has revealed defects which must seriously undermine its claim to be suitable for universal application. And when we are discussing this point it will be just as well to recall that the decades after 1917 were decades of general technical advance, that a backward, non-communist (but also authoritarian) country like Japan also made remarkable strides towards industrialisation, and that Russia, with its huge population and vast natural resources, would certainly have made considerable material advances had its regime been capitalist. The Communist Party of the Soviet Union undeniably changed the face of Russia and created a new society; but it remains to be asked whether it did so in the best way possible, and whether the 'Soviet achievement'* justifies the harsh methods used to bring it about.

Arguments about Stalin's dictatorship often centre around this very point of whether the end justified the means. To revolutionaries this may well be the sole criterion of judgement. Future generations, looking back from a transformed and richer society, may, as Russians now do, hold that Stalin's

*See J. P. Nettl, *The Soviet Achievement*, particularly the final chapter, which accepts the necessity of Stalin, pointing out that whereas often exponents of terror have achieved no lasting result, Stalin did transform his country for the benefit of future generations.

particular ruthlessness was an unfortunate aberration born of haste and defective equipment, which was corrected after his death and which in no way invalidates the principles upon which Communism is founded. But the point which more objective observers may want to make is that the monolithic party system lends itself to dictatorship, that the need for united action in the immense task of transforming society admits of no opposition, and that ruthless suppression of individual dissenters is an almost inevitable corollary. Stalin may or may not have been necessary; he may have been a unique exception; but monolithic communism presents the opportunity for such dictatorship, for its maintenance, and for its recurrence.

There is a paradox, too, in a system which encourages belief in a new man, a transformed humanity with a new social morality of service and altruism, but which on the way towards the achievement of that morality is prepared to use every form of deceit, brutality and viciousness in order to expedite it. Is it surprising if the vanguard of the new order becomes corrupted by its techniques, loses sight of the goal, ends by devoting its energies to the immediate issues, including the in-fighting and the power struggles as well as the multitudinous bureaucratic decisions of a planned economy? Reason might dictate that half a million opponents of the regime should be eliminated lest they distract the others in their efforts to build communism; or that a thousand farmers who resist the flooding of their land for a reservoir or power station be exterminated, that others may live more abundantly. It may be reasonable to butcher peasant factory workers for bad time-keeping, in order to encourage the others to jump several centuries from rural, agricultural ways to those required of the industrial life. But such reason is liable to run riot and to destroy the possibility of the good society in the name of which it is employed. Such reason, it can be argued, did run riot under Stalin; and such reason can never be the proper tool anywhere for promoting a harmonious society of cultured and fulfilled individuals.

Besides, even in the area of proudest achievement, the economic sector, serious doubts persist. Undoubtedly the successes of central planning are there. But central planning is something of a two-edged sword, mistakes and errors of judgement having repercussions throughout the whole system. And, worse still, as the economy has become highly complex, serious doubts have arisen as to whether the system can really cope, for it is riddled with waste and inefficiency. Observers can point out that individual initiative is stifled and worker productivity is low, that pricing and production quotas remain arbitrary, unrelated to real costs or 'economic' capacity.

In fact, much of the Soviet economy resembles what in capitalist society has been known only in the abnormal conditions of wartime. Then, to remedy desperate shortages of, for example, aero-engines, a capitalist government might have made special, priority provision for the rushing into production of so vital a commodity. Men and materials might have been devoted, regardless of cost, to the desired end. A badly machined part might have been discarded, an unsatisfactory engine scrapped *in toto* rather than waste time on looking for faults or redeeming useful parts. But no-one would have pretended that such production was economically sound. Once peace-time conditions returned, so the efficiency of competition in the open market would be restored; once again, only those engines produced more cheaply or with notably enhanced performance over rivals would be likely to sell. But in Russia it is normal for the aero-engine factory to have a target of units to produce and a given work-force to employ. The factory may even reach its target. But whether its product is efficiently and economically produced or not will be difficult to determine; all the evidence suggests that by capitalist standards Russian industry is inefficient. Calculations based upon total work forces and estimated gross national products would indicate that, in the mid-sixties at least, the Soviet worker produced only about one third of his American counterpart.

The most notable area of failure under communism, however, has not been industry but agriculture. Productivity in the collective farms has been particularly low, due, it seems, to a failure in the mechanism for pricing and planning and to an inbuilt discouragement of individual initiative. (In contrast, production from small private plots has been good.) The

Soviet economists are aware of the problem and some wish to experiment with market measures, with real profitability tests enabling the farms to decide what to grow, and how much, at what price, and with direct profit-sharing amongst the workers. Some Western experts will argue that farming can only flourish when the farmer is enabled to enjoy the peculiar relationship that springs from the ownership of the land, from long contact, forward planning and personal return for initiative and labour expended. The fact remains that Russian collective farming, for all the theoretical advantages of size and rational organisation, has lagged far behind the production of comparable land in the uncollectivised world. Intensified individual farming of proper-sized holdings, with expanded educational training in rural areas, and geared to the supply and demand of the open market, would, it is claimed,* raise agricultural output enormously at a time when all the world needs maximum production of foodstuffs. (The alternative of increasing the scale of collective farming in the world would be a disaster.) Soviet propagandists are aware that in the battle to capture the allegiance of developing nations, their agricultural record remains inferior to that of capitalist lands. But what havoc would the introduction even of limited market techniques in agriculture (and in industry) cause to the ideology and practice of communism?

Russian shortcomings and difficulties have also made themselves felt in the attempt to rationalise the economic planning of the communist bloc countries. Here Comecon (The Council of Economic Mutual Assistance),** which endeavours to ensure that trade and development throughout the bloc serves the interests of all members, revealed strong differences of opinion, as the most powerful member, Russia, sought in the early days to gear production and foodstuffs to the needs of Russia and of bloc inter-dependence. The freedom of the other members to follow their own interests may be much

*See Roy D. and Betty A. Laird, *Soviet Communism and Agrarian Revolution* (Penguin, 1970).

**Founded in 1949, Comecon now consists of Bulgaria, Czechoslovakia, German Democratic Republic, Hungary, the Mongolian People's Republic, Poland, Rumania and the U.S.S.R.

Foundations of the post-war world (above) Cologne

(below) London's East End

(above) Potsdam Conference: Churchill, Truman and Stalin, Potsdam, July 1945 (below) The mushroom shadow

(above) The first Pan-African Conference, Manchester 1945

(below) Dr. Dubois, Founder of Pan-Africanism

Commonwealth Prime Ministers (above) 1949 (below) 1969

Architects' post-war dreams (above) Dawn Palace, Brasilia

(below) Cumbernauld New Town – angled for the people?

(above) Korea, 1950

(below) Vietnam, 1970

Progress?
(above) Concorde

(below) First men
on the moon

(above) Tokaido express

(below) Traffic jam, M1

increased now, but their progress is still crippled by lack of genuine price levels and lack of a convertible currency to facilitate trade between themselves and with outside countries. Prices tend to approximate to international price levels outside the bloc, for these are based on the only genuine criterion of supply and demand (thus an Italian journalist could speculate that if, one day, socialism managed to take over the whole world, *one* country with a capitalist regime would have to be kept, so that the actual level of prices could be known!).[13] All the junior Comecon countries are experimenting, with varying degrees of boldness (Hungary, Czechoslovakia and Rumania to the fore), with profitability and with decentralisation; and these do not accord well with central planning or direction.

It is worth observing, too, that Comecon enables Russia to exert considerable political pressure on the other members. The socialist trading system generally may have favoured the Russians in the beginning, but they have found that the economic implications of the Chinese Communist victory have since proved distinctly unpalatable. Russia, by 1949, had laboured long and hard. The Russian workers were sustained by the hope of material rewards, but socialist fraternity now demanded that the backward millions of China be helped to advance. The price of equalising would have entailed lowering the Russian level yet further, and so it did not take place. Here surely is one of the underlying causes of Sino-Soviet hostility. Stalin's legacy of national self-sufficiency has combined with bureaucratic and racial arrogance and jealous dogmatism to prevent the creation of 'a socialist commonwealth stretching from the seas of China to the Elbe'.[14]

Economic relationships have a profound effect upon other aspects of society, a fact not a little disquieting to the Russian establishment. Internal economic reform in Russia, as in the other communist states of Eastern Europe, threatens to have major repercussions in the political field. If the introduction of the profit motive and the play of market forces is sanctioned, these must reduce the role of the bureaucracy. And this means politician as well as planner. Economic reform, it is feared, might set in train political change. And the sort of political change that might follow greater economic freedom might be the demand for more political freedom; free discussion and the right to hold opinions different from the single, permitted Party viewpoint. But such freedom would weaken the Party's hold, would question the indispensibility of the Party, might even posit alternative forms of government, allowing the ever-waiting capitalists to return to power. It is extremely difficult for the entrenched Party bureaucrats to lessen their grip without releasing a tide of experiment and innovation that might sweep them out of existence. Their sole means of supremacy is the political machine which they have formed and which they control through censorship, propaganda and a monopoly of decision-making. Out of such a situation dictators have consolidated their personal rule. It is such a situation that prevents the cultural flowering of the Russian people; and it is such a situation which led to the greatest crime (and standing indictment) of Russian communism in modern times: the invasion of Czechoslovakia on the night of 20 August 1968.

The Soviet Union and its fellow members of the Eastern European Mutual Assistance Treaty (Warsaw Pact, signed 1955) were by 1968 pledged to respect one another's sovereignty. But the experiment in freedom launched by the Dubcek regime with such popular support in Czechoslovakia posed just that threat of free expression, particularly in the daily press, that would most readily have started the innovating and perhaps irreversible tide most feared by the ruling cliques of Eastern Europe. Russia itself could hardly have escaped. Socialism with a human face was what the Czechs had begun to build. But their success would assuredly have changed not only the face of socialism, but the faces of the ruling socialists throughout East Europe. That was the reason that this hopeful, spontaneous, exhilarating experiment in a small, advanced ally had to be crushed. The doctrine of respect for sovereignty had perforce to be changed by the conquering Russian armies to one that recognised in future only 'limited sovereignty'; limited, that is, to actions approved by Russia. Thus although the carefully fostered Soviet image of international rectitude, of friendship for small nations and of helpfulness to peoples seeking independence was shattered, the bureaucrats were saved; saved to pursue the common good according to the revealed truths of communism, so jealously guarded in the Kremlin citadel.

But is this really the way forward for the needy millions of the developing world or for those multitudes labouring under the inequalities of capitalism? Can fine objectives really be served by rotten methods? Arthur Koestler provides one very definite word of warning in his moving novel, *Darkness at Noon*. He uses in it a quotation that is somewhat older than communism but which nevertheless contains timely observations for to-day's unwary idealist, and an apt commentary upon recent events:

> When the existence of the Church is threatened, she is released from the commandments of morality. With unity as the end, the use of every means is sanctified, even cunning, treachery, violence, simony, prison, death. For all order is for the sake of the community, and the individual must be sacrificed to the common good. (Dietrich von Nieheim, Bishop of Verden, *De schismate* liber III, A.D. 1411)*15*

The People's Republic of China

No discussion of contemporary Russia can be conducted without specific reference to the People's Republic of China, triumphantly established by Mao Tse-tung in 1949, and especially to Sino-Soviet relations. And the Russian experience must be borne in mind as China's progress and outlook are examined, until some comparison can be drawn.

In 1949 China was as backward, rural and demoralised as a nation could be, and it was overpopulated, famine-ridden and poverty-stricken as well. To-day, its seven hundred and forty million people seem to share a consciousness of unity and achievement – notably in new communications, new industries, schools and hospitals – and an egalitarianism that has prevented starvation even if it has not yet raised the general level of prosperity very high. The Chinese People's Republic is a post-war phenomenon, up-to-the-minute, pragmatic, flexible, immediate. Its message to the world, and to the developing world in particular, is one of sheer, determined effort, of disciplined self-help. China, war-torn and disintegrating when the Communists gained power, had become, a decade later, a proud and progressive world power. Troubled, divided and mistaken though it has been at times since, it has continued to make material advance and to initiate political and social experiment. China, populous, rural and poor, speaks to the underprivileged two-thirds of mankind, also populous, rural and poor. China's speech is of revolution, of force, of social transformation, but it does not rely on speech alone. China has set a new course and pointed a new way for others to follow.

The way is hard, but full of promise. The Chinese leaders have studied closely the Russian experience and have adapted and altered Russian methods to suit Chinese conditions. They have made their own interpretation of Marxism and have criticised what they deem to be Russian deviations from the true path and Russian revisions of the one creed. They have found much to criticise in the Soviet Union, just as they have exposed many evils amongst the countries of capitalism, and they have sustained their own people by projecting their moral and ideological rectitude, just as they have appealed to the dispossessed and down – trodden of the world in the name of historical inevitability. But can the Chinese revolution really be exported and is its promise really being fulfilled in China itself?

It is necessary to begin, again, as with Russia, by paying tribute to the heroic achievements of the Chinese people under the determined leadership of the Communist Party. Mao Tse-tung, dynamic guerilla leader and revolutionary Marxist theoretician, has been impatient for results and a hard task-master, but one flexible in approach. His country has pursued an erratic course since 1949, compromising with capitalism at first, while building a people's dictatorship capable of re-organising and planning the entire national economy. After a decade of power, during which Lenin's principal of democratic centralism was implemented in an effort to establish the industrial base for socialism, Mao Tse-tung was forced to place greater reliance on agriculture and to experiment in new forms of social organisation and political control. The first decade had seen the implementation of the first 5 year plan, in 1953, and an experiment in critical self-appraisal, launched in 1956, but terminated the following year, when socialism itself seemed to be in question. In 1958 the Party had launched a 'Great Leap Forward' to develop the economy at a rapid pace, but this too had not met expectation and in the following year economic targets had been reduced substantially. Neverthless as the vehicle for the 'Great Leap Forward', the Chinese leaders had created, from their early experiments in mutual aid and agricultural co-operatives, the organised People's Commune,[16] and this unit of economic, social and political administration has emerged as one of the principal features of subsequent Chinese life, so far as Western observers can judge.

In the first decade Russia had given to China a considerable measure of help, in the form of skilled technicians, know-how and plant, but already by 1959 a rift between the two major capitals of the communist world was becoming visible. In 1960 the Russians withdrew their experts from China. The Chinese were now on their own, and they were further handicapped by three bad harvests. Nevertheless, experiment and effort continued, the vast manpower of the nation being harnessed to huge power and communication works, and physical progress and economic growth went on impressively. By 1962 the New Model Commune had been tested and was ready for general application. In 1964 the regime officially admitted that its main emphasis was now on agriculture.

The People's Commune, designed to unite State and society, is one of the most interesting innovations in China. As officially defined, 'the People's Commune is the basic unit of our socialist structure, as also of the power structure of our socialist state. It brings together industry agriculture, commerce, education, and military affairs'.[17] Formed initially by merging a number of agricultural collectives, the Commune has permitted a reduction of local government organisation, leaving the Communist Party cadres to maintain control, and has proved to be an effective unit for conducting the two-way traffic of information necessary to work out and implement the State plan. Communes vary in size, depending on geographical location and proximity to a city. A sample, visited by the French agronomist René Dumont, varied from 10,000 to 75,000 inhabitants; one typical Commune, with a population of 30,000, in 7,000 households, had a work force of approximately ten thousand, with another third of the total at school, and the remainder at home as housewives or elderly people.

The Commune is sub-divided into brigades, which are further divided into work teams (a work force of 3,000 might have ten or twenty brigades and a hundred or more work teams). The Commune has a Council formed of representatives from Brigade Committees, meeting twice yearly, and a weekly General Purposes Committee. It will elect a Director and Deputy Director, who will be advised by a number of administrative sections concerned with, for example, accounts, sales, stock, and general works. Some Communes will also incorporate a science team to conduct research and initiate new methods, crops and products (the Commune quoted above had a science team in 1965 composed of 32 graduates, 43 technicians and 360 peasant members, many undergoing training).

Here then is a unit of local government and production, with a hierarchy of subdivisions and a Council which will work out an annual Commune Plan as a component part of the State Plan. The Commune Plan will incorporate the annual output (broken down into items), the amount of this to be marketed, gross income, members' earnings and investment allocations (the latter will not only be in terms of money but also of work, for it is here that tremendous progress has been made in China with more than ten, and often twenty, percent of effort being put into investment projects, as a general rule). The Commune is often large enough to experiment and to diversify its work teams, thus permitting a high degree of specialisation of labour and the acquisition of sophisticated techniques. Light industry can be encouraged in rural communities, growing from agricultural machinery workshops, and a peasant population can thus be introduced to an ever-increasing number of modern skills, managerial as well as mechanical. Education at all levels combines academic and manual work in order to remove barriers between individuals and to prevent the entrenchment of a bureaucratic class or mentality. The fullest attention is given. to social awareness both during formal education and in after-work classes, in a sustained attempt to induce maximum output and a full community spirit. The Commune has succeeded in giving a measure of decentralised responsibility. Its small work teams, the members of which receive work points for labour given and benefit financially according to their work-point total, and the fixed land-tax system (not rising with productivity) have managed to stimulate initiative and boost production steadily, something not achieved in Russian and Cuban commune experiments.

The Communes, still innovating, still investing heavily in the future, provide a prototype economic, social and political unit which may turn out to have great relevance to emerging Africa and to other areas of Asia, though the level of expertise, confidence and pride attained in China, and the extent of the natural resources available in so vast and populous a country, must not be underrated when application of the system elsewhere is envisaged. At any rate, the Chinese policy of 'walking on two legs', of employment for all, at no matter how low a level at first, in co-operative endeavours designed to raise gradually the level of technical work, would seem a common sense example to poor lands everywhere.

During the evolution of the system in China, however, the top Party officials have found much else to preoccupy them, and not only in the realm of foreign affairs. Ever conscious of the Russian precedent, Mao Tse-tung in particular has become aware of hitherto unsuspected dangers to the cherished socialist system; dangers that have prompted renewed political innovation at home.

Whatever the real causes of the Sino-Soviet quarrel, however much the split derived from great-power considerations as opposed to differences of ideological interpretation, there seems little doubt that, as time went on, Mao Tse-tung became increasingly worried by what he observed in Russia. There, he felt convinced, socialism had been overturned by a new privileged class of bureaucratic 'capitalists', entrenched in power and content to further its own interests through the exploitation of the mass of the people. What he was observing was, in part, the impact of industrialisation and the emergence of the technical experts at the top; the process which Galbraith has ascribed to advanced communist and capitalist countries alike. But the implications for Mao had a more fundamental horror. He had hitherto assumed that once the dictatorship of the proletariat had begun, the evolution of socialism into communism would be a relatively straightforward process, albeit one requiring discipline and effort. Now, he concluded, socialism could be overturned by the bureaucracy, by the new 'capitalist' class concerned more with 'efficiency' and its own privileges than with the morality of communism and the development of all individual citizens. What had happened in Russia could happen also in China.

His antidote was vigilance, and the ruthless rooting out of those bureaucrats who had chosen to 'follow the capitalist way'. Mao, for a time in the early sixties overshadowed in a power struggle at the top which favoured the Head of State, President Liu Shao-Ch'i, began to reassert himself, late in 1965, and to encourage the purification of the now well-established state bureaucracy. To this end he launched a theoretically more egalitarian and certainly anti-bureaucratic 'Great Proletarian Cultural Revolution'.

The course and consequence of the Cultural Revolution in China can hardly have been anticipated at the outset: and details are by no means clear yet. Part of the appeal of its purpose undoubtedly lay in genuine resentment against the rigours and regimentation of life under the Party bureaucrats. Officially it was designed to

smash revisionism, seize back that portion of power usurped by the bourgeoisie, exercise all-round dictatorship of the proletariat in the superstructure including all spheres of culture, and strengthen and consolidate the economic base of socialism so as to ensure that our country continues to advance in giant strides along the road of socialism.[18]

Affirming in 1966, in a letter addressed to the youthful Red Guards conducting the Cultural Revolution, that 'it is right to rebel against reactionaries' Mao Tse-tung recommended them to:

express your wrath against and your denunciation of the landlord class, the bourgeoisie, the imperialists, the revisionists and their running dogs, all of whom exploit and oppress the workers, peasants, revolutionary intellectuals and revolutionary parties and groups.

The better educated Chinese were exhorted to 'combat egoism', 'eschew privilege', and above all 'serve the people'. A new ethos of equality was demanded. The educated man was to receive no rights and privileges above the labourer.

The Cultural Revolution was also a direct appeal to the spontaneity of the proletarian masses, to a renewal of revolutionary fervour, placing individual commitment and participation in the advance of socialism before the smooth but heartless working of the state bureaucratic machine. It sought fresh ideas and new personnel for that machine, and, through a 'three-in-one combination' of Party, Army and Masses, and through a process of 'struggle-criticism-transformation', it hoped to ensure that the correct, Marxist line was followed. How 'struggle-criticism-transformation' might be implemented in a factory was explained in the following terms:

Establishing a three-in-one revolutionary committee; carrying out mass criticism and repudiation; purifying the class ranks; consolidating the Party organisation; and simplifying the administrative structure, changing irrational rules and regulations and sending office workers to the workshops.

The Cultural Revolution plunged China into chaos. Fiercely resisted both at the grass-roots and at the top, it disrupted life and led to bloodshed and open fighting. Throughout 1966 and much of 1967 the revolutionary youth supporting Mao Tse-tung struggled with the established structure, much of which repudiated the need for change. The outcome was in doubt until Mao made use of the army under Lin Piao to restore order and reach a measure of compromise. Chairman Mao emerged successful, President Liu Shao-Ch'i's 'renegade clique' was smashed and the President himself – 'hidden traitor and scab...crime-steeped lackey of the imperialists, modern revisionists and Kuomintang reactionaries' and 'the chief person in power taking the capitalist road' – was discredited. By 1969 the Ninth National Congress of the Chinese Communist Party could look back upon a glorious phase of struggle and look forward with determination to the consolidation of victory:

The Great Proletarian Cultural Revolution is the broadest and most deep-going movement for Party consolidation in the history of our Party. The Party organisations at various levels and the broad masses of Communists have experienced the acute struggle between the two lines, gone through the test in the large-scale class struggle and undergone examination by the revolutionary masses both inside and outside the Party. In this way, the Party members and cadres have faced the world and braved the storm and have raised their class consciousness and their consciousness of the struggle between the two lines. This great revolution teaches us: Under the dictatorship of the proletariat, we must educate the masses of Party members on classes, on class struggle, on the struggle between the two lines and on continuing the revolution. We must fight revisionism both inside and outside the Party, clear the Party of renegades, enemy agents and other elements representing the interests of the exploiting classes, and admit into the Party the genuine advanced elements of the proletariat who have been tested in the great storm. We must strive to ensure that the leadership of Party organisations at all levels is truly in the hands of Marxists. We must see to it that the Party members really integrate theory with practice, maintain close ties with the masses and are bold in making criticism and self-criticism. We must see to it that the Party members will always keep to the style of being modest, prudent and free from arrogance and rashness and to the style of arduous struggle and plain living. Only thus will the Party be able to lead the proletariat and the revolutionary masses in carrying the socialist revolution through to the end.[19]

The Cultural Revolution continues, but now under military

auspices and within the general regimentation of a national life that remains as firmly as ever dedicated to the achievement of communism, and is newly vigilant against the danger from within as well as from without. But while Mao fights successfully against alternative views of progress under the dictatorship of the proletariat, views like those of Liu Shao-Ch'i, preferring strict Party obedience, proletarian discipline and rational planning of industry, can he really hope to triumph over the pressures of the industrial state, once a high level of economic development has been reached? Mao and the army may have routed the bureaucrats; will the technocrats of the future succumb so easily in China and wherever the Chinese way is emulated?

During the course of the Cultural Revolution the Chinese openly castigated the Russian leaders since Stalin for turning, through 'peaceful evolution . . . the world's first state under the dictatorship of the proletariat into a dark fascist state under the dictatorship of the bourgeoisie'.[20] Naturally the Kremlin replied in kind. Looking back, the Russians saw in the 'Great Leap Forward' the beginnings of error, for it was this that disturbed the accepted process of industrialisation and set back agriculture alarmingly. Worse than such 'revisionism', however, was the Chinese policy on the international level of rivalling Russian leadership of world communism; a policy which was nothing short of 'petty bourgeois adventurism and great-power chauvinism'.[21] The Russians also criticised the 'urban and rural "communes" in which people were to live like soldiers', and, when the Cultural Revolution got under way, it too was exposed as a crude and violent bureaucratic and military dictatorship, devoid of 'culture' and thoroughly un-Marxist. The cult of personality, carrying to extremes the veneration of Chairman Mao, was of course only too familiar to Russians of the Stalin generation, as indeed were the apparent purges of the Party organisation. Russians who watch China to-day are, therefore, inclined to see the historic parallel with their own experience and to expect that the Chinese will eventually emerge from the tunnel, as they believe themselves to have done.

Russia, erstwhile sympathiser and senior partner in communism, is therefore openly critical of present-day China, now rival for communist leadership as well as claimant upon Russian resources. Chinese life may indeed be highly regimented but it is probably true also that there is no longer starvation amongst China's many millions, and the Chinese leadership can properly claim there is little point in talking of general concepts of individual freedom and fulfilment if the bulk of the population is unable to subsist. Credit must be given, therefore, to an autocratic regime which has achieved something more than subsistence for all its citizens. However, doubts may remain as to whether the same regime can be capable of nourishing those freedoms which give life meaning above mere existence and by which it justifies its remaining in power. The assessment of Chairman Mao reached by Professor Stuart Schram seems relevant to this consideration:

> Mao has, in my opinion, done very little to show the way to a free, spontaneous society not founded simply on the pursuit of self-interest. The moral pretensions of his Cultural Revolution are largely vitiated by the crudeness and mediocrity of the slogans, the narrow and primitive fanaticism which inspires the whole movement, and Mao's willingness to rely on naked military control in order to maintain his own power.

Professor Schram nevertheless adds that 'as one of the first and most influential to reject the seemingly implacable logic of advanced industrial society, even though he was totally incapable of imagining a viable alternative, Mao may be remembered as a Janus-like figure looking forward to the future, despite the limitations resulting from his deep roots in the past.'[22]

Mao Tse-tung thus joins the Galbraiths and the Duvergers of the world in deploring the values and warning of the dangers of modern industrial society, whatever his shortcomings as a builder of a better alternative may be. Those leaders of developing countries who would dismiss his practical achievements must first raise the level of all their own peoples above the subsistence line before their right to criticise will be granted. The foundation of life and livelihood for all must be laid before the development and cultivation of the individual can be widely pursued. It is deplorable if the machine which lays the main foundation then blocks the avenues of individual development; it is worse if the foundation itself is never achieved.

Republic of India

There are many reasons for looking at India immediately after China. India is the next most populous country in the world (with about 550 million citizens); India too is Asian and developing, seeking to modernise its economy and its outlook and to make its mark upon the world. Independent since 1947, India too is an ancient land with a new national government. But India seeks a different way to that of China and is proud to be a democracy in the Western sense. India wishes to move forward through debate and consent, to utilise the incentives of a capitalist economy within a pattern of socialist planning. India pursues non-alignment in a foreign policy designed to diminish the areas of world tension. A multi-racial, multi-lingual, secular state, a federal republic with a mixed capitalist-socialist economy, India battles against grinding poverty, bursting population, internal division and external pressure. India, member of the Commonwealth, 'beacon of democracy in Asia', is China's rival.

India is unique and does not lend itself to ready European generalisation. It is easy to question the validity of India's nationhood, riven and split by religion, language, geography and tradition as it is, bound merely, it seems, by the experience of foreign rule and the struggle against that rule. But it is possible that firm leadership at the centre, improved communications, and the shared experience of independence can yet unite the diverse Indian peoples, and overcome political, economic and social liabilities of formidable dimensions. It is just possible that India may yet prove to be a serious rival to the ostensibly more successful and dynamic Peoples Republic to its North and East.

India's federal union provides a strong central government over seventeen states and ten small, centrally administered territories. Its Constitution, which came into force on

26 January 1950, is dedicated to achieving justice, liberty, equality and fraternity for all citizens, and incorporates a number of fundamental individual rights. Power resides in the President and two Houses of Parliament, Rajya Sabha (Council of States) and Lok Sabha (House of the People), through democratic electoral processes and prime-ministerial and cabinet government. The Constitution also sets out clear economic objectives:

> To ensure the right of the citizens, men and women equally, to an adequate means of livelihood; to ensure the distribution of ownership and control of material resources of the community as best to subserve the common good; and to prevent concentration of wealth and means of production to the common detriment. (Article 39)

To build popular participation in political affairs into the experience of a largely illiterate peasant country (five-sixths live on the land), the government, as well as tackling the problem of illiteracy itself, has given much attention to the development of the village *panchayat* or elected council, giving more authority to these basic units and grouping them in a pyramid structure with increasing local government responsibilities. To the *panchayats*, Community Projects have been added, designed to stimulate new methods of agriculture and develop local leadership and technical skills through civil, or light industrial, engineering schemes. Redistribution of land is further evidence of government concern. Nothing less than a revolution in farming, education, living standards and general agricultural and industrial production is aimed at; but it has to be 'revolution by consent'.

Politics and economics are closely interwoven and the largely capitalist economy was given a socialist emphasis when the Indian Parliament, in 1954, voted in favour of a 'socialist pattern' of society designed, as Prime Minister Nehru said, 'to make the business of building up India a co-operative enterprise of all the people'.[23] In 1956, an Industrial Policy Resolution stated that 'The State shall progressively assume a predominant and direct responsibility for setting up the new industrial undertakings and for developing transport facilities.

It will also undertake State trading on an increasing scale'. It went on to divide industry into three categories. In the first, heavy industry, the State would take exclusive responsibility for future development. This included mining, minerals, shipbuilding, aircraft, heavy machinery, electrical equipment. The second, chemical production, road and sea transport and industry not in the first category, would be jointly developed by the State and private enterprise. The third category, textiles, cement, paper and consumer goods, would generally remain in private hands.[24]

Already, in 1951, India had begun its first 5-Year Plan. Under a planning commission, basing its blueprints upon wide debate in order to achieve general consent, the first Plan gave principal attention to the agricultural sector, publicising new methods and improving seed and stock, building irrigation and power projects, producing fertilizer, encouraging land redistribution and making credit available. Targets for production were set in both agriculture and industry.

The second 5-Year Plan, commencing in 1956, carried forward the new emphasis on the public sector, placing greater stress on industrialisation as a means of raising living standards and advancing the people from 'the cow-dung age to the nuclear era'. But agriculture was not neglected and Community Projects were extended in a bid to reach all India's 600,000 villages. Efforts were made to decentralise industrial processes in order to supply employment away from the major cities, and to state more precisely the respective roles of government and private enterprise. Though the State concentrated upon financing and controlling the crucial areas of mining, steel, atomic energy and machine tools, it is notable that in the first decade the government of 'mixed economy' India was responsible for a mere 8% of the national income, in contrast to capitalist America's more than 20%.

The government of India, faced with a colossal task of modernisation, and choosing to move by consent, has continued into its fourth plan to harness public and private investment and to encourage overseas funds, notably from Britain, Russia and America. A stagnant economy has begun to pulse with

new energy; India has begun to move from its own unique form
of static traditionalism towards modernity. But it remains
precariously poised, still engaged in the struggle to outpace
with rising standards the dramatic expansion in population.
Family planning has been embarked upon energetically, but
still self-sufficiency in food has not been achieved. Progress has
been uneven. Under Prime Minister Nehru, in office from 1947
until his death in 1964, a certain momentum of development
was maintained, despite the brief war with China in 1962 and
the consequent need to devote more resources to defence. But
economic growth had been too slow – 2.5% against a planned
5% – and bad harvests and the outbreak of hostilities with
Pakistan in 1965 set back development and cast long shadows
over the future. Under Prime Minister Shastri (1964–5) and
his successor, Indira Gandhi, the ruling Congress Party has
lost its unity and prestige, though it is true that its reformed
wing, under Mrs Gandhi, surged to victory in the impressive
1971 General Elections. Mrs. Gandhi has since translated her
concern for the mass of the people into energetic attacks upon
corruption and into greater measures of social welfare. She
could yet prove to be the leader India so sorely needs.

Since independence, the Indian government has endeavoured to utilise five main instruments in its struggle to
bring its vast population (increased by 200 millions since
independence) to an acceptable standard of living in a just and
stable society. First of all, it has concentrated upon the provision
of services such as education, and of public works (for example
hydro-electric schemes), and it has managed railways and
developed industries such as shipbuilding, fertilizer production
and atomic energy. Secondly it has undertaken the promotion
of such schemes as village improvement through general
community development and specific measures such as hand-
textile subsidies. Thirdly it has provided the legal framework
and direction of movement through such means as labour
legislation, the abolition of caste and the emancipation of
women. Fourthly it has channelled energy by restricting
specific activities by licensing, prohibition or foreign-exchange
control. Finally it has exercised its coercive power to direct or

redirect resources, through taxation and in some instances through the compulsory redistribution of land. It has attempted to lay down central policies, while permitting the States a degree of responsibility for their execution, but it would be a mistake to assume that it has yet been entirely successful. Its twin aims, as re-stated to the United Nations in 1968 by Mrs Gandhi ('to build a democracy and develop a technologically mature society – a formidable endeavour in a country of our size'),[25] remain as yet aims.

For the problem of modernisation in India has been as much concerned with traditional attitudes and practices as with innovation of techniques and organisation. There is in Hinduism, the dominant religion of India, a fatalism and resistance to change which permeates much of the popular outlook upon life; a concept of acceptance of the status quo which makes resistance to change a virtue and makes India's struggle to introduce progress and scientific method even more difficult than is general in rural peasant societies. Fortunately, part of Mahatma Gandhi's strength as a nationalist leader was to emphasise reform of traditional Hinduism, and much progress has in fact followed. But it is well to be aware of the specifically Indian factors operating. Another is the existence of the caste system, splitting Indian society into mutually exclusive levels, the most worrying being the untouchable community at the bottom. Untouchability has been prohibited by law, and the lowly status of women also has been rejected by the Constitution. But practices long followed cannot easily be removed overnight.

Added to caste within the majority religion, there is communal violence between different religions. This also is too rife for the safety of the Indian body politic and bodes ill for the internal peace and co-operation needed for development. India is a secular state where all religions are protected. But old hatreds need time to die.

Yet another practice shows no sign of death. On the contrary, 'grease money' lives on and prospers. In India outright bribery, and money to galvanise the processes of law, or administration, into action, are rampant. And these old evils have proliferated in that new attendant evil of state development, the swelling bureaucracy; in India too often underpaid and always, it seems, open to temptation. India is fortunate in the number and quality of its top civil servants, but the bureaucratic system as a whole absorbs a great deal of corruption. This and a tax structure more concerned to redistribute wealth than to allow its creation in the first place, have permitted to flourish an essentially anti-social morality embracing public and private dealing. The adulteration of cement, of milk and of flour unfortunately matches the greasing of legal, educational or administrative palms at many levels. To eliminate both will require tough leadership at the top and also at many intermediate national and State levels.

This leadership is not strongly in evidence. More than foreign aid, more than increase of foodgrains, or rising industrial production, India needs clear-headed and even ruthless leadership. And with leadership, India needs know-how; expertise at the technical, scientific level, at the factory managerial level, and the civil service principal level. Like every developing country, India is short of skills, but more than most, India needs a change of attitudes and practices to encourage the acquisition of these skills through proper, rigorous training. Fortunately, there is another less prevalent but valuable Indian tradition, that of service to the community, of contempt for mere materialism. If this tradition can be fostered and harnessed to high standards and public service, then India need not fail.

The same tradition was reflected in the strong moral streak that ran through the great leaders of the Indian nationalist struggle, Mahatma Gandhi in particular, but also Jawaharlal Nehru in whose hands the first decades of independent India rested. Morality, service, an emphasis on the spiritual values, these were qualities which Gandhi hoped would inform the Indian masses and constitute the peculiarly Indian contribution to world affairs: a spirituality to counter the prevailing materialism of the Western world. Nehru, who at home presided over a mixed, capitalist-socialist economy (a primitive approach to that democratic socialism that is perhaps the best hope for a co-operating world), hardly succeeded abroad in injecting a new spirituality into the veins of world diplomacy. Nevertheless the foreign policy which he so persistently argued for India had significance for a changing world and retains significance to-day.

India was the first great nation to shake off imperial control after the Second World War, and India immediately assumed the duty of opposing imperialism everywhere in the interests of emergent peoples. This was particularly so in Asia and amongst those developing peoples anxious for freedom, economic as well as political. Such peoples needed self-government first; and second they needed peace. International peace, therefore, became a pre-occupation of Indian foreign policy, and non-alignment, a refusal to join military alignments in the emerging cold war era, its principal expression.

Non-alignment was not, however, a merely negative refusal to take sides: it had a more positive aspect in its cultivation of international friendships, its respect for the internal affairs of others, its support for the United Nations, its devotion to the cause of freedom for dependent peoples, and its pursuit of international economic co-operation. Non-alignment fostered co-operation, particularly amongst the developing nations themselves, along regional lines, and sought to co-ordinate their efforts to avoid involvement in big power manoeuvrings as well as to eliminate a world of big bloc domination. So far as India itself was concerned, non-alignment received general approval inside the country, thus strengthening national unity and avoiding the polarisation of attitudes between right and left, the fate of many aligned nations.

Looking back on the policy of non-alignment in 1967, the then Foreign Secretary of India, C. S. Jha, pointed[26] to the peace initiatives, the reduction of nuclear testing, and the solid and practical work for peace done by the non-aligned nations in twenty years. He pointed to the disappointment experienced by India when attacked by China in 1962, but denied that non-alignment and neutrality were the same thing, or that non-alignment was incompatible with defence forces. Far from neutrality, the non-aligned countries, fifty in number at that time, felt passionately and took initiatives on numerous issues; and the non-aligned must of course be ready to support their views of right and wrong against attack. Nevertheless, international peace, the reduction of tensions, the ending of hostile blocs and the promotion of co-operation in development, would remain integral to non-alignment, relevant in 1967, as in 1947, to a world in change.

Nehru, passionate advocate of non-alignment, gave to India wide influence in the post-war world of developing and developed nations. Yet he overlooked the immediate needs of India's own defence and did not seem to observe that in his own cabinet strong adherents of both the Cold War ideologies battled for supremacy. Nehru, it has been said, and the remark was directed as much to his domestic as his foreign policy, was dazzled by his own words and failed to notice his own lack of deeds. In this he illustrated yet another trait of the 'Indian personality', one only too familiar to politicians the world over:

> a tendency to mistake affirmations for achievements, the failure to face up to the implications of hard choices, the habit of regarding the promises of one's own or of others as tantamount to performance, exulting in the willingness of the spirit to the extent of overlooking the weakness of the flesh, a preoccupation with what might be or even with what ought to be unmatched by a careful examination of existing reality.[27]

So Nehru was caught napping by a China that chose in 1962 to violate the sacred principles of Panchsheel (the five principles of peace) so fraternally drawn up between India and China in 1954. His idealism in foreign affairs may here have ignored the realities of international power politics. Nevertheless Panchsheel – 'respect for each other's territorial integrity; non-aggression; non-interference in each other's internal affairs; equality and mutual benefit; peaceful co-existence' – continues as an ideal standard of international conduct.

In domestic affairs, too, Nehru was prone to speak toughly but condone abuses in practice. There, too, it was China that put Indian example to the test; for China was openly contemptuous of an Indian 'democracy' that failed to fill the peasant's belly with food. But there too Nehru's words were wise. They stand yet in proud contrast to Chinese precept, as relevant to the seventies, as when he spoke them in 1959, and they testify to India's importance in a contemporary world as preoccupied as ever with the problems of development:

> It is sometimes said that rapid progress cannot take place by peaceful and democratic methods and that authoritarian and coercive methods have to be adopted. I do not accept this proposition. Indeed, in India today any attempt to discard democratic methods would lead to disruption and would thus put an end to any immediate prospect of progress. From the long term point of view also I believe in the dignity of the individual and in as large a measure of freedom for him as possible, though in a complex society freedom has to be limited lest it injure others.[28]

Japan

Japan too has necessarily considered the same basic question as that posed by Nehru. As the Japanese Foreign Minister, Takeo Miki, put it in a speech in Canberra in 1968, during which he weighed the manner in which the struggle against the common enemies of mankind – poverty, ignorance, disease and hunger – might be won:

> In an Asian framework, should we accomplish this through communism, or through liberalism and democracy?
>
> Through totalitarian control by authority, or through democracy based upon the individual's self-awareness and self-restraint?
>
> Through bureaucratic control, or through the creative ingenuity of private citizens?
>
> Through revolutionalism that pays no regard to sacrifices, or through innovationism that respects human dignity?
>
> Which of the two is the more effective in our war against our common enemies? The answer is being tested on the Asian stage. Could we not say that Japan is providing tangible evidence that economic construction through liberalism and democracy is more effective than economic construction through communism?

He then proceeded to outline three fundamental aims of Japanese assistance policy towards Asia, emphasising:

(1) Japan's international responsibility as the only advanced industrial nation in Asia, (2) that a solution to the problem of poverty through democratic means is the best counter-measure to the threat of communism, and the key to Asian stability, and (3) that improvement of living standards among the Asian peoples would eventually contribute to expanded trade for Japan.[29]

How is it that Japan finds itself so well placed in Asia and how well is it championing democracy and fulfilling the obligations of its unique position?

The history of the rise to power of the Japanese Empire is both astonishing and impressive. It belongs, in major part, however, to the nineteenth century, dating principally from 1868. Then a major reform and policy change opened Japan's doors to the techniques of the Western world, directed Japanese energies towards modernisation, and began a process that was to lead eventually to constitutional government. Japan's success in its endeavours can be measured by its ability to inflict defeat on China in 1894–5 and, more importantly, on Tsarist Russia in 1904–5. Involved in the First World War as a result of its 1902 treaty with Britain, Japan emerged from that struggle as one of the world's great powers. But the ill-effects of the inter-war depression allowed militarism and expansionism to dominate the Japanese government and in the Second World War Japan overreached itself, and as a result was subjected to bombardment, unconditional surrender, and foreign occupation. Nevertheless, from the ashes of Hiroshima and Nagasaki, and from the humiliation and destruction of defeat, Japan quickly arose with renewed drive to recapture the economic leadership of Asia and to make itself, more than ever before, a power in the world.

The relevance of Japanese experience to those countries of the world struggling to develop today does not appear to be immediate. Japan started over a century ago when the gap dividing industrial and non-industrial nations was not so wide. Nevertheless, the Japanese reliance then upon agriculture to provide the investments to finance its industrial expansion may still have significance; and the recent, post-war surge of Japanese development, admittedly with large American assistance, but also under a genuinely democratic constitution, is worthy of emulation.

Japan is a small, insular country, half as big again as the United Kingdom, but with a population almost twice as large (over 101 million in 1970). Like the United Kingdom it has few natural resources and must earn its living in the world by trade. Literate, energetic, disciplined, the Japanese people have a long cultural tradition, which draws heavily on China, as well as immense skills founded on Western technology, particularly in the manufacturing, electrical and electronic industries. The Japanese are renowned in the popular mind for their ships, cars, radios, cameras, their town planning, photography, flower arranging, unarmed combat, suicide rate and their administrative thoroughness, as displayed recently in the 1964 Olympic Games and the highly successful Expo '70. Their country is believed to be overcrowded, with problems of housing, traffic congestion and pollution. Like every people their qualities are varied, and their popular image something of a distortion; but the Japanese are unique in many ways, not least in their regional success.

In government, the Japanese owe much to the post-war American Administration which lasted formally until 28 April 1952, when the Japanese Peace Treaty, signed with forty-eight other nations, came into force. It was the Americans who in the main drafted the democratic Constitution which came into operation in May 1947. This firmly placed sovereignty in the hands of the Japanese people and ended the divine claims of the Emperor, who was nevertheless retained as the symbol of the State and of the unity of the people.

The 1947 Constitution adopted a parliamentary system of government. The Diet, composed of two houses – the House of Representatives (486 seats), which is senior, and the House of Councillors (250 seats) – is the supreme legislative branch. All its members are directly elected by the citizens, male and female, the voting age being twenty. Government follows the

JAPANESE GOVERNMENT

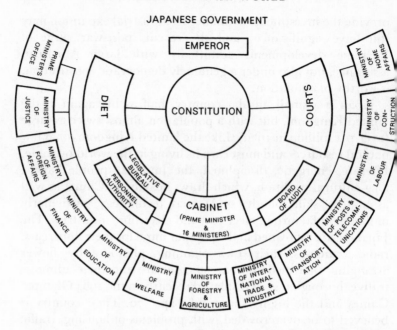

Prime Ministerial and Cabinet pattern, as illustrated in the diagram, and at least half of the Cabinet Ministers must be drawn from the Diet to which they are all responsible. The Judiciary is completely independent of the executive and legislative branches of government, the whole judicial power resting in the Supreme Court and such inferior courts as are established by law. Japanese Government since the war has been dominated by conservatives, their present ruling party, the Liberal-Democratic Party, being founded from conservative elements in 1955. Its main opposition comes from the Socialist Party, established in the same year, which aims at a socialist society through peaceful change.

The 1947 Constitution, highly democratic and conceived in the spirit of the American New Deal of the 1930s, cannot be said to be ideally suited to the singular character and experience of Japan, and it has suffered some stress and strain, particularly since the regaining of independence in 1952. Nevertheless it has proved an adequate framework for the economic and social achievements of successive Japanese governments, during the past quarter of a century of continuous material progress.

The Japanese economy, which draws much of its strength from traditional practices, has achieved staggering growth since the period of reconstruction ended in 1952. Just as in the case of government, it is not always easy to describe economic structures and methods in terms drawn from the West. But it is true that much of the Japanese success has rested on government planning and the willing co-operation of private business. It must be stressed that Japanese society has never been strongly individualistic in the Western sense and that social discipline and responsibility have long been held in high regard: in fact 'the overriding tradition has been... to assume that it is the moral duty of the state to regulate and control the economy for the general welfare'.[30] It is the government which has taken the initiative in economic planning, and it is economics that has been in modern times its central and most abiding preoccupation.

In 1968, Japan's gross national product reached 51,092,000 million yen, and as such became the third highest in the world. It has expanded by over ten percent per annum since 1947, a rate faster than that of any other country. (The 1970 GNP increase was 16·6%, at a value in U.S. dollars of $177,570 million, though the rate was observed to be falling in the last quarter of the year.) The principal sectors of expansion have been in heavy engineering and chemicals, with ships, textiles, electrical machinery and equipment (particularly radio and television sets) and cars being amongst the most notable exports. Manufacturing production has soared, and with it domestic and foreign trade, and the general standard of living; road and railway building, airports and harbours, and other 'social overhead capital' items have also received increasing attention in the last few years, with some remarkable achievements, such as the trunk road network and the super-express Tokaido railway line. Behind all these achievements have lain not only government planning blueprints and considerable technical innovation, but a quality labour force rich in skills and prepared to save and so provide the capital for further expansion.

The pace and extent of change and growth however have
created many urgent problems; problems summarised by
Premier Eisaku Sato in 1969 as: '"dehumanisation"...the
price for material development and scientific and technological
progress'.[31] In the long, post-war boom, social progress has
been uneven and has not kept pace with economic progress.
Agricultural incomes, in spite of intensive husbandry and
increasing mechanisation, have fallen behind those in industry,
and the flight from the land has resulted in urban overcrowding, serious shortages of accommodation and severe air and
water pollution. High land prices, lengthy commuting, smog,
the sheer persistent weight of numbers, the sense of individual
insignificance and lack of participation in decision-making
which are prevalent in advanced industrial societies, have all
in some measure touched Japan, though admittedly in forms
directly moulded by Japan's unique development.

The impact of modern worker mobility on family life has
been the more severe for the tradition of extended family
responsibilities towards the weak and the old. The wholesale
importation of the American system of education after the war
has also had unfortunate effects upon a people still hierarchical
in outlook. And the Japanese criteria of success and failure have
heightened the already intense educational strains as children
struggle to get or remain on the secondary education escalator
that can lead them to the top, and as students strive to reach
the prestigious universities that, again, can give them a lead in
the newly competitive, materialistic society.

The operation of parliament, dependent as it is upon the
cut and thrust of debate, does not always accord with the
Japanese language and habits of speech which are elaborately
formal, impersonal, and indirect. The Liberal Democrats have
been so long in office that they have become contemptuous of
opposition, while the Socialists have shown a rigidly 'all or
nothing' attitude which has led to parliamentary violence and
party walk-outs. Such attitudes do not bode well for democratic
processes which depend for their success upon majority respect
for minority views and sincere minority acceptance of majority
rule. Even where there has been a measure of success, in the

great Japanese corporations, practices widely accepted would hardly appeal to peoples who do not share the Japanese view of society. For the Japanese worker, joining a firm, at whatever level, is a commitment for life, and in return he is assured of employment and of a wide range of benefits – food at cost, numerous allowances and services relating to recreation, health and housing – on top of his admittedly low salary. The business corporation will concern itself with every aspect of the worker's life and in return expects and receives group loyalty and dedication.

There are of course many other unique aspects of Japanese life, and such disharmonies and discontinuities as exist are due largely to the very success of the Japanese people in achieving general affluence at so rapid a pace. They have at least generated the means to smooth out the irritations of change. Thus it is that the latest national development plan, for the fifteen years to 1985, gives high priority to environmental factors, and attempts to remove the imbalance between urban and rural living, to spread prosperity evenly throughout the different regions of Japan, and to counter the threats posed by pollution, traffic congestion, and inadequate housing: in short, to 'emphasise a respect for humanity, the protection of nature and the preservation of existing, favourable conditions'.[32]

The National Plan, as ever, posits a 'mixed governmental-private formula' for the successful conclusion of projects in three major fields: communication and transport; agriculture, manufacture, distribution and tourism; and conservation. Japan is crowded, mountainous, with a premium on usable land, so the Plan has as its main target the enforcement of proper land usage on a nation-wide basis, designating areas for agricultural, industrial, living, recreational and communication purposes. But it is not only in domestic terms that the Japanese are now thinking. Another quotation from Prime Minster Sato indicates new directions of thought:

As in the case of an individual, an affluent state, in international relations, is charged with certain responsibilities commensurate with its affluence. And just as an individual, as a citizen, finds something to live for in serving society, so the Japanese, as a people, should be able to find life worth living by contributing in one field or another to the security and prosperity of the international community of nations.[33]

Japanese foreign policy, directed as a trading nation's must be towards peace, has also emphasised nuclear disarmament in the post-war period. Now it has begun to concern itself seriously with developmental assistance, particularly in Asia, in an effort to create those conditions of wellbeing that are essential both to world peace and world trade. Governmental and private finance, and considerable technical training, both overseas and in Japan itself, are helping to translate this policy into practice, and although the definition of 'aid' remains loose, including investment and export credits and loans as well as outright grants and technical assistance, 1968 OECD tables placed Japan fourth amongst the world's aid-givers.

The Preamble to the Japanese Constitution specifically recognises the world context of Japanese national aims. Deliberately it states:

> We the Japanese people, desire peace for all time... We desire to occupy an honoured place in an international society striving for the preservation of peace and the banishment of tyranny and slavery, oppression and intolerance, for all time from the earth.

And material success has now turned Japan's attention towards the responsibilities inherent in such aims. Premier Sato has up-dated their expression in terms of the international and national contribution yet to be made by his country:

> In the case of Japan, I consider that the most worthy target we can set for ourselves would be to direct the creative capacity of the Japanese people to man's welfare and particularly to the peace and stability of Asia. The great political task for Japan in the 1970s is to channel the energy of the Japanese people in this direction. Externally, if Japan were to become, despite her limited defence capacity a stabilising force in the international community through economic co-operation and the high intellectual standards and the common sense of 100 million Japanese, and if, internally, she were able to become a country creative in

the field of thought and culture, then, and only then, could Japan be considered worthy of being called a first-class nation.[34]

The Japanese Premier sets high standards for his people. But already, despite the problems remaining before them at home, they are able to speak to the world with authority. Their sacrifices have not been in vain; their efforts, their restraint, their reinvestment, have created a measure of abundance unsupported by material resources which is a triumph of human skill over adversity. Demonstrably the Japanese have earned the right to be heard with respect.

The United Kingdom of Great Britain and Northern Ireland

Our country is a small insular nation not well endowed with natural resources. Therefore, international commerce is the one and only way to maintain and advance its prosperity. Accordingly, the development of the ...economy cannot be separated from the prosperity of the world economy as a whole.[35]

These words, spoken of his own country by the Japanese foreign Minister, Kiichi Aichi, in 1969, could as easily have been written of Britain at any time in the past one hundred and fifty years. For Britain, since the beginning of the nineteenth century, as Japan since the beginning of the twentieth, has lived by trade though the skills and drive of its people. Britain today, like Japan, must seek to implement the logic of One World: peace, harmonious intercourse, the steadfast promotion of prosperity for all the world's peoples.

Britain and Japan are not, of course, alike in tradition, character or social structure. The contribution to the world's historical experience of Britain – the oldest industrial nation, the foremost European power of the imperial age, and the country with the most enviable record of political stability – has been unique. Its world contact has been long, its reach far-flung, its impact both productive and destructive. Its major world role may now be ended, but its business is by no means finished and it has more of value than its past record of achievements and mistakes to contribute to the contemporary world.

Britain in 1970 is an ordered, collectivist polity of 56 million people. It is fortunate in its dedicated civil service and well equipped with a central and local government structure which relies first of all on a population long accustomed to the operation of democratic machinery based upon majority decision, and also upon political parties which 'accept the rules of the game laid down by prevailing conceptions of authority'.[36] The rule of law, moderation and respect for privacy in general characterise a society which has recently been enriched by immigrant communities, and thus has acquired a valuable potential for exemplary multiracial living. To the foreign observer, traditional pageantry and culture and the enviable public broadcasting and television services may stand out for commendation: for a thoughtful native it is still possible to proclaim that Britain is 'the most stubborn, the most practical, the most tolerant, the most civilised society on earth'.[37]

There is, on the other hand, much that is wrong with Britain today, as Mr T. A. Neal's recent history[38] does not fail to observe: pockets of poverty remain amid general posperity; there are real problems concerning the creation of wealth as well as its distribution; race relations are not yet assured of harmony; moral values are changing and uncertain; inhibiting, anachronistic attitudes, dating from former, more splendid days, are too common; and there is bitter communal strife in Northern Ireland which also has its roots in the past. Abroad, Britain's proclaimed concern for equity and for aid in development is not always matched by its trading practices or its level of assistance; at home the welfare state, built since the war, has in the view of some sapped the nation's initiative too much public welfare breeding too little private responsibility. Yet it is the concept of the welfare state, however controversial its application may be, that constitutes the main part of Britain's interest for the contemporary world. The blueprint for *Social Insurance and Allied Services*, drawn up by William Beveridge in 1942, remains a statement of ideals worthy of wide consideration.

Beveridge, while carefully enunciating the principles of his scheme of social security, based upon income security, also outlined what are worthwhile goals for any civilised society. Summarised in paragraph 456 of his *Report*, these goals constitute a concise statement of welfare state philosophy as well as a useful yardstick of social judgement. Beveridge broadened his vision by emphasising that the plan for social security was being put forward as part of a general social policy programme:

It is part only of an attack upon five giant evils: upon the physical Want with which it is directly concerned, upon Disease which often causes that Want and brings many other troubles in its train, upon Ignorance which no democracy can afford among its citizens, upon Squalor which arises mainly through haphazard distribution of industry and population, and upon the Idleness which destroys wealth and corrupts men, whether they are well fed or not, when they are idle. In seeking security not merely against physical want, but against all these evils in all their forms, and in showing that security can be combined with freedom and enterprise and responsibility of the individual for his own life, the British community and those who in other lands have inherited the British tradition have a vital service to render to human progress.

To eliminate these five evils – Want, Disease, Ignorance, Squalor, Idleness (unemployment) – and to promote their opposites is the proper task for the enlightened community. Beveridge wished to make a start by laying down a series of minimum standards and his *Report* was devoted to establishing minimum income levels which would eliminate want by taking account of the number in the family, whether the individual was employed or unemployed, ill, disabled or old. Each of the remaining evils could be tackled in like manner if the government assumed its proper responsibilities: disease could be reduced through a national health service designed to prevent illness as well as to treat the sick, with medical services provided according to need and not merely according to ability to pay; ignorance required facilities for education geared to the ability of the children and not simply to the income of the parents; squalor would disappear with adequate housing at prices that could be afforded, combined with town and country planning; idleness could no longer haunt the land once governments undertook to create jobs, to re-train the redundant, and to eliminate areas of particular depression through appropriate, particular remedies.

Beveridge saw such actions as necessary social responsibilities; only national legislation would suffice and only a total scheme, interlocking and all-embracing, made sense. Thus, for example, care for the environment, general education and instruction in hygiene, could combine to reduce ugliness, superstition and infection and to promote beauty, knowledge and health; and the provision of full employment, apart from reducing the demands on resources, would create the funds to pay social security benefits and finance the overall scheme. An assault on one evil might have repercussions on others, but an assault upon all together would dramatically multiply the benefits. Such a common, co-ordinated assault constitutes the welfare state.

Post-war British governments, notably the Labour Administration successful in the 1945 elections, have endeavoured to implement, sustain and improve upon Beveridge's ideal. Previous, piecemeal legislation on social security was consolidated between 1945 and 1948, the main Act being the 1946 National Insurance Act which established a contributory scheme embracing all people of working age. Similarly, the National Health Service Act, 1946, set up a free and complete medical service, to be paid for from Exchequer and National Insurance funds; and the 1944 (Butler) Education Act established a system of primary, secondary and post-secondary education, free to all in the first two stages and with free provision in the third for those of suitable ability. The extent of the post-war housing shortage necessarily involved the government, which alone was capable of tackling so large a problem, and successive Housing Acts and Town and Country Planning Acts have provided direct and indirect support, laid down standards and sited and established New Towns. Unemployment was tackled not only by special provision but through a multiplicity of financial measures and controls designed to foster and expand the whole national economy.

By 1948, three years after the end of a war which had, like no other before it, spread death, injury and destruction through all levels of the community, the main structure of the welfare state had been built. The British people had chosen to act as a community to insure against risks and hazards which are largely communal in origin. But the significance of their decision lies in the extent to which they preferred to avoid a single, monolithic, take-it-or-leave-it scheme. Reflecting numerous compromises, accepted as the blueprints were being worked out, the British welfare state retains within it many opportunities for the exercise of choice by the individual, particularly in the realms of health, education and housing. Choice – the freedom for those who can afford it to choose, for example, private medical treatment or private schooling for their children – remains a subject of considerable passion. Many believe that a society of limited resources should devote all that it has to one single scheme to which all people should have access according to their needs (medical) and abilities (educational), without provision of privileges for those with greater incomes. In contrast, others feel equally passionately about the individual's right to choose how to spend his income, particularly in such important fields as health and learning; and they argue not only about freedom of choice, but also about incentives to work, and rewards for bearing the burdens of responsibility. Given that the capitalist system is based upon a realistic appraisal of human nature, they maintain, a basic welfare scheme which provides minimum standards (naturally at as high a level as possible) for all, but which permits a wide degree of choice above that minimum, to those able and willing to choose, is the only logical course. Beveridge was, after all, a Liberal, and there is no reason why a liberal democracy should not tackle social evils through debate and with variety, which are the essence of liberal democratic thinking.

British society, a quarter of a century on, is deeply divided about its welfare and educational institutions. The arguments now are less concerned about whether there should be a state structure at all than about the form that structure should take and the degree to which it should be comprehensive and exclusive. The structure itself, for all its inadequacies, omissions and inefficiencies, is largely taken for granted. It is also impressive. At least in part, it is reducing wastage of human resources, increasing the development of individual talents, ensuring work, sustaining retirement, guarding the environment and promoting culture and recreation.

Whatever the world decides in judgement upon the British welfare state in practice, its ideals at least may, as Beveridge hoped, render 'a service to human progress'. And there is one other ideal, in this highly selective survey, which has equal claim to distinction. It is the ideal of Commonwealth.

The Commonwealth, no longer the 'British Commonwealth', will be treated as a working institution in the next chapter, though it will not be out of place here to say that it, too, falls short in practice of its proclaimed theory. As an association it is the product of many peoples, its form dictated by the victories, defeats and compromises of history, by the impact of nationalism upon imperialism and of protection upon free trade, by the vision or lack of vision of a host of soldiers, administrators, merchants and politicians. But central to this modern, multiracial partnership of free peoples, is the experience of British rule, of British traditions of government and public administration. And for the creation of a Commonwealth ideal of co-operation out of the Imperial practice of domination much credit must be given to the British themselves. Slow to change, and in the end too exhausted by the Second World War to give adequate assistance, the British did at last endeavour to measure up to those responsibilities which a developed, industrial power must exercise towards colonial possessions demanding their right of self-rule. A real effort was made to train civil servants, doctors, teachers and politicians, to provide economic assistance, and in general to prepare new regimes by peaceful transition from dependence to independence. And because the world remains divided, uncertain, and beset with the major difficulties of development and racialism, the value of preserving links, no longer enforced, was rightly stressed. Could not newly independent nations remain in association with their former ruler and the already existing members of an expanding, ex-imperial community? Could not a fraternal association replace an imperial one?

The idea was stressed and an ideal emerged. Though fundamentally a 'concert of convenience',[39] an association to which members belong through self-interest, the Commonwealth has become aware of its unique opportunities as a forerunner of wider, hopefully universal, co-operation. It has declared its dedication to racial equality, to the settlement of disputes by discussion, to mutual aid in development, and to co-operation in scientific and social research. Here too is a yardstick of action, this time on the international plane. Though bedevilled by contradictions and smirched by occasional lapses in practice, the ideal remains intact. If at times in Britain itself faith in its future seems to wane, there can be little real doubt of the common sense utility of its existence. And the world can ill afford to lose organs of co-operation of such potential, however imperfect they may appear to be.

The British, even though they first seek their own salvation, can be seen to have interests more closely tied to the world in which they live than do most peoples. Britain, ex-hub of an Empire radiating to all continents of the globe, retains relevance to the developing world through its present Commonwealth membership. With the developed industrial world it must trade to live, and, ambivalent, off-shore European island though it may be, it has the skills and energies necessary to contribute to the growth of continental Europe. A mature, ordered society, free of speech and assembly, affluent by most standards, it offers a degree of social and civil security not widely found. To some, Great Britain, in Dean Acheson's words, may have 'lost an Empire and not yet found a role':[40] to others, it is set on a course peculiarly relevant to our modern age: at home striving after social justice; abroad seeking after world co-operation.

The Socialist Federal Republic of Yugoslavia
If Britain offers us an example of a liberal, democratic,

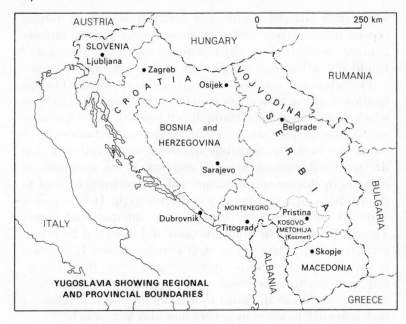

**YUGOSLAVIA SHOWING REGIONAL
AND PROVINCIAL BOUNDARIES**

capitalist state with comprehensive social welfare services,
Yugoslavia is a communist state employing many of the
capitalist devices of the free market, and with an unusually high
concentration of innovation and experiment in the fields of
politics and daily work. Perhaps more than any other country,
Yugoslavia is facing up to the problems of modern industrialisation, with new parliamentary measures and systems of
worker self-management designed to facilitate the participation of ordinary people in the making of those decisions
which most affect their daily lives.

A country today of some twenty million people grouped into
a federation of six republics, with five recognised ethnic groups
and three official languages, Yugoslavia achieved statehood
only at the close of the First World War, in 1918. Constituted
as a monarchy in 1921, it emerged from the Second World
War in 1945 as a communist republic, the only such territory
to come under communism by the efforts of its own people
without assistance from the Russian Army. The main architect
of the successful partisan struggle against Nazi occupation

during the war, and of unity since, is Marshall Tito, first Prime Minister of Yugoslavia, and President from 1953. Upon his assumption of power in 1945, Tito embarked upon a ruthless policy of consolidation and centralisation in an effort to eliminate opposition and to develop rapidly a backward country much devastated by war.

The creation of a centralised economic structure along Russian lines had been completed by 1947, with the federal government exercising a monopoly over all branches of activity in the state, and the Government Planning Commission taking all important economic decisions. In short, 'all human activity was linked up in a huge all-inclusive state organisation'.[41] For a time the genuinely democratic traditions established in wartime and the general enthusiasm of the Yugoslav peoples carried this bureaucratic system forward with impressive momentum. Between 1945–8 a record annual production rise of 15% was achieved and the destruction of wartime was repaired. But such progress was not maintained. As the Yugoslavs observe today, looking back upon the first years of their revolution: 'with the passage of time the inherently bureaucratic system became truly and oppressively bureaucratic. Partisan democracy was gradually corroded by the "modern" bureaucratic state machinery'.[42] Power, ever wider in scale, became tightly concentrated, with the ruling circles becoming divorced from the people; corruption and the abuse of power proliferated; and the workers grew apathetic and indifferent in their attitude towards work as conditions came more and more to resemble pre-revolutionary days, the state simply replacing the old capitalist boss. Economic stagnation grew, and political enthusiasm waned. The bureaucratic system stunted the creative energy of the people and, as planned targets were not fulfilled, so the bureaucrats adopted ever harsher coercive measures.

Fortunately for the Yugoslavs, a realisation of what was happening dawned before the bureaucratic system had become deeply entrenched. In dramatic circumstances a reappraisal of the revolution was made and radical changes implemented; changes which are still in the course of development today and which, though they are not devoid of contradictions and difficulties, command both interest and respect.

The dramatic circumstances which helped to redirect the Yugoslav revolution revolved round the break with Stalinist Russia which occurred in 1948. The Yugoslavs could not accept complete Russian hegemony of the communist bloc, and would not subordinate all Yugoslav interests to those of Russia. As a result, Stalin denounced Tito's government, and Yugoslavia was expelled from the economic organisations of the Eastern bloc and denied Russian aid. This action in turn provoked the Yugoslavs to examine the Russian bureaucratic state in detail and to look for deformities, similar to those they found there, within their own system of administration. They became aware, as the Chinese were to become aware later, of the dangers to the revolution posed by a bureaucracy which was usurping the rights belonging to the working people. They reacted, sharply, to reverse the steady expansion of state control which had advanced through all spheres of public life. They tackled both government and industry with a determination to rely above all upon the producer rather than the state; to jettison the unwarranted, mushrooming, autocratic bureaucracy and instead to build up by degrees a truly self-governing society. In 1950, changes were begun which hinged upon the three basic principles which have guided Yugoslavia's development since. The principles were simply stated:

> first, the process of withering away of the state cannot be postponed indefinitely for some future date, but must begin immediately;
> second, the Communist Party of Yugoslavia must be dissociated from the state apparatus, lest it be deprived of its essential characteristics of a class party and become a part of the government apparatus;
> third, state ownership must be transformed into social (public) ownership under the management of the direct producers, i.e. workers.[43]

Yugoslavia, barred from Eastern bloc society but unwilling to approach too closely to the West, proceeded to develop domestically many aspects of both the socialist and capitalist

NATIONAL AIMS AND VIEWPOINTS

systems, while in foreign policy it championed the doctrine of non-alignment. At home the Yugoslav economy was transformed into what has been described as 'market socialism',[44] a system under which there is no private ownership of industry but in which the role of government in guiding the economy is indirect, closely resembling the generalised controls over credit and finance common in Western economies. Politically, not only did the Communist Party step aside from detailed decision-making, but the Federal Government to a remarkable extent decentralised authority to the Republics and to smaller local units (the Communes). Central planning merely allocated major investment funds and established broad priorities and guidelines for their use as well as directing such national utilities as are favoured by central control (e.g. power and broadcasting). Direct control of individual enterprises was firmly placed in the hands of the workers engaged in them.

The results have been impressive in many ways. The average national growth rate since 1953 has been superior to that of all European countries except Western Germany; mineral output and industrial expansion have increased dramatically, as has tourism; illiteracy was reduced from 20 per cent to 5 per cent between 1953 and 1961.[45] The constitutional and industrial changes, which have recaptured individual enthusiasm and fulfilled social goals to such an extent, may thus bear closer scrutiny particularly in respect of self-government and worker management.

The Yugoslav Constitution, modified in 1969 and 1971, does not lend itself to brief summary, for each of the six Republics has its own constitution, modelled upon the Federation which supplies the framework for their operation. The political basis of the system is the self-governing Commune and power radiates upwards from this unit rather than downwards from the central government. It is the Federal Government which guarantees the security of the state, conducts foreign policy, preserves the social ownership of all means of production and all mineral and other resources; and it is the Federal Assembly (illustrated on p. 284) which provides the model for the Republics and the central bond and meeting place of the representatives of the nation; but it is the Commune which is the most direct and vital influence upon the lives of the individual citizens, best fulfilling the Yugoslav commitments to direct democracy, local autonomy and a varied, competitive economy.

There are 501 Communes today in Yugoslavia, ranging from 5,000 to 100,000 in population. Varying greatly in area, composition and complexion, they do have basic characteristics in common, discharging all those functions – economic, educational, cultural, health and welfare – not confined by the Constitution to the Federation or the Republics.

In the economic sphere, the Commune can pursue a definite policy, having authority to lay down the operating conditions in such sectors as catering, retail trade, skilled crafts and privately owned agriculture, and to determine the level of taxes to be levied on each. It can invest, on its own or jointly with others, in modernisation of industrial, transport, trade or other undertakings. It can site new projects, fix rates for public services, and promote public discussion of the activity of any working organisation in its territory, from elementary school to giant industrial complex, to ensure that its policies conform fully to worker self-management principles and to the interests of the community. It manages the 'reserve fund', established through taxes on industrial enterprises, for the relief of those enterprises in difficulty (or bankrupt) and it also maintains an unemployment fund.

In the educational and cultural sphere, the Commune has a remarkable degree of autonomy. It decides upon its own system of education, has power to establish and regulate all types of school except the universities and schools founded by economic enterprises. It sets the level of educational taxes which are managed by the Commune's own educational assembly and distributed to all educational and cultural institutions.

Regarding health and welfare, the Commune establishes its own medical institutions – from outpatient clinics to hospitals – with which insured persons draw up their own contracts. The Commune also has much administrative and legal work, is responsible for public law and order and for the regulation and inspection of such activities as transport and education. It is, in fact, a state in miniature and it has properly established democratic institutions to enable it to fulfil its functions in accordance with the wishes of its members.

The organ of government in the Commune is the Communal Assembly. This 'parliament' of two chambers comprises a Council, elected by all citizens, and a Chamber of Working Communities which is elected by employed persons only, the manufacturing, wholesale and retail trades, educational, scientific, cultural and public health organisations all sending representatives. In the larger Communes this Chamber of Working Communities will in fact be divided into three, with an economic chamber, a chamber of health and welfare, and a cultural-educational chamber. But as well as the Communal Assembly there are other grass-roots organisations vitally interested in opinion-forming and legislation-promotion, such as the trade and professional unions, the League of Communists, the Socialist Alliance, the Youth League, and the Veterans Federation. These bodies are all organised at Commune level, as also at Provincial, Republic and Federal levels, to further the interests of their members.

Yugoslavia is composed of the Socialist Republics of Serbia, Croatia, Slovenia, Bosnia-Herzogovina, Macedonia and Montenegro. There are two autonomous provinces – Vojvodina and Kosovo – within Serbia. The republics reflect the various national communities in Yugoslavia and each has its own constitution and parliament with a wide range of executive, administrative and legislative functions. The Republican Assemblies mirror the Federal Assembly (except that it has an additional Chamber of Nationalities).

The role of the Federation, according to the Constitution, is to 'realise and safeguard the sovereignty, territorial integrity, security and defence of Yugoslavia, the international relations of Yugoslavia, the unity of the socio-economic and political system, the economic unity of the country, the course and co-ordination of general economic development, and the basic rights and freedoms of man and citizen; and [to] . . . co-ordinate [the] . . . political, economic, cultural and other common

YUGOSLAV GOVERNMENT

FEDERAL ASSEMBLY

5 Chambers : 620 Members

Elects the President of the Republic and relieves him of his functions

Elects the President and Vice-Presidents of the Federal Assembly and relieves them of their functions

Decides on functions of commissions of the Federal Assembly

Elects presidents and members of commissions of the Federal Assembly

Chamber of Nationalities (140)

Economic Chamber (120)

Permanent Committees and Commissions

Chamber for Education and Culture (120)

Chamber for Social Welfare and Health (120)

Socio-Political Chamber (120)

Permanent Commissions

Commission for Elections and Nominations

Commission for Legislative and Juridical Affairs

Social Control Commission

Commission for Petitions and Complaints

Administrative Commission

Commission for Establishment of Authenticity of Texts in Languages of Peoples of Yugoslavia

Foreign Affairs Committee

Committee for National Defence and Security

Committee for Organizational and Political Affairs

Committee for Social Plan and Finances

Committee for Socio-Economic Relations

Budget Committee

Committee for Industry, Housing and Crafts

Committee for Transportation

Committee for Agriculture

Committee for Commerce and Tourism

Committee for Communal Affairs

Committee for Educational and Cultural Affairs

Committee for Social and Health Affairs

Committee for Labour Affairs

Commission for Mandates and Immunities

interests'. The Federal Parliament, as the diagram illustrates, is composed of five Chambers, with a total membership of 620 deputies, and is designed to reflect the interests of the Republics and the working groups as well as the wishes of the body of citizens as a whole.

The most important Chamber in the Federal Assembly is the Chamber of Nationalities which plays a predominant role in the parliamentary system and which is elected by the six Republican and two Provincial Assemblies (the Republics each sending twenty delegates, the Provinces ten). Of the four Chambers of Working Communities, the Socio-Political Chamber alone is elected by all the citizens of the country, the Economic, Education and Culture, and Social Welfare and Health Chambers being elected by Communal Assemblies. A Federal Executive Council conducts national affairs, and it, too, represents democratically the federal structure of the state, with three members from each Republic and two from each Province. A collective Presidency, similarly constituted (see diagram), is responsible for proposing Federal policies.

The peoples of Yugoslavia, showing their will to unite (this was previously held to be fragile, owing too much to the leadership of President Tito), have thus created out of their diversity a highly democratic and decentralised polity. And these qualities of their political institutions are even more manifest in their arrangements for worker-management in all collective enterprises.

It was in 1950 that the Basic Law on the Management of Economic Enterprises (better known as the Law on the Transfer of Factories to the Management of Workers) de-nationalised Yugoslavia's factories and began the handing over of them to the workers engaged in their operation. This remarkable and uprecedented decision was based upon several assumptions about man and society, some of which have already been mentioned. For a start, something had to be done to end the current stagnation; and as in the political realm, the obvious answers seemed to lie in breaking the stranglehold of the central bureaucracy. The Yugoslavs also felt convinced that until a condition of abundance had been achieved, there would exist a need for the market forces of supply and demand, to stimulate individual initiative by permitting a direct return for energy and effort expended. It was agreed that the worker should feel involved and directly concerned in the success of his factory; that the individual industrial enterprise required the authority to take its own decisions, raise its own capital and enter if necessary into international competition. No enterprise should be allowed to operate against the interests of society, so government, local and central, should continue both to scrutinise, and, by outline national plans, credit or exchange controls, or local environmental requirements, to provide a framework inside which the enterprise must operate; but to a large extent there should exist the same oportunities, risks and rewards as under capitalism. And this, in rough outline, is the form of market socialism which, by progressive, expanding legislation since 1950, Yugoslavia has implemented and continued to develop.

The outstanding difference between capitalism and market socialism is, of course, that under the latter there is no private ownership of the means of production. In Yugoslavia, further-more, tremendous efforts have been made to involve all work-people in the conduct of their own affairs. Thus the Constit-ution lays down that, on joining the work force of any collective enterprise, the worker automatically acquires the right to participate in its management. Thereafter, strict rules specify the degree to which he has direct and indirect participation (in person or through elected representatives) in the decision-making processes.

Worker management is expressed through a number of assemblies and representative councils. In any enterprise it is the Workers' Council that is the highest organ of management. This Council, directly elected by the workers, decides on the basic framework of the enterprise's operation. It elects the Management Board and supervises its activity. It decides on the 'hiring and firing' of workers, determines production and expansion plans, and participates in the appointment of the Director of the enterprise. According to law, enterprises of less than thirty workers do not elect a Council but manage the

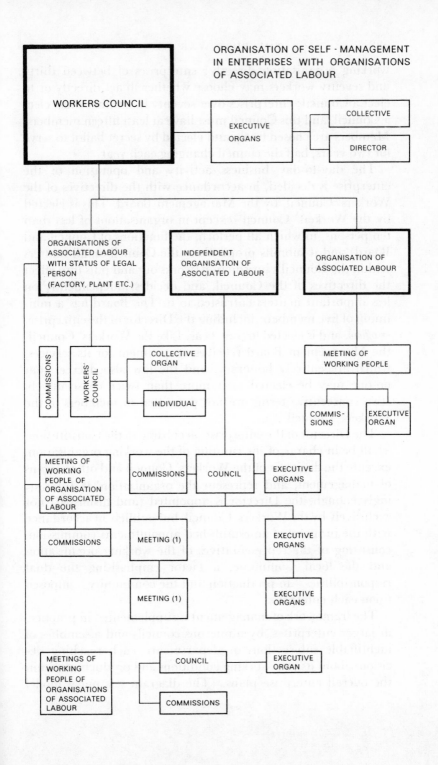

ORGANISATION OF SELF - MANAGEMENT
IN ENTERPRISES WITH ORGANISATIONS
OF ASSOCIATED LABOUR

WORKERS COUNCIL

EXECUTIVE ORGANS

COLLECTIVE

DIRECTOR

ORGANISATIONS OF ASSOCIATED LABOUR WITH STATUS OF LEGAL PERSON (FACTORY, PLANT ETC.)

INDEPENDENT ORGANISATION OF ASSOCIATED LABOUR

ORGANISATION OF ASSOCIATED LABOUR

COMMISSIONS

WORKERS' COUNCIL

COLLECTIVE ORGAN

INDIVIDUAL

MEETING OF WORKING PEOPLE

COMMISSIONS

EXECUTIVE ORGAN

MEETING OF WORKING PEOPLE OF ORGANISATION OF ASSOCIATED LABOUR

COMMISSIONS

COMMISSIONS

COUNCIL

EXECUTIVE ORGANS

MEETING (1)

EXECUTIVE ORGANS

MEETING (1)

EXECUTIVE ORGANS

MEETINGS OF WORKING PEOPLE OF ORGANISATIONS OF ASSOCIATED LABOUR

COUNCIL

EXECUTIVE ORGAN

COMMISSIONS

working organisation directly; enterprises of between thirty and seventy workers may choose whether to act directly or to elect a Council; enterprises over seventy in number must elect a Council, and this Council must have at least fifteen members. Members are chosen freely and elected by secret ballot to serve for two years, half the council changing each year.

The day-to-day business activity and operation of the enterprise is decided, in accordance with the directives of the Workers' Council, by the Management Board. This is elected by the Workers' Council (except in organisations of less than ten persons, in which all perform the functions of Council and Board) and it submits proposals to the Council on all matters within the Council's jurisdiction, works out and puts into effect the directives of the Council, and decides independently on less important matters entrusted to it. The Board has a minimum of five members, including the Director of the enterprise, *ex officio*, and is elected for one year. Like the Workers' Council, the Management Board receives no payment for its services, which are entirely honorary, and the law also decrees that no-one may be elected to it more than twice consecutively (two consecutive terms are not permitted to members of the Workers' Council).

The Director of the enterprise, according to the Constitution, 'shall be in charge of the running of the working organisation, execute the decisions of the Workers' Council and other organs of management, and represent the organisation'.[46] Interestingly enough, the Director is appointed (and dismissed) not exclusively by the Workers' Council, but publicly in accordance with the proposal of an established appointments commission, consisting of the representatives of the working organisation and the local Commune, a factor emphasising the dual responsibilities – to production and the community – imposed upon each enterprise.

The framework of management is supplemented in practice, in larger enterprises, by numerous councils and assemblies of identifiable sub-sections or departments, each reaching decisions about its own working conditions and production within the overall enterprise plans. (The diagram sets out a model scheme of such an organisation). In this way every worker may exercise an influence on his immediate working circumstances and upon the broad policy-decisions of his organisation.

The system is based upon an assumption, by no means universally accepted, that working people desire such a degree of involvement and responsibility; it also implies that the Yugoslav workers have the ability, as well as the interest, to make a success of worker management; a success not only in terms of personal satisfaction but of optimum production and social benefit. Critics, and even enthusiasts of the system, point out that to some extent all these assumptions are premature. Nevertheless they provide worthwhile goals and in the meantime involve the participation of increasing numbers of workers in democratic processes and in the experience of service on councils and management boards. In so far as deficiencies in the operation of the system are the result of lack of education and of inexperience, these are fast-diminishing handicaps.

Meanwhile deficiencies and difficulties in worker management certainly do exist and are readily admitted. But some misconceptions should be removed as to the sort of management which the ordinary worker can, in fact, conduct. No one pretends that the man at the work-bench can weigh up and overrule the advice of the technical or scientific expert. The fact will remain that the management executives will continue to play the crucial role in drawing up technical plans, for example for production, financing, or marketing. Worker management does not lie here, but rather in the determination of production relations, that is the conditions and the results of associated work, the fulfilment of the personal and social interests of the producers. Thus the workers will decide upon the framework and the aims of work: they will determine the proportion of enterprise earnings to be devoted to personal income, and the proportion to be accumulated for future expansion (capital formation). They will, in brief, decide upon the short and long-term implications, for themselves and for the enterprise and for the community, of the studies, analyses and programmes worked out by their technical experts.

In this task there remain conflicts of interest which have not

yet been resolved. Because market socialism requires workers
to 'share the fate of their products', that is the rewards of
success or the penalties of failure, inequalities can exist between
workers of similar skills in different enterprises. Even within
the same enterprise the fact that some skilled operators or
managers contribute more than others to the success of the
venture creates pay differentials, and these are often disputed.
Although a rough guideline decrees that top salaries should be
no more than five times as great as those at the bottom, this is
not easy to implement in practice. Again, different groups
interpret their interests differently and not all can easily be
harmonised in an agreed plan. As well, personal power still
corrupts and leads to abuse in individual cases, even under
aspiring socialism.

These faults are admitted by the Yugoslavs. Western
observers have confirmed them, adding that in practice the
Board of Management, often composed of professional and
highly skilled personnel, seems to govern, not the Workers'
Council, and that the ordinary worker is apathetic on most
issues other than the rate of his own pay. Furthermore, there is
a marked disparity between the industrial, prosperous North
of the country and the relatively barren South (though in the
South tourism is beginning to even this out) and the autonomous enterprise system and the fact of local and regional
self-government together make it difficult for the Federal
Government to raise funds to assist Southern development.
Another problem created by understandable worker reluctance
to dismiss redundant colleagues is gross over-employment in
many enterprises, with consequent inefficiency and high costs
which, in turn, adversely affect Yugoslav competition in
international markets. Within the country, such critics as
Milovan Djilas have remarked with bitter disillusion that many
of the worst faults of capitalism, for example unemployment,
economic disruption and petty tyranny, are still present in
Yugoslavia. And the fact that Djilas can be imprisoned for
expressing his views implies that the country has not yet
achieved as free and open a society as it would have outsiders
believe.

It remains true, however, that the Yugoslavs are making a courageous effort not only to build a modern, progressive, industrialised nation from a collection of backward and divided peoples, but to do so with genuine regard for the interests of the mass of the people, expressed in terms of individual fulfilment, individual initiative and individual responsibility, inside a framework of social ownership and democratic local government. Man is perhaps not destined ever to become perfect; the Yugoslav system itself is still far short of its goals though it continues to adjust and develop; but given these reservations, what is being attempted in Yugoslavia continues to provide valuable lessons. Yugoslavia is a laboratory both of industrialisation in terms of worker-participation in management and of political decentralisation in terms of citizen participation in decision-making.

Its economy, as has been somewhat timidly observed, 'shares with other socialist economies social ownership of the means of production and a measure of economic planning, and with the capitalist economies a high degree of enterprise initiative, competition and the separation of ownership from control as in the large capitalist corporations. As such it offers an alternative system which is of interest to some of the newly developing countries as they seek economic forms appropriate to their situations and needs'[47]. In fact, its significance is much wider. It is of immediate interest to all countries prepared to face up to the problems of citizen-disillusion and worker-alienation in a contemporary world of confusingly complex industrial technology and over-centralised political bureaucracy.

The Republic of Cuba

The Republic of Cuba represents communism in a form very different from that of Yugoslavia. In Castro's Cuba only the tiniest of minorities has taken the helm in the name of the people, without any pretence at democracy, without any framework whatsoever of institutions, local or central, to involve the participation of the people. In Cuba, in contrast, equality is expressed through poverty. There are equal shares for all – but of virtually nothing! The slogan of advance might be phrased 'from each according to his ability, to each according to availability'. And as yet very little is available.

The largest Caribbean island, with a population estimated in 1967 at 7,937,200, Cuba gained its independence from Spain in 1898, but immediately became subject to United States supervision and intervention. In spite of periodic attempts to establish constitutional government, it also succumbed to a series of ruthless and corrupt dictatorships, culminating in that of Fulgencio Batista, who was finally overthrown by the revolutionary forces of Fidel Castro on 1 January 1959, after a two-year campaign. Great luxury in the midst of general misery, official corruption, police brutality, and widespread rural neglect were features of life in Batista's Cuba. There was also American investment, in industry, tourism and gambling, transport and agriculture, to the extent of approximately 956 million dollars.

Castro came to power sworn to end corruption and the gross inequalities of Cuban life, and to bring real democracy to an oppressed people. It was not surprising that he resented the former American involvement in Cuban rottenness, both its investments, which drew away Cuban resources, and its military support for the detestable Batista dictatorship. And resentment soon led to action. Within three years Cuba had seized most American investments, resisted an American-sponsored invasion (April 1961), proclaimed itself a socialist State (1 May 1961), and been excluded from the activities of the Organisation of American States (January 1962).

The United States responded to Cuban hostility by ending its own Cuban trade and finally encouraging all the American countries to place an embargo upon Cuba, a move facilitated by Cuban readiness to encourage revolutionary groups inside the other States of South and Central America. Cuba meanwhile turned to Russia to sell its vital sugar crop and to find the imports it needed for survival and expansion.

It is against this wider international background that domestic Cuban events must be seen. American rejection of Cuba, as a communist pariah in the American hemisphere, has helped to cripple the Cuban economy and jeopardise the social experiments of the Castro regime. But American hostility has also provided a focus for the national endeavour and unity of the Cuban people. Russian enthusiasm for the first communist regime in the Americas has been tempered by subsequent ideological and economic differences and there is little doubt that the Soviet-Cuban relationship has been difficult, and, for Cuba, uneasy and dangerous.

Castro soon moved away from his promise of democratic government. As he later explained, his revolutionary supporters constituted less than one per cent of the Cuban population. They themselves were not experts in government, nor did they know quite what they wanted for the Cuban people. They wished an end to corruption, to the sterile squabbling of other political groups, and to illiteracy and poverty. They knew that the resources of the country and the scarcely developed skills of the people would permit no easy solutions: only a great and sustained effort would bring prosperity. Castro and his gradually emerging communist supporters determined to direct that effort along socialist lines, through centralised, dictatorial government, the nationalisation of all production and distribution, and through state planning.

Despite a lack of trained planners, planning in Cuba was extended throughout the land and into every home. Total mobilisation of the nation was required. Industrialisation was embarked upon initially, but prematurely as it turned out, for skills and materials were lacking and the more hopeful agricultural sector became dislocated. After 1963, greater emphasis on agriculture produced better results. Meanwhile tremendous changes in Cuban life were dictated. Educational and medical facilities were stepped up, geared specifically to the nation's needs. Rural life was fostered with rural development increasingly stressed. Virtually under siege, Cuba devoted its resources to investment rather than consumption, some 30% of the national income going to build future expansion. In such circumstances, with money of relatively little importance, there being hardly anything to spend it on, great emphasis was placed upon work – necessary, socially useful work – as the proper source of individual fulfilment. The value of shared voluntary labour was stressed, not only because this was essential to the building up of the economy but also for its own sake. With the ending of the depressed, rural, cane-cutter class and the termination of seasonal immigrant cutters, it became necessary to mobilise city workers to bring in the vital four-month sugar harvest. This task, uneconomically conducted because of poor skills and the costs of the transport, housing and feeding of short-term workers, was utilised to end rural-urban differences, promote class and national solidarity, and create an awareness of national utility in each individual.

An end of wage-work and a beginning of new attitudes towards personal fulfilment through useful service were high amongst the ideals of the Revolution, in particular of Che Guevara, Castro's most celebrated lieutenant. Guevara despised the European communist regimes for their preoccupation with wages and money incentives. The 'new man' he sought to mould would not need money. The struggle to free men from the habits of capitalist thinking would be no easy one, Guevara recognised, but discipline and fairness and sustained 'social engineering' through education would, he believed, triumph in the end, producing 'a future in which work will be man's greatest dignity, in which work will be a social duty as well as a true human pleasure and the ultimate act of creation', instead of the 'unfortunate necessity'[48] it had become under capitalism. Guevara and Castro sought to develop conscience rather than material incentive. The value of work was regarded as having more importance in human terms than in terms of economic efficiency, though obviously as skills and social conscience improved, so also would efficiency as measured in economic terms. The purpose of the State was nothing less than to supply all the needs of the workers so that they in turn could labour for the good of all, while in the process money would become as obsolete as slavery.

Such idealism, critics have pointed out, has been but imperfectly realised in practice. Rather it is a new form of slavery that has emerged. The Cuban State (satirised as *Castro and Company Inc* in a book by Castro's first President, the non-communist Manuel Urrutia) owns the worker's house, directs his employment, supplies his ration card, controls his movement from place to place, dictates the education of his children and the job and training they will ultimately receive, and conducts his press and radio services. It has mishandled his country's economy, wasted his assets, cut him off from his natural trading partners, deprived him of foreign investment, and embarked him upon ill-devised plans that continue to devalue his latest efforts. And it has left him no opportunity to complain: opposition can so easily lead to loss of house, or job, or food, even family or all of these state-controlled factors. Castro permits malcontents to leave; the five-year waiting list to do so is the measure of the discontent he has provoked.

Nevertheless such criticism, which comes easily to those whose standpoint derives from the different conditions of the West, with conventional political attitudes far removed from the total state allegiance demanded by Castro's Cuba, over-looks real achievements and considerable popular enthusiasm. There are certainly grounds for misgiving. Few Westerners would relish the regimentation and dependence of the Cuban citizen. And there has been in Cuba as well that all too common tendency for the bureaucratic machine to grow until it dwarfs the individual and acquires an inhuman momentum of its own, only mitigated in this instance by the prevalent Caribbean inefficiency. There are terrible shortages, there is widespread rationing, there have been planning blunders and wastage. But there is also a real sense of equality, of sharing in a difficult but worthwhile task. And the fruits of an education designed to integrate the individual into society and to redirect his energies away from personal gain towards the common good have not had a chance to mature and so cannot yet be condemned out of hand. Cuban communism is more of an enthusiasm than a creed: a means of perpetuating that sense of solidarity and purpose that seems to appear in other societies only in times of war or crisis (it is of course true that Cuba has been in a crisis situation for over a decade now and it might be wondered just how long its people can preserve their effort). The Revolution has released a wealth of talent that must otherwise have been wasted; it has harnessed the hopes of the young that they can change the world by their own efforts.

The Cuban population, now fully literate, is healthier and better educated than ever before and its government, for all its faults, can still be described by a far from ideologically sympathetic journalist as the 'fairest and most humane in Latin America'.[49] Cuba may be drab, austere, inefficient; it also eschews racial prejudice and commercialism. It may have no institutions of popular government, but Castro's personal magnetism continues to inspire much support, and the revolution continues to develop.

1970 provides sufficient example of this. Above all, 1970 was characterised for Cubans by the immense effort to achieve a sugar harvest of ten million tons. 'TEN MILLION' was blazoned on hoardings, in the press, on television, over the air; squads of cutters were mobilised not only from all over Cuba but from friendly powers throughout the world, even the foreign ambassadors and their missions joining in token sessions in the field. The total·harvested was hailed as it mounted, individual achievements applauded. Revolutionary honour and national economy alike were made to depend on raising the magic total, and no effort was spared. Then, on 26 July, Castro addressed a huge rally to admit failure. The target had not been reached. The shortfall was some 15%, representing a notable increase, in fact, but nevertheless constituting a shortfall. Having centralised the government in his own hands, having devoted the nation's resources to this major project, both to win economic progress and to rejuvenate political confidence, Castro could only blame himself. And he did so, squarely. He recognised, perhaps for the first time, that the task he had set himself was beyond reason, was overcentralised and impossible; and he admitted that the Cuban people were entitled to share the formulation as well as the implementation of the Cuban dream. He admitted his own mistakes, and accepted that there had been planning errors. And he promised change. Cuban socialism would henceforward be based upon democratic institutions, and institutions, moreover, from which the revolutionary party would remain distinct. It will be difficult henceforward to delay such action and still preserve wide national support.

In ten years, Castro has taken a relatively poor and backward nation by the scruff of the neck and shaken it into new and radically different patterns of life. Using his powerful personality and magnetic oratory, and centralising all decisions upon himself, Castro has turned a downtrodden exploited people into a self-aware nation seeking salvation through socialism. He has not succeeded in his vision, nor yet has he failed. For Cuba the issue remains in doubt. The Cuban people may build a Cuban form of socialism capable of expanded production and of an equitable distribution of wealth; a new Cuban personality may emerge free from self-interest, fulfilled in work, satisfied in social achievement. Or mistakes and hardships may breed their own despair; the glamour of the revolution may fade and the Cuban attempt may sink into the squalor of intrigue and factionalism.

Succeed or fail, however, the attempt retains relevance for the wider world. If it succeeds, then there will be lessons of more than local validity. If it fails, then its failure must be analysed; again the lessons should be of general interest. Only ignorance of the attempt and carelessness as to its outcome are inexcusable in a world so much in need of inspiration and example.

United Republic of Tanzania
Cuba is preoccupied with development: development more or less from scratch, through self-help and from a position of dignity based upon independence. So, in the very different context of East Africa, is Tanzania. And just as Cuba owes its present course largely to the efforts of one man, so does Tanzania owe an immeasurable debt to its national leader; a man very different from Castro but one equally central to his nation's progress: Julius K. Nyerere.

It was Nyerere who led mainland Tanganyika from dependent colonial status into independent nationhood. It is he who has continued to initiate and direct policy since independence, stressing all the while that independence is but the first step

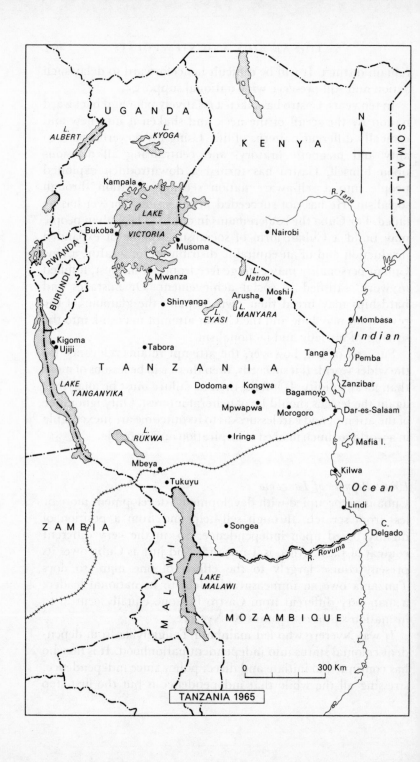

TANZANIA 1965

in the realisation of freedom, that immense effort is still required to win a struggle more important than that first one against the alien regime: the new struggle to fight 'poverty, ignorance, and disease' and to achieve national unity, political integration and economic development...to build a society both socialistic and democratic'.[50] In the working out of his own political philosophy, directed to the particular circumstances of his people, and in the practical development of Tanzania, politically, socially and economically, Nyerere has made a unique and valuable contribution that deserves wide notice and encouragement.

Tanganyika, former German colony and British Mandated Territory since World War One, with a land area of 341,150 sq. miles and, in 1967, a population of 12 million, attained independence, after peaceful development, on 9 December 1961. In 1964, after a revolution had occurred in Zanzibar, Tanganyika united with that small island (population 300,000) to form the United Republic of Tanzania, with Nyerere as President. It is mainland Tanganyika, however, that forms the basis of this discussion, Zanzibar for the moment retaining a somewhat distinct identity.

In working for independence, Nyerere had forged an effective political weapon, the Tanganyika African National Union (TANU), and it was this party which assumed the responsibilities of self-government shortly before independence and which took over the complete administration of the country in December 1961. Since that date Tanganyika's story has been the story of Nyerere and of TANU. President and Party have worked out together the development plans for the country and the means of implementing them. They have sought to maintain independence through reliance on self-help, to promote development through co-operative effort and to raise the level of skill and understanding through the adaptation of education to fit the immediate needs of the community. Faced with a largely rural, undeveloped land, they have placed emphasis on agriculture rather than industry, upon the countryside rather than the city; confronted with a largely backward population they have perforce concentrated on supplying leadership from the centre and recommending solutions from above, but they have not ignored the need for popular participation in government and, building upon deep-rooted African traditions of local assembly and debate, they have constructed political representation on genuinely democratic processes. Partly through foresight, partly through trial and error, the young nation has developed both a serviceable political machine and an economic programme based upon careful planning of scarce resources. Together these are directed to the basic needs of a society in transition. It is too early to be confident of Tanzanian success. It is not too early to be excited about Tanzanian determination to succeed.

Nyerere's major decision as President has been to opt for a One Party Democracy, a decision in favour of TANU as the only vehicle of political expression, serving as the focus of national endeavour and aiming at national consensus rather than the furtherance of particular interests. Such a vehicle can only succeed, however, if, to change the analogy to one of Nyerere's own, it 'acts like a two-way all-weather road along which purposes plans and problems of the Government can travel to the people at the same time as the ideas, desires and misunderstandings of the people can travel direct to the Government'. But here the difficulty is acute. For the problem remains how to guide an unsophisticated peasant nation along the right development lines without riding roughshod over local opinion and without building up an insensitive, ruling elite drawn from party into administration and government. One answer has been to stress the qualities of leadership needed by the better-educated few, and to insist upon the interdependence of all members of the community at local as well as national level. TANU must lead by example, must seek no special privilege, must strive continuously to raise the level of the people's life. TANU members, it was decided after independence, must adhere to a rigorous code:

1. All men are my brothers and Africa is one.
2. I will serve my country and all its people.
3. I will take every opportunity to help myself overcome poverty, ignorance, disease and injustice.

4. Bribery is the enemy of justice; I will never receive or offer a bribe.
5. Leadership is a trust; I will not exploit my position or the position of another for personal advantage.
6. I will educate myself to the extent that I am able and use my knowledge for the benefit of all.
7. I will co-operate with all my fellows to build our country.
8. I will always be truthful and abstain from promoting discord.
9. I will be a trustworthy member of TANU and a loyal citizen of Tanganyika and Africa.[51]

It is not pretended that TANU members have never fallen below such idealism in practice. But the President has been vigilant and the Party determined. By 1967 TANU had refined its principles in the light of experience and with more precise regard to the needs of the nation. At its meeting at Arusha in January 1967 it adopted policies of socialism and self-reliance and resolved upon a standard of personal and governmental behaviour, since enshrined as the Arusha Declaration (5 February 1967). Both policies and resolution merit examination. They were preceeded by the following statement of beliefs and aims:

a) That all human beings are equal;
b) That every individual has a right to dignity and respect;
c) That every citizen is an integral part of the Nation and has the right to take an equal part in Government at local, regional and national level;
d) That every citizen has the right to freedom of expression, of movement, of religious belief and of association within the context of the law;
e) That every individual has the right to receive from society protection of his life and of property held according to law;
f) That every individual has the right to receive a just return for his labour;
g) That all citizens together possess all the natural resources of the country in trust for their descendants;
h) That in order to ensure economic justice the State must have effective control over the principal means of production; and

i)   That it is the responsibility of the State to intervene actively in the economic life of the Nation so as to ensure the well-being of all citizens and so as to prevent the exploitation of one person by another or one group by another, and so as to prevent the accumulation of wealth to an extent which is inconsistent with the existence of a classless society.

Now, therefore, the principal aims and objects of TANU shall be as follows:

a)   To consolidate and maintain the independence of this country and the freedom of its people;

b)   To safeguard the inherent dignity of the individual in accordance with the Universal Declaration of Human Rights;

c)   To ensure that this country shall be governed by a democratic socialist government of the people;

d)   To co-operate with all political parties in Africa engaged in the liberation of all Africa;

e)   To see that the Government mobilises all the resources of this country towards the elimination of poverty, ignorance and disease;

f)   To see that the Government actively assists in the formation and maintenance of co-operative organisations;

g)   To see that wherever possible the Government itself directly participates in the economic development of this country;

h)   To see that the Government gives equal opportunity to all men and women irrespective of race, religion or status;

i)   To see that the Government eradicates all types of exploitation, intimidation, discrimination, bribery and corruption;

j)   To see that the Government exercises effective control over the principal means of production and pursues policies which facilitate the way to collective ownership of the resources of this country;

k)   To see that the Government co-operates with other States in Africa in bringing about African Unity;

l)   To see that the Government works tirelessly towards world peace and security through the United Nations.

In the policy statement that follows this section of the official record, careful attention is given to a definition of socialism and democracy, and then the meaning and application of self-reliance in Tanzania is spelled out. It states firmly that Tanzania is at war: that the enemy is poverty and oppression; that the weapon for victory is not money but hard work, that is, the labour of the people, co-operatively given in a planned, nationwide programme of development. External aid may be welcome at times but it can never be sufficient and may often carry strings that endanger independence. 'Independence means self-reliance' and self-reliance in Tanzania means rural development first, an increase in agricultural production to provide more food and the money for other needs.

Again and again it stresses hard work as the prerequisite for development: 'we know what is the foundation and what is the fruit of development; between MONEY and PEOPLE it is obvious that the foundation is the people and their HARD WORK, especially in Agriculture. This is the meaning of self-reliance.' Therefore the document emphasises the following priorities and proceeds to expand upon them:

a) The Land and Agriculture,
b) The People,
c) The policy of Socialism and Self-reliance, and
d) Good leadership.

The obligation to work and pay one's way, to develop one's capacities, to seek education and to apply learning for the common good are made clear. TANU will lead the way. And from the top downwards TANU will inspire by example. Thus the National Executive Committee resolved:

1. Every TANU or Government leader must be either a Peasant or a Worker, and should in no way be associated with the pratices of Capitalism or Feudalism.
2. No TANU or Government leader should hold shares in any Company.
3. No TANU or Government leader should hold Directorships in any privately-owned enterprises.
4. No TANU or Government leaders should receive two or more salaries.
5. No TANU or Government leaders should own houses which he rents to others.

6. For the purposes of this Resolution the term 'leader' should comprise the following: Members of the TANU Nation Executive Committee; Ministers, Members of Parliament, Senior Officials of Organisations affiliated to TANU, Senior Officials of Para-Statal Organisations, all those appointed or elected under any clause of the TANU Constitution, Councillors and Civil Servants in high and middle cadres.
(In this context 'leader' means a man, or a man and his wife, a woman or a woman and her husband)[52]

In this manner TANU laid down the broad lines of a commitment to socialism based upon human equality and public ownership; to self-reliance based upon personal labour, with emphasis on the rural community; and to a high standard of personal behaviour in leadership. Further statements drawn up by President Nyerere have amplified the spirit of dedication to development here displayed. In the fields of both education and development-planning, Nyerere (his title *Mwalimu* – The Teacher – is easily explained) has tackled what are universal problems in a manner particularly relevant to the circumstances of his own people.

Having subjected the system of education left behind by the departing imperial power to close analysis, Nyerere found it necessary to redefine the proper role of education in a primitive peasant country. Education, he concluded, must be much more closely related to the needs of the community, much more utilitarian in equipping the individual for his future place in society. There must indeed be provision for producing skilled technicians and professionally qualified personnel, but for the bulk of the population rural techniques are what matter most, along with an ethic of social commitment. Broadly, education should aim to equip each citizen with 'an enquiring mind; and ability to learn from what others do, and reject or adapt it to his own needs; and a basic confidence in his own position as a free and equal member of the society, who values others and is valued by them for what he does and not for what he obtains'. Education must be interspersed with local improvement schemes and each school must, as far as possible, incorporate farm production sufficient to meet the needs of the school itself. Education must reflect the socialist aims of the nation and encourage social qualities and the knowledge of the mutual interdependence of the members of society. Planning and participation in decision-making must be experienced (here the advantage of having a farming enterprise associated with each school is further emphasised). And for those who have the capacity to travel beyond a reconstituted primary system the same assumptions apply: 'Further education for a selected few must be education for service to the many. There can be no other justification for taxing the many to give education to only a few'.[53]

Development too has received the President's personal touch:

> Development brings freedom, provided it is development of people. But people cannot be developed; they can only develop themselves. For while it is possible for an outsider to build a man's house, an outsider cannot give the man pride and self-confidence in himself as a human being. Those things a man has to create in himself by his own actions. He develops himself by what he does; he develops himself by making his own decisions, by increasing his own knowledge and ability, and by his own full participation – as an equal – in the life of the community he lives in. Thus, for example, a man is developing himself when he grows, or earns enough to provide decent conditions for himself and his family; he is not being developed if someone gives him these things. A man is developing himself when he improves his education – whatever he learns about; he is not being developed if he simply carries out orders from someone better educated than himself without understanding why those orders have been given. A man develops himself by joining in the subsequent decision; he is not being developed if he is herded like an animal into the new venture. Development of a man can, in fact, only be effected by that man: development of the people can only be effected by the people.[54]

And there is no denying that the problems of development facing the people of Tanzania are manifold. The primitive state of the economy, the enormous difficulties in spreading modern knowledge and in raising the quality of life become immediately apparent upon reading the opening chapter of

Arthur Hopcraft's *Born to hunger* (mentioned already above).
There the effects of malnutrition, superstition and ignorance of
elementary hygiene are described, along with the heroic efforts
being made to combat them. A start has had to be made from
virtually nothing, and already much has been achieved.

Already there has been an impressive growth of *ujamaa*
villages, where collective farming and the introduction of
modern techniques and amenities have been combined. *Ujamaa*,
meaning 'familyhood', stresses the basic socialism as well as
the self-reliance of Tanzanian development and the pioneer
village of Mbambara has already begun to attract international
attention as well as to win domestic emulation. The government is reluctant to impose solutions, but the second five-year
plan for development (1969–74) includes provision for the
spreading of *ujamaa* villages through educational and financial
incentives, in the belief that they provide the key to advancement in terms both of social consciousness and material progress. The National Development Plan, affecting every sector
of the economy, continues in its second five year period to lay
emphasis on rural development, though particular attention
is also paid to industry (the major enterprises have been
nationalised), communications, education, health and
tourism.

Political development has also proceeded impressively, the
acid test of One Party Democracy coming in 1965 when TANU
faced its first post-independence National Elections. Already
the administrative structure of the country had been reorgan-
ised, with administrative personnel being appointed on merit,
and chiefly authority being phased out. Already it had been
established that national unity could best be served by the
proscription of parties other than TANU. Already, it has to be
admitted, bureaucracy and some TANU impatience with
popular wishes had begun to cramp local initiative and undermine democratic expression, particularly as local election
candidates were being pre-selected by TANU and could not
be opposed. Now, however, it was decided that in each constituency there would be a genuine contest between *two* selected TANU candidates. And even in the eyes of some sceptical

observers, the results of this election converted the theory of One Party Democracy into practical reality. With honesty and impartiality the official machine responded to local preference to the extent of dismissing three-quarters of the incumbent members of parliament, including Cabinet Ministers. The election is proof at least to Andrew Maguire, who concluded his study of Tanzania with this event, that 'Tanzanian voters may already count themselves among those few electorates of the world who truly have a choice'. Confidence can also be placed in Maguire's further comment: 'That the choice is theirs, and that they have exercised it fully, are impressive achievements for the Tanzanian nation'. And it can also be observed that the November 1970 National Elections have provided additional evidence of a genuinely democratic procedure at work.

In its democratic emphasis, Tanzania might seem to resemble more an African Yugoslavia-in-the-making than an African counterpart to Cuba. But comparisons of this sort are probably not helpful. Tanzania is simply the most successful and dedicated African exponent of development based upon a mixture of traditional virtues and modern techniques in the face of widespread ignorance and poverty. Like its neighbour Zambia, under the inspiration of Kenneth Kaunda, and like the early Convention Peoples Party of Ghana, under Nkrumah, Tanzania stresses hard work and co-operative effort. Its peculiar advantages lie in an absence of tribal divisiveness, in the blessing of a local *lingua franca*, Swahili, and above all in the personal qualities of *Mwalimu* Julius Nyerere.

For it is the gifted Nyerere who has chivvied and prodded and coaxed and guided Tanzania along lines of advance that have both stressed humanity and ensured stability. Fair treatment, honest administration, dignity and purpose have distinguished his leadership, and he has tried to make these the hallmarks of leadership at all levels of his administration. He has sought to harness education to the development alike of individual and nation; he has sought to make impossible all forms of exploitation, whether of one individual by another, or one group by another, or of the countryside by the town; he has sought to foster national unity through pride of achievement in common endeavour.

It is, of course, too early to pass judgement; but at least one experienced observer is prepared to comment and prophesy:

> President Julius Nyrere is the only African Head of State who has evolved a political system based on African Traditions. ... it seems likely that he will succeed in carrying out his full programme; and if he does the egalitarian Tanzanian nation which he will have created cannot fail, by its example, to influence, not only other states in the African continent, but also developing countries in other parts of the world.[55]

NOTES

[1]President Nixon, State of the Union Address, 22 January 1970.

[2]President Nixon, Inaugural Address, 20 January 1969.

[3]President Johnson, Inaugural Address, 20 January 1965.

[4]President Johnson, address to Congress, 15 March 1965.

[5]President Johnson, State of the Union Address, 4 January 1965.

[6]President Johnson's speech at University of Michigan, 22 May 1964. Reprinted with Walter Lipmann's comment, and other speeches in '*The Great Society – a plan*' (U.S.I.S., American Embassy, London, 1965).

[7]Martin Luther King, *Chaos or Community* (Penguin, 1969), p. 27.

[8]Eldridge Cleaver in an interview given to *Playboy* and reprinted in *New Statesman*, Vol. 80, No. 2054, 31 July 1970.

[9]See Martin Luther King, *op. cit.*, pp. 15–16.

[10]Hyman Bookbinder, Assistant Director, U.S. Office of Economic Opportunity, 29 December 1966. Quoted by Martin Luther King, *op. cit.*, p. 15.

[11]*Essentials of Scial Security in the United States* (U.S.I.S. London), p. 2.

[12]See A. Werth, *Russia Hopes & Fears* (Penguin, 1969), p. 52.

[13]P. Sormani, quoted in A. Werth, *op. cit.*, p. 217.

[14]I. Deutscher, *op. cit.*, p. 91.

[15]Quoted in A. Koestler, *Darkness at Noon* (Penguin, 1965

edition), p. 81. Pages 81–4 add some powerful additional arguments.

[16]See Leonard Barnes, *African Renaissance* (Gollancz, 1969), Appendix D. This is a summary of the Chinese Commune based on R. Dumont, *Chine Surpeuplée* (Paris, 1965).

[17]*Ibid.*, p. 288.

[18]This and following quotations are taken from the 'Report of the Ninth National Congress of the Communist Party of China' (1 April 1969), printed in *China Reconstructs*, Vol. XVIII, No. 7 (July 1969), pp. 16–17.

[19]*Ibid.*, p. 25. This is the best expressed passage in the *Report*. Respect for Chinese efforts to improve the lot of mankind is not easy to sustain beyond a page or two of Chinese polemic in the English language.

[20]*Ibid.*, p. 12.

[21]I. Alexandrov in *Pravada*, 16 August 1967. Quoted in A. Werth, *op cit.*, p. 274.

[22]Stuart R. Schram, *The Political Thought of Mao Tse-tung* (Penguin, 1969), pp. 143–4.

[23]N. G. Jog, *Understanding India* (Indian Ministry of Information, Coimbatore, 1966), p. 38.

[24]*Ibid.*, pp. 38–39.

[25]Mrs. Indira Gandhi, Address to UNO, 14 August 1968. See *India 1968* (Information Service of India, 1968), p. 11.

[26]C. S. Jha, 'Non-alignment for a Changing World', a paper read at the International Diplomatic Seminar at Salzburg on 8 August 1967.

[27]Raghavan Iyer, 'The Indian Personality' in Guy Wint (ed.), *Asian Handbook* (Penguin, 1969), pp. 551–2.

[28]Jawaharlal Nehru, *India Today & Tomorrow* (Azad Memorial Lectures, 1959, published by the Indian Council for Cultural Relations, New Delhi), pp. 28–9.

[29]Takeo Miki, *Japan's Foreign Policy*, Speech to Australian National University, 29 July 1968 (Japan Reference Series, No. 8–68, Ministry of Foreign Affairs, Japan), pp. 8–9.

[30]Ardath W. Burks, *The Government of Japan* (methuen, 1966), p. 174. This 'University Paperback' provides a good account of the whole operation of Japanese government.

[31] Eisaku Sato, in *New Tasks for Japan* (Japan reference series, No. 3–69), p. 10.

[32] *Japan Information Bulletin*, XVI, No. 17 (1 September 1969), p. 134.

[33] Eisaku Sato, *op cit.*, pp. 6–7.

[34] *Ibid.*, pp. 12–13.

[35] Kiichi Aichi, *The Search for National Security* (Japan Reference Series, No. 4–69), p. 4.

[36] Samuel H. Beer, *Modern British Politics* (Faber, 1965), p. ix.

[37] Charles Owen, *The Opaque Society* (Allen & Unwin, 1969), p. 111. This stimulating enquiry into the views of young Britons about their country asks many pertinent questions worthy of further discussion and debate.

[38] T. A. Neal, *Democracy and Responsibility: British History 1880–1965* (Macmillan, 1969). See Chapter 26 & Epilogue.

[39] J. D. B. Miller, *The Commonwealth in the World* (Duckworth, 1958), p. 271.

[40] Dean Acheson, 5 December 1962.

[41] D. Bilandzic, 'Some Aspects of the Yugoslav System of Self-government and Worker Management' in *Studies*, No. 28 (Belgrade, 1968), p. 12.

[42] *Ibid.*, p. 16.

[43] *Ibid.*, p. 21.

[44] Erich Heinemann, 'The Economic Machinery' in Harrison Salisbury (ed.), *op. cit.*, p. 67.

[45] Neville Brown, *A History of the World in the Twentieth Century* (*pt. 3: 1945–68*), p. 131.

[46] D. Bilandzic, *op. cit.*, p. 34.

[47] Ware, *op. cit.*, ii, p. 710.

[48] Andrew Sinclair, *Guevara* (Fontana, 1970), p. 58.

[49] J. Horgan, 'Cuba To-day' in *Irish Times*, 24–30 May 1969.

[50] G. Andrew Maguire, *Toward 'Uhuru' in Tanzania* (O.U.P., 1969), p. 16.

[51] *Ibid.*, p. 321 (quoted from TANU official sources).

[52] From *The Arusha Declaration*, 5 February 1967. (This can be found in the *Third World File*, published by Third World First, Britwell Salome, Oxfordshire, England.)

[53] Julius K. Nyerere, *Education for Self-reliance* (Dar es Salaam, March 1967).
[54] Julius Kl Nyerere, *Freedom and Development*, quoted in *The Peoples Plan for Progress (Second Five-year-plan, 1969–74)*, (Dar es Salaam, 1969), p. 5.
[55] Judith Listowel, 'Tanzania and Her Future' in *Round Table*, No. 239 (July 1970), p. 275.

CHAPTER SIX
The Challenge of Co-operation

Our one world, richly endowed with national diversity, poorly equipped for international unity, must of necessity learn to strengthen those organs of co-operation that already exist and create a new and better frame-work for the husbanding and utilisation of its patently limited resources. The year 1970, twenty-fifth anniversary of the founding of the United Nations, and European Conservation Year, seems a suitable moment in time to survey those areas of co-operation which best illustrate hope for the future.

There are, of course, many fields where international co-operation is well-established and where there is a long history of fruitful collaboration, and this is as true in the cultural as in the political sphere. Natural Science, for example, has traditionally shared its discoveries, and even if to-day ideological barriers have closed off whole areas of research and experiment, still there remains a degree of information exchange and multilateral endeavour that is impressive; and the enormous and often unpredictable impact of technology, the application of science, has been felt powerfully the world over, serving not only to destroy distance but also to undermine difference. In religion there has been a notable movement away from exclusiveness towards ecumenism, and towards respect and understanding of others; in the visual arts, national boundaries have long proved to have no relevance, forms of expression commanding interest internationally. All these fields deserve more than the mere glance that space allows here. Then there are examples of merging sovereignties, such as that proposed by the European Economic Community, and of international associations, such as the Commonwealth; as well as the United Nations Organisation itself, not yet worldwide in membership, not yet given committed support even by those who belong, but still representing the highest expression of our world-consciousness; these too must be considered in a closing chapter which sees co-operation on a world scale not only as an exciting challenge but as a last chance for survival.

THE CULTURAL CONTEXT

The course of the twentieth century has been characterised above all else by the scientific and technological revolutions which have transformed both man's thinking and his living. The revolutionary changes took place early in the century: their effect has been cumulative ever since, the past twenty-five years seeing an acceleration particularly in technological innovation. And this innovation has been ever more social in its consequences as more and more the pattern of work and leisure has been altered and the traditional values of society have been brought into question.

Scientific discovery had moved with snowballing momentum throughout the eighteenth and nineteenth centuries; moving with confidence and certainty as it revealed natural laws and explained the intricate working of the material world. The twentieth century dawned to new, fundamentally new, discoveries. In the physical sciences, for example, the supposedly indivisible atom was found to have structure and parts, subsequently the electron, proton and neutron being identified; the absolute nature of space and time, according to the Newtonian system, was also questioned, then disproved by the youthful Einstein, in 1905, in his Special Theory of Relativity,[1] relating not only to space and time but to mass and energy; Max Planck's quantum theory, enunciated in 1899, allowed Einstein and Max Born in the next three decades to alter the accepted view of another aspect of energy, its structure. In mathematics, statistical reasoning provided a highly developed tool for making judgements of probability; geometry, topology, differential calculus were extended, while new insights into whole numbers led Whitehead and Russell to alter many previously accepted assumptions. In biology, Mendel's late-nineteenth century experiments in plant-breeding provided the clue to the modern understanding of heredity, based on the knowledge of genes, while in 1900, Hugo de Vries introduced the fact of mutation; research into the nature of living matter launched the twentieth century science of biochemistry; cells, chromosomes, viruses and nucleoproteins in turn yielded their secrets and sparked off new enquiry.

The material world proved to be not so certain, not so unvarying in its laws and therefore so predictable, as had been assumed. The major developments of earlier theories and these major new insights took science forward in new directions, progressively altering human attitudes as well as human circumstances. The way in which they did so has been summarised succinctly by Professor J. Bronowski[2]:

> In place of the quantitative principle, the scientist of the twentieth century thought of himself as pursuing a concept of structure. In place of the principle of continuity, the scientist recognized that the underlying structure of the small-scale world is discontinuous. In place of the principle of determinism or cause and effect, he recognized that the smallest units of matter and energy follow laws which can only be described by probabilities and whose predictions are therefore always surrounded by an area of uncertainty. In place of the impersonality of science came an understanding that the operations of the scientist enter inextricably into his findings. These were revolutionary changes in the outlook of science, and they make it appropriate to speak of a second scientific revolution.
>
> The total effect of the new outlook was to overthrow the stark and mechanical image of the scientist serving an inhuman truth, remote from the everyday world, which the nineteenth century set up. Its place was taken by a richer image in which the scientist saw himself as carrying out an essentially human and personal activity, from which he must create an order, an understanding of the world by the projection of his own mind.

This was the most subtle change which took place in the view of science and all of knowledge. The twentieth century broke with the view that knowledge is passive, that it accumulates the facts that nature provides like a card index, and that the scientist need do nothing more than keep the index accurate and tidy. Instead it saw knowledge as a constant activity.

Professor Bronowski has also noted the impact of the scientific outlook upon daily life:

A scientific outlook did come to penetrate into the daily life of the time and some of the new scientific concepts, at times diluted or distorted, became part of current thought. In areas where the scientific point of view was accepted – and these were constantly growing, both geographically as more people came in contact with modern techniques and in wider areas of daily life – people came to respect facts and to approach them rationally and empirically. This was particularly noteworthy not only in practical matters relating to industry or travel but in the field of health where new knowledge supplanted traditional practices at a strikingly rapid rate.

Perhaps the most significant evidence of the extent to which science had entered the outlook of the twentieth century was the acceptance of change as a continuous and fundamental phenomenon, and adaptation to its accelerating pace. Not only was this true of the western countries where the expectation of change had become a well-established attitude. In the historically more static societies of the East, where change had been looked upon as defection from eternally established norms, it became the order of the day.

Equally fundamental was the concept of new potentialities which science brought and the public accepted. All over the world people who for centuries had taken poverty and disease for granted saw in the methods and the fruits of science a new possibility of human fulfilment. In the first half of the twentieth century this vision altered the outlook of mankind.

Specific concepts from the new science were incorporated into attitudes and thought. Chief among these was the idea of relativity. Though often enough misunderstood, the idea of relativity as a revolutionary concept in physics impressed on moralists, artists and the man in the street the notion that, from other points of view, reality may appear different, and yet be as valid as that which they themselves perceive.

The concept of uncertainty also entered the popular mind and many people learned to think statistically in terms of chance and probability rather than in terms of the certainty of direct cause and effect. Concepts derived from psychological studies of learning and conditioning and Freudian analysis of personality formation entered into the lore associated with the rearing of children. The scientist's sense that the observer is inevitably a part of that which he observes was reflected in the inner perspective of the modern writer. And the fact that physics became concerned with atomic structure also influenced painters and sculptors to portray what they saw as discontinuous structure rather than as surface appearance.

In the swiftly changing world of the twentieth century science was thus an ever-growing force, constantly yielding new facts and new capabilities which brought changes in structures, activities and relationships, often before it had developed the means to deal with the results of such changes.

Looking merely at the post-war world, scientific discovery can be seen to have resulted in remarkable technological innovation and to have led to highly important biological advances, perhaps not all to be welcomed. This is not the place to review new developments, to point to individual extensions of the technological or biological frontiers or to assess their relative importance for the future. Here, concern must be with the cumulative total effect of such changes. Each one may have been pursued with brilliance, but taken all together they have created a new world, with neither plan nor direction, that has, almost without being noticed, rendered many traditional values and practices obsolete. Considered separately, the perfection of computerised, automated machinery, the revolution in tele-communications, the creation of new and wonderful materials, the extension of mass production, mass consumption and mass urban living, may be impressive; the mastery of new techniques to control disease, replace defective human parts, prevent ageing, or conduct genetic engineering may command admiration and respect. Considered collectively they may engender a profound disquiet. As Professor Bronowski has observed, the changes they have produced individually have sometimes preceded the means to cope with them. The changes they have wrought collectively have multiplied the problems of coping. The mass production of the motor car, for example, facilitated personal mobility enormously; it has also produced choked road systems in the advanced countries, while attempts to build express services to meet motoring demands threaten themselves to destroy city life and pedestrian movement; and the poisonous by-products of combustion pollute animal and vegetable life alike. Locally, nationally, even internationally, men try to cope with specific ills, try to adjust to specific benefits. All are so busy with the 'trees' of technology that they remain unconscious of the vast new 'forest' that has changed the face of their world.

This phenomenon has been well described by Michael Harrington whose book, *The Accidental Century*[3], is so titled to emphasise the unplanned totality composed of the many individual advances of our time. We have arrived where we are by accident and, what is worse, we are unconscious that we are in a new world. It is the lack of consciousness that Harrington attacks. We have some hope if we realise our predicament, none if we do not. Harrington's most precise illustration of the point is the megalopolis; that continuous urban sprawl that has invaded the highly populated centres of production in the developed world. The megalopolis has revolutionised the lives of those who dwell within it. Its technical culture, its automobile, its endless extent, have created the affluent teenager, rearranged the structure of family life, cut off man from nature and from escape from himself; it has helped produce 'purposeless materialism, congestion and insensate disorder.'[4] And it has grown piece-meal without direction. Its revolution has been 'without conscious revolutionists'.[5] And this is symptomatic of the technological revolution as a whole:

Each new invention, like the automobile, television, nuclear power, space rockets, was a triumph of the human intelligence. But the totality of these innovations, with all of their revolutionary consequences, was an increasingly puzzling, even mysterious, society. As the parts became more ingenious and minutely calibrated, the whole became more irrational to those who had unwittingly fabricated it.... Technological progress was achieved by a radical method of breaking life up into specific functions which could be measured and engineered. In such a sub-divided existence there was no vantage point for the comprehension of the whole. Bureaucratic, scientific man was losing his intellectual hold on reality even as he pragmatically conquered it.[6]

The paradox of this situation in the light of past endeavour is striking. Whereas the 'conscious revolutionist of the past' proposed visions which outstripped reality, the 'unconscious revolutionists of the present create realities which outstrip their vision'.[7]

Harrington is concerned to show how 'technological ingenuity is now subverting Western economic, political, and social assumptions'.[8] How abundance and leisure, for example, is playing havoc with an ethic based upon scarcity and hard work. More specifically, he would endorse the criticisms of capitalism, voiced in chapter four above, asserting that 'practically every ethical, moral, and cultural justification for the capitalist system has now been destroyed by capitalism. The idyll of the free market, risk-taking, inventiveness, the social virtue of making money, all these have been abolished by the very success of capitalism itself.'[9] In recommending a socialist alternative he is clear that technology will continue to reshape man's environment. He simply asks us to view this re-shaping with our eyes open, co-operating together to become its master not its servant. For 'either Western man is going to choose a new society – or a new society will choose, and abolish, him'.[10]

More 'unconscious', accidental revolution will lead us to that technically brilliant, humanly barren world so gloomily predicted by Huxley and Orwell; or to overpopulation, or pollution, or holocaust – the other possibilities open to us. Harrington here reinforces the necessity of a world view; for a world problem demands a world response. Scientists themselves have not been slow to urge co-ordination on a similar scale. Some scientists have a vested interest: oceanologists, and meteorologists, for example, can only conduct their researches on a global basis. But they provide only more vivid examples of a general truth applicable to all scientists as to all men. It is therefore something of an encouragement to witness not only the deliberations of so many international professional scientific bodies, but the voluntary assumption of watchdog responsibilities by such as the members of the Pugwash movement (founded in 1957 to face up to the possibility of nuclear war, and gaining its name from the venue of its first meeting, Pugwash, in Nova Scotia). Science, it has even been admitted by one outstanding scientist, 'has become too important to be left to scientists, or politicians'.[11] All men must take a hand in its management, for only then can they ensure that it is properly directed towards the defeat of war and famine and the promotion of human welfare. Once again, awareness of the issue is the prerequisite starting point to remedial action.

Following upon the huge growth in material technology – with its associated ills and blessings – the twentieth century has witnessed also great advances in social technology, stimulated as often as not by the changes which material technology has wrought. Developments in the social sciences have been comparable, in fact, to those in the natural sciences.

At the beginning of the twentieth century, scientific method had scarcely begun to be applied to human behaviour. The 'behavioural' sciences were in their infancy. The pace of technical change, the extent of industrial and urban growth, and the dislocations of major wars combined to promote interest and development in the new disciplines. The social sciences offered at least some assistance in dealing with overcrowded living conditions, migration of peoples, economic crises and concomitant stresses in social living which brought new dimensions to such problems as delinquency, crime and mental illness.

Economics, political science, psychology, anthropology, sociology and history were all developed at least in part as separate disciplines with distinct social purpose and relying upon new statistical techniques of investigation and the marshalling of evidence. Advances were made in all these fields in the years prior to the Second World War, and each discipline responded to developments in the others. The early years of the century were particularly noted for the new insights of such distinguished thinkers as Emile Durkheim, Max Weber, Franz Boas and Sigmund Freud, while the inter-war period was distinguished by the absorption and spread of the new knowledge.

The period of the Second World War and after saw a quite remarkable expansion in the social sciences, in response to the demands of war, Cold War, increasing population and the urgent needs of such things as economic development and welfare state management. Unequal in extent and pace, this expansion has nevertheless been worldwide in operation, responding to problems equally worldwide, however unevenly concentrated. Psychologists have pursued their enquiries into personality development and thought processes, with direct benefit to the education of the young and the rehabilitation of the casualties of modern life; anthropologists have subjected to analysis advanced as well as primitive societies; political scientists have investigated the principles of domestic adminis-tration and international order; economists have studied the urgent task of maintaining a high level, expanding, stable economic system and have introduced sophisticated fiscal and monetary techniques; teams from many disciplines have co-ordinated their skills in the investigation of specific societies or problems, and interdisciplinary studies have proliferated as individuals within separate specialisms have followed their researches into neighbouring disciplines or have responded simply to the need to link distinct if neighbouring fields. Not yet universally acclaimed, social scientists by the middle of the century had at least made an impact upon the increasingly complex and demonstrably 'single' world in which all men now live: 'they had established, and gained widespread though not universal acceptance for, the idea that "the behaviour of man, like the behaviour of materials, is characterized by certain uniformities and patterns that can be studied systematically".'[12]

Equally, in the sphere of literature and the arts, men responded to the upheavals of war, and the impact of technology and mass education which helped to break down the distance between nations and the barriers between cultures. Reacting to the profound, fast-moving and worldwide social changes, literary and artistic pioneers sought with renewed intensity a meaning to life, an explanation of man's nature, a revaluation of society. They expressed themselves in a wide variety of forms, often quite revolutionary in their break from the past, particularly in Europe. Yet, although 'expression remained infinitely varied in terms of the multitude of languages and of visual and musical idioms which embodied the world's manifold cultures, and of the individuality of the creative artist', nevertheless it is true also that 'by mid-century artists all over the world had begun more self-consciously to recognize that whatever their own culture they had common aspirations and problems.... In both the West and in the East they refreshed themselves by drawing on forms from many parts of the world. More and more, in spite of national feeling, barriers of language and other idioms, and of conflicting political ideologies which extended to different conceptions of the function of the arts in society, they and their audiences became aware of each other on a world scale'.[13]

The work of creative artists early in the century had had an impact similar to the work of natural and social scientists in their respective fields, so that 'the outlook and styles of western writers, painters, sculptors, architects and composers ... were as different after Marcel Proust and James Joyce, Picasso, Le Corbusier, Debussy and Schönberg as was the outlook of science after the work of Planck, Einstein, Heisenberg, Mendel and Freud'.[14] After the Second World War, in an era now dominated by the knowledge of man's capacity to destroy utterly or enrich infinitely the world in which he lived, the process of exploration and innovation continued, with inter-war confusion and fear in many cases heightened. In literature, some pursued the battle against the apparent chaos, meaninglessness and absurdity of existence; others followed Orwell in attacking the oppressive, authoritarian tendency of society, an imposed order hostile to the human spirit. Music, too, reflected new emotional intensity, with greater abstraction and ambiguity and the employment of more dissonances: Stravinsky's music transformed modern opera and ballet; Webern's took Schönberg's abstract theories further, introducing popular instruments into the orchestra. In the wider world, 'pop' music was carried by the mass media to unprecedented audiences and across all frontiers.

Painters and sculptors increasingly expressed themselves in abstract form; in painting, the emphasis was on colour for its own sake, or upon texture (Nicholas de Stael, Jackson Pollock); in sculpture, organic abstractions relating parts to one another and to the work as a whole (Giacometti, Moore), or constructivist abstractions, with mathematical proportions, dominated. Some sculptors were working in new materials, such as celluloid (Gabo), though most employed metal. Architecture, too, responded to new materials and advances in engineering. Frank Lloyd Wright established similar organic principles, with buildings or entire communities seen as a related whole; Gropius, Le Corbusier and van der Rohe were other pioneering giants whose work continued into the post-war period, emphasising social as well as technical requirements. Functional and economic considerations too often had to take precedence over artistic, but post-war architecture has nevertheless continued to experiment vigorously.

Though only the most outline trends of Western cultural development are hinted at here, some mention of the cultural impact of the Russian revolution must be made. After an early period of artistic liberation, particularly in painting, communism demanded of its artists that they serve as instruments of the state, that their creative talents be employed to reflect or project ideology. Writers and artists, to Stalin, were 'engineers of human minds'; socialist realism was conceived as best suited to express the struggles and triumphs of the working class; the artist, deeply involved in the revolutionary struggle, must depict the joy, the heroism, the attainment of the people. In practice, particularly after the Second World War, the inflexible framework imposed by the state severely limited the freedom of the artist to express himself, while the xenophobia of the Russian leadership tended to cut the Russian artist off from movements outside his country. In some ways, of course, the ideological confidence of Marxism served to sustain the artist who did not suffer from the doubts of his Western counterparts; but in other ways the dead bureaucratic hand of the administration stifled growth, prevented innovation, and generally stultified artistic expression.

Ideological division was thus to some extent imposed upon the cultural world. In an opposite manner, however, strides were made in the direction of breaking down the geographical barriers to cultural exchange. In its confident, imperial period, Europe had made considerable impact upon Asian and African cultures, subjecting their traditional conventions to often ruthless assault. Western 'superiority' attracted many educated non-Westerners away from local forms of expression, but Western arrogance stimulated others to a reappraisal and sometimes a re-discovery of their traditional culture. As the twentieth century advanced, the accumulated results of both Western and non-Western scholarship – translations of ancient classics, photographs of ancient art and architecture, knowledge of unsuspected civilisations – combined with the loss of European self-confindence to ensure that the cultural flow was not merely one-way from West to East. And while the reverse flow cannot yet be said to have made a deep impression, it has already made a significant impact, with painting, sculpture and dance most easily overcoming the barrier of language.

Post-war developments in the sciences and the arts, then, would seem to underline the interdependence of all peoples, serving further to stimulate the wakening knowledge of the oneness of the world. National boundaries are seen to be irrelevant to the search for truth or beauty, a point further emphasised if some analysis is afforded man's quest for meaning through religion. For the Churches of the developed world, too, have responded, albeit slowly and ponderously, to industrial civilisation, mass communication, materialism and the assaults of unbelief; elsewhere the great living religions of Asia, the Middle East and Africa have also begun to adjust to modern pressures.

In the developed world, the twentieth century has thrown

up forces which have in some cases diminished, in other cases strengthened religious belief. For example, many working class people, already ill-served by churches badly adapted to city life, turned further away from religion which seemed either irrelevant to their struggle for more rights and better conditions or, worse, actively concerned to preserve a status quo in which church leadership enjoyed a position of privilege. Also, scientific knowledge and worldwide culture contact helped to erode the certainty of religious belief and turn intellectuals away from even nominal church support. The technological revolution secularised the everyday world, giving man the self-confidence to agree with Nietzsche that 'all the gods are dead and man must be mature enough to go on from there', or, with Marx that 'religion is the sign of the oppressed creature, the sentiment of a heartless world and the soul of soulless conditions. It is the opium of the people.'[15] Technology was hailed as a force liberating man from superstition, bigotry and selfish vested interest; religion was condemned as a tool of the privileged order, the defender of delusion, the exploiter of the weak. On the other hand, science and technology did not appear to have all the answers and religious leaders, forced by so much criticism and apathy to re-examine the basis of their faith, instituted reforms of doctrine and practice, helping to provide an acceptable sanctuary for many who were dismayed by the evident evils of the time.

Christianity, the main religion of the developed world, has responded to denunciation and opportunity by trying to heal its own divisions. The Roman Catholic Church, long a conservative force, has in the post-war period made remarkable strides towards accepting the need for change, for less authoritarian control, for more concern with social conditions. It has been in the forefront of resistance both to atheistic communism and general materialism, and under the leadership of Pope John XXIII (1958–63), moved noticeably in the direction of the reformed, Protestant Churches. The Protestant Churches too have fostered ecumenism within the Christian fold and established friendly relations with other religions. The World Council of Churches was formed by the various Protestant denominations, in 1948, as part of their defence against communism, but it has to be observed that deep divisions continue to frustrate concerted action. In the broadest sense, however, Christianity has expanded even in the post-war period, both numerically and geographically. If it has declined at home, it has increased abroad, particularly in Africa, where its record of education and medical and social service is good. It continues to attack the evils of the material world – disease, ignorance, slavery – while offering to men everywhere a vision of a higher, spiritual world.

In the developing countries, religion itself has been under less assault, but it has had to serve in many instances as a stabilising force in conditions of national upheaval, and the Moslem, Hindu and Buddhist faiths have been in some degree affected by technical, secular forces. Islam, in particular, has had to play a leading part in the struggle for independence of peoples in the Middle East, and its adhesion to a traditional way of life has continued to win converts, especially in Africa. But Islam has yet to come to terms with much that is modern in the world. Hinduism, especially in India, where its role in the nationalist movement was very important, has had to reform many of its aspects: but its strength has always lain in its ability to absorb new teachings, and the appeal of its ancient religious idealism, its emphasis on the transience of all things, and its search for meaning makes it attractive in contemporary terms, even in the developed world. Buddhism, like Christianity and Islam a missionary creed, has also revived its prestige and effectiveness in this century, partly through spearheading nationalism, providing both leadership and mass following. This has been most notable in Burma and Ceylon, but has been a feature elsewhere in South East Asia and India, and also in Japan and even China, where the communist regime has permitted Buddhism to continue, its morality in no way conflicting with the ideals of revolutionary progress.

In the religious, as in the whole cultural sphere, there has been a two-way traffic between the developed (largely Western) and the developing (largely Eastern). For example, as well as the penetration of the East by Western scholarship and

science, 'the West, by its contacts and by its efforts of understanding, has by its invasion in the East made the eastern
cultures and religions an event of great purport in its own
quest, and an important part of its own native crisis in religion
and culture'.[16] All the great religions have spread beyond
the confines of their traditional areas, just as cultural expression
throughout the world has begun to take on 'a quality of
universality'.[17] International religion, therefore, can underpin
that international society which is the hopeful part of the
world's development. For although modern materialism,
passively, and modern communism, actively, stand in opposition to religion, promising the good life here and now based on
plenty, the very success of economic development has served
to emphasise man's spiritual needs: the provision of material
necessities, in fact, merely freeing man to attend to moral and
spiritual matters, the affairs of religion. And religion can here
usefully be defined as 'an attempt or a great series of attempts
at discovering the meaning of the universe and adjusting
human life to it. Not just how the world works, which is the
concern of science, or how society is to be ordered, which is
the affair of politics, but what is the meaning of the whole
thing'.[18]

But, before he can devote his sole attention to the purpose
of life, man must ensure the continuance of life. 'The affair of
politics' must claim his urgent attention. The sciences, the arts
and the churches may increasingly stress things universal,
while valuing the rich individual contribution of separate
cultures, but it is politics which must face up to the challenge
of co-operation: the peaceful ordering and development of
our one world. The national strands of the tapestry of world
culture may be individually bright and attractive, but it is
through political endeavour alone that they can be woven
into a more satisfying (and today vital) whole. The challenge
is one of survival. To formulate it is to begin to look into the
future, a task altogether beyond the purpose of this book. But
there are some models of international co-operation which can
at least serve as a basis for further discussion, and at best may
point the way towards closer world harmony. Accordingly,

it seems appropriate to look in turn at the international context and at three types of approach to the world's most pressing political problem; the merging of sovereignties, in the European Economic Community; association across barriers of wealth and colour, in the Commonwealth; and co-operation within a single international body – the United Nations Organisation.

THE INTERNATIONAL CONTEXT

The nation state lives in a world of nation states. How is that world to be ordered? National sovereignty and a world enforcement agency (a world government or a supra-national United Nations police force) are incompatible. Either sovereignty must be superseded or the nation state must learn to curb the use of its sovereignty in the service of some higher end. World government has attracted many theorists, complex though the problems of participation and administration are admitted to be. Already, the nation state is demonstrably an insufficient unit. This is identifiable not only in terms of food and manufactures but through a host of alliances and relationships, both geographical and functional (from postal traffic or fisheries to flying rights or coffee production). The interdependence of peoples and economies is widely recognised, and yet the nation state remains the most solidly founded and staunchly defended unit of human organisation. It cannot simply be ignored. So the most realistic avenue of advance might be to try to approximate the society of states to the society of men and to build from that society something closer to a community; a community in which the parts are prepared to adapt themselves to the interests of the whole, and in which greater awareness, built upon improved communications, will enable the long-term interests of the whole to be discerned beyond the, perhaps conflicting, short-term interests of the parts. And, even more important, a community must be built that will be flexible, not rigid. It is the ability to adjust to new circumstances that must be the outstanding characteristic of any new international arrangement. As J. W. Burton, one of Britain's leading international relations theorists, has put it:

The issue, Sovereign States or World Government, side-steps the basic problem; the pressing issue is whether local-ities – be they States or other organized groups – acting separately or within a world organisation, are capable of responding to the demands made upon them by altering circumstances.[19]

Only if peaceful change is readily possible can a genuine inter-national community survive in the fast-moving times in which we now live; times which, we must recognise, are radically different from preceding eras. Today, to quote Burton again, 'Power in the form of force or the threat of force now plays a less important role than it did before 1945, due to the restraints imposed on nuclear States by mutual deterrence, and on all States by an altered political environment'.[20]

This 'altered political environment' comprises such innov-ations as technological developments in armaments and in communications, particularly in news services, which have increased aversion to war; the democratisation of foreign policies; the growth in the number of non-aligned states. It is an environment which places ever increasing importance upon the ability of the nation state to keep its own house in order: itself to facilitate change, to respond to the altering needs of its own people. For the real danger lies in the internal upheavals of states: 'It is from rival interventions and counter-interventions in domestic revolts and civil wars, rather than from direct attacks of nations against one another, that the peace of the world is likely to be threatened in the coming years.'[21] 'Peace and security is a function of domestic policies and not of inter-national structures'.[22] The State, communist or free-enter-prise, must, in the interests of peace and security, fulfil its obligations to its own people 'constructively and not restrict-ively, that is, to facilitate adjustment to change, and not to afford protection against it'.[23]

This then is the new international context inside which the search for peace and security takes place. Our world is still a world of violence; of repressive regimes and violent reaction; of ill-founded governments propped by foreign support, and of uprisings, also with foreign backing. These are the national sources of international conflict which remain to be tackled, nationally and internationally, through a broad awareness of the issues at stake. New circumstances require new approaches, new imaginative insights, a new readiness to pursue new courses. How has the post-war world responded in practice?

CO-OPERATION: THREE MODELS
The European Economic Community
The immediate origins of the European Economic Community (EEC or Common Market) can be given only briefly here. Common post-war problems, the urgent needs of co-operation under the Marshall Plan (achieved through the Organisation for European Economic Co-operation – OEEC, established April 1948) and the military insecurity which found its answer in the North Atlantic Treaty Organisation (NATO, set up in April 1949), provided in their different ways some practical follow-up to the theoretical dreams of European unity formulated by the wartime resistance movements. So too did the quiet deliberations of the Council of Europe, which provided, from August 1949, a regular forum for the discussion of continental problems. But the most immediate and concrete forerunner of the EEC was the European Coal and Steel Community (ECSC).

Created in 1952, ECSC grew from a plan put forward two years earlier, in May 1950, by the French Foreign Minister Robert Schuman. His proposal was to integrate the coal and steel industries, the basic components of industrial society, as a conscious first step towards wider European economic and political integration. Six nations took up the proposal, France Western Germany, Italy, Belgium, the Netherlands and Luxembourg, and signed the Treaty of Paris in April 1951 accepting ECSC membership. In August 1952, the Treaty of Paris came into operation, establishing a number of important management institutions. It is in this ECSC and its institutions that the model for the wider EEC is to be found.

Conscious of their pioneering role, the makers of the ECSC set up machinery out of all proportion to the limited fields of coal and steel with which they had to deal. They realised at once that it would be necessary, owing to the nature of the two industries (fluctuating demand, fierce competition, heavy investment needs, etc.), to delegate powers from the separate governments to a central authority, and that the decisions of that authority must be binding, though subject to appeal. So they created an executive, an assembly, a consultative committee, a court and a council. Around this framework, it was hoped, an integrated European economy could in due course be built. And, despite set-backs in the coming years, this hope is largely being fulfilled through the present-day European Economic Community.

The importance of the ECSC structure was the supranational element which it contained: its authority to override national viewpoints in the interest of the Community. This authority was carefully regulated and guarded, and the whole scheme was introduced with a five-year transitional period. By the time that period had expired the ECSC had clearly proved its merits, and much else had happened besides.

A significant set-back to the progress towards European integration had occurred with the failure of a French-inspired European Defence Community, initiated in 1950 and finally abandoned, through French opposition by this time, in 1954. But this failure did not deter the ECSC Assembly which had already set up a Committee to investigate further integration. Jean Monnet, Chairman of the ECSC's High Authority, established an Action Committee for the creation of a United States of Europe, which worked hard on public opinion inside the six member states of the Community. Then, in May and June, 1955, the Foreign Ministers of the Six met at Messina to follow up advice from the ECSC Assembly to explore the pooling of atomic energy resources and the building of a European customs union. Paul-Henri Spaak, Belgian Minister of Foreign Affairs, another great Europeanist, was then instructed to head an integration Committee to formulate specific proposals. He presented a blueprint to the ECSC Assembly in March 1956, and in February 1957 the Prime Ministers of the Six agreed on terms for the establishment of a European Economic Community. The Treaty of Rome, the foundation of the EEC, was then signed on 25 March 1957, alongside a further treaty establishing Euratom, the atomic energy pool. The Treaty of Rome was ratified by all Parliaments by December, and on 19 March 1958 the European Economic Community was born. It now remained for the six members to enlarge the membership of their community and to extend its economic integration into the political sphere.

The Preamble to the Treaty of Rome makes the purposes of the EEC clear. The governments of Belgium, West Germany, France, Italy, Luxembourg and the Netherlands:

> Determined to establish the foundations of an ever closer union among the European peoples,
> Decided to ensure the economic and social progress of their countries by common action in eliminating the barriers which divide Europe,
> Directing their efforts to the essential purpose of constantly improving the living and working conditions of their peoples,
> Recognising that the removal of existing obstacles calls for concerted action in order to guarantee a steady expansion, a balanced trade and fair competition,
> Anxious to strengthen the unity of their economies and to ensure their harmonious development by reducing the differences existing between the various regions and by mitigating the backwardness of the less favoured,
> Desirous of contributing by means of a common commercial policy to the progressive abolition of restrictions on international trade,
> Intending to confirm the solidarity which binds Europe and overseas countries, and desiring to ensure the development of their prosperity, in accordance with the principles of the Charter of the United Nations,
> Resolved to strengthen the safeguards of peace and liberty by establishing this combination of resources, and calling upon the other peoples of Europe who share their ideal to join in their efforts,
> Have decided to create a European Economic Community. ...[24]

The institutions of the EEC, built on the experience of the ECSC, were designed to implement these purposes and were carefully set out in Articles 137 to 187 of the Treaty, with

further provision being made for a consultative Economic and
Social Committee (Articles 193–7).

The main authority of the EEC was placed in a Ministerial
Council, which was given the task of co-ordinating the general
economic policies of the member states and of taking final
decisions. A European Assembly, drawn from the Parliaments
of the members, was created as a deliberative body, making
recommendations only. The working executive, the Commission, established under the chairmanship of Professor Hallstein,
was charged with the day-to-day business of the Community,
its decisions requiring ratification by the Council. The other
major institution, the Court of Justice, was formed to 'ensure
observance of law and justice in the interpretation and
application' of the Treaty (Article 164).

Once established, the Common Market's daily experience
has inevitably worked to underline the necessity of harmonising
policies within the member nations as well as of combining in
joint Community action. So many common enterprises depend
on individual attitudes. As Pierre Urri, French economic
planner, has put it, many questions required to be answered,
'such as how much disparity in taxation systems can be allowed
without causing damage to the Common Market; how much
autonomy is permissable in trade policy to enable each country
to pursue its own foreign policy; which industrial and commercial agreements have a purely local significance and which
affect the Common Market as a whole; how much disparity
in company law can be allowed between one country and the
next?'[25] Such matters would have to be tackled pragmatically
and with tact. And in the years since 1957 the tackling of them,
and others like them, have given the Common Market both
a firm shape and considerable strength.

In the economic sphere, the EEC has opened up to its
industrial enterprises a market of some 175 million persons and
created a great reservoir of skill and capital, with no internal
tariff barriers. The institutions for managing this market have
operated with skill, though not always according to the blueprint, and not always with complete success (agricultural
problems have been among the most difficult to resolve, as well

as those relating to expanding the membership). The vital problem of reaching collective decisions affecting several countries has been met in practice through the close co-operation of Council and Commission. The latter body has become the most significant European institution, being given responsibility also for the ECSC and Euratom in 1967, and has worked assiduously to establish the real interests of the Community as a whole and to relate these to the immediate circumstances of the members. This problem, the fundamental and universally relevant problem, of balancing those supra-national and national interests which may appear to be in conflict, has thus found in the EEC one form of answer:

> The European Common Market, with its common authoritative body (the Council of Ministers), its rules of procedure laid down in the Rome Treaty, and its institution (the Commission) for carrying out the decisions of this body by means of discussion and control, is the most original solution yet put forward to solve the problem. The Community does not simply ignore national attitudes, psychological differences and divergent interests; it provides a strictly realistic solution in order to counter the divergences in the initial outlook and circumstances of the countries concerned; a group of men – the Commission – have been appointed to think out and propose new formulae, to create a balanced approach and to provide a concrete idea of the common interest. Supranationalism and co-operation between countries are therefore not contradictory terms in the Community system. It is based on co-operation, but co-operation better organised and made more effective because a body of men can stimulate the parties involved into joint action.[26]

Furthermore, supra-nationalism in the EEC does not mean that a country has to put itself at the mercy of its fellow members without a guarantee that a common interest is being served, because ensuring that 'majority decisions can be taken (by the Council) only on a proposal put forward by the Commission, and that these proposals can be altered only by unanimous agreement in the Council, has led to a dialogue between the parties concerned'.[27]

In practical terms, then, the six member nations of the EEC

have responded to the challenge of co-operation at supra-national level in the economic sphere. How far have they progressed towards political integration? Here the old adage that 'when we are agreed, the problem is economic; when we do not agree then it is political' does not quite hold water, but it has sufficient truth to emphasise how blurred indeed are the economic and political dividing-lines today. Nearly every major economic decision carries with it political implications. Ultimately, a more general merging of sovereignty may be necessary before the goal of replacing 'opposing passions with common objectives'[28] can be won. This is a formidable under-taking and initiatives to enlarge the Community will have much bearing upon the end result.* Here it can only be remarked that the basis of final success is an early recognition of the difficulties, the inbred national outlooks, fears and vested interests, which must be overcome. So far at least, the European Economic Community has shown itself able to respond to some aspects of these difficulties. Its record stands as both an achieve-ment in itself and an inspiration to proceed further.

Nevertheless, it remains true that neither the direction nor the character of the Common Market has assumed definite form. Both its opponents and its protagonists employ an element of faith, pessimistic or optimistic, in their analyses. Critics taking a broad, world view, can point to this experiment in European integration as an example of the rich, affluent nations combining to protect their rich affluence at the expense of the developing nations. EEC discrimination against the manufact-ures and foodstuffs of the Third World, the exclusive nature of the Rome Treaty, the failure of the original Six to shoulder wider world responsibilities, have contributed to the brand-ing of the EEC as an economic extension of the military and political alignments of the capitalist West and as a large, better organised segment of the old Europe, designed for the advancement of its own citizens to the detriment of those left outside. Rather than contributing to the abolition of all boundaries, the Community might simply entrench new

---

*On 1 January 1973 the Six became the Nine, with the enlargement of the EEC to include Britain, Denmark and the Republic of Ireland.

boundaries more firmly than the old. Besides, even within the Community, no agreement has been reached between those who, following General de Gaulle, seek a *'Europe des Patries'*, inside which national sovereignties remain intact, and those others whose desire is full European union.

It remains a matter of faith. Certainly it is possible, with the same world interests at heart as held by the critics above, to see in the EEC at least a movement in the right direction. Whether a *'Europe des Patries'* or not, its existence must serve to heighten awareness of one another amongst members, and should serve to lessen the sanctification of sovereignty as an end in itself. And if a European Community can generate more wealth, then there is hope that this wealth can be used responsibly in the widest possible sense. A Common Market, enlarged to include Britain, Denmark, Ireland and eventually others, might look towards the developing world and to embark upon related policies of trade and aid that would be more effective than anything possible from unco-ordinated individual nations (to his credit, this was one of the chief arguments for British membership advanced by George Brown when he was British Foreign Secretary). The Common Market is at least addressing itself to the problems and creating a vigorous supra-national instrument that may be used, finally, to constructive purpose by men of good will and world awareness.

The Commonwealth

In contrast to that of the European Economic Community, Commonwealth membership involves no erosion of sovereignty. The Commonwealth offers an alternative response to the challenge of co-operation. A loose association of partner nations, combining to serve, primarily, their trade and development needs, the Commonwealth has rightly been described as a 'concert of convenience'[29]. It came into existence through the shared experience of British rule – as a former Governor General of Canada put it, through 'a common historical recollection and a framework of values and institutions'.[30] It persists beyond the end of Empire because it suits the members that it should do so. It does not compromise their independence and autonomy; it does provide a range of important services and serve a variety of valuable purposes. And by its very existence, even in the face of external criticism and some internal strife, it emphasises those aspects of our single world which are so essential for the survival of man: multiracial co-operation; development across the frontiers of wealth; dissemination of information and understanding amongst peoples, as well as governments, of all races, creeds and continents. The Commonwealth, in the words of its first Secretary-General, Arnold Smith, helps, in a real way, 'to make the world safe for diversity'.[31]

Emerging only in the period since the war as an association of demonstrably independent nations, the Commonwealth has continued to evolve since the crucial days of 1947 when India and Pakistan requested membership. Their decision to belong – 'the most spectacular event in the constitutional evolution of the modern Commonwealth' – set the tone and pace of the new association, which freed itself further from the nominal shackles of British domination when, in 1949, it decided that members could belong as Republics, without even indirect allegiance to the British Crown. But the boldest step, and one which has reinforced the claim of the Commonwealth to be an association of relevance to the real issues facing mankind, occurred in 1961. In that year South Africa decided to alter its constitutional status to become a Republic, and to make formal request at the impending Commonwealth Prime Ministers' Conference to continue in Commonwealth membership. So great however was the opposition to South Africa's policy of apartheid, vehemently expressed not only by African members but by others of all races, that South Africa withdrew the application, and left the association. The Commonwealth was seen to take a stand on human dignity and equality. And it has since expanded its multiracial membership and thus enhanced its world stature.

The institutions and machinery of the Commonwealth are in keeping with its voluntary nature. The Commonwealth 'is not a political union or federation; it is not a military alliance, and it is not an economic bloc'.[32] So it has no Assembly.

or Council or Commission. What it does have, and the establishment is as recent as 1964, is a Commonwealth Secretariat designed to provide administrative services independent of the control of any one member. Dedicated, like the institutions of the EEC, to the 'common objectives' of the association as a whole, the Secretariat also gives a sense of continuity to the Commonwealth's purposes. The other main organ of the Commonwealth is the periodic Commonwealth Prime Ministers' Meeting, a deliberative gathering to discuss major common issues and world affairs of import to the association.

Called today at two-year intervals, or when exceptional circumstances dictate, this Prime Ministers' Meeting has emerged as the chief expression of the Commonwealth personality. In the long tradition of Colonial and Imperial Conferences, dating from 1887, to-day's Meetings are of an informal character, whose chief value lies in the opportunity they provide for: 'frank discussion between the Commonwealth's leaders for a full and candid exchange of views in the light of which each Commonwealth Government can formulate and pursue its separate policies with deeper knowledge and understanding of the views and interests of its fellow members', as the final communique of the 1957 Meeting put it.[33] First called Prime Ministers' Meetings in 1944, they are more properly 'Meetings of the Heads of Governments of the independent Commonwealth nations', as not all of these nations in fact maintain the office of Prime Minister. With only two exceptions, the Meetings have taken place in London, and they have been held in 1944, '46, '48, '49, '51, '53, '55, '56, '57, '60, '61, '62, '64, '65, '66 (Lagos), '69 and 1971 (Singapore).

At frequent intervals and with rapidly expanding numbers, the Heads of Government (there were five in attendance in 1946, thirty-one, or their deputies, in 1971) have grappled with the major issues of the day: issues of world affairs – decolonisation, nuclear disarmament, communist expansion – and more especially issues vital to the association itself; Britain's application to join the EEC; immigration to Britain: Rhodesia's unilateral declaration of independence; multi-racialism and the issue of arms sales to South Africa.

In 1969 the dominant concerns were Rhodesia ('no independence before majority African rule' – NIBMAR), the
Nigerian Civil War, and Britain's action in restricting the
flow of East African Asians with British passports who were
becoming increasingly anxious to settle in Britain. All of these
matters were politically explosive, all were passionately
debated. The unilateral declaration of Rhodesia's independence by a haughty Mr. Ian Smith in November 1965, had
been the occasion of the previous exceptional meeting at Lagos.
Of particular concern to African members, who feared an
extension of apartheid under this minority white government
and who demanded that Britain face up more resolutely to its
trusteeship responsibilities, it provided a litmus test for the
Commonwealth's multiracial idea. So, too, in a different way,
did the issue of East African Asians. Having opted for British
Citizenship on the independence of their adopted countries,
these people now found Britain's doors all but closed against
them and, with mounting difficulties facing them in Africa,
their plight raised basic moral principles. The secession of
Nigeria's Eastern region, 'Biafra', was not on the Conference
agenda, being an internal Nigerian matter, but it was nevertheless discussed, in an effort to bring an end to bloodshed and
destruction in Africa's major black nation.

The important thing about the Conference was that, in
spite of its divisive issues, cordiality and debate were successfully maintained. The Commonwealth as a whole remained
adamantly against minority rule in Rhodesia, and the British
Prime Minister promised to continue to consult his Commonwealth colleagues; the Secretary-General was requested to
conduct an examination of migration problems; the range of
economic and social co-operation was examined and full support affirmed for the value of their continued association by
which they 'could form a better understanding of one another's
problems and attitudes and of their growing interdependence'.[34]

In 1971, in Singapore, the mood was less cordial. The new
Conservative British Government of Edward Heath wished to
keep open its option to sell arms to South Africa, for the defence

of the naval route around the Cape. The African members, supported by almost all the other members of the Commonwealth, interpreted the British policy as one designed to give comfort and support to a country whose apartheid practices have been universally condemned. Britain seemed to be siding with the enemy of Black Africa, and furthermore, seemed bent on breaking a United Nations embargo on such arms sales. Unfortunately this African issue overshadowed the other issues before the members of this first meeting in Asia, and prevented more constructive work in the development sphere.

If the Prime Ministers' Meetings are the high-level occasions when co-operation is planned and views exchanged, theSecretariat keeps the Commonwealth's daily life-blood flowing. Secretary-General Arnold Smith described his work at the beginning as that of encouraging consultation at all levels inside the Commonwealth, of looking after the details of Commonwealth affairs while the Prime Ministers, 'meeting less often to talk longer on fewer subjects',[35] dealt with the major problems. His subsequent periodic *Reports* illustrate handsomely just how much detailed work there is, and how broad and deep are the interests linking the Commonwealth members: developments in world politics, the organisation of aid and trade, programmes of technical assistance, a host of commodity reports and studies, research, tourism, educational and medical co-operation, and many other matters of both enduring or topical importance. Taken together, the common pursuit of these matters, as Arnold Smith said in his *Report* of October, 1968, can help 'to develop significantly the dialogue and the practical co-operation which are needed across the differences of race, geography, wealth and poverty which otherwise could fragment our planet'; can, indeed, 'contribute one of mankind's bridges to a more peaceful future'.[36]

The Secretariat sits, in fact, on top of a pyramid of Commonwealth-wide bodies, professional, trade, communication, sporting, cultural, parliamentary, to name but some. As the useful pamphlet, *The Commonwealth at Work*, published by the Commonwealth Institute, itself a central chain in the Commonwealth information network, puts it: 'in almost every field of human endeavour some Commonwealth organisation is quietly at work'; at work of a functional nature which, with 'all the common understanding, personal friendships and professional links which are part of it'[37] gives the Commonwealth its real strength.

One example of what this means in practice lies in the field of education:

Under a Commonwealth Scholarship and Fellowship Scheme, the governments between them give over 1,000 scholarships a year so that students from elsewhere in the Commonwealth can come to their universities and colleges.

India, for example, offers 45 scholarship and five fellowships a year and Canada receives more than 200 students from other Commonwealth countries.

A dentist from Ghana can study in New Zealand, a teacher from the Solomon Islands can get further training in Australia; an Indian can read chemistry in Canada; a Malaysian can study agriculture in India.

The Association of Commonwealth Universities arranges for hundreds of professors and lecturers to go on exchange or secondment to each others' universities.

A Commonwealth Education Conference, attended by Ministers, officials and academics, is held every four years. In between there are specialist conferences on such matters as the teaching of science and mathematics, the techniques of agricultural training, and the teaching of English as a second language.

Each summer hundreds of British teachers go out to Africa and conduct refresher courses for the staffs of the local schools. Each autumn hundreds of teachers from all over the Commonwealth come to Britain to do a year's training in British colleges. Some put in an extra term lecturing on their countries in the schools for the Commonwealth Institute.

Indian teachers (as well as doctors and technicians) are working in Nigeria and Uganda, Canadian teachers in Africa, Asia and the West Indies, and teachers from Australia and New Zealand in Asia and the Pacific islands.

In addition, consultation between educationists on every subject, from the supply of textbooks to teacher training, goes on all the time at all levels.

Education in one form or another comes into most of the ·

activities in which the peoples of the Commonwealth help each other, because so much of that help is at present needed by the developing countries.[38]

Another vital sphere is that of aid and development. Here Commonwealth aid schemes have always emphasised the provision of skills, through training schemes or the secondment of necessary experts. Examples of such schemes in action are quietly impressive:

> One of the most effective schemes for mutual aid is the Colombo Plan, started in 1950. Under this Plan, the needs of developing countries in South East Asia, whether they are in the Commonwealth or not, are co-ordinated through a small secretariat in Colombo, with the aid programmes of Australia, Britain, New Zealand, the United States, and Japan, so that each country gives or receives whatever help is needed in the simplest and most convenient way.
>
> Some of the help takes the form of grants or equipment for development projects, but most of it is used to provide expert advice or overseas training for students of all kinds.
>
> Canadian engineers helped to build the great Warsak dam in West Pakistan. Australia has sent about a thousand expert advisers on assignments in Malaysia, India, and other countries in South East Asia, and has trained many Asian students in her universities and technical colleges. Some of the Asian countries are also helping each other in similar ways. India, for example, had already by 1963 trained more than two thousand people from other Colombo Plan countries and agreed, in 1968, to set up a technical training institute in Malaysia.
>
> The Colombo Plan is so successful that a similar organisation has been set up for Africa – the Special Commonwealth African Assistance Plan (SCAAP). Under this Plan, Canada and Ghana co-operated in establishing a new trades training centre at Accra; eighty Africans have gone to study in New Zealand; and several expert advisers from New Zealand are at work in Africa.
>
> In Britian, the Ministry of Overseas Development helps the developing world to the tune of over £200 million a year. Over 75% of this aid goes to the Commonwealth, and Britain has sent about 5,000 teachers and other experts overseas.
>
> Moreover, at a conference held in Nairobi in 1967, a

Commonwealth Technical Assistance Scheme was agreed by all Commonwealth governments. Under this, Commonwealth governments will work together on development projects, each contributing whatever resources in men, money, materials and technical expertise they can provide; and the Commonwealth Secretariat itself now has a group of economic experts who can be sent wherever their advice is most urgently needed.[39]

These examples form but a small part of the whole interlocking network of relationships, which now criss-cross the Commonwealth. No longer is London the central dynamo of an empire with power radiating out to the periphery, though it is true that it remains of great importance in the Commonwealth scheme of things as the headquarter seat of many organisations; no longer can Britain claim supremacy or even a position of *primus inter pares*. As Professor Silock, of the University of Malaya, put it in 1964:

> The Commonwealth is no longer a wheel with only one centre of force and drive. If it is to survive at all, it will be as a lattice of increasing intercommunication and interaction. No monopoly of initiative and concern should be expected of the government, the people, or the press of the "mother country".[40]

'No *monopoly* of concern', perhaps, but real concern for the future of this living Commonwealth should certainly be felt in Britain. For the world would be the poorer for the severing of the links which it continues to nourish. The Commonwealth has set itself ideals to live up to, ideals of equal opportunity, non-discrimination and democratic principles, and it has been truly said that 'the Commonwealth is nothing unless it asserts ideals and Britain nothing within the Commonwealth unless she offers an example of striving to achieve those ideals.'[41]

It has been further observed, by *The Times*, that 'the function of the Commonwealth is only to be found in the work it actually does'.[42] From the brief indication above of the extent and nature of the Commonwealth in action, it must be admitted that it does, without doubt, a great deal of work. For all the strife, divisions and disagreements which beset it from time to time – arguments which at least testify to its vitality – the Commonwealth can claim much positive achievement, while its potential for the expansion of co-operative endeavour and mutual awareness remains immense. Whatever the future holds for it, the Commonwealth has provided a model of international association from which the world as a whole may profit.

The United Nations

Something of the purpose and structure of the United Nations, founded in 1945, has already been mentioned in Chapter 1 (pp 43–47). But how has the Organisation functioned since then, and how does it measure up to the problems of the contemporary world, twenty-five years on?

In some respects the United Nations was established deliberately as an Organisation that was more than the sum of its parts, that had an element of supra-national authority about it, even though it was founded upon respect for the 'sovereign authority of all states' (Article 2, i), and even though it further prohibited intervention in the domestic affairs of states (2, vii). For the Charter vested in the Security Council the power of decision as to whether the peace was threatened or aggression had occurred and charged it with deciding upon the appropriate action to be taken. Member states of the Organisation assumed obligations which, in some circumstances, might infringe their freedom of action, and they recognise that it is possible for the Assembly to alter the rules of the Organisation to impose further obligations, in so doing binding all members, whether they have agreed with the change or not.

The Assembly is the first of six main organs of the U.N. It is composed of all member states and each member has one vote. The Assembly meets once a year in regular session, commencing on the third Tuesday in September, though special sessions can also be convened. Its main functions are to discuss and make recommendations on the principles of international co-operation and on any problem affecting peace and security (providing the Security Council is not already handling the

issue); to initiate studies and make recommendations to promote international co-operation or collaboration in the political, economic, social, cultural, educational and health fields
and in that of international law; to receive and consider
reports from the Security Council and other organs; to supervise its trusteeship agreements; to elect members to the Security
Council and other organs; to consider the budget and apportion contributions among members.

The relationship of the Assembly to the Security Council
reflects the fact of big power sovereignty. By virtue of its
capacity to function continuously, the Security Council has
been made the principal watchdog of world peace. Composed
of five permanent members (China, France, the Union
of Soviet Socialist Republics, the United Kingdom and the
United States of America), and ten* non-permanent members,
elected by the General Assembly for two-year terms, it is
required to maintain peace and security, investigate disputes
and recommend settlements, formulate plans to regulate armaments, determine the existence of threats to peace or acts of
aggression and recommend appropriate action, call on members to apply economic sanctions to stop aggression or to take
military action against an aggressor. It also recommends the
admission of new members, exercises trusteeship in 'strategic
areas', makes recommendations concerning the appointment
of the Secretary General and submits annual and special reports
to the Assembly. The Security Council has, to help it, a subsidiary Disarmament Commission, established in 1952, to bring
about 'general and complete disarmament'.

Resulting from the particular experience of the Korean War,
the relationship between Security Council and Assembly was
modified in November 1950 by the 'Uniting for Peace' resolution, adopted by the Assembly. This states that if the Security
Council fails to act on an apparent threat to the peace, breach
of the peace, or act of aggression, because of lack of unanimity

*On 17 December 1963 a proposal to amend the Charter by raising the non-perman-
ent seats from six to ten was accepted. This came into force on 31 August 1965, bringing
the total number of seats up from 11 to 15. At the same time the membership of the
Economic & Social Council was raised from 18 to 27.

between its five permanent members, the Assembly itself may take up the matter within twenty-four hours – in emergency special session – and recommend collective measures.

The third major organ of the UN is the Economic and Social Council. Composed of twenty-seven members, nine of which are elected each year for a three year term, this Council is responsible for the economic and social activities of the UN and is charged with initiating studies, reports and recommendations in this broad field, with promoting human rights, supervising the many specialised agencies and co-ordinating their activities. It has a number of functional and regional economic commissions and special committees all designed to bring specialist expertise to bear on particular economic and social problems.

The Trusteeship Council, the International Court of Justice and the Secretariat form the remaining three principal organs. The Trusteeship Council is composed of those states which administer UN Trust Territories and an equal number of those which do not. Its function is to supervise the administration of Trust Territories by way of questionnaires, reports and visits.

The International Court of Justice, situated at the Hague, in the Netherlands, is the principal judicial body of the UN. All members of the UN are automatically parties to the Statute of the Court. The Court consists of 15 full-time judges, elected by the General Assembly and the Security Council, voting separately, and chosen on the basis of their qualifications, not their nationality (though no two judges can be nationals of the same state).

The Secretariat comprises the Secretary-General and 'such staff as the organisation may require'. The Secretary-General, the Chief Administrative Officer of the UN, is required to bring to the attention of the Security Council any matters he deems fit, and to make an annual report on the work of the UN. He is assisted by an international staff recruited on the highest standards of efficiency, competence and integrity, drawn from as wide a geographical spread as possible.

With the avowed object of preventing war, the Charter gave to the Great Powers recognition of their status with permanent seats on the Security Council, and gave to each one of them the power to veto action, to protect its own special interests. This built-in authority, this special peace-keeping duty, and the great international Agencies placed under its wing, have given to the United Nations a unique position in the post-war world. Not yet universal, it commands a much wider membership than did its predecessor, the League of Nations. And if its actions have been abused, sometimes for being too presumptuous, or too biassed, more often just for being ineffective, nevertheless it has to its credit much solid achievement in the quarter-century of its existence; achievement not only in peace-keeping but also in the fields of decolonisation, disarmament and refugee welfare, and in the myriad areas of the specialist agencies, from education and health, to agriculture and economics.

'A human institution marked by a familiar human blend of sincerity and deception and self-deception'[43], the United Nations has been noisily at the centre or quietly on the edge of a succession of post-war crises. From the petition of Iran in January 1946, demanding an end to Russian 'interference', to the present day, the going has been tough. Greece, Palestine, Indonesia and Kashmir were all storm-centres of the '40s. Then, in June 1950, the Korean War burst upon the world, involving the United Nations for the first time in active military campaigning, and dramatically influencing the future of the Organisation. For, during this war, the United Nations condemned the aggression of Communist China, and long after the Assembly kept the Peking Government from its membership and from the place on the Security Council that it should have occupied.* The Suez and Hungarian crises of 1956, the much more pre-occupying and embroiling Congo conflict of 1960, the policing mission in Cyprus, to separate Greek and Turkish Cypriots, and the long-drawn out Middle Eastern presence between Arab and Jew, the application of economic sanctions against the rebel regime in Rhodesia, these are the high-lights of the story up to the 'seventies. There have been obvious failures and humiliations – impotence in face of the Vietnam War, inability to bring peace to the Middle East,

---

*Nationalist China was replaced by Communist China in the UN on 25 October 1971.

scant attention when the chips were down over the Cuban missiles (though of some service in ending that crisis). But it is partly to the credit of the United Nations that the world has survived these threats and conflicts and that something is being done to heal the sores that remain: the 1952 Disarmament Commission works on steadfastly to reduce tension; the Commission on Refugees cares for millions of the dispossessed; the great expansion in membership of the Organisation itself (127 members, by October 1970) speaks volumes for its success in urging decolonisation; the World Bank, FAO, UNESCO, the World Health Organisation, the International Labour Organisation, the United Nations International Children's Emergency Fund, the United Nations Relief and Works Agency, and its many other organs, have all born eloquent testimony to its care and concern to achieve the full development of men everywhere.

Of course the record is incomplete. The United Nations has no magic cure for the world's ills. As Sydney Bailey has put it (quoting Ernest Gross at the beginning), the United Nations is essentially:

> 'a set of rules and a set of tools'. The rules are contained in or derived from the Charter and are binding; the tools must be fashioned and adapted for each job. One tool is to provide a means of discussion and negotiation, whether in public or in private. Another tool is to place an element of the United Nations where a job needs doing. This United Nations 'presence' may perhaps be a group of technical assistance experts, or an operation for helping refugees, or a visiting mission of the Trusteeship Council, or an executive authority such as was established in West New Guinea (West Irian), or a UN force of the kind needed in the Middle East and the Congo, or a truce observation unit like that sent to the Kashmir area, or a single diplomat such as the representatives of the Secretary-General sent to or stationed in Jordan or Laos.[44]

More prosaically, in the words of Andrew Boyd, the United Nations is 'a do-it-yourself kit – with incomplete instructions and a price tag'.[45] It is a universal implement at the service of world peace and development, but it will succeed only to the extent to which its members are prepared to use it, and only in proportion to the skill and devotion of the officers they appoint and the resources they release.

Certainly, by 1970, the United Nations had developed problems. The General Assembly and the Security Council, designed as agencies of mediation and conciliation, had tended to be, through the rivalries of the Great Powers and the greatly expanded membership of the Organisation, arenas in which to display debating skills or from which to make appeals to outside world opinion. From this point of view, America, host nation of the UN's permanent headquarters, has been most affected, its delegates conscious of the need to appeal to the American public close at hand (and to be seen to succeed in debate) as well as to the representatives of world opinion in the Assembly Chamber. This has sometimes placed distorting pressures notably absent from the representatives of more closed societies whose public is in any event further away.

. Financial worries, too, inhibit UN action. U Thant (1961–72) even more than his predecessors, Trygve Lie (1946–52) and Dag Hammarskjöld (1953–61), was plagued by mounting deficits, as individual nations chose to with-hold their contributions towards the cost of operations of which they disapproved (e.g. Russia in relation to the Congo). U Thant, in his public pronouncements of 1970, became increasingly concerned that global solutions be found for global problems, for these would not respond to piecemeal remedies. He believed that: 'UN decisions should be enforceable; that all member-States should accept the compulsory jurisdiction of the International Court of Justice in legal disputes between nations; that a UN standby military force – a permanent peacekeeping corps – should be available; and that every nation should belong to the UN'.[46]

This last point was peculiarly relevant to the future of the UN, for the spectacle of Formosa, an American puppet state, representing China, only tarnished the Organisation in the eyes of Asia: and the absence of the real China prevented any successful initiatives on the major world conflict of that moment, the Vietnam War. Furthermore, without the most populous nation in the world, the UN could not really adapt itself to express and attempt to solve the outstanding world problems of the present and the future. A world organisation can only command world attention and respect if it is truly representative of all the world's peoples.

Certainly, U Thant's plea was in line with the view of Dag Hammarskjöld that the UN should be used, not as mere 'static conference machinery' but as a 'dynamic instrument' for resolving, or even better, averting conflict. Others have regarded the UN more as an 'Aunt Sally', a useful scapegoat for blame, or target for abuse, or as a sacred shrine before which versions of history can be acted out so that nations anxious to back down from intransigent positions can retreat without loss of face. In these roles too, the UN has served the cause of peace. There are dangers, of course, in placing unreal hopes in an international organisation which has not the resources to override Big Power opposition. A myth of world government, attached to the UN, may serve as a hope to many peoples and as a focus of idealism, but it can lead to disillusioned reaction when expectation, however unreal its basis, is disappointed. Some, therefore, would argue that the existence of the UN is double-edged and that it must be carefully protected from any notion of coercive power, for it is the nation states of the world that are the reality and the peoples of the world are not yet ready to yield to dictation from others, whether foreign states or international bodies.

Such arguments may reflect the imperfect state of our international relations, or of man himself. What must be true is that man and nations require greater awareness of the problems of humanity, of the conditions of the world community and of the steps which must be taken to ensure its survival, let alone its enrichment. The United Nations Organisation, like life in general, will give out to its members in direct proportion to the effort they choose to put into it.

COMMUNITY

EEC, Commonwealth, UN: all may contribute towards the elimination of conflict and the promotion of harmonious development that are today the urgent tasks facing man. What they must help to build is a self-conscious, global community of mankind: a community conscious of its common opportunities, common dangers, common culture and common material resources. Perhaps the early agonies of the twentieth century will prove to have been the birth pangs of just such a community. Certainly the century has already created something unprecedented: a nuclear, technological, Big Power world that necessitates an equally novel response of just such a kind.

One method of consolidating this community, building on the experience both of success and failure in multi-state associations and on the fact that modern technology has now reduced the world to a 'spherical village', might be a progressively extended federation of nations, region after region, until all the world is included: 'the gradual federation of nations into a unified world'.[47]

But whatever form it takes, political action must be accompanied, if not preceded, by economic action. Many will accept, with Mr. Kiichi Aichi, the validity of the ' $200 standard of living theory'. The Japanese Foreign Minister has expressed this in terms of Communist China:

> If Communist China's per capita national income exceeds $200 a year, the Chinese people's way of thinking would undergo a considerable change and they would no longer be influenced by the 'Quotations from Chairman Mao Tse-tung' alone.
>
> At the present time, per capita national income still lingers at around $70 in many Asian nations. If they are helped to treble that sum systematically, I believe it will go a long way toward removing the causes of international tensions.[48]

There is no need to accept the ideological undertones in recognising the basic reality of this point of view: men must first eat before they can live. And the scale of the world problem will require something more than that minimum of aid asked by the Pearson Commission (1% gnp) from the developed lands. As Martin Luther King has put it, 'True compassion is more than flinging a coin to a beggar; it understands that an edifice which produces beggars needs restructuring'.

In fact, as well as political and economic change, a moral shift is needed. Here Martin Luther King is more definite:

> Truth is found neither in traditional capitalism nor in classical Communism. Each represents a partial truth. Capitalism fails to see the truth in collectivism. Communism fails to see the truth in individualism. Capitalism fails to realise that life is social. Communism fails to realise that life is personal. The good and just society is neither the thesis of capitalism nor the antithesis of Communism, but a socially conscious democracy which reconciles the truths of individualism and collectivism . . .

And to arrive at this 'good and just society' nothing less than a revolution is needed:

> The stability of the large world house which is ours will involve a revolution of values to accompany the scientific and freedom revolutions engulfing the earth. We must rapidly begin to shift from a 'thing'-oriented society to a 'person'-oriented society.
>
> . . . A true revolution of values will soon look uneasily on the glaring contrast of poverty and wealth. With righteous indignation, it will look at thousands of working people displaced from their jobs with reduced incomes as a result of automation while the profits of employers remain intact, and say: 'This is not just'. It will look across the oceans and see individual capitalists of the West investing huge sums of money in Asia, Africa and South America, only to take the profits out with no concern for the social betterment of the countries, and say: 'This is not just'. It will look at our alliance with the landed gentry of Latin America and say: 'This is not just'. The Western arrogance of feeling that it has everything to teach others and nothing to learn from them is not just. A true revolution of values will lay hands on the world order and say of war: 'This way of settling differences is not just'. . . .
>
> A genuine revolution of values means in the final analysis that our loyalties must become ecumenical rather than sectional. Every nation must now develop an overriding loyalty to mankind as a whole in order to preserve the best in their individual societies.[49]

The choice, for the moment, remains with us: 'non-violent co-existence or violent co-annihilation'; 'community' or 'chaos'.

But the exercise of choice requires a knowledge of the alternatives. The people of the world, particularly of the affluent world (for the poor are only too well aware of their poverty) must be given an accurate 'state of the planet' picture, so that adequate action can be taken on a worldwide scale. It is to the dissemination of information, and ultimately to a radical redistribution of resources, therefore, that such groups as Third World First (born in Oxford University in 1969) are dedicated.

Third World First recognises the existence of '300,000,000 humans on the earth who are inhumanly treated... mentally and physically stunted by malnutrition,... (who) will die young... cannot help themselves... cannot feed their families ... through no fault of their own... are diseased, illiterate, and hungry'. And recognising also that the problem here presented can only be tackled by governmental action, Third World First sets out to let 'the populations of the developed countries know about the problem and its causes' and to ensure that the desire to see the problem solved is nurtured. Working especially through students and student organisations, this group has established an Educational Trust to disseminate information, 'to promote the case of the Third World and create as much awareness as possible in as large a constituency as possible'.[50] Already, some thirty thousand young people in Britain are contributing a proportion of their income and time in response to an appeal brought home to them with directness and simplicity.

A world community, then, where people are at last "free and equal in the opportunities to exercise their abilities', and where at last all men will recognise that 'our true nationality is mankind'[51] has become a necessity. Its achievement will require dedication and sacrifice from the rich, who have, after all, so much to give, and to lose through not giving. In the 1970s, more urgently than ever before in the past, the supplication of Shakespeare's *King Lear* should be both motto and battle cry:

So distribution should undo excess, and each man have enough.

DAMMED COUNTRY

Of all the dams built by rich nations for poor nations, the one built by Russia for Egypt is in a class of its own. The high dam at Aswan is the biggest and most expensive in the world. The late President Nasser spent over 1,000 million dollars on it and in the process changed the course of history. It made his political fortunes, but spread such ecological havoc that his country may never get over it.

This is not just Nasser's fault. The blame must be shared by an entire generation distracted by politics and bemused by technology.

There was no excuse for all the eminent international experts who did not see what was coming, since at least one did. The distinguished Egyptian hydrologist, Dr Abdel Aziz Ahmed, warned that the dam's conception was 'foreign to Egypt and a complete reversal of time-honoured Nile irrigation policy.' To build it, he said, would be 'Unwise and extremely hazardous.'

These were some of the things he rightly predicted would go wrong:

(1) The dam, built without sluices, would trap an annual 134 million tons of Nile sediment, 'containing vulcanic materials which produce the most fertile soil on the face of the earth.' Since practically all cultivated soil in Egypt was formed and nourished by the sediment, for which no adequate man-made substitute has yet been devised, the lack of it would strike at the heart of Egyptian agriculture.

(2) The silt-free water would scour the river bed downstream, eroding the Nile's banks and undermining every barrier-dam and bridge on its 600 mile course from Aswan to the sea.

(3) Evaporation, seepage, and changes in underground water movements would cause such colossal losses in the lake forming behind the dam that Egypt would almost certainly end up with less water than it had before.

Dr Ahmed couldn't think of everything. He failed, for instance, to anticipate the decimation of marine life in the eastern Mediterranean, erosion of the delta coastline by sea current, a rise in soil salinity threatening to put millions of acres irreversibly out of cultivation, an unnerving increase in the exhausting water-borne disease called bilharzia, a potential invasion from the Sudan of a killer-mosquito carrying the deadliest kind of malaria. What he did predict, though, has come true with a vengeance.

Without the Nile sediment, much of Egypt's six million cultivated acres need chemical fertiliser already, as all farmland will in the next few years.

Furthermore, without the flood to flush the earth of soil salts, salinity is reaching alarming levels.

On the other side of the ledger is a clear and substantial gain: the conversion of 700,000 acres from flood to canal irrigation. With double-cropping, that has added half again to the yearly production of these lands. Yet here, too, the Nile has found a way to strike back. The fellaheen working on these converted lands were not afflicted with bilharzia before. They are now.
Washington Post.

(Reprinted from the *Guardian* 20 November 1971)

NOTES

[1] Ware *op. cit.*, p. 132. Einstein's 'General Theory of Relativity' was published in 1916.

[2] See his chapter, 'The New Scientific Thought', in Ware, *op. cit.*, pp. 121–58. These extracts come from p. 149 and pp. 157–8.

[3] Michael Harrington, *The Accidental Century* (Penguin, 1967).

[4] *Ibid.*, p. 17.   [5] *Ibid.*, p. 18.   [6] *Ibid.*, pp. 23–4.   [7] *Ibid.*, p. 14

[8] *Ibid.*, p. 112.   [9] *Ibid.*, p. 87.   [10] *Ibid.*, p. 218.

[11] J. D. Bernal, *Science in History* (Penguin, 4 vols, 1969), iv, p. 1299.

[12] Ware, *op. cit.*, i, p. 564. (The internal quotation is from C. Dollard, 'Strategy for Advancing the Social Sciences' in *The Social Sciences in Mid Century*, p. 12.)

[13] Ware, *op. cit.*, ii, p. 1194–5.

[14] *Ibid.*, p. 1193.

[15] See T. B. Bottomore and M. Rubel, (eds.) *Karl Marx, Selected Writings* (Penguin, 1963), p. 41.

[16] H. Laemer, *World Cultures and World Religions* (Lutterworth, 1960), p. 322.

[17] Ware, *op. cit.*, ii, p. 1310.

[18] Geoffrey Parrinder, *The World's Living Religions* (Pan, 1964), pp. 198–9.

[19] J. W. Burton, *International Relations: a General Theory* (C.U.P., 1965), p. 266.

[20] *Ibid.*, p. 1.

[21] G. F. Hudson, *The Hard and Bitter Peace* (Pall Mall, 1966), p. 287.

[22] J. W. Burton, *op. cit.*, p. 264.

[23] *Ibid.*, p. 265.

[24] The Treaty is printed in full in Sturat de la Mahotière, *The Common Market* (Hodder, 1961), pp. 148–92.

[25] Pierre Uri, 'From Economic Union to Political Union' in John Calmann (ed.), *The Common Market* (Blond, 1967), p. 56.

[26] *Ibid.*, p. 58.   [27] *Ibid.*, p. 59.   [28] *Ibid.*, p. 62.

[29] See page 277 above.

[30] George Vanier, 'A New Tradition in the World' in *Commonwealth Journal*, viii, No. 6 (December 1965), p. 246.

[31]Arnold Smith, 'The Need for Commonwealth', in *Round Table*, No. 223 (July 1966), p. 224.

[32]*What is the Commonwealth?* (Commonwealth Institute, 1968), p. 1.

[33]P. N. S. Mansergh, *Documents and Speeches on British Commonwealth Affairs, 1952–62*, p. 532. Quoted in Hamilton, Robinson and Goodwin (eds.) *A Decade of Commonwealth 1955–64* (Duke University Press, Durham N.C., 1966), p. 118. This is a volume that repays study.

[34]*Final Communique, Meeting of Commonwealth Prime Ministers, London, 7–15 January 1969*, p. 4.

[35]*Maclean's Magazine*, 21 August 1965, p. 40.

[36]*Second Report of the Commonwealth Secretary General: Sept. 1966–Oct. 1968*, pp. 3–4.

[37]*The Commonwealth at Work* (Commonwealth Institute, n.d.) pp. 2–4.

[38]*Ibid.*, p. 2–3.   [39]*Ibid.*, p. 3.

[40]Letter to *The Times*, 2 June 1964, quoted in H. Victor Wiseman, *Britain and the Commonwealth* (Allen and Unwin, 1965), p. 129.

[41]H. Victor Wiseman, *op. cit.*, p. 18.

[42]*Ibid.*, p. 55, quoting *The Times*, 4 January 1969.

[43]Andrew Boyd, *United Nations: Piety, Myth and Truth* (Penguin, 1964), p. 20.

[44]S. D. Bailey, *The United Nations* (Pall Mall, 1963), pp. 118–9.

[45]Boyd, *op. cit.*, p. 17.

[46]*Irish Times*, 25 August 1970.

[47]*Q: Operation Survival* (1970), p. 7 *Q* is a London based movement which urges the peoples of the world to combine to force their governments into world federal union.

[48]Kiichi Aichi, 'Ideals and Realities in National Security' in *The Search for National Security* (Min, For. Aff., Japan, 1969), p. 19.

[49]Martin Luther King, *Chaos or Community*, pp. 177–82.

[50]Third World First, Britwell Salome, Nr. Watlington, Oxfordshire, England.

[51]Robert Gardiner, *A World of Peoples*, pp. 10 and 91.

APPENDIX A

Chronology 1945–1970

AN OUTLINE OF EVENTS

1945	Feb.	Yalta Conference
	April	Roosevelt dies
		Truman President
	April–May	San Francisco Conference (U.N.)
	May	Hitler's death announced
		Surrender of Germany
	July	Potsdam Conference (G.B. election: Labour victory)
	6 Aug.	A-bomb on Hiroshima
	8 Aug.	U.S.S.R. declares war on Japan
	14 Aug.	Surrender of Japan
	Oct.	United Nations inaugurated
1946	Jan.	1st meeting U.N. General Assembly, London
	Feb.	Trygve Lie U.N. Secretary General
	April	U.N. Assembly at Geneva: dissolves L. of N.
	April–May	Commonwealth Prime Ministers Meeting
	June–July	U.S. tests A-bomb at Bikini
	July–Dec.	Peace treaties negotiated with European allies of Germany
	Oct.	U.N. General Assembly at New York
		French Union established
	Dec.	Baruch Plan (nuclear) adopted by U.N.
1947	March	Truman Doctrine
	June	Marshall Plan for European recovery
	Aug.	Independence of India and Pakistan

	Oct.	Cominform (Communist Information Bureau) established
	Dec.	4-power conference on Germany breaks down
1948	Jan.	Independence of Burma
		Gandhi dies
	Feb.	Independence of Ceylon
		Czechoslovakia communist coup
	March	Masaryk dies
		O.E.E.C. established
		Russia interferes with access to W. Berlin
	May	Rajagopalachari Governor-General of India
		Israel proclaimed. Arab-Israeli war begins
	June	Yugoslavia expelled from Cominform
		W. Berlin airlift begins (Blockade completed July)
	Aug.	Korean Republic established
	Oct.	Commonwealth Prime Ministers' Meeting
	Nov.	Truman re-elected
1949	Jan.	Comecon (Council for Mutual Economic Assistance) formed as riposte to Marshall Plan
	April	Newfoundland enters Canada
		N.A.T.O.
		Commonwealth Prime Ministers' Meeting
	May	Berlin blockade lifted
		Council of Europe
	Aug.	U.S.S.R. A-bomb
	Sept.	German Federal Republic established
	1 Oct.	People's Republic of China proclaimed
1950	Jan.	India Republic
	Feb.	British election. Labour returned
	May	Schuman Plan for European Coal and Steel community
	June	N. Korea invades South: Truman sends troops
	Aug.	Independence of Indonesia
	Nov.	Communist China into Korean War

	Dec.	Independence of Libya
1951	Jan.	Commonwealth Prime Ministers Meeting
	Feb.	U.N. General Assembly condemns Communist China as aggressor in Korea
	March	Schuman Plan (E.C.S.C.) initialled by 6 states.
	May	Persian oil nationalised
		German Federal Republic into Council of Europe
	July	Colombo Plan
	Sept.	A.N.Z.U.S. pact
	Oct.	G.B. elections: Conservative victory, W.S. Churchill Prime Minister
1952	Feb.	King George VI dies
	April	Japan regains sovereignty
	July	15th Olympics, Helsinki
		Cairo coup: Farouk deposed
	Aug.	Treaty of Paris: E.C.S.C.
	Oct.	Mau Mau rising in Kenya
	Nov.	U.S.A. H-bomb
		Eisenhower presidential victory
1953	Jan.	Chinese 1st 5-year plan
	5 March	Stalin dies
	6 March	Malenkov Prime Minister and 1st C.P. Secretary (Khruschev replaces as 1st Secretary within week)
	11 March	Hammarskjöld U.N. Secretary General
	May	Everest conquered
	June	E. German rising
		Commonwealth Prime Ministers' meeting
	July	Korea: armistic at Panmunjom
		Central African Federation
	12 Aug.	U.S.S.R. H-bomb
	Oct.	Anglo-Egyptian Agreement on Suez Canal
1954	Jan.	Sudan self government
		Harwell atomic pile
	April–July	Geneva Conference on Korea and Indochina

	May	4 minute mile (Bannister)
		Dien Bien Phu defeat of French in Indo-China
	July	Indo-China war ends
	Sept.	S.E.A.T.O.
	Oct.	W. German sovereignty: enters N.A.T.O. and W.E.U.
	Nov.	Algerian war of independence begins
1955	Jan.–Feb.	Commonwealth Prime Ministers' Meeting
	Feb.	Bulganin (Khrushchev's nominee) succeeds Malenkov as Prime Minister
	April	Winston Churchill resigns as Prime Minister: Eden replaces
		Bandung Afro-Asian Conference
		Einstein dies
	May	Austrian peace treaty
		G.B. election: Conservatives returned
		Warsaw Pact
	May–June	Messina Meetings on European unity.
	July	4-power Conference at Ceneva: G.B./France/U.S.A./U.S.S.R.
	Sept.	Peron resigns from Argentinian presidency
1956	Jan.	Independence of Sudan
	Feb.	Khrushchev denounces Stalin at 20th Congress of C.P.S.U.
		In China '1000 Flowers Bloom' Policy
	March	Pakistan Republic
	April	France leaves Indo-China
		Cominform dissolved
	May	G.B. first atomic power station (Calder Hall)
	June–July	Commonwealth Prime Ministers' Meeting
	June	Last G.B. troops leave Suez Canal
		Nasser President of Egypt
		Polish workers' rising
	26 July	Nasser nationalises Suez Canal
	Oct.	Gomulka to power in Poland
	23 Oct.	Hungarian uprising
	29 Oct.	Israel invades Egypt
		Anglo-French offensive in Egypt
	Nov.	Russia crushes Hungarian rising

Eisenhower re-elected
U.N. cease-fire in Egypt
Suez Canal blocked
16th Olympic Games at Melbourne

1957	Jan.	Eden resigns Prime Minister; Macmillan replaces
	March	Independence of Ghana
		Treaty of Rome establishes European Economic Community (E.E.C.)
	April	Suez re-opened
	May	G.B. H-bomb
	June–July	Commonwealth Prime Ministers' Meeting
	July	Independence of Malaya
	Sept.	Sibelius dies
	Oct.	Sputnik, first earth satellite (U.S.S.R.)
1958	Jan.	Federation of West Indies
		1st U.S.A. satellite
	Feb.	United Arab Republic established
	March	Khrushchev replaces Bulganin as Prime Minister
	May	De Gaulle returns to power in France
		Chinese 'Great Leap Forward' Policy
	July	Iraq Republic
		U.S.A. troops to Lebanon
		G.B. troops to Jordan
	Oct.	Guinea Republic
		Marshall Law Pakistan – Ayub Khan to power
		Pius XII dies – John XXIII Pope
		Geneva: suspension of nuclear tests talks
		De Gaulle President of 5th Republic; French Community
		U.A.R./U.S.S.R. Aswan Dam project
1959	Jan.	Castro to power in Cuba
		Alaska 49th State of U.S.A.
	April	Lui Shao-ch'i Head of State, People's Republic of China
	June	St. Lawrence Seaway

	Sept.	Lunik V hits moon
		Khrushchev visits U.S.A.
		Tass public attack on China – Sino-Soviet quarrel in open
	Oct.	G.B. election: Conservatives returned
	Dec.	Archbishop Makarios 1st President of Cyprus

1960 Jan.   Camaroun Republic
                    Camus dies
      Feb.   Macmillan 'Wind of Change' speech
                    France A-bomb
      March   Sharpeville massacre in South Africa
      April   Togo Republic
                    Chinese attack Russian 'revisionism'
                    Russia withdraws technicians from China
      1 May   U.S.A. U-2 shot down over Russia
      14–17 May   Abortive summit conference at Paris
                    Brezhnev succeeds Voroshilov as President of
                       U.S.S.R.
                    Kariba dam
                    Pasternak dies
                    Commonwealth Prime Ministers' Meeting
      June   Independence of Madagascar
                    Congo Republic (Kinshasa)
      July   Ghana Republic
                    Somali Republic
                    Mutiny in Congo
                    Independence of Ivory Coast, Dahomy,
                       Niger, Upper Volta, Congo (Brazzaville),
                       Chad & Central African Republic
      Aug.   Cyprus Republic
                    17th Olympics at Rome
      Oct.   Independence of Nigeria
      Nov.   Kennedy elected President of U.S.A.
                    Independence of Mauritania
      Dec.   Ghana-Guinea-Mali union

1961 Feb.   Lumumba dies
      March   Commonwealth Prime Ministers' Meeting
                    Beecham dies

	April	Gagarin orbits earth: first man in space (U.S.S.R.)
		Cuba – 'Bay of Pigs' invasion attempt
		Independence of Sierra Leone
	May	Shepard into space: up and down rocket (U.S.A.)
		South African Republic (outside Commonwealth)
	June	Khrushchev and Kennedy meet in Vienna
	July	Hemingway dies
		G.B. application to join E.E.C.
	Aug.	E. Germans build Berlin Wall
	Sept.	Hammerskjöld dies
		Syria leaves U.A.R.
	Nov.	U. Thant U.N. Secretary General
		U.N. condemns apartheid
	Dec.	Independence of Tanganyika
		India takes Goa
1962	Jan.	Independence of W. Samoa
	Feb.	Glenn: first U.S. orbit
	March	Algerian-French truce
	May	W. Indies Federation dissolved
	July	Independence of Burundi & Rwanda
		Independence of Algeria
		Telstar
	Aug.	Independence of Jamaica
		Independence of Trinidad and Tobago
		Mont Blanc tunnel $7\frac{1}{2}$m.
	Sept.	Commonwealth Prime Ministers' Meeting
	11 Oct.	Pope John XXIII opens 2nd Vatican Council
	20 Oct.	Indian-Chinese war in Assam
	Oct.	Independence of Uganda
		Cuban missile crisis
	Nov.	U. Thant re-elected Sectretary General
	Dec.	Tanganyika Republic
1963	Jan.	De Gaulle vetoes G.B. entry to E.E.C.
		Katanga secession ends

April	John XXIII : *pacem in terris* : world community for peace
May	O.A.U. founded, Addis Ababa
June	John XXIII dies. Paul VI Pope
	Partial nuclear test ban treaty: U.S.A./U.S.S.R./G.B.
Aug.	U.N. Security Council arms embargo on S. Africa
	Braque dies
	'Hot line' installed Washington–Moscow
Sept.	Malaysia
Oct.	Nigeria Republic
22 Nov.	President Kennedy assassinated. Johnson President
Dec.	Independence of Zanzibar
	Central African Federation of Rhodesias and Nyasaland ended
	Independence of Kenya

1964	March	U.N. peace force to Cyprus
	April	Tanzania – Union of Tanganyika and Zanzibar
	May	Nehru dies
		Quotations from Chairman Mao published
	June	U.N. forces leave Congo
	July	Commonwealth Prime Ministers' Meeting
		Independence of Malawi
	Aug.	Tonkin incident
	Sept.	Independence of Malta
	Oct.	18th Olympics at Tokyo
		Khrushchev replaced by Brezhnev (1st Secretray C.P.S.U.) and Kosygin (Prime Minister)
		Communist China nuclear bomb
		G.B. elections: Labour wins; Wilson Prime Minister
		Independence of Zambia
	Nov.	Johnson elected President of U.S.A.
	Dec.	J.B.S. Haldane dies
		Kenya Republic

1965	Jan.	Churchill dies
	Feb.	U.S. bombardment of N. Vietnam
		Independence of Gambia (21st member of Commonwealth)
	18 March	First space walk (U.S.S.R.)
		U.S. marines into S. Vietnam
	April	U.S. troops into Dominican Republic
	June	Commonwealth Prime Ministers' Meeting
		U.S. space walk
	July	Mariner IV (U.S.A.) photographs Mars
	Aug.	Singapore secedes from Malaysia
	Sept.	India-Pakistan war over Kashmir
		Schweitzer dies
	Oct.	G.B. death penalty abolished
	Nov.	Cultural Revolution in China – early beginnings
		U.D.I. of Rhodesia: G.B. applies sanctions
	Dec.	2nd Vatican Council ends

1966	Jan.	Tashkent agreement: ends Pakistan-India war
		Commonwealth Prime Ministers' Meeting at Lagos
		Giacometti dies
		Military coup in Nigeria
	Feb.	Military coup in Ghana
	March	G.B. elections: Labour returned
	April	Luna 10 orbits moon (U.S.S.R.)
	May	Independence of Guyana
	July	Malawi Republic
		Nigeria army mutiny; Gowan to power
		U.S. moon-orbit
	Sept.	Verwoerd assassinated
		Commonwealth Prime Ministers' Meeting
		Independence of Botswana
	Oct.	Independence of Lesotho
	Nov.	Independence of Barbados
	10 Nov.	Wilson announces new G.B. approach to be made to E.E.C.
	Dec.	U. Thant re-elected U.N. Secretary General

1967	27 Jan.	Space treaty on nuclear weapons U.S./ U.S.S.R./G.B.
	5 Feb.	Arusha Declaration
	March	Kodaly dies
	12 March	Sukarno replaced by Suharto in Indonesia
	18 March	*Torrey Canyon* aground: oil pollution disaster
	28 March	Paul VI *populorum progressio*
	30 March	Commonwealth round-the-world cable completed
	31 March	Malinovsky dies
	April	Sierra Leone military coup
	19 April	Adenaur dies
	21 April	Greek military coup
	27 April	Expo '67 opens Montreal
		Chinese denounce Liu Shao-ch'i
	11 May	G.B. 2nd application for E.E.C. membership
	28 May	Sir Francis Chichester completes sailing round world alone
	30 May	Eastern Region of Nigeria announces secession as Republic of Biafra
	5-10 June	Arab-Israeli War (6-day)
	6 June	East African Community agreed
	Aug.	Cultural Revolution in China
	20 Sept.	*Q.E.II* launched
	8 Oct.	Che Guevara dies
	18 Oct.	Venus IV (U.S.S.R.) lands on Venus
	19 Oct.	Mariner V (U.S.A.) passes within 2,000 miles of Venus to measure and photograph
	2 Nov.	Opening of official celebration of 1917 Russian Revolution 50th Anniversary
	18 Nov.	G.B. £ devalued by 14.3%
	20 Nov.	U.S. population passed 200m.
	27 Nov.	De Gaulle rejects G.B. 2nd E.E.C. bid: bid remains on table
	3 Dec.	1st human heart transplant by Dr. Barnard at Cape Town
	17 Dec.	Mr. Holt, Prime Minister Australia, drowns (J. Gorton P.M., 9 Jan. 68)
1968	1 Jan.	Cecil Day Lewis made Poet Laureate

5 Jan.	Dubcek replaces Novotney as Czech C.P. 1st Secretary
22–3 Jan.	N. Korea seizes *U.S.S. Pueblo* spyship
12 March	Independence of Mauritius
23 March	Dresden Meeting of E. European Communist Leaders
4 April	Martin Luther King murdered
6 April	P. Trudeau replaces Lester Pearson as Prime Minister Canada
8 May	Moscow Meeting of E. European Communist leaders
13 May	Vietnam peace talks open in Paris
4 June	Robert Kennedy assassinated (dies 6 June)
27 June	Czech '2000 words' article published (see Appendix D)
1 July	Non-proliferation of nuclear weapons Treaty signed U.S.S.R./U.S.A./G.B.
14 July	Warsaw Meeting of C.P. leaders of U.S.S.R., Hungary, E. Germany, Poland, Bulgaria
29 July– 1 Aug.	U.S.S.R.–Czech meetings at Cierna
4 Aug.	Czechs meet with Warsaw 5 (above) at Bratislava
20–21 Aug.	Invasion of Czechoslovakia by U.S.S.R. and allies
6 Sept.	Independence of Swaziland
26 Sept.	Dr. Caetano replaces Dr. Salazar as Prime Minister of Portugal
Oct.	Civil Rights campaign in N. Ireland. Derry disturbances.
	Liu Shao-ch'i removed from presidency of China
9–13 Oct.	Wilson and Smith meet on board *H.M.S. Fearless* to discuss Rhodesia settlement
5 Nov.	R. Nixon wins U.S. Presidential election
Dec.	U.S. 'Apollo VIII' manned lunar orbit
1969 4 Jan.	U.N. Convention on Racial Discrimination in force
7–15 Jan.	Commonwealth Prime Ministers' Conference, London

17 Jan.	Jan Palach suicide in Prague
24–31 March	Sino-Soviet clash on Amur river border
	President Ayub Khan replaced by Yahya Khan in Paskistan
28 March	General Eisenhower dies
1–20 April	9th Communist Party Congress in China
7 April	G.B. representation of People Act: votes at 18
17 April	Husak replaces Dubcek in Czechoslovakia as 1st secretary C.P.
28 April	De Gaulle resigns President of France
1 May	O'Neill replaced by Chichester Clarke as Prime Minister, N.I.
1 June	G.B. Open University founded
5–17 June	Moscow International Conference of Communist Parties
15 June	G. Pompidou President of France
5 July	Tom Mboya assassinated, Kenya
20 July	U.S. 'Apollo XI' moon landing. Armstrong and Aldrin first men on moon
Aug.	Sino-Soviet Border clashes, Sinkiang and Far East
29 Aug.	Free elections in Ghana (Busia Prime Minister 23 Sept.)
3 Sept.	Ho Chi Minh dies
1 Oct.	Report of Pearson Commission on International Development
21 Oct.	Willi Brandt Chancellor of W. Germany, replacing Dr. Kiesinger
Nov.	Indian Congress Party splits
13–15 Nov.	Washington march of 250,000 against Vietnam War
Dec.	G.B.: Permanent abolition of capital punishment for murder
1970 1 Jan.	U.S. Creates Council of Environmental Quality
15 Jan.	End of civil war in Nigeria proclaimed by Federal Government (10–11 'Biafran' resistance collapsed)
2 Feb.	Bertrand Russell dies
18 Feb.	Nixon 'state of world' survey: 'Nixon Doctrine'

14 March	Expo '70 opened Japan
24 April	China – first earth satellite
29 April	South Vietnam–U.S. invasion of Cambodia
4 May	4 anti-war students killed in Kent State University, U.S.A. unrest
5 May	U. Thant proposes U.N. Volunteer Corps for underdeveloped countries
6 May	Political crisis – Irish Republic
27 May	Ceylon: Mrs. Banderanaike Prime Minister on defeat of Mr. Senanayake
18 June	G.B. General Election, Conservatives defeat Labour: Heath Prime Minister
21 June	Sukarno dies
27 July	Dr. Salazar dies
7 Aug.	3-month Egypt-Israel cease fire
28 Aug.	W. Samoa member of Commonwealth
4 Sept.	Salvador Allende wins Presidential election in Chile (confirmed 28 Oct. as President)
8–10 Sept.	3rd non-aligned summit conference, Lusaka
17–27 Sept.	Civil war in Jordan: army defeats guerillas
21 Sept.	Tunku Abdul Rahman resigns Prime Minister Malaysia; Tun Abdul Razak replaces
28 Sept.	President Nasser dies; Sadat replaces
10 Oct.	Independence Fiji 31st commonwealth member
30 Oct.	Tanzania elections; Nyerere continues
5 Nov.	Middle East ceasefire extended further 3 months
9 Nov.	De Gaulle dies
12–13 Nov.	E. Pakistan flood disaster
3 Dec.	G.B. Industrial Relations Bill published
7 Dec.	W. Germany–Poland Treaty, normalising relations, signed
	Pakistan elections
20 Dec.	Gomulka resigns Polish leadership after riots; Gierek replaces
27 Dec.	India Parliament dissolved; elections to be held March '71

United Nations Declarations and Conventions

(i) UNIVERSAL DECLARATION OF HUMAN RIGHTS
Adopted and proclaimed by the General Assembly of the United Nations on 10 December 1948

PREAMBLE

Whereas recognition of the inherent dignity and of the equal and inalienable rights of all members of the human family is the foundation of freedom, justice and peace in the world,

Whereas disregard and contempt for human rights have resulted in barbarous acts which have outraged the conscience of mankind, and the advent of a world in which human beings shall enjoy freedom of speech and belief and freedom from fear and want has been proclaimed as the highest aspiration of the common people,

Whereas it is essential, if man is not to be compelled to have recourse, as a last resort, to rebellion against tyranny and oppression, that human rights should be protected by the rule of law,

Whereas it is essential to promote the development of friendly relations between nations,

Whereas the peoples of the United Nations have in the Charter reaffirmed their faith in fundamental human rights, in the dignity and worth of the human person and in the equal rights of men and women and have determined to promote social progress and better standards of life in larger freedom,

Whereas Member States have pledged themselves to achieve, in co-operation with the United Nations, the promotion of universal respect for and observance of human rights and fundamental freedoms,

Whereas a common understanding of these rights and freedoms is of the greatest importance for the full realization of this pledge,
Now, Therefore,

THE GENERAL ASSEMBLY

proclaims

THIS UNIVERSAL DECLARATION OF HUMAN RIGHTS as a common standard of achievement for all peoples and all nations, to the end that every individual and every organ of society, keeping this Declaration constantly in mind, shall strive by teaching and education to promote respect for these rights and freedoms and by progressive measures, national and international, to secure their universal and effective recognition and observance, both among the peoples of Member States themselves and among the peoples of territories under their jurisdiction.

Article 1

All human beings are born free and equal in dignity and rights. They are endowed with reason and conscience and should act towards one another in a spirit of brotherhood.

Article 2

Everyone is entitled to all the rights and freedoms set forth in this Declaration, without distinction of any kind, such as race, colour, sex, language, religion, political or other opinion, national or social origin, property, birth or other status.

Furthermore, no distinction shall be made on the basis of the political, jurisdictional or international status of the country or territory to which a person belongs, whether it be independent, trust, non-self-governing or under any other limitation of sovereignty.

Article 3

Everyone has the right to life, liberty and security of person.

Article 4

No one shall be held in slavery or servitude; slavery and the slave trade shall be prohibited in all their forms.

Article 5

No one shall be subjected to torture or to cruel, inhuman or degrading treatment or punishment.

Article 6
Everyone has the right to recognition everywhere as a person before the law.

Article 7
All are equal before the law and are entitled without any discrimination to equal protection of the law. All are entitled to equal protection against any discrimination in violation of this Declaration and against any incitement to such discrimination.

Article 8
Everyone has the right to an effective remedy by the competent national tribunals for acts violating the fundamental rights granted him by the constitution or by law.

Article 9
No one shall be subjected to arbitrary arrest, detention or exile.

Article 10
Everyone is entitled in full equality to a fair and public hearing by an independent and impartial tribunal, in the determination of his rights and obligations and of any criminal charge against him.

Article 11
(1) Everyone charged with a penal offence has the right to be presumed innocent until proved guilty according to law in a public trial at which he has had all the guarantees necessary for his defence.

(2) No one shall be held guilty of any penal offence on account of any act or omission which did not constitute a penal offence, under national or international law, at the time when it was committed. Nor shall a heavier penalty be imposed than the one that was applicable at the time the penal offence was committed.

Article 12
No one shall be subjected to arbitrary interference with his privacy, family, home or correspondence, nor to attacks upon his honour and reputation. Everyone has the right to the protection of the law against such interference or attacks.

Article 13
(1) Everyone has the right to freedom of movement and residence within the borders of each state.

(2) Everyone has the right to leave any country, including his own, and to return to his country.

Article 14

(1) Everyone has the right to seek and to enjoy in other countries asylum from persecution.

(2) This right may not be invoked in the case of prosecutions genuinely arising from non-political crimes or from acts contrary to the purposes and principles of the United Nations.

Article 15

(1) Everyone has the right to a nationality.

(2) No one shall be arbitrarily deprived of his nationality nor denied the right to change his nationality.

Article 16

(1) Men and women of full age, without any limitation due to race, nationality or religion, have the right to marry and to found a family. They are entitled to equal rights as to marriage, during marriage and at its dissolution.

(2) Marriage shall be entered into only with the free and full consent of the intending spouses.

(3) The family is the natural and fundamental group unit of society and is entitled to protection by society and the State.

Article 17

(1) Everyone has the right to own property alone as well as in association with others.

(2) No one shall be arbitrarily deprived of his property.

Article 18

Everyone has the right to freedom of thought, conscience and religion; this right includes freedom to change his religion or belief, and freedom, either alone or in community with others and in public or private, to manifest his religion or belief in teaching, practice, worship and observance.

Article 19

Everyone has the right to freedom of opinion and expression; this right includes freedom to hold opinions without interference and to seek, receive and impart information and ideas through any media and regardless of frontiers.

Article 20

(1) Everyone has the right to freedom of peaceful assembly and association.

(2) No one may be compelled to belong to an association.

Article 21

(1) Everyone has the right to take part in the government of his country, directly or through freely chosen representatives.

(2) Everyone has the right of equal access to public service in his country.

(3) The will of the people shall be the basis of the authority of government; this will shall be expressed in periodic and genuine elections which shall be by universal and equal suffrage and shall be held by secret vote or by equivalent free voting procedures.

Article 22

Everyone, as a member of society, has the right to social security and is entitled to realization, through national effort and international co-operation and in accordance with the organization and resources of each State, of the economic, social and cultural rights indispensable for his dignity and the free development of his personality.

Article 23

(1) Everyone has the right to work, to free choice of employment, to just and favourable conditions of work and to protection against unemployment.

(2) Everyone, without any discrimination, has the right to equal pay for equal work.

(3) Everyone who works has the right to just and favourable remuneration ensuring for himself and his family an existence worthy of human dignity, and supplemented, if necessary, by other means of social protection.

(4) Everyone has the right to form and to join trade unions for the protection of his interests.

Article 24

Everyone has the right to rest and leisure, including reasonable limitation of working hours and periodic holidays with pay.

Article 25

(1) Everyone has the right to a standard of living adequate for the health and well-being of himself and of his family including food, clothing, housing and medical care and necessary social services, and the right to security in the event of unemployment, sickness, disability, widowhood, old age or other lack of livelihood in circumstances beyond his control.

(2) Motherhood and childhood are entitled to special care and assistance. All children, whether born in or out of wedlock, shall enjoy the same social protection.

Article 26

(1) Everyone has the right to education. Education shall be free, at least in the elementary and fundamental stages. Elementary education shall be compulsory. Technical and professional education shall be made generally available and higher education shall be equally accessible to all on the basis of merit.

(2) Education shall be directed to the full development of the human personality and to the strengthening of respect for human rights and fundamental freedoms. It shall promote understanding, tolerance and friendship among all nations, racial or religious groups, and shall further the activities of the United Nations for the maintenance of peace.

(3) Parents have a prior right to choose the kind of education that shall be given to their children.

Article 27

(1) Everyone has the right freely to participate in the cultural life of the community, to enjoy the arts and to share in scientific advancement and its benefits.

(2) Everyone has the right to the protection of the moral and material interests resulting from any scientific, literary or artistic production of which he is the author.

Article 28

Everyone is entitled to a social and international order in which the rights and freedoms set forth in this Declaration can be fully realized.

Article 29

(1) Everyone has duties to the community in which alone the free and full development of his personality is possible.

(2) In the exercise of his rights and freedoms, everyone shall be subject only to such limitations as are determined by law solely for the purpose of securing due recognition and respect for the rights and freedoms of others and of meeting the just requirements of morality, public order and the general welfare in a democratic society.

(3) These rights and freedoms may in no case be exercised contrary to the purposes and principles of the United Nations.

Article 30

Nothing in this Declaration may be interpreted as implying for any State, group or person any right to engage in any activity or to perform any act aimed at the destruction of any of the rights and freedoms set forth herein.

Note:

By Resolution 2200 (XXI) of 16 December 1966, the General Assembly of the United Nations adopted and opened for signature, ratification and accession the following international instruments:

(a) the International Covenant on Economic, Social and Cultural Rights;

(b) the International Covenant on Civil and Political Rights;

(c) the Optional Protocol to the International Covenant on Civil and Political Rights.

The International Covenants on Human Rights were adopted unanimously. The Optional Protocol to the International Covenant on Civil and Political Rights was adopted by a majority of 66 to 2, with 38 abstentions.

Each of the Covenants will enter into force three months after the date of the deposit with the Secretary-General of the United Nations of the thirty-fifth instrument of ratification or instrument of accession. Subject to the entry into force of the International Covenant on Civil and Political Rights, the Optional Protocol will enter into force three months after the date of the deposit with the Secretary-General of the tenth instrument of ratification or instrument of accession.

The United Nations has thus taken a further step towards the promotion of universal respect for, and observance of, human rights and fundamental freedoms for all without distinction as to race, sex, language or religion, following upon the proclamation by the General Assembly on 10 December 1948 of the Universal Declaration of Human Rights as a common standard of achievement for all peoples and all nations.

(ii) UNITED NATIONS DECLARATION ON THE ELIMINATION OF ALL FORMS OF RACIAL DISCRIMINATION

The General Assembly,

Considering that the Charter of the United Nations is based on the principles of the dignity and equality of all human beings and seeks,

among other basic objectives, to achieve international co-operation
in promoting and encouraging respect for human rights and fundamental freedoms for all without distinction as to race sex, language
or religion,

Considering that the Universal Declaration of Human Rights
proclaims that all human beings are born free and equal in dignity
and rights and that everyone is entitled to all the rights and freedoms
set out in the Declaration, without distinction of any kind, in particular as to race, colour or national origin,

Considering that the Universal Declaration of Human Rights
proclaims further that all are equal before the law and are entitled
without any discrimination to equal protection of the law and that all
are entitled to equal protection against any discrimination and
against any incitement to such discrimination,

Considering that the United Nations has condemned colonialism
and all practices of segregation and discrimination associated
therewith, and that the Declaration on the granting of independence
to colonial countries and peoples proclaims in particular the necessity
of bringing colonialism to a speedy and unconditional end,

Considering that any doctrine of racial differentiation or superiority is scientifically false, morally condemnable, socially unjust and
dangerous, and that there is no justification for racial discrimination
either in theory or in practice,

Taking into account the other resolutions adopted by the General
Assembly and the international instruments adopted by the
specialized agencies, in particular the International Labour
Organisation and the United Nations Educational, Scientific and
Cultural Organisation, in the field of discrimination,

Taking into account the fact that, although international action
and efforts in a number of countries have made it possible to achieve
progress in that field, discrimination based on race, colour or ethnic
origin in certain areas of the world none the less continues to give
cause for serious concern,

Alarmed by the manifestations of racial discrimination still in
evidence in some areas of the world, some of which are imposed by
certain Governments by means of legislative, administrative or other
measures, in the form, inter alia, of apartheid, segregation and
separation, as well as by the promotion and dissemination of doctrines
of racial superiority and expansionism in certain areas,

Convinced that all forms of racial discrimination and, still more
so, governmental policies based on the prejudice of racial superiority

or on racial hatred, besides constituting a violation of fundamental human rights, tend to jeopardize friendly relations among peoples, co-operation between nations and international peace and security,

Convinced also that racial discrimination harms not only those who are its objects but also those who practise it,

Convinced further that the building of a world society free from all forms of racial segregation and discrimination, factors which create hatred and division among men, is one of the fundamental objectives of the United Nations,

(1) Solemnly affirms the necessity of speedily eliminating racial discrimination throughout the world, in all its forms and manifest-ations, and of securing understanding of and respectfor the dignity of the human person;

(2) Solemnly affirms the necessity of adopting national and international measures to that end, including teaching, education and information, in order to secure the universal and effective recognition and observance of the principles set forth below;

(3) Proclaims this Declaration:

Article 1

Discrimination between human beings on the grounds of race, colour or ethnic origin is an offence to human dignity and shall be condemned as a denial of the principles of the Charter of the United Nations, as a violation of the human rights and fundamental freedoms proclaimed in the Universal Declaration of Human Rights, as an obstacle to friendly and peaceful relations among nations and as fact capable of disturbing peace and security among peoples.

Article 2

(1) No State, institution, group or individual shall make any discrimination whatsoever in matters of human rights and fun-damental freedoms in the treatment of persons. groups of persons or institutions on the grounds of race, colour or ethnic origin.

(2) No State shall encourage, advocate or lend its support, through police action or otherwise, to any discrimination based on race, colour or ethnic origin by any group, institution or individual.

(3) Special concrete measures shall be taken in appropriate circumstances in order to secure adequate development or protection of individuals belonging to certain racial groups with the object of ensuring the full enjoyment by such individuals of human rights and fundamental freedoms. These measures shall in no circumstances

have as a consequence the maintenance of unequal or separate rights for different racial groups.

Article 3

(1) Particular efforts shall be made to prevent discrimination based on race, colour or ethnic origin, especially in the fields of civil rights, access to citizenship, education, religion, employment, occupation and housing.

(2) Everyone shall have equal access to any place or facility intended for use by the general public, without distinction as to race, colour or ethnic origin.

Article 4

All States shall take effective measures to revise governmental and other public policies and to rescind laws and regulations which have the effect of creating and perpetuating racial discrimination wherever it still exists. They should pass legislation for prohibiting such discrimination and should take all appropriate measures to combat those prejudices which lead to racial discrimination.

Article 5

An end shall be put without delay to governmental and other public policies of racial segregation and especially policies of *apartheid*, as well as all forms of racial discrimination and separation resulting from such policies.

Article 6

No discrimination by reason of race, colour or ethnic origin shall be admitted in the enjoyment by any person of political and citizenship rights in his country, in particular the right to participate in elections through universal and equal suffrage and to take part in the government. Everyone has the right of equal access to public service in his country.

Article 7

(1) Everyone has the right to equality before the law and to equal justice under the law. Everyone, without distinction as to race, colour or ethnic origin, has the right to security of person and protection by the State against violence or bodily harm, whether inflicted, by government officials or by any individual group or institution.

(2) Everyone shall have the right to an effective remedy and protection against any discrimination he may suffer on the ground of race, colour or ethnic origin with respect to his fundamental rights

and freedoms through independent national tribunals competent to deal with such matters.

Article 8

All effective steps shall be taken immediately in the fields of teaching, education and information, with a view to eliminating racial discrimination and prejudice and promoting understanding tolerance and friendship among nations and racial groups, as well as to propagating the purposes and principles of the Charter of the United Nations, of the Universal Declaration of Human Rights, and of the Declaration on the granting of independence to colonial countries and peoples.

Article 9

(1) All propaganda and organizations based on ideas or theories of the superiority of one race or group of persons of one colour or ethnic origin with a view to justifying or promoting racial discrimination in any form shall be severly condemned.

(2) All incitement to or acts of violence, whether by individuals or organizations, against any race or group of persons of another colour or ethnic origin shall be considered an offence against society and punishable under law.

(3) In order to put into effect the purposes and principles of the present Declaration, all States shall take immediate and positive measures, including legislative and other measures, to prosecute and/ or outlaw organizations which promote or incite to racial discrimination, or incite to or use violence for purposes of discrimination based on race, colour or ethnic origin.

Article 10

The United Nations, the specialized agencies, State and non-governmental organizations shall do all in their power to promote energetic action which, by combining legal and other practical measures, will make possible the abolition of all forms of racial discrimination. They shall in particular study the causes of such discrimination with a view to recommending appropriate and effective measures to combat and eliminate it.

Article 11

Every State shall promote respect for and observance of human rights and fundamental freedoms in accordance with the Charter of the United Nations, and shall fully and faithfully observe the provisions of the present Declaration, the Universal Declaration of

Human Rights and the Declaration on the granting of independence
to colonial countries and peoples.

Note:

The United Nations General Assembly, on 21 December 1965,
adopted an International Convention on the Elimination of all forms
of Racial Descrimination, in order to implement the principles
embodied above. (The text of this Convention may be obtained from
any United Nations Information Office) The Convention came into
force in 1969, and early in 1970 the Committee on the Elimination of
Racial Discrimination, for which it made provision, began its work.
This Committee is the first U. N. body especially set up to deal with
allegations that human rights are being violated in independent
countries and Territories.   (D.W.H.)

(iii) DECLARATION ON THE PROMOTION AMONG YOUTH
       OF THE IDEALS OF PEACE, MUTUAL RESPECT AND
       UNDERSTANDING BETWEEN PEOPLES

Adopted by the United Nations General Assembly

The General Assembly of the United Nations, on December 7, 1965,
adopted by acclamation a Declaration on the Promotion among
Youth of the Ideals of Peace, Mutual Respect and Understanding
between Peoples. In adopting the Declaration the Assembly took into
consideration the fact that in the 'conflagrations which have afflicted
mankind it has been the young people who have had to suffer most
and who have had the greatest number of victims'. It was convinced
that young people wished to have an assured future and that peace,
freedom and justice were among the chief guarantees that their
desires for happiness would be fulfilled.

The Assembly also had in mind the important part being played by
young people in every field of human endeavour and the fact that
they were destined to guide the future of mankind.

Proclaiming the Declaration the General Assembly called upon
Governments, non-governmental organisations and youth movements to recognize its principles and to ensure their observance by
means of appropriate measures.

The full text of the Declaration is given below.

The General Assembly,

Recalling that under the terms of the Charter of the United Nations
the peoples have declared themselves determined to save succeeding
generations from the scourge of war,

Recalling further that the United Nations has affirmed in the Charter its faith in fundamental human rights, in the dignity of the human person and in the equal rights of men and nations,

Reaffirming the principles embodied in the Universal Declaration of Human Rights, the Declaration on the Granting of Independence to Colonial Countries and Peoples, the United Nations Declaration on the Elimination of All Forms of Racial Discrimination, General Assembly resolution 110 (II) of 3 November 1947 condemning all forms of propaganda designed or likely to provoke or encourage any threat to the peace, the Declaration of the Rights of the Child and General Assembly resolution 1572 (XV) of 18 December 1960, which have a particular bearing upon the upbringing of young people in a spirit of peace, mutual respect and understanding among peoples,

Recalling that the purpose of the United Nations Educational, Scientific and Cultural Organization is to contribute to peace and security by promoting collaboration among nations through education, science and culture, and recognizing the role and contributions of that organization towards the education of young people in the spirit of international understanding, co-operation and peace,

Taking into consideration the fact that in the conflagrations which have afflicted mankind it has been the young people who have had to suffer most and who have had the greatest number of victims,

Convinced that young people wish to have an assured future and that peace, freedom and justice are among the chief guarantees that their desire for happiness will be fulfilled,

Bearing in mind the important part being played by young people in every field of human endeavour and the fact that they are destined to guide the fortunes of mankind,

Bearing in mind furthermore that, in this age of great scientific, technological and cultural achievements, the energies, enthusiasm and creative abilities of the young should be devoted to the material and spiritual advancement of all peoples,

Convinced that the young should know, respect and develop the cultural heritage of their own country and that of all mankind,

Convinced furthermore that the education of the young and exchanges of young people and of ideas in a spirit of peace, mutual respect and understanding between peoples can help to improve international relations and to strengthen peace and security,

Proclaims this Declaration on the Promotion among Youth of the Ideals of Peace, Mutual Respect and Understanding between

Peoples and calls upon Governments, non-governmental organizations and youth movements to recognize the principles set forth
therein and to ensure their observance by means of appropriate
measures:

Principle 1

Young people shall be brought up in the spirit of peace, justice,
freedom, mutual respect and understanding in order to promote
equal rights for all human beings and all nations, economic and
social progress, disarmament and the maintenance of international
peace and security.

Principle 2

All means of education, including as of major importance the
guidance given by parents or family, instruction and information
intended for the young should foster among them the ideals of peace,
humanity, liberty and international solidarity and all other ideals
which help to bring peoples closer together, and acquaint them with
the role entrusted to the United Nations as a means of preserving and
maintaining peace and promoting international understanding and
co-operation.

Principle 3

Young people shall be brought up in the knowledge of the dignity
and equality of all men, without distinction as to race, colour, ethnic
origins or beliefs, and in respect for fundamental human rights and
for the right of peoples to self-determination.

Principle 4

Exchanges, travel, tourism, meetings, the study of foreign languages, the twinning of towns and universities without discrimination
and similar activities should be encouraged and facilitated among
young people of all countries in order to bring them together in
educational, cultural and sporting activities in the spirit of this
Declaration.

Principle 5

National and international associations of young people should be
encouraged to promote the purposes of the United Nations, particularly international peace and security, friendly relations among
nations based on respect for the equal sovereignty of States, the final
abolition of colonialism and of racial discrimination and other
violations of human rights.

Youth organizations in accordance with this Declaration should take all appropriate measures within their respective fields of activity in order to make their contribution without any discrimination to the work of educating the young generation in accordance with these ideals.

Such organizations, in conformity with the principle of freedom of association, should promote the free exchange of ideas in the spirit of the principles of this Declaration and of the purposes of the United Nations set forth in the Charter.

All youth organizations should conform to the principles set forth in this Declaration.

Principle 6

A major aim in educating the young shall be to develop all their faculties and to train them to acquire higher moral qualities, to be deeply attached to the noble ideals of peace, liberty, the dignity and equality of all men and imbued with respect and love for humanity and its creative achievements. To this end the family has an important role to play.

Young people must become conscious of their responsibilities in the world they will be called upon to manage and should be inspired with confidence in a future of happiness for mankind.

South Africa's Apartheid Policy

The Government of the Republic of South Africa, believing that its unique historical, cultural, racial and economic circumstances have combined to present it with a uniquely difficult and complex challenge, has adopted a programme of development without parallel in the rest of the world. This programme – apartheid, or the separate development of the various peoples within the borders of the Republic – has been condemned as racialist, authoritarian, selfish, evil, debasing and inhuman by most other nations, yet its exponents regard their critics as uninformed or ill-intentioned, see their own policy as enlightened and their society as one of the last repositories of uprightness and Christian virtue in a defeatist and largely immoral world. They believe that they have analysed their problem intelligently and honestly and they appeal only for understanding and sympathy while they carry it out to the benefit of all their peoples, white, coloured and black. It is important in view of the incompatibility of these two claims that we make an effort to understand their thinking in order to determine whether they do deserve our sympathy or whether, after all, our censure is more appropriate.

There were, in 1970, 21.3 million South Africans. Of these, 3.8 million were white, 2 million were coloured (mixed blood) and 0.6 million of Asian origin. The rest, 14.9 million were black Africans, ('Bantu'), the largest groupings of which were the Xhosa (over 3.5 million) and the Zulu (about 3.5 million). In this mixed-race nation, occupying an area of 472,359 square miles ($5\frac{1}{4}$ times the size of Great Britain) it is the whites and the whites only who wield political power (they also administer South West Africa (Namibia), an area of 317,725 squares miles). The ruling decisions are white decisions. Apartheid

is a white policy and its ultimate objective is the security and preservation of the white 'nation'. It is the white South Africans who see
themselves faced with the choice of whether to build one integrated
society or several separate societies. They have long made it clear
that integration is not their aim. To them, history and nationalism
together argue decisively against an integration that could only
swamp white culture, submerge white identity, and inevitably
deprive white people of the economic fruits of their three centuries of
endeavour. Yet integration tends to occur naturally when diverse
communities are thrown together. So an active policy to prevent
integration, a fully detailed plan of contrary development was called
for: a policy of separate development. Whites have in fact followed
policies of racial segregation since the Union was founded in 1909.
In 1948 apartheid became official State policy when the Nationalist
Party took power. Later, in 1954, the Nationalist Government appointed a Commission under the Chairmanship of F. R. Tomlinson
to work out the details of policy in the light of prevailing conditions.
More specifically, the Commission was asked to determine 'the socio-
economic development of the Bantu areas within the Union of South
Africa'.[1]

The Tomlinson Commission adopted the widest interpretation of
its brief and made the most comprehensive survey of the South
African problem. It outlined the historical development of South
Africa's communities; pointed out as a fact of life the distinct,
autonomous nature of the three hundred year old European nation
determined to preserve its identity; and given that determination,
saw no hope of a unified society arising in South Africa through
evolutionary development. It pointed out that when the existence
of a people is at stake 'purely rational considerations play a relatively
unimportant role'[2] and added that unsympathetic foreign criticism
would tend only to harden the will to resist. Integration as a policy
was seen to be too risky, for once political equality and unity became
the goal it would be impossible to control events: there could be no
second thoughts. Yet the 'Bantu' would not forever acquiesce in the
present situation of subjection. The Commission described the problem in a nutshell:

> On the part of the European population, there is an unshakeable
> resolve to maintain their right of self-determination as a national
> and racial entity; while on the part of the Bantu there is a growing
> conviction that they are entitled to, and there is an increasing
> demand for, the fruits of integration, including an ever greater

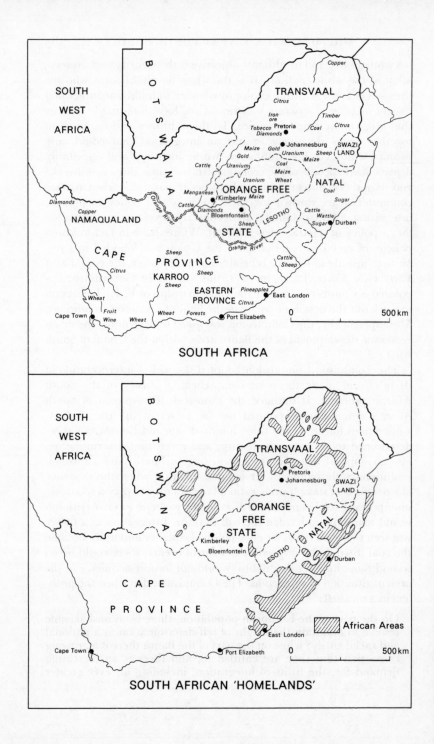

SOUTH AFRICA

SOUTH WEST AFRICA

BOTSWANA

Copper

TRANSVAAL

Citrus

Iron ore

Timber

Tobacco
Diamonds

Pretoria

Coal

Citrus

Johannesburg

SWAZI LAND

Maize

Gold

Gold

Uranium

Cattle

Uranium

Coal

Sheep

Maize

Uranium

Maize

Wheat

NATAL

Manganese

ORANGE FREE

Coal

Kimberley

Maize

Sugar

Diamonds

Cattle

Diamonds

Bloemfontein

LESOTHO

Cattle
Wattle

Namaqualand

Copper

Sheep

Orange River

Sugar

Durban

CAPE

STATE

Orange River

PROVINCE

Sheep

Cattle
Sheep

Citrus

KARROO

Sheep

Sheep

EASTERN
PROVINCE

Pineapples

East London

Citrus

Wheat

Cape Town

Fruit
Wine

Wheat

Wheat

Forests

Port Elizabeth

0   500 km

SOUTH AFRICA

SOUTH AFRICAN 'HOMELANDS'

SOUTH WEST AFRICA

BOTSWANA

TRANSVAAL

Pretoria

Johannesburg

SWAZI LAND

ORANGE FREE

STATE

Kimberley

Bloemfontein

LESOTHO

NATAL

Durban

CAPE

PROVINCE

African Areas

East London

Cape Town

0   500 km

Port Elizabeth

SOUTH AFRICAN 'HOMELANDS'

share in the control of the country.[3] Thus the choice before the
white nation was simple: As the Bantu come to share our Christian
principles and our civilisation, and their sense of duty and of
responsibility develops, all rights and privileges, as well as duties
and responsibilities have to be accorded them either (a) together
with the Europeans (i.e. as part and parcel of the European community); or (b) together as Bantu (i.e. their own communities).
There can be no middle course in the future. Indeed, the present
so-called middle way leads, as already pointed out, inescapably
towards integration. The only alternatives available are, therefore,
either the path of ultimate complete integration (i.e. of fusion with
the Europeans) or that of ultimate *complete* separation between
Europeans and Bantu.[4]

Believing that 'The policy of separate development is the only means
by which the Europeans can ensure that future unfettered existence,
by which increasing race tensions and clashes can be avoided, and
by means of which the Europeans will be able fully to meet their
responsibilities as guardians of the Bantu population', and that 'The
European population should, therefore, be willing to take the necessary action and to make the sacrifices required to put this policy into
effect', the Commission gave its unequivocal decision that 'the only
solution is the separate development of European and Bantu'.[5]

The Tomlinson Report has the ring of honest conviction about it.
It assumed from the beginning that the white community could not
retain its identity (and wellbeing) if a policy of integration was pursued. It affirmed its belief that the white community wished above
all else to retain its identity. It therefore planned and recommended
a policy of separate development. But this policy was going to prove
costly; enormously costly. So the white community must be under
no illusions as to the price. The Report spelled it out, summarising
its long and detailed analysis in such paragraphs as the following:

> The initial step towards the practical realisation of separate devel-
> opment of Europeans and Bantu, lies in the full-scale development
> of the Bantu Areas.
>   The development of the Bantu Areas will have to embrace a
> fully diversified economy, comprising development in the primary,
> secondary and tertiary spheres.
> . . . .
>
> For the first ten year programme, an amount of approximately
> £104,000,000 will be required, about £55,000,000 of which will
> be of a private-economic nature, and about £49,000,000 of a
> socio-economic nature. The Commission foresees that the present
> budget of the Department of Native Affairs, will probably have

to be doubled during the following ten years. A large proportion of these capital investments and expenditures will, in any case, have to be incurred, whether development of the Bantu Areas takes place or not.

The present geographical pattern of the Bantu Areas is so fragmentary that it will not be possible to carry out in all respects, the programme of development proposed by the Commission. Consequently, the Commission is convinced of the necessity for a policy which will aim at the consolidation of the Bantu Areas, on the basis of the historico-logical homelands of the principal ethnic groups.

It is the conviction of the Commission, that the development programme must be tackled in the spirit of an act of faith, in the same manner in which many other great undertakings in the Union have already been launched as acts of faith at times when the chances of success were at their minimum, or were totally denied by some people. If it is permissible for the Commission to draw a comparison, it would like to point out that the task set in its Report cannot be described as impossible, indeed not even as exceptionally difficult, when it is compared with the task of reconstructing the war-devastated countries after 1945. And these countries succeeded in their task.

The choice is clear: either the *challenge* must be accepted, or, the inevitable *consequences* of the integration of the Bantu and European population groups into a common society, must be endured.[6]

The Tomlinson Commission thus reached a clear and definite solution: complete apartheid based on a high economic investment. Leaving aside for a moment the dubious initial premises upon which the Commission founded this solution let us look at the way in which apartheid has been implemented in the years since 1954. The facts make gloomy reading and we note straight away that, in admittedly changing circumstances, the Tomlinson recommendations were quickly abandoned. Tomlinson assumed that the white community which had always resisted cultural integration would not now change its tune; but somehow imagined that it would be prepared to change its economic spots and make a massive financial effort in order to secure apartheid. Sadly, white South Africans have preferred to keep the cake of economic integration and to eat it at the same time, by forcing through social separation and insisting that black South Africans foot the bill in terms alike of financial sacrifice and personal hardship. The inescapable conclusion reached in 1968, after 20 years of Nationalist Government, was that 'separate development' is a contradiction in terms: 'The truth is that where there was separation there was no development; and where there was development there was no separation'.[7]

Certainly much has happened in South Africa, since 1954. There has been considerable expenditure on African welfare; schools, hospitals, factories and other amenities have been built, and a start has been made on the consolidation of African 'homeland' Bantustans. This latter work, indeed, lies at the very heart of the Nationalist Government's policy. Believing firmly in the 'multi-national' nature of South African society it sees that its major problem is, in its own words, 'to protect the position of each population group and to give them full opportunities for political, economic and cultural development without doing injustice to or hampering the development of other population groups'.[8] To this end the Bantu Authorities Act, 1951, and the Promotion of Bantu Self-government Act, 1959, were enacted to make provision for the recognition and development of 'Bantu' national units. In 1963 the first of these units, the Transkei, achieved a form of self-government, gaining for its people a territory, a flag and an anthem, and a legislative assembly with powers 'to make laws regarding taxation, education, agriculture, inferior courts, public works, regulation of traffic, labour matters, welfare services and other local matters'.[9] Seven other Bantustans are projected to be given 'independence' as and when their peoples are deemed capable of managing their own local affairs.

By 1968, in the educational field, the Government could also report progress:

> even now four out of every five Bantu children are at school. . . . The total Bantu school enrolment is over two million. This is more than twice what it was only ten years ago. . . . most Coloured and Indian children are at school. . . Opportunities for vocational and technical education for the non-white peoples are also being continually expanded. . . . And in recent years university facilities for the Bantu have been considerably enhanced. There are now three Bantu university colleges with a combined student roll of 1,161. In addition more than 1,600 Bantu are enrolled with the University of South Africa. The Coloured people, too, have their own university college. . . . Last year it had 481 students. In the same year the University College for Indians in Durban had more than 1,000 students enrolled.[10]

In terms of health there was similar encouragement:

> Some 336 hospitals, containing 70,000 beds for Non-Whites, are

strategically sited throughout the country. Of these, 111 hospitals are in the Bantu homelands and cater exclusively for Bantu. A nominal registration fee is paid on entry; otherwise, practically all Bantu patients receive free attention, including X-ray, surgical, and other specialist treatment.

Out-patient treatment, general nursing, preventive and maternity services (including ante-natal and post-natal services) are free to everybody at hospitals, Government Health Centres, Local Authority poly-clinics and district nursing clinics, even in the remotest areas.[11]

Social Welfare had not been neglected:

At present about 200,000 Bantu receive Old Age Pensions; 675 receive assistance as needy ex-soldiers, more than 14,000 receive blind persons' benefits and about 62,000 disability benefits.[12]

In terms of job provision, a start had been made in the sitting of industrial plant adjacent to the 'Bantu' homeland areas.[13] As well as these provisions, a sympathetic commentator has observed,

Hundreds of miles of contour walls were built to combat erosion; hundreds of miles of flood walls, thousands of miles of fencing, thousands of boreholes. Irrigation schemes were introduced, dams built and afforestation projects launched. Demonstration farms were set up, and instruction given on veterinary practice and stock breeding.[14]

Much has been done, much spent. And it is the proud boast of the white Pretoria Government that all this has been granted at the expense of the white taxpayer. This boast must be challenged on two counts: first it must be stressed that despite progress far too little has been done; second it must be stated emphatically that in more than one way it is the non-whites who are paying, and paying not only for their own limited amenities but also for the boom in white prosperity. Inside South Africa, supporters of apartheid as well as opponents who reject every aspect of the policy, have expressed their reservation about the extent and the pace of Government action. In *A Report on the Republic of South Africa 1968–9*, already referred to above, Legum and Drysdale quote Afrikaner officials or government supporters to make this point. Thus, Dr. J. Adendort, General Manager of the Bantu Investment Corporation, commented upon the inadequacy of funds for the Bantustans:

At the present rate of development the Bantu homelands will never be in a position to absorb the increases in Bantu population and assure decent living standards.

Calvinist Professor Adrian Pont expressed doubt as to whether the apartheid policy could survive the present low level of investment:

Can the policy of separate development lay claim to justice if a faster development tempo is not envisaged and if thousands of Africans capable of skilled work cannot find employment opportunities in their homelands and are, at the same time, excluded from more skilled and better paying jobs in the White areas? How can we, with the clock at five to twelve, continue travelling at an ox-wagon pace when the world is being subjected to ever faster change; when the modern standard of living is steadily increasing and the African – in close contact with a fast progressing economy – finds his requirements and his desire for an improved standard of living also increasing? How can we, if the tempo is not increased, want to hold back the African who has grown up in this atmosphere (of economic prosperity) to a primitive way of life, either by forcing him to a poverty-stricken homeland where he cannot make a living, or by allowing him into the White areas only as a low-paid worker who will never have the opportunity of progressing? How can we allow the policy to fail because, due to the neglect of all our striving for an acceleration of the tempo of development in the homelands, the backlog of the homelands, and their inhabitants becomes steadily greater in relation to the standard of living of the urban Africans who are caught up in the fast-progressing world current?

Finally, Legum and Drysdale back their own comment with statistics unfavourable to the government view:

What 20 years of apartheid rule has brought home to the country is the losing battle against African numbers and against the basic inequities of living standards between whites and blacks. Dr. H. M. Stocker, former director of the S. A. Bureau of Statistics, laid out some of the statistical facts of South African life in November. The White national income per head was R1,400 to R1,500 a year – more than 10 times that of the other three races combined. The national income per head for urban Africans was R120 to R130 a year, and for Bantustan Africans R30 to R35 a year. The non-White population was doubling itself twice as fast as the Whites and the natural increase rate of the Africans (3 per cent a year) was currently one of the highest in Africa and should double the present African population to reach 26 million in the 1990s.

Dr. Stocker said there were five times as many Africans as Whites under the age of 15, and the cost of rearing these children was largely born by the Whites. The African school population had also doubled in the past eight years to exceed two million; but 70 per cent of them were below Standard 3 and the high drop-out rate at primary school level led to social and economic problems.

Sixty per cent of Africans over 15 years were illiterate, compared with 50 per cent of the population of the underdeveloped countries of the world and 82 per cent of the population of Africa as a whole.[15]

X-Ray, a publication of the Africa Bureau (London) adds that the oft-proclaimed Pretoria assertion that more is spent on education for Africans in South Africa than elsewhere is false, giving the following comparison with Zambia:

Education of Africans	Zambia	South Africa
Money spent	R55m	R40m
Spending per child	R58	R16
Proportion of pupils in secondary schools	7%	4%
Proportion of teachers with degrees and professional qualifications in secondary schools	59%	22%
Number of full-time university students	1,250	1,600
Number taking secondary school leaving exam	5,467	2,289[15(a)]

Further, the United Nations Information Service has pointed out that though central and local government contributions to white education amount to $333 million, they total only $20.3 million for African education. *Per capita* expenditure on education for African children is in fact less than one eighth of that for white children.[15(b)]

Other opponents of the regime are more outspoken. Brian Bunting, South African-born journalist and M. P. who was long hounded and harrassed before being forced to leave his country, has declared unequivocally in his book, *The Rise of the South African Reich*, that separate development means simply 'that in return for limited rights of self-government in the Reserves, the Africans are to lose all rights in the remaining White Areas of South Africa, where they will enjoy the status only of 'temporary sojourners'.[16] Of the Bantustans he concludes that they 'are no more than a device for perpetuating the supply of African labour on the cheapest and safest possible terms to White South Africa'.[17] That the Bantustans are principally a 'divide and rule' device by the Pretoria government is a conclusion more than upheld by Ràndolph Vigne's *The Transkei – a South African Tragedy*, an analysis of the one 'self-governing' example attempted so far. Vigne, another South African harrassed into exile, exposes the political hypocrisy of a 'self-government' that preserves final authority in white hands and allows Pretoria to ride roughshod over Transkei aspirations. He also presents an 'economic outlook as grim as the political one. [For]... The Transkeins can expect, if they are the fortunate ones who are allowed to work outside the Transkei, only the lives of rightless migrant labourers. For the rest there is ever increasing poverty at home. For many the future can only mean starvation.'[18] It is perhaps worth adding that the projected Bantustans total a mere 13% of South Africa's total area.

To men such as Bunting and Vigne the significant story of South Africa under the Nationalist Government has clearly not been one of a booming white economy with benevolent trusteeship towards the 'Bantu', but one of a legalised oppression that has regimented and controlled the non-white population with an ever increasing intensity; that has provided the unfranchised majority with inadequate returns for its labour and which has, moreover, exacted a horrific price in human suffering on behalf of purely political policies designed to ensure continued white supremacy. It is in the legislation of control that this story lies, and it is in terms of degradation and suffering that the true price is being paid.

South Africa's legislation of control can be divided conveniently into those acts which restrict or direct non-whites, and those which are designed to prevent opposition to apartheid from any direction whatever. In this latter category fall such Acts as the Suppression of Communism Act, 1950, the Public Safety Act, and the General Law Amendment Acts, 1962, 1963 and 1965, which together provide the government with a formidable armoury of powers to proscribe opposition organisations, to declare states of emergency, to arrest and imprison without charge or trial. This legislation applies to the population as a whole and erodes what is normally accepted as 'the rule of law' in any civilised society. Arbitrary legal decision can remove or threaten anyone who appears to 'rock the boat' of state by questioning too closely or opposing too vehemently the official apartheid policies.

But it is in the former category of laws, those designed to circumscribe everyday non-white behaviour, that the most repressive side of the state reveals itself. Such legislation as the Group Areas Acts of 1950 and '57, enabling residential segregation; the Bantu Education Act, 1953, putting control of learning in all-white hands; the Bantu (Abolition of Passes and Consolidation of Documents) Act, 1952, replacing passes with reference books for all 'Bantu' but not relieving the personal inconvenience and harrassment associated with the compulsory carrying of the document; and the mass of industrial legislation limiting trade union activity, imposing job reservation

for whites only and generally enforcing the low wage migratory
labour policy; and administrative law, such as the Bantu Laws
Amendments Acts, 1963 and 1964, which remove African rights in
urban areas; all these can merely give an indication of the regulation
and restriction surrounding the non-white population.

Apartheid, from the sports field to the park bench, is well known
outside South Africa; so is the practice of regarding the Chinese as
'black' and the Japanese as 'white' to suit economic and political
ends, revealing the tortuous workings of a political theory based on
skin colour. But the raw edges of apartheid, as it is practised, are less
well known. They have been well illustrated by Cosmas Desmond in
The Discarded People, a book which describes the bitter degradation
and suffering occasioned by the ruthless and insensitive resettling of
people to fit the apartheid blueprint; the uprooting of men, women
and children (mostly, in practice, women and children) from their
established community and accustomed area, often where farming
was conducted and work was available, to geographically 'neater'
areas, too often barren, where plots have been inadequate, facilities
deplorable and work non-existent. It is in this way, as well as in their
depressed wages, limited work opportunities and lack of rights, that
the African pays the price of white prosperity. The 'homelands' are
admitted to be inadequate, malnutrition and disease are recognised
to be rife, but political ideology dictates separation, so Africans must
move. As Father Desmond observes:

> Families are being broken up because, while the White economy
> demands the presence of African workers in the urban areas, the
> apartheid ideology calls for as many Africans as possible to live in
> their 'homelands' ... For the sake of the comfort of the White
> man the Black man must be deprived of his right to live with his
> wife and family. This in a professedly Christian country which has
> a public holiday to celebrate Family Day.[19]

The information garnered by Father Desmond from all over South
Africa in 1969, added to the fund of his own previous experience of
resettlement, notably the transfer of his mission flock to Limehill,
Natal, in 1968, make a depressing record of the physical and mental
subjection of helpless peoples; a process, furthermore, accompanied
by misleading official propaganda which speaks only of 'voluntary'
removal to 'well prepared' locations, smothering over the actual
conditions of human misery involved. Having surveyed many resettlement areas, Father Desmond concludes that too often they are
merely dumping grounds for those whose labour is no longer needed

by the white economy; dumping grounds where the means of livelihood are notoriously lacking. Angrily he condemns both the comfortable, distant theoretician and the unknowing, unthinking, mass
of the white electorate:

> there must be something inherently wrong with a social system
> under which such atrocities can take place. The poverty, suffering,
> and broken families caused by the resettlement schemes are not
> accidental; they are an inevitable consequence of the policy of
> separate development. They are allowed to happen because they
> are part of the price of White economic security. And there are
> few, if any, White men in South Africa who do not benefit from
> this economic security and who do not share in the guilt for the
> steps which are taken to ensure it. We cannot absolve ourselves of
> this guilt simply by handing out relief or calling on the Government
> to make better preparations before they move people.[20]

And here Father Desmond puts his finger on one of the subtlest
and most damning aspects of the apartheid policy: its effect, not just
on its victims, but on those who, wittingly or unwittingly, are its
perpetrators. 'We are all liable', he warns, 'to become so conditioned
by our social environment that we just do not think of applying the
same standards for Africans as for Whites.' A selfish and inhuman
policy corrupts its operators. Franz Fanon in Algeria warned of the
hurt of colonialism to the coloniser, and Nadine Gordimer, in an
outraged introduction to Father Desmond's book, here repeats the
similar observation of Sartre: 'It is enough that they show us what
we have made of them for us to realise what we have made of ourselves'. 'Why', asks Nadine Gordimer, 'should people have to live
like this in a prosperous country at peace? Is there any aim or gain
that could be worth it?'[21]

Advocates of apartheid will return, in answer, to their basic premise: the survival of the white nation is *only* possible through separate
development; multiracialism or gradual integration will *inevitably*
lead in the end to the subjection of White to Black. Confusedly they
will on the one hand point to the absolute uniqueness of South
Africa's situation while on the other stress the lessons to be learned
from independent Black Africa. South Africa *is* unique. Comparison
with others cannot be appropriate. Rather, South Africans should
recognise that they are better placed than any other people to make a
success of racial partnership. The South African White minority is
so substantial, providing key personnel and vital expertise, that it
could never be simply pushed aside by an enfranchised Black major-

ity. And if a multiracial partnership seems to be a risky undertaking then all that can be said is that the risks are hardly greater than those inherent in oppressive apartheid, with all the frustrations and hatreds it engenders, and they would at least be risks in a nobler cause. Present policies of job reservation and racial discrimination are proving increasingly debilitating to the economy; complete separation is both physically impracticable and morally indefensible. Eventually the South African peoples must work together and the sooner they begin the less harm will have been done.

Afrikaners, it can be observed, are not averse to assuming for themselves the role of guardians of Western values and Christian standards in a decadent world of liberalism, communism and permissiveness. Their country may indeed have a role, but it is not as the repository of godliness and good living. If all white South Africans had sufficient faith in their values to live up to them and to wish to assist the more backward non-white peoples to acquire them (the reference is not to total culture but to truth, integrity and fellowship as well as the range of technical skills) and thus to assist in the building of a common society based on equality before the law, equal opportunity and just reward for labour, then they might indeed be a shining beacon amongst the world's peoples. As it is their society, built on the accident of birth and skin pigmentation, stands a pariah amongst nations, an affront to human dignity, a provocation to racial discord constituting a real threat to international peace. As such South Africa touches the selfish interests of all people. Because it also represents a moral affront it commands attention, condemnation, and active opposition.

NOTES

[1]Tomlinson Commission for the socio-economic development of the Bantu Areas within the Union of South Africa, *Summary of the Report* (Government Printer, Pretoria, 1955).

[2]*Ibid.*, p. 104.

[3]*Ibid.*, p. 105.

[4]*Ibid.*, p. 106.

[5]*Ibid.*

[6]*Ibid.*, pp. 207–8 and p. 211.

[7]Colin Legum & John Drysdale (eds.), *A Report on the Republic of South Africa 1968–9*, p. 4 (quoting Sir de Villiers Graaf, August 1968).

[8]*State of S. Africa Year Book 1969*, pp. 70–1.

[9]*Ibid.*, p. 73.

[10] *Education for Success* (S.A. Dept. of Information Pretoria, n.d.), p. 1.

[11] *Health and Healing* (Department of Information, Pretoria, 1969), p. 4.

[12] *State of S. Africa Year Book 1969*, p. 81.

[13] See *Taking Factories to the People* (Department of Inf., Pretoria, 1968).

[14] John Fisher, *The Afrikaners* (Cassell, 1969), p. 338.

[15] Legum and Drysdale, *op. cit.*, pp. 4–5.

[15(a)] *X-Ray*, vol. 1, no. 10 (May 1971).

[15(b)] See *Objective: Justice* (UN Office of Public Information), vol. 2, no. 3 (July 1970), pp. 27–8.

[16] Brian Bunting, *The Rise of the South African Reich* (Penguin, 1969).

[17] *Ibid.*, p. 490.

[18] Randolph Vigne, *The Transkei – a South African Tragedy* (Africa Bureau, n.d.), p. 25.

[19] Cosmas Desmond, *The Discarded People* (Christian Institute of S.A. Braamfontein, 1970), p. 19. (Later published by Penguin)

[20] *Ibid.*, p. 20.

[21] *Ibid.*, p. 5.

APPENDIX D
Two Thousand Words

The *Guardian* 16 July 1968

THE CZECH MANIFESTO WHICH HAS ANGERED
THE KREMLIN

This is the manifesto, published by a group of 70 writers, scientists, and others, which has brought to a head the campaign against Czechoslovakia in the Soviet Union and other East European countries.

It is entitled simply '2,000 words' and was published in four Czechoslovak newspapers on June 26. It was disowned in moderate terms by the Government and the Communist Party presidium, but Prague Radio and the newspapers have reported a huge volume of support for it.

The document does not bear out the claim of the Moscow 'Pravda' that its authors advocate 'the use of force of arms' to support a national leadership acceptable to them, or the setting up of local committees 'to raise power.' It is possible, therefore, that the Warsaw Summit decisions will be based on a misreading of it.

2000 WORDS

The life of our nation was first threatened by the war. Then followed another bad time with events which threatened the nation's spiritual health and character.

The majority of the nation hopefully accepted the programme of socialism. But its direction fell into the hands of the wrong people. It would not have mattered so much that they did not have enough statesmanlike experience, practical knowledge, or philosophical education, if at least they had possessed more common wisdom and decency, if they had been able to listen to the opinions of others, and if they had allowed themselves to be replaced gradually by more capable people.

The Communist Party, which after the war possessed the great trust of the people, gradually exchanged this trust for offices, until it had all the offices and nothing else. We must put it in this way, and those among us who are Communists know it to be so and their disappointment over the results is as great as the disappointment of the others.

The incorrect line of the leadership changed the party from a political party and an ideological alliance into a power organisation which became very attractive to egotists avid for rule, calculating cowards, and people with bad consciences. Their influx into the party affected the nature and the conduct of the party.

Its internal arrangement was not such that honest people could gain influence in it without shameful incidents, or that such people could change it to bring it continuously into line with the modern world. Many Communists fought this decline but they did not succeed in preventing what happened.

The situation in the Communist Party was the pattern and cause of a similar situation in the State. The fact that the party was linked with the State led to the party's losing the advantage of distance from executive power. There was no criticism of the activity of the State and economic organisations. Parliament forgot its procedures, the Government forgot how to rule, and the directors how to direct. Elections had no significance and the laws lost their value.

We could not confide in our representatives in any committee, and if we could trust them we could not ask them to do anything because they could effect nothing. It was still worse that we could no longer trust even one another. Personal and collective honour declined.

Honesty led nowhere and it was useless to speak of any appreciation for ability. Therefore most people lost interest in public affairs. They were concerned only with themselves and with money. These bad conditions also brought the result that now one cannot even rely on the money.

Relations among people were spoiled, joy in work was lost. To sum up, a time came on the nation which threatened its spiritual health and character.

We are all responsible for the present state of affairs. The greater responsibility rests with the Communists among us. The main responsibility, however, rests with those who were component parts or instruments of uncontrolled power. It was the power of an opinionated group placed, with the help of the party apparatus, everywhere from Prague to each district and commune.

The apparatus decided what one might or might not do, and the apparatus directed the cooperatives for the cooperative members, the factories for the workers, and the national committees for the citizens. No organisation actually belonged to its members, not even the Communist organisation.

The main guilt and the greatest deception of these rulers was that they presented their arbitrariness as the will of the workers. If we wanted to believe this deception we would now have to blame the workers for the decline of our economy, for the crimes against innocent people, for the introduction of censorship which made it impossible for all this to be written about. The workers were to blame for the mistaken investments, for the losses in trade, for the shortage of apartments.

Naturally, no sensible person believes in such guilt on the part of the workers. We all know and, in particular, each worker knows, that in practice the workers did not decide anything. It was someone else who made the worker-officials vote.

While many workers thought that they ruled, the rule was executed in their name by a specially educated group of officials of the party and State apparatus. In effect, they took the place of the overthrown class and themselves became the new authority.

For the sake of justice, we will say that some of them long ago recognised this as an unpleasant game of history. We know them now by the fact that they redress wrongs, correct mistakes, return the taking of decisions to the membership and the citizens, and limit the authority and the numbers of the apparatus of officials. They are with us against obsolete views in the party membership.

But many of the body of officialdom are still opposing changes and they still have weight, they still hold instruments of power, particularly in the districts and in the communes, where they may use these instruments secretly and without fear of impeachment.

From the beginning of the current year we have been in the revival process of democratisation. It began in the Communist Party, we must say this, and the people among us outside the party who, until recently, expected no good to come from us, also know it. We must add, however, that this process could not have begun elsewhere. After a full twenty years only the Communists could live something approaching a political life; only Communist criticism was in a position to offer a fundamental assessment, only the opposition within the Communist Party had the privilege of being in contact with the enemy.

The initiative and efforts of the democratic Communists, therefore, are only an instalment in the repayment of the debt owed by the entire party to the people outside the party, whom it kept in a position of inequality. Therefore, no gratitude is due to the Communist Party, although it should probably be acknowledged that it is honestly striving to use the last opportunity to save its own and the nation's honour.

The rivival process is not introducing anything very new. It is bringing ideas and suggestions, many of which are older than the errors of our socialism, and others, some of which emerged from under the surface of what was actually visible. They should have been expressed long ago, but they were suppressed.

Let us not cherish the illusion that these ideas are now victorious through the force of truth. Their victory was decided rather by the weakness of the old leadership which obviously had first to be weakened by a rule of 20 years in which no one hampered it. Obviously all the undesirable elements hidden in the foundations and the ideology of this system had to mature until they came to full fruition.

Therefore, let us not over-estimate the significance of the criticism from the ranks of writers and students. The source of social change is the economy. Words have a significance only if they are spoken under conditions which have already been duly prepared. 'Duly prepared conditions in our country' – unfortunately, we must understand this term to mean our general poverty and the complete disintegration of the old system of rule, in which politicians of a certain type calmly and peacefully compromised themselves at our expense. Thus truth is not victorious – truth simply remains when everything else goes to waste. There is no cause for a national celebration of victory, there is merely cause for new hope.

We turn to you in this moment of hope, which is still threatened, however. It took several months for many of us to believe that they could speak out and many still do not yet believe it. Nevertheless, we have spoken up, and so many things have been revealed that somehow we must complete our purpose of humanising this regime. Otherwise the revenge of the old forces would be cruel. We turn mainly to those who so far have only waited. The time which is coming will be decisive for many years.

The time which is coming is summer, with its vacations and

holidays, when, according to old habit, we will want to leave everything. We can be certain, however, that our dear adversaries will
not indulge in summer recreation, that they will mobilise the people
under obligation to them, and that even now they are trying to
arrange for calm Christmas holidays.

Let us be careful, therefore, of what will happen. Let us try to
understand it and respond to it. Let us renounce the impossible
demand that someone higher up must always give us the only possible
interpretation of things and the one simple conclusion. Each of us
will have to draw his own conclusions of his own responsibility.
Conclusions mutually agreed on can be arrived at only by discussion,
and this needs the freedom of expression which actually is our only
democratic achievement of the current year.

In the forthcoming days we will have to show initiative of our own
and determination of our own. Primarily we will oppose views,
should they arise, that it is possible to conduct some sort of democratic
revival without the Communists, or possibly against them. This
would be both unjust and unreasonable.

The Communists possess developed organisations and in these
we should support the progressive wing. They have experienced
officials and, last but not least, they also have the decisive levers and
buttons in their hands. Their Action Programme has been submitted
to the public. It is a programme for the initial adjustment of the
greatest inequalities and no one else has any similar specific programme. We must demand that local action programmes be submitted in each district and each commune.

Here, suddenly, we shall be taking very ordinary and long-awaited
right steps. The Czechoslovak Communist Party is preparing for the
congress which will elect a new Central Committee. Let us demand
that it be better than the current one. If the Communist Party now
says that in the future it wants to base its leading position on the
confidence of the citizens and not on force, let us believe this as long
as we can believe in the people whom it is now sending as delegates
to the district and regional conferences.

People have recently had fears that the progress of democratisation
had stopped. This feeling is partly a manifestation of tiredness due
to the agitated events and is partly due to the fact that the season of
surprising revelations, resignations from high places, and intoxica-
ting speeches of unprecedented verbal boldness is past.

However, the struggle of forces has merely become less obvious to
a certain extent. The fight is now being waged for the substance and

for the working of the laws, for the extent of practical steps. In addition, we must give the new people, the Minister, prosecutors, chairmen, and secretaries, time to work. They have the right to this time so that they can either make good or be proved unfit. Apart from this, one cannot at the moment expect more of the central political organs.

The practical quality of the future democracy depends on what becomes of the enterprises and what will happen in them. In all our discussions it is the economists who have the last word. One must seek out good managers and see to it that they get good positions.

It is true that, compared with mature countries, we are badly paid, and some are even worse off. We can demand more money – it can be printed, but at the same time its value will diminish. Let us rather demand that directors and chairmen explain to us what they want to produce and at what cost, to whom they want to sell their products, and at what price, and as regards the profits what part of it is invested in the modernisation of production, and what part can be distributed.

Under apparently boring headlines a very hard struggle is going on in the press relating to democracy and the manager. As producers the workers can intervene in this struggle by the choice of the persons whom they elect to the enterprise managements and enterprise councils. As employees they will do best for themselves when they elect as their representatives in the trade union organs their natural leaders, capable and honest people, regardless of party allegiance. If at this time we cannot expect more from the present central political organs then we must achieve more in the districts, notably as regards the Communists.

Let us demand the resignation of people who have misused their power, who have harmed public property, or who have acted dishonestly or brutally. We must find ways to induce them to resign, for instance, through public criticism, resolutions, demonstrations, demonstrative work brigades, collection drives for gifts to them when they withdraw, strikes, and boycotts of their doors.

However, we must reject methods which are illegitimate, indecent, or gross since they might use them to influence Alexander Dubcek. We must decry the writing of insulting letters with such emphasis that any letter of this kind, which they may yet receive, could only be considered a letter which they had sent to themselves. Let us revive the activity of the National Front. Let us demand public meetings of the national committees. Let us set up special citizens' committees and commissions to deal with questions about which no official admits to know anything.

It is simple: a few people convene, they elect a chairman, keep regular minutes, publish their findings which demand a solution, and refuse to let themselves be intimidated. Let us change the district and local press, which has degenerated into a mouthpiece of official views, into a platform of all the positive political forces; let us demand the establishment of editorial councils composed of representatives of the National Front, or let us found new papers.

Let us establish committees for the defence of the freedom of expression. Let us organise a special service to ensure order at our meetings. If we hear strange news let us check on it, let us send delegations to the people concerned and let us publish their replies, possibly nailed to trees. Let us support the security organs when they persecute genuine criminal activity; we do not mean to cause anarchy and a state of general insecurity. Let us avoid disputes among neighbours, let us renounce spitefulness in political affairs. Let us reveal informers.

The heavy holiday traffic throughout the republic will arouse interest in the constitutional arrangement of the Czechs and Slovaks. We consider that federation is a method of solving the nationality question. Apart from this, it is one of the important measures aimed at democratising conditions. But this measure will not of itself ensure better living conditions for the Slovaks. The problem of the regime – whether in the Czech regions or in Slovakia – is not solved by this. The rule of the party-State bureaucracy may still survive – in Slovakia even better, because it has 'ensured greater freedom.'

The recent great apprehension springs from the possibility that foreign forces may interfere with our internal development. Being faced with all these superior forces, the only thing we can do is to hold our own decently and not to start anything. We can assure the Government that we will give it our backing, if necessary, even with weapons, as long as the Government does what we gave it the mandate to do: and we can assure our allies that we will observe our treaties of friendship, alliance, and trade. Excited reproaches and underground suspicions must necessarily make the position of our Government more difficult.

At any rate, we can ensure equal relations only by improving our internal conditions and by carrying the process of revival so far that one day at elections we will elect statesmen who will have sufficient courage, honour, and political wisdom to establish and maintain such relations. This, by the way, is the problem of absolutely all governments of all small countries of the world.

This spring, just as after the war, we have been given a great chance again. Once again we have the possibility of taking into our hands our common cause, which for all practical purposes we call socialism, and giving it a shape which will better correspond with our former good reputation and with the relatively good opinion which we once had of ourselves. This spring has just ended and will never come back again. In the winter we shall know everything.

With this we conclude our statement to the workers, farmers, officials, artists, scientists, technicians, and everybody. It was written at the suggestion of the scientists.

(Reprinted from the *Guardian*
16 July 1968)

The more powerful people then betook themselves to another method of assuaging the strife of men: they sought by attacking whole nations and subduing and reducing them to subjection, to establish whether in the state or in the realm of religion a single order or rule which should embrace them all; but always, as unvarying experience proves, rather with the effect of making things worse than with any good result. For there is inborn in human nature a love of liberty — for liberty man's mind is convinced that it was made — and this love can by no means be driven out: so that, wherever and by whatever means it feels that it is being hemmed in and impeded, it cannot but seek a way out and declare its own liberty. Inevitably resistance, opposition, rebellion follow whenever force becomes an element in the government of men.

Greetings from Prague: a New Year card from the Institute of Micromolecular Chemistry, Czechoslovak Academy of Sciences. The text is from J. A. Comenius's *The Way of Light*, published in 1668.

(Reprinted from the *Guardian* 7 January 1969)

Index